By Members of the FRCC Guidebooks Committee

Edited by Steve Scott

LAKE DISTRICT ROCK

WARNING
You climb at your own risk. You are the sole judge of conditions. You take responsibility for your own actions.
The information in this guide is derived from a number of sources. While every effort is made to check its accuracy please do not presume that any of the material in this book is accurate. Neither the publisher nor anyone involved in the publication of this book can be held responsible for omissions, mistakes, nor held liable for any personal or third party injuries or damage, howsoever caused, arising from its use.

A catalogue record for this book is available from the British Library

ISBN 978-0-85028-057-9

Designed by Wired Guides
Typesetting Peter Sterling

Maps prepared by Don Sargeant
Reproduced by permission of Ordnance Survey on behalf of HMSO.

Published by Wired Guides and The Fell and Rock Climbing Club of the English Lake District Limited - Industrial and Provident Societies Reg. 30506 R

Nowt but a Fleein' Thing E8 Dave Birkett — Alastair Lee

FRCC

The Lake District is a fantastic compact mountainous area in the north west of England containing so much and attracting so many with its scenery, culture and huge range of activities. Scattered amongst these fells is a stunning collection of crags with routes for everyone. This guidebook gives a selection of more than 1,500 routes which will keep most people happy for a lifetime. As well as the popular crags of Shepherd's in Borrowdale and Raven Crag, Langdale, there are many lesser known crags, such as Boat How Crags and another Raven Crag, on High Stile; a visit to either would be well rewarded. You'll find all styles of climbing here; thuggy cracks, fingery walls and smeary slabs, trad or sport, on an array of different rock – volcanic ashes, limestone, granite, sandstone and slate.

The Fell and Rock Climbing Club (FRCC) has been producing definitive rock climbing guides to the Lake District since 1922. These authoritative guides are produced by an energetic and enthusiastic group of climbers who really know the area and this guide brings together a comprehensive selection of the best climbs on offer.

Whilst the FRCC has its origins in the Lake District, its membership is now spread throughout the United Kingdom with activities covering many aspects of "fell and rock". Offering an extensive meets programme and also a collection of well-situated huts and cottages principally in the Lake District, but also in Scotland. The Club has a long history and remains very active, ever open to new members who don't necessarily need to be climbing high 'E' numbers – a keen interest in the fells, whether for rock climbing, walking, mountaineering, ski touring or fell running is our shared enjoyment. Take a look at the Fell and Rock Climbing Club website: www.frcc.co.uk

I have had the pleasure of being involved with FRCC guidebook production for many years and it is always exciting as a new one nears publication. I would like to thank Steve Scott and the guidebook team for their work and their commitment to making this project happen. As you flick through its pages I am sure you will want to get out and climb these Lake District crags – not only those you may have been to before, but also others which may have been off the "crag radar". I hope this guide will inspire you to get out and enjoy these magnificent crags and challenging routes!

Ron Kenyon – President FRCC

Collie Step, Moss Gill, Scafell — 📷 FRCC Archive

CONTENTS

WE ARE WIRED

In terms of guidebooks, Britain is one of the richest countries in the world. Since the word Go, activists and clubs combined to record the efforts of the day, meticulously noting the pioneering ascents of explorers so that those who came after could follow in their footsteps and marvel at their achievements. This all began back in 1909 in Snowdonia when JM Archer Thomson & AW Andrews wrote the first complete guidebook to the mountain crag of Lliwedd.

For over a century the clubs have maintained this incredible record of first ascents. These have been chronicled and revised to give climbers the most up-to-date and accurate account of climbing in Britain. These organisations have undertaken the gargantuan task of publishing definitive guidebooks to put this knowledge into the hands of climbers. This work has depended on volunteers, climbers who are committed to contributing something invaluable to the rest of us, putting something back into the world they love.

Wired is a new concept that brings these clubs together. Under this banner, the voluntary guidebook producers share their collective knowledge, skill and enthusiasm to take the information they have spent so long creating and use it in new and creative ways.

www.wired-guides.com

Wired Guides are published by a co-operative of UK definitive guidebook publishers including: the **British Mountaineering Council**, **The Climbers' Club**, the **Fell & Rock Climbing Club** of the English Lake District, the **Scottish Mountaineering Club**, and the **Yorkshire Mountaineering Club**. Wired guidebooks aim to document the whole of the UK describing the very best – world-class – rock climbing these beautiful green islands have to offer.

The **Wired Guides** collaborators:

The **Fell & Rock Climbing Club** of the English Lake District publishes definitive guidebooks documenting the Lake District National Park and Cumbria.

www.frcc.co.uk

The **BMC** first became involved in publishing Peak District guidebooks in 1972 and has had a continued involvement ever since. Today it produces definitive guides to the gritstone and limestone crags of the Peak District and Lancashire. With gritstone guides to Stanage, Burbage, Millstone and Beyond, Froggatt, Over The Moors, The Roaches and Lancashire as well as Peak Limestone, it maintains the definitive record of over a century of climbing in this great area.

www.thebmc.co.uk

The Climbers' Club published the world's first ever guidebook in 1909 and is today still one of the world's largest definitive guidebook publishers with guidebooks covering Snowdonia, Pembroke, the South West and South of England. The club has eight huts in: Scotland, the Lake District, the Peak District, Cornwall, Pembroke, and Snowdonia. Club membership is open to all experienced climbers.

www.climbers-club.co.uk

The **Scottish Mountaineering Club** founded in 1889 has recorded new routes in its annual journal since 1890. It now publishes 16 guidebooks to climbing in Scotland, plus a number of scrambling and hillwalking guides. All profit from SMC guidebooks goes to the Scottish Mountaineering Trust, a registered charity, which has distributed more than £1 million to projects in the Scottish mountains since 1990.

www.smc.org.uk

The **Yorkshire Mountaineering Club** publishes definitive guidebooks documenting Yorkshire's gritstone and limestone.

www.theymc.org.uk

Steve McClure on *Hell's Wall (E6 6c)*, Bowderstone Crag, Borrowdale Lake District. Photo: Keith Sharples

USING THIS GUIDEBOOK

CHARACTER
The district offers a superbly varied climbing experience with roadside, high mountain, sport and bouldering venues. The complex geology presents amazingly varied rock, with granites, volcanic ashes and lavas, limestone and sandstone all represented. The whole district forms a dome with radial drainage creating deep valleys, like the spokes of a wheel, with England's highest mountain Scafell Pike in the centre. You will generally be climbing in a spectacular mountain setting or amongst trees and bracken in a beautiful valley.

CONDITIONS
Year round climbing can be enjoyed, even on the high crags as the maritime air is generally mild and can be wet. In the spring, summer and autumn wet weather generally moves through quickly followed by a day or two of cooler showery conditions before the next weather front. When high pressure prevails, long stable periods of dry warm weather can be enjoyed, sometimes for several weeks!

LOGISTICS
The North West of England has superb air, rail and road links making it easy to reach. The stunning lake and mountain scenery and huge range of activities makes this a very popular tourist destination. With so many attractions it gets very busy in holiday periods with congested roads around the main centres – Ambleside and Keswick.

www.visitcumbria.com/tourist-information-centres/

Fly: Liverpool Manchester Newcastle Blackpool – 2hrs drive

Train: Windermere and Penrith

ojp.nationalrail.co.uk/service/planjourney

Moving Around
A car is easiest. However, it is feasible by bus. These run throughout the district in summer, but are less frequent out of season.

www.lakedistrict.gov.uk/visiting/planyourvisit/

MAPS
- BMC Harveys 1:40,000 Lake District
- Harveys Super Walker 1:25,000
- OS Explorer 1:25,000 OL4, OL5, OL6 and OL7
- OS Landranger Sheet 90

A compass is useful.

ACCOMMODATION
There's loads…

www.lakedistrict.gov.uk/visiting/wheretostay/

CONDITIONS
All year venue – check the forecast. MWIS and the Met Office offer reliable forecasts.

www.mwis.org.uk/english-welsh-forecast/LD/

www.metoffice.gov.uk/public/weather/national-parks-forecasts/lake-district

Midges: Aren't generally as bad as in Scotland, but are a nuisance late May to early September.

LAYOUT
Bases, crags and climbs are sequenced by reference to the FRCC definitive guidebooks, working clockwise around the district, starting from Langdale in the South. See area map inside front cover.

Crag Guide
The crag guide is a useful tool for choosing where to climb. It gives an indication of the character of the crag and the range of grades available.

Icons
See inside rear cover flap for an iconography key.

Gear
A comprehenisve rack is required for the trad climbs. Quickdraws and a full weight rope for sport climbs. Some sport routes require a 70m rope.

Bouldering
Please see www.LakesBloc.com

Corrections, New Routes, etc.
www.frcc.co.uk

AID & FIXED GEAR
Check everything. Some of the fixed abseil points may be OK, but there is a lot of rubbish around; use your judgment and if you are in any doubt back things up. The mountain crags are bolt free and should remain that way. When abseiling watch out for climbers below you.

Colin Downer has done an immense service for climbers using Bramcrag Quarry. If you meet him make sure that you thank him, but a contribution to www.cumbriaboltfund.com is better; a box is in Needlesports Keswick.

Please don't threaten access; parking considerately.

GRADES

Trad climbs use British grades and sport climbs use French grades. Grade ranges are colour coded – **Green**, **Blue**, **Red** and **Black** (see inside rear cover flap for grade colouring). To make choosing routes quick and easy these are shown in the text and on the topos.

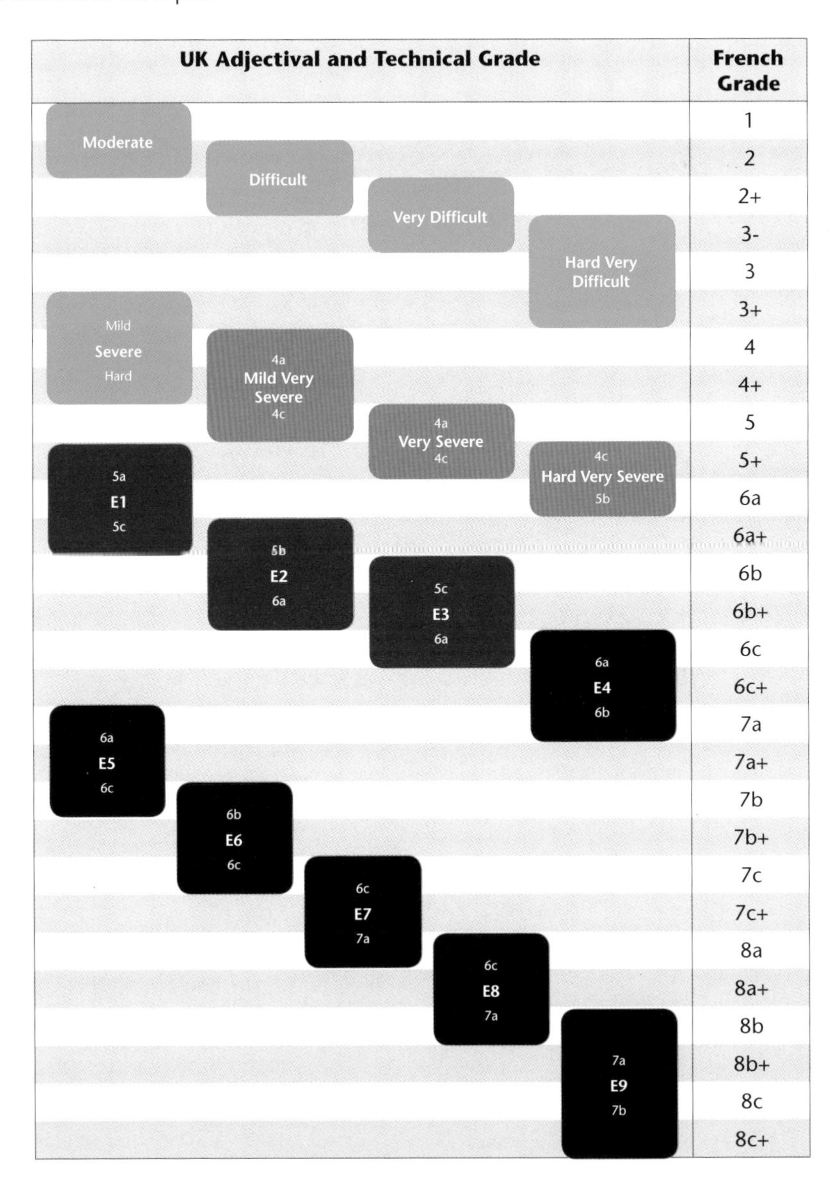

CRAG GUIDE

Area	Crag	#	←VD	S	VS	HVS	E1	E2	E3	E4	E5→
Langdale	Raven Crag Walthwaite	12		2	3	4	3				
	Scout Crags	11	8	2	1						
	White Ghyll	29		5	7	4	8	3	2		
	Stickle Barn Crag	12	2	1	5	2	1	1			
	Pavery Ark	25	5	2	3	4	2	5	1	1	2
	Raven Crags	24	3	8	5	7	1				
	Gimmer Crag	38	4	7	12	6	6	2	1		
	Bowfell Area	44	4	2	6	6	13	7	1	1	4
	Pike of Blisco Area	64	14	12	18	10	5	2	2		1
	Kettle Crag	12	1	3	8						
Dow & Slate	Dow Crag	44	4	7	5	6	3	4	1	6	8
	How Crags	12	2	5	4		1				
	Hodge Close	13				1	2	3	1	1	5
	Cathedral Quarry	6				1	2	1		2	
Eskdale & Duddon	Bell Stand	17		2	3	4	1	4	1		2
	Hare Crag	19	2	2	6	1	4	1	2		1
	Heron Crag	6			2		2		1	1	
	Brantrake Crag	26	7	3	7	4	2	1	1		1
	Esk Buttress	19		1	2	3	2	2	4	2	3
	Hardknott Crag	4						2	1	1	
	Stonestar	6			1	1	1	3			
	Wallowbarrow Crag	10	2	2	6						
	Brandy Crag	20	1	2	1	5	6	2	2	1	
	Burnt Crag	8						2	3	1	2
	Upper Great Blake Rigg	7						2	2	1	2
	Far Hill Crag	8					1	1	3	3	
	Gaitscale Area	76	8	19	18	12	5	8	4	1	1
Scafell & Wasdale	Scafell Crag	38	3	6	10	7	2	3	3	2	2
	The East Buttress	32			4	6	6	3	5	3	5
	Pikes Crag - Pulpit Rock	6	2	1	1	2					
	Piers Gill Crag	20	2	5	5	3	2	3			
	Round How	8			3	2	3				
	Buckbarrow	13		1	5	2	5				
Gable & Pillar	Kern Knotts	14		1	2	1	2	4	1	3	
	The Napes, Tophet Wall	29	6	6	5	2	3	1	1	2	3
	Gable Crag	12			3	3	1	1	4		
	Boat How Crags	13			1	2	1	2	4	1	2
	Pillar Rock	64	6	10	20	11	8	7		1	1
	Mirk Cove	22	3	3	3	5	4	3	1		
Buttermere & St Bees	Yew Crag Knotts	12	1	1	2	1	5	2			
	Zorro Buttress	4				1	2	1			
	Maidenstone Buttress	8	1		2	3	1	1			
	Buckstone How	11		1	1	6	1	2			
	Great Round How	9	2	2	3		2				
	High Crag	16		2	4	3	6		1		
	Eagle Crag	8			3	1	2		2		
	Grey Crag	17	5	5	7						
	Raven Crag High Stile	12	3	3	1		2	1	1	1	
	Newlands Valley Crags	16	1	4	6	2	3				
	St Bees	57	1	2	3	11	13	8		14	5
Borrowdale	Lower Falcon Crag	12			2	2	3	5			
	Reecastle Crag	22			1	1	3	3	3	2	9
	Goats Crag	21	1	4	1	4	4	4		3	
	Shepherd's Crag	41	6	3	11	6	9	4	2		
	Black Crag	12		1	4	2	2	1	1	1	
	Quayfoot Buttress	7	1		1	3	1	1			
	Bowderstone Area	19	1	3	5		1			1	8
	Eagle Crag	8			1			2	3	1	1
	Bleak How	8				4	2	1	1		
	Upper Heron Crag	9					2	6		1	
	Sergeant Crag Slabs	6			1	3	1	1			
	Combe Ghyll Area	25	8	5	9	3					
	Gillercombe	6	2	2	2						
	Steel Knots	17			3	4	1	4	3	2	
	Goat Crag	8				1	1	1	2	1	2
Eastern	Bramcrag Quarry	76		1	13	25	17	16	1	1	2
	Castle Rock of Triermain	20	2	3	2	2	6	3	1	1	
	Lower Swirl Crag	9				1	1	3	2	2	
	Raven Crag, Thirlmere	13			1		1		2	4	5
	Iron Crag	13					3	2		2	6
	Eagle Crag	8		1	3	2		2			
	Scrubby Crag	5		1	2	2					
	Dove Crag	12		1			1	2			8
	Raven Crag, Threshthwaite	9						1	2	3	3
	Buckbarrow Crag	19	1	6	3	3	1	1	2	1	1
	Gouther Crag	7	1	2		2	2				
EV	Armathwaite	24	2	2	3	1	6	3	5	1	1
	Chapel Head Scar	57				1	8	12		11	25
			←F3	F4	F5	F6a	F6b		F6c	F7a	F7b→

Approach	Aspect	Sun	Altitude	Notes	Page
5 mn	S		180m	A wonderful crag for a half-day; close to the road and sunny.	30
10 mn	S		210 .. 275	A range of pleasant and accessible craglets.	34
½ hr	W		400m	Imposing gill walls and a sunny aspect create a classic Lakeland venue.	37
15 mn	S		220m	Clean, sunny, quick to dry, and so easy to access!	48
1 hr	SE		540m	Possibly one of Langdale's most important venues with big enchainment options.	49
15 mn	SW		200m	Sunny, roadside, year-round climbing.	62
1 hr	S		525m	One of Lakelands sunniest high crags.	72
1 .. 2 hr	N, NE, W		550 .. 775	Mountain crags of immense atmosphere.	92
20 .. 25 mn	SW		550 .. 580	An idyllic setting and yet only a short walk walk from the Three Shire Stone.	109
½ hr	W		300m	Easier routes and a less frequented climbing venue.	114
1 hr	E		610m	First class climbing throughout the year and right across the grading spectrum.	119
1 hr	SE		550m	Well positioned overlooking Levers Water on rough sound rock.	134
2 mn	SW		170m	Climbing at Hodge Close is an adventure!	138
5 mn	NW		150m	An impressive hole of high quality slate.	143
15 mn	S		210m	A sunny, quick-drying 15m face of rough granite - similar to a gritstone edge.	149
10 mn	SW		170m	A collection of steep clean buttresses and blank slabs of rough granite.	150
½ hr	SE		250m	Biggest low-level crag in Eskdale - dries quickly.	153
10 mn	NW		90m	A fine collection of granite crags situated close to the road.	154
1 ½ hr	SE		490m	Without doubt one of the finest and most impressive crags in the district.	158
5 mn	W		440m	An imposing and impressive crag near the top of Hard Knott Pass.	165
5 mn	SW		150m	An excellent crag for a short day or evening,	168
15 mn	SW		210m	Defines the traditional crag with a selection of good routes in the VD - VS range.	171
20 mn	S		450m	A fantastic crag for confident climbers.	175
20 mn	S		350m	The best crag in the valley for the hard climber.	176
15 mn	S		590m	A hard man's dream - steep, clean, fast drying.	179
40 mn	NW		450m	A brilliant crag of superb clean rock.	180
40 .. 50 mn	S, SE		640 .. 670	Open clean outcrops arranged above Gaitscale Gill.	181
1 ½ hr	N		790m	Magnificent crag for climbers of all grades.	190
1 ¾ hr	SE		750m	Simply the best crag in the Lake District for anybody climbing at VS and above.	204
1 ¾ hr	W		760m	Large crag offering grandstand view of *Central Buttress* - and sunshine all day.	216
1 ¾ hr	SW		730m	A small compact wall of excellent rock - reminiscent of Bosigran.	221
1 ¾ hr	W		670m	Lovely rough mountain rock with late afternoon sun.	222
25 .. 30 mn	S, SE		300 .. 350	Accessible low lying crags often in condition when the high crags are shrouded in mist.	225
1 ½ hr	SW		520m	A superb crag providing high quality climbing on steep rough rock.	233
1 ¾ hr	SE, SW		650m	Magnificent area with routes of all ages and grades.	236
1 ½ hr	N		800m	A superb high mountain crag giving atmospheric climbing on excellent rock.	248
2 hr	NE		700m	This crag has a unique feeling of remoteness - well worth the effort to get there.	252
2 ½ .. 3 hr	N, S, E, W		600+	A great remote crag attractive to seekers of solitude.	256
3 hr	N		675 ..770	One of the most beautiful and remote coves in the Lake District.	285
15 mn	SW		350m	Good climbing on clean rock.	297
25 mn	SW		430m	Great routes, an open sunny aspect and absorbing climbing - well worth the walk.	300
15 mn	SW		380m	A compact, quick-drying, sunny buttress with a lovely outlook.	301
10 mn	SW		400m	Very accessible, steep and exposed. Comfortably sound with memorable experiences.	302
¾ hr	NW		520m	A superb outlook, dries very quickly catching the early evening sun.	307
¾ hr	NE		450m	Some of the most enjoyable routes in the valley, start early to make the most of the sun.	308
1 ¼ hr	NW		600m	An impressive buttress offering great climbing.	315
1 ½ hr	SE		700m	A series of short, superbly positioned buttresses.	318
1 ½ hr	SW		610m	Stunningly situated on the Ennerdale face of High Stile. Rough, firm and quick drying rock.	322
1 ¼ hr	W		400 .. 480	A quiet backwater offers varied climbing on contrasting crags.	326
20 mn	W		5m	Something for everyone – or just sunbathe, watch the sea and dream of paradise.	332
10 mn	W		180m	Long, exciting and memorable with a reputation for loose rock and tricky protection.	340
5 mn	NW		300m	Excellent crag where strong fingers are a considerable asset.	345
10 mn	SW		400m	An idyllic setting, splendid views, quick drying.	347
5 mn	W		140m	Roadside climbing across the grades and maybe the Lakes' best climber's cafe!	348
20 mn	W		260m	A superb crag in a wonderful location, one of Borrowdale's best.	362
2 mn	NW		135m	Very accessible high quality climbing on superb compact rock.	366
5 .. 20 mn	W, SW		90 .. 220	Something for everyone - easy trad to high 'sport'.	370
¾ hr	NE		500m	This crag has real character!	374
35 mn	NW		270m	A great venue on good rock.	376
1 hr	NE		440m	A crag with altitude.	378
1 hr	W		400m	Superb climbing on immaculate rock; justifiably one of the valley's most popular crags.	379
½ .. 1 hr	W, S, NE		300 .. 475	Outcrops of beautiful, clean, rough rock in this heavily glaciated valley.	380
40 mn	SE		480m	A impressive classic buttress and a bit more!	388
20 mn	SE		240m	Excellent rock and the right side of the valley for climbing in the morning sunshine.	392
1 hr	NE		350m	Impressive crag by any standard, giving considerable challenging routes.	394
10 mn	W			A high-quality sport venue with fun climbing - very popular.	398
10 mn	W, S		275 .. 300	The magnificent north crag and much friendlier south crag.	411
15 mn	SW		330m	Slightly out of the way - a steep wall of excellent rock which offers high quality climbs.	416
20 mn	E		350m	A steep and impressive place with a high density of quality hard routes.	417
40 mn	E		350m	All ranges of extreme with the hardest in the district lurking here.	420
1 ½ hr	SE		395m	Sunny, open climbing in a delightful situation.	424
1 ½ hr	SE		710m	Superb climbing in an atmospheric mountain setting.	426
1 ¼ hr	NW		580m	One of the most impressive pieces of rock in the district!	427
¾ hr	SE		450m	For those operating at E3 and above this is one of the best crags in the Lakes.	432
½ hr	SW		335m	Excellent climbing across the grades in a secluded valley.	437
½ hr	NW		330m	A delghtful isolated crag.	438
10 mn	SW		50m	A quality sandstone outcrop in a beautiful woodland setting.	446
15 mn	SW		70m	Brilliant all-year sport climbing destination - though beware of bird restrictions.	454

ACKNOWLEDGEMENTS

In 2013, with an ageing title, the FRCC team started work on a new 'the best of' selection of rock climbs in the Lakes – the guide would be comprehensive, have total photodiagram coverage, be vibrant and inspiring. Ben Ranson worked up the original design and Ron Kenyon and Peter Simcock persuaded the committee that it should go ahead.

Lake District Rock is collated from the output of the authors and past-editors of all FRCC Guides, together with the volunteers who contribute to the FRCC Guidebook committee. We have leaned heavily on the work of Max Biden and Phil Rigby who created the original photodiagrams. Many other active local climbers have been involved checking manuscripts, photodiagrams, and providing information or comment; of special mention are John Adams, Dave Birkett, Dave Bodecott, Duncan Booth, Steve Crowe, Mark Hetherington, Adam Hocking, James McHaffie, Craig Matheson, Rob Matheson, staff of Needlesports, Keith Phizacklea, Ted Rogers, Cath Sullivan and Al Wilson. The technical team: Jane Beagley (VG Graphics), Don Sargeant and Peter Sterling, produced the maps, photodiagrams and set the pages. To those of you who submitted photographs, without your input our output would be so much poorer.

Special thanks to the FRCC committee, John Barrett, Ron Kenyon and Richard Tolley for their unstinting support for the project, Trevor Langhorne for always being on hand to check proofs and edit text and Sandra for her patience. If there is anyone that I have missed please don't be upset.

With this purchase you are supporting the huge effort and investment made by volunteers collecting, storing and reproducing the record of climbing in the Lake District, for which we thank you. I hope that you enjoy climbing here and that you find inspiration in all our guides – please give us your feedback and report corrections and new routes at www.frcc.co.uk

Wired is an exciting collaborative venture between the not-for-profit guidebook publishers. Our vision is to become the publisher of choice for climbers in Britain. Neil Foster brought the definitive guidebook publishers together in 2014, the BMC supported design work, and Wired was born. Lake District Rock is the first book published in the Wired series.

Authors

Max Biden, James & Kerrie Bumby, Barry Clarke, Al Davis, Colin Downer, Andy Dunhill, Mark Eddy, Rick Graham, John Holden, Paul Jennings, Ron Kenyon, Trevor Langhorne, Peter Latimer, Jim Loxham, Al Phizacklea, Colin Read, Stephen Reid, Phil Rigby, Steve Scott, Justin Shiels, Peter Sterling, Richard Tolley, Nick Wharton & Bill Young.

Images

Action Photo Research — Ron Kenyon, Keith Sanders, Peter Sterling & Richard Tolley

Photo Diagrams
(MB) Max Biden, (SC) Steve Crowe, (AD) Andy Dunhill, (JH) John Holden, (SH) Stuart Halford, (PJ) Paul Jennings, (RK) Ron Kenyon, (TL) Trevor Langhorne, (AP) Al Phizacklea, (CR) Colin Read, (PR) Phil Rigby, (SR) Stephen Reid, (ES) Eric Shaw, (RT) Richard Tolley, (NW) Nick Wharton & (BY) Bill Young

Steve Scott – FRCC Guidebook Editor
March 2015

LAKELAND GUIDEBOOKS

Early Years

By the end of the Victorian age the pastime of rock climbing was becoming popular as an enjoyable gymnastic and social pursuit in its own right, disconnected from mountaineering in the Alps. Edwardian climbers were becoming more technically proficient, practising on local outcrops, and they were keen to learn about the routes that had already been explored. Much of the information had been recorded in club Journals and log books maintained at hotels, the chief of these being the Wasdale Head Hotel and in Wales, the Pen-y-Gwyrd Hotel.

At that time the Fell and Rock was a very young club, yet in1908 Scantlebury had proposed the formation of a guidebook committee and the year after Seatree, the President, raised the matter again announcing that "in the near future, it would be probable that small handbooks [of] climbs in the Lake District would be published." Information had appeared in FRCC Journals from 1907. Then, in 1909, The Climbers' Club published the first modern guidebook, Lliwedd by Thompson and Andrews. Immediately, Geoffrey Winthrop Young asked Siegfried Herford to chronicle the cliffs of Scafell. As ever while undertaking the route checking Central Buttress was climbed. The results were published in the 1914 FRCC Journal. The FRCC work continued, but was later abandoned as others were producing material that fitted the bill. The intervention of the hostilities stalled further work.

Editor - RST Chorley

After the war matters were slow to gather momentum, until finally, with the appointment of Chorley as Editor in 1921, a series of guides selling at two shillings (10p) each and covering the whole District was planned. The first Doe (Dow) Crag appeared in 1922, with the full series completed by 1926. These are amazing hand finished artefacts much sought after by todays collectors. The same material was also reproduced in the FRCCJs.

The 1930s – Harry Kelly

A new decade; a new Editor. Harry Kelly had been involved from the off and the 2nd series took the form of The Climbers' Club guides – compact, pocket-sized, hard backed. The photodiagrams were replaced by Heaton Cooper's magical line drawings and Kelly's terse succinct descriptions condensed the material to four volumes. Kelly continued as Editor with little change producing a 3rd series and several re-prints.

Frustration and Pirates

Paul Ross and Mike Thompson exasperated at the FRCC's lethargy in updating Borrowdale – the 1953 guide had merely been re-printed in 1960 – produced their own private guide in 1966. They used the **XS** grade (today superseded by **E**xtreme grades) and from inception to publication the whole thing took just 6 weeks! The establishment of the FRCC responded by threatening legal action, but nothing came of it, although the FRCC were galvanised and their Borrowdale guide appeared in 1968 just as the 2000 private copies sold out.

Post-Kelly – John Wilkinson

The Club realised that the guides needed to be modernised and the pace of publication stepped up: John Wilkinson was drafted in. His impact was immediate and pronounced. The cover was re-designed with bright graphics and new plastic encapsulated covering was road tested by Wilkinson who threw one repeatedly at a wall for over an hour! Wilkinson changed the font, introduced maps and embraced the extension to the adjectival grading system and later **E** grades. The simple compact size was retained. Heaton Cooper remained as illustrator and his watercolours featured at the front of the books. Wilkinson's output was prodigious and Rocksport commented on the fluidity of the FRCC guidebook 'machine'. Wilkinson presided over the 4th and 5th series handing over to David Miller in 1978.

Lakeland Climbers Guide Books

Steve Clegg, Colin Read and Bob Wilson, frustrated by the dull and wordy FRCC guides, set about covering the District in three small volumes. Lake District North (1978) and Lake District South (1979) were inexpensive, slim, succinct books with line topos and no colour. In his introduction Steve describes the minimalist approach that would be taken "to describe climbs of merit" - 500 climbs are contained in a mere 130 pages with all of the extraneous 'dross' excluded. His suggestion that "climbers wishing to discover them are welcome to do so, but please keep it to yourself." makes the climbing of these dirty and obscure lines sound like a bad habit. This team introduced the linking of the best pitches from different routes to produce a better climb.

Hard Facts and Ken Wilson

In 1977 Ken Wilson let rip; in Mountain 57 he complained that all of the major publishers were failing to produce what climbers wanted, leaving the market open to selective guidebook producers who would "cream off the best routes, ignore history and ethics … and kill off definitive guides."[1] The FRCC could be providing better value as its authors and Editor seemed to be unable to produce clear succinct route descriptions and this resulted in more volumes than was necessary. The Club had spurned the invitation to produce a selective guide to the Lakes from members Eilbeck, Cram and Roper and then complained of copyright infringement when this team successfully turned to Constable. Wilkinson wasn't at fault in all of this – he had achieved an awful lot in a short period, he wanted to run with the selective but was overruled by the committee. Many of his new ideas were in the pipeline when he stepped down after eleven productive years.

Constable

The selective guide wasn't a new concept. The trio of members rejected by the FRCC committee turned to Constable and the guide was published. Defending definitives to the hilt Terry Sullivan published a 'damning indictment'[1] of "composite, scissor and glue… cut price guidebooks" in the 1976 FRCCJ. He raised the ethical question about collective ownership by the climbing community of the intellectual property recorded and distributed by the clubs and challenged commercial use and gain from this information. The climbing community are being resold what they already own! This strong notion was somewhat diluted by what had gone before, with the FRCC committee turning it's back on this popular idea – the guide has run into 4 editions with 2 reprints and sold over 15,000 copies.

Rejuvenation - David Miller & Dave Armstrong

Leading young climbers Armstrong, Berzins, Cleasby, Matheson, Sowden and Whillance were drafted onto the committee and their ideas fundamentally altered the appearance and utility of the guides. The most noticeable changes are the colour action photographs on the covers and the introduction of Al Phizacklea's meticulous and accurate crag diagrams. These diagrams, drawn from photographs projected onto Al's living room wall, have become iconic and appeared in all of the guides until 2007 when colour photodiagrams replaced them. The 6th series morphed into the 7th as the concept of the series became redundant and Armstrong implemented his rolling programme of one guide per year. The main improvement was the inclusion of the diagrams within the text and more action images appeared.

Topos

Disappointed by the lack of a guide to the Duddon Al brought his skills into play to produce a superbly crafted topo sheet – The Duddon Valley Crag Guide: Still Britain's crappest guidebook. The hand copied 4 stapled sheets of A4 contain an amazingly comprehensive, simple and clear guide to the whole valley. Together with his incisive comments and tourist guide notes Al introduced decimalised **E** grades to help visitors with the broad range of difficulty encounterted. The classic *Shifter* on Burnt Crag is graded **E3.4** while neighbour *Innocenti* gets **E3.6**. If you can get hold of one – grab it!

Many other topos to bouldering and micro-crags have emerged and remain popular.

Rockfax

No review would be complete without Rockfax. The Lakes Rockfax was published in 1994 and authors Andy Hyslop and Paul Cornforth concentrated almost exclusively on sport climbing on limestone in the south, quarried slate, sandstone at St Bees, micro-granite and rhyolite. It offered hand-drawn simple line topos and finally sold out in 2012.

Professionalism – Al Phizacklea; Stephen Reid

After Al singlehandedly produced the 1996 Scafell, Dow & Eskdale guide It was clear that the workload for the Editor needed to be better organised and resourced. Ron Kenyon held the fort for a few years after being installed as Business Manager to take on production matters. Stephen Reid took over in time for Langdale in 1999 and to further strengthen the team photograph and diagram sub-editors were appointed.

Stephen carried the editorial mantle for twelve years embracing the opportunities made available by changes in print and paper technology to modernise the guides. A milestone was the first FRCC selective guide, Lake District Rock (2003). Conceived as a centenary tribute to the FRCC

[1] With thanks to Stephen Reid: A History of Lake District Climbing Guidebooks FRCCJ 2006.

Guidebook Editors. This was a full colour production and the swan-song for Al's diagrams, also now enhanced by colour. Then in a flourish the 2007 Gable & Pillar guide saw the introduction of the full colour photodiagram coverage that we are used to using today. Phil Rigby was responsible for much of the work in this and the next three guides, handing over to Max Biden to finish the Langdale diagrams.

The FRCC were approached by Cicerone to provide technical input to their winter guide to the District that Brian Davison authored and Stephen edited this as a joint publication. Photo Editor Nick Wharton persuaded the committee to hire a plane to take the crag images. This was completed in one flight on a beautiful crisp winters day. Reinforcing the popularity of winter climbing in the Lakes this first edition of 3,000 sold out in 6 years.

An Outsider – Steve Scott

The second edition of the winter guide was under pressure and Kendal local Steve Scott was drafted in to oversee the work. Offering little in the way of innovation, yet filling the void that would be left this 2nd edition contained all of the new material and for the first time a well-researched first ascent section. With the support of the professional editorial team at Cicerone, in a blindingly rapid four months, the guide was prepared and appeared on time in November 2012.

Steve then set about revitalising what looked like an ageing definitive series. After much discussion contemporary limpbound card covers with flaps were introduced and a sans-serif font was adopted offering a crisp, clear typeface for the user. After careful research the size was increased, the final decision influenced by the version that fitted in Al's jacket pocket! This allowed the action shots to be showcased and the photodiagrams to be clearer in use.

The long-awaited Langdale guide, although a compromise as the material had been designed for the 'old' size, indicated how things would be developed. However, with the Scafell & Wasdale 'CB Centenary Edition' the full benefit of the larger format was utilised.

The current 'series' will be completed with the publication of Dow Coppermines & Slate, Eskdale & Duddon, and Borrowdale. What comes next? Well who knows...

At his first guidebook committee meeting Steve pressed the FRCC to consider starting work on a selective guide to replace the outdated, but still popular, Lake District Rock. The committee backed this project and work began in the autumn of 2013. After the loss of the page-setter Ben Ranson to proper work, the project stalled.

In 2014 Neil Foster prompted the BMC to host a meeting of the not-for-profit guidebook producers. The discussion focussed on the issues that these publishers faced as the market polarised to support private selective output. From these talks **Wired** has been conceived to produce a series of selectives and strengthen awareness of the quality and authority of the work of the clubs producing definitives. Lake District Rock Wired published by the FRCC is the first of that series.

Steve Scott – FRCC Guidebook Editor

DEFINITIVE GUIDEBOOKS

The FRCC publishes a complete range of definitive guidebooks documenting all of the climbing areas of the Lake District in summer and winter.

Langdale

With some of the most varied, enjoyable and popular climbing in the Lake District; describing over 850 routes with comprehensive, high-quality, photodiagram coverage and Harveys maps.

Max Biden ISBN: 978-0-85028-054-8

Buttermere & St Bees

Describes High Crag, Eagle Crag and Grey Crag, the newly developed Raven Crag on the Ennerdale face of High Stile, plus the Newlands Valley and the sunny sandstone cliffs of St Bees.

Colin Read & Paul Jennings ISBN: 978-0-85028-048-7

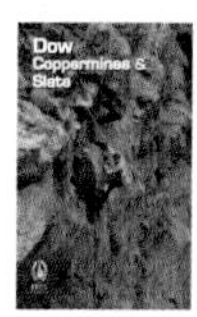

Dow, Coppermines & Slate

A guide to the most easily accessible mountain crag in the District, a secluded esoteric valley and fingery, wild slate this guide offers something for everyone.

John Holden

Borrowdale

This popular valley offers a lifetime of superb roadside cragging, some of the most accessible 'hard' venues in the Lakes and a couple of classic mountain crags.

Justin Shiels, Andy Dunhill, Trevor Langhorne, Steve Scott, Richard Tolley, Ron Kenyon & Peter Latimer

Eskdale & Duddon

Quiet, friendly outcrops above trees and bracken in a popular valley; a majestic mountain venue; esoteric gems and hard test-pieces, all worth seeking out.

Al Phizacklea & Mark Eddy

Eastern Crags

From Thirlmere north to Carrock Fell and south to Kendal, east to Patterdale and beyond. The home of fantastic crags: Castle Rock, Raven Crag (both of them) and Dove to name a few.

Al Davis & Nick Wharton ISBN: 978-0-85028-051-1

Scafell & Wasdale

Inspiring action shots, Harveys maps and extensive photodiagram coverage get you to your chosen climb. Published to coincide with the centenary of the first ascent of the *Central Buttress*.

Al Phizacklea & Ron Kenyon ISBN: 978-0-85028-055-5

Eden Valley & South Lakes Limestone

The crags and quarries described in this guide are scattered over a large area of North, East and South Cumbria outwith the Lake District.

Ron Kenyon, Nick Wharton & John Holden

ISBN: 978-0-85028-052-4

Gable & Pillar

A guide to the traditional home of Lakeland climbing. This guide describes hundreds of the finest mountain routes in the most superb of locations.

Phil Rigby & Stephen Reid ISBN:978-0-85028-047-0

Lake District Winter Climbs

The FRCC winter climbs guidebook to the Lake District and Cumbria is published jointly with Cicerone Press.

Brian Davison

ISBN: 978-1-85284-716-6

Definitive Guidebooks

A BRIEF HISTORY OF CLIMBING IN THE LAKES

What would the early climbers in the Lakes think if they could look down on the routes being climbed today? Broad Stand was descended by Samuel T Coleridge in 1802 and in 1826 John Atkinson (a local cooper/shepherd) ascended Pillar Rock: his ascent was given due prominence in two county papers.

In the late 19th century Wasdale Head became a regular haunt for climbers at the then named "Huntsman Inn". Many of these climbers were venturing to and developing the Alps, Norway and beyond. The fells and crags round Wasdale Head were not on the same scale but gave many challenges on Scafell, Gable and Pillar. Initial interest was directed at gullies but as confidence grew the ridges and walls were explored. In 1886 Walter Parry Haskett Smith soloed the iconic *Napes Needle* **HS** on the front of Great Gable with only a pole to safeguard his ascent and descent. In 1892 Godfrey Solly moved things on with *Eagle's Nest Ridge Direct* **MVS** – a bold route he felt was unjustifiably dangerous and gave due warning when recording it.

One of the first ever bouldering guides was produced in 1898 by Oscar Eckenstein and Aleister Crowley to the Y-Boulder. The Abraham Brothers (Ashley and George) ran a photography business in Keswick and were closely involved with the climbing scene with many first ascents but also capturing the climbs of the Lakes, and beyond, which helped to promote rock climbing. Owen Glynne Jones was attracted to the Lakes when he saw an Abrahams' photograph in a shop window in The Strand in London – which in due time led to many routes bearing his name – the classic *Jones' Route Direct from Lord's Rake* **HS** being one of them as well as *Kern Knotts Crack* **VS**. Jones spent considerable time on *Kern Knott's Crack* and he is reputed to have been able to climb the Crack and descend *Kern Knotts Chimney* **HS** in seven minutes.

In 1903 Fred Botterill led *Botterill's Slab* **VS** in nailed boots with a rucksack and carrying an ice axe. At one point, not wishing to be parted from his ice axe he seized it between his teeth whilst raising his hat to a lady on the screes below! Sadly, shortly afterwards there was a terrible accident when four climbers were killed attempting to reach Hopkinson's Cairn on Scafell Pinnacle – this tragedy marked the end of the "Golden Age" of exploration around Scafell and caused a lull in proceedings. In 1912 Siegfried Herford and George Sansom successfully completed this route, *Direct from Lord's Rake to Hopkinson's Cairn* **S**.

This pair then went on to climb *Hopkinson's Gully* **MVS** and *Girdle Traverse of Scafell* **MVS** and then in 1914 *Central Buttress* **HVS/E1**, which was a huge breakthrough in standard. The Great War was then to dominate the world and with it take the lives of many climbers, including Herford, and a future generation.

Following the War Harry Mills Kelly arrived on the climbing scene pioneering many new routes and classics of today including *Rib and Slab* **HS**, *Tophet Wall* **HS**, *Moss Gill Grooves* **MVS** and *Grooved Wall* **VS**.

That other "big" crag in the south of the Lakes – Dow Crag – attracted climbers from the late 19th century onwards. J I Roper pushed up standards on the crag with *Great Central Route* **HVS** and *Black Wall* **HVS** then H S Gross and G Basterfield completed the three Eliminates – *A,B* and *C* **VS** – together with an epic *Girdle Traverse* **VS** with 7½ hours of climbing.

In 1922 C D Frankland and Bentley Beetham spied and climbed *Brown Slabs Arete* **D** but it was 25 years before Beetham returned to develop Shepherds Crag.

East Buttress of Scafell is an impressive area of rock – this was first breached by Colin Kirkus, Ivan Waller and Marco Pallis in 1931 with *Mickledore Grooves* **VS** – the ascent led to further routes, spearheaded by Maurice Linnell, with *Great Eastern Route* **VS**, *Overhanging Wall* **HVS**, *Morning Wall* **MVS** and *The Yellow Slab* **HVS**.

In 1937 the first member of the Birkett clan appeared on the scene. Jim Birkett, a quarryman from Little Langdale often accompanied by Len Muscroft and Charlie Wilson, went on to dominate Lakeland climbing for the next 12 years or so. On Scafell's East Buttress they climbed *May Day Climb* using combined tactics, now **E1** its first free ascent by Alf Mullan in 1938 was the first extreme lead in the Lakes, as well as the *Girdle*

Traverse **HVS**. In 1939 they made the first successful ascent of the north face of Castle Rock with *Overhanging Bastion* **VS** – reported by the press with their usual accuracy as "Lakeland Everest Conquered". This was followed shortly afterwards by *Zig Zag* **VS** and others elsewhere including *F Route* **VS** and *Haste Knot* **VS**.

Bill Peascod could see the Lakeland fells from his home in West Cumbria and a new world, away from the mines, was discovered when he made a bike ride into the Buttermere valley. He developed his climbing skills and began a flow of new routes with *Eagle Front* **VS**, *Dexter Wall* **VS**, *Sinister Groove* **VS**, *Cleopatra* **VS** and many more. He emigrated to Australia in the 1950s but came back in the 1980's and continued to produce new routes.

In the 1940's Arthur Dolphin appeared on the scene producing new routes on Great Gable with *Demon Wall* **VS** and *Tophet Girdle* **HVS**. Well practised on Yorkshire gritstone his route *Kipling Groove* **HVS** was much bolder in conception than its contemporaries – named due to it being "ruddy 'ard". More climbs followed, often with Pete Greenwood: *Deer Bield Buttress* **E1** (now collapsed), *Sword of Damocles* **E1**, *Pegasus* **HVS**, *Hell's Groove* **E1** and *Trespasser Groove* **HVS**. Sadly in 1953 Dolphin was killed when he fell from easy ground below the Dent du Geant in the Alps – a huge loss. In 1956 Greenwood hung up his climbing gear until he was enticed back onto rock, by Paul Ross, 33 years later when opening up Spout Head Crag on Great End.

Paul Ross started climbing in 1953, soloing routes at his nearby Shepherd's Crag and climbed his first new route *Troutdale Pinnacle Superdirect* **HVS** to be followed by many more initially in Borrowdale and Thirlmere areas. *Post Mortem* **E3** has given many epic ascents. Many have been relieved to reach the top of *The Bludgeon* **E1** but just remember that Ross's only protection was a peg at the bottom of the big flake because he thought if he put a sling on the pinnacle it would collapse if he fell onto it! Many more tales - best told round a camp fire.

Allan Austin started his climbing on his Yorkshire grit and was particularly active in Langdale where he developed Pavey Ark with *Golden Slipper* **HVS**, *Astra* **E2** and *Red Groove* **E1**. He was involved in a day of frenzied activity on Esk Buttress as two rival teams raced for *Central Pillar* **E2**. Austin, Jack Soper and Matey Metcalf were talking in the Old Dungeon Ghyll pub of plans to go and climb this "plum". Unfortunately for them an informant of Pete Crew overheard this and contacted Crew who made a dawn start and was well established on the route when Austin's party appeared – their compensations were *Red Groove* **E1** and the aptly named *Black Sunday* **HVS**.

Some climbers go for quantity – Les Brown went for quality. He was on the first ascent of Nuptse, with Chris Bonington, in 1961. He had an eye for lines – *Gormenghast* **HVS**, *Side Walk* **E2**, *The Balrog* **E2** and *The Nazgul* **E3**, a tremendous "last great problem" climbed in typical Brown secrecy – inquisitive competitors were told he was exploring Far East Buzzard Crag. *Praying Mantis* **E1** was the first and his only new route on Goat Crag.

... and some go for quantity - Ray McHaffie! Mac was born in Carlisle and before he took up climbing he was the leader of a gang of teddy boys. During one fracas with a rival gang he was struck in the face with an axe and lost the sight of an eye. Luckily he discovered rock climbing! His first new routes were in 1959 and in 1962 he climbed *Interloper* **E1** and *The Niche* **E2** with Ado Liddell. He pioneered and unearthed many, many routes and also crags – including Sergeant Crag, Grange Crag and Piers Gill Crag. Also known as the Jaws of Borrowdale – the route *White Noise* **E3** was so named by Jeff Lamb after leading it to the accompaniment of Mac's distinctive voice. Mac's son James continues the McHaffie legacy.

In the 1960s a West Cumberland group of climbers including Geoff Cram, Bill Young, Chris Eilbeck, and Bill Lounds formed the Pillar Group and began to develop Pillar Rock producing a wealth of excellent routes including *Electron/Thanatos* **HVS**, *Necromancer* **E1**, *Gondor* **E2** and *Puppet* **E2**. In those days one could drive all the way up the valley to below Pillar Rock thus making access much easier – but still not a road side crag.

Add Towards the end on the 1960's Colin Read and John Adams produced cutting edge routes around the Lakes with *Deimos* **E3** and *Phobos* **E2** as well as the mega-traverse of *Lord of the Rings* **E2** which took two days to complete. Read unfortunately had a serious accident to his hand but returned to climbing, years later, to continue to claim first ascents marked up in his "black book".

The decades come and go and each one brings forward new climbers and often attitudes. The 1970s was quite a decade. In the South Lakes Rob Matheson came on the scene, often with his father Murdoch. Dow Crag was the arena for his first forays with *Catacomb* **E1**, *Tarkus* **E1**, *The Pink Panther* **E2**, *Hesperus* **E2** and *Holocaust* **E4**.

Pete Livesey adopted a professional approach – a very focused and able sportsman, being "the best" at all sports that he did – rock climbing

was one of them. Training, pre-inspections and preparation of routes was part of his approach. He had a galvanising effect on the Lakeland scene in 1974 with a series of routes of an increased standard to what the locals were producing. Quality not quantity was his aim - *Raindrop* **E1** was his first new route but he upped the game with *Eastern Hammer* **E3**, *Dry Grasp* **E4**, *Rough* **E4** and *Tumble* **E4**, *Lost Horizon* **E4** then *Bitter Oasis* **E4** and *Footless Crow* **E5**.

There was some controversy when Tut Braithwaite and Rod Valentine climbed *The Cumbrian* **E5** with 3 points of aid – the route was however done in the traditional way – i.e. ground up – and the route needed cleaning hence the need for the aid points. There were reverse arguments, by the traditionalists about the routes *Peccadillo* **E4**, *The Graduate* **E4**, *Cruel Sister* **E3** and *Fine Time* **E5** which were pre-inspected and had preplaced slings – these routes were omitted from the 1973 Langdale guidebook. A clash of the changing cultures.

The Lakes scene polarised North and South with in the 'North "Carlisle MC" corner' Pete Whillance, Jeff Lamb, Pete Botterill, Steve Clegg and Dave Armstrong etc. and in the 'South corner' Rob Matheson, Ed Cleasby, Rick Graham, Bill Birkett, Andy Hislop, Al Phizacklea etc. With the new approach, training regime and newly developed outcrops of Chapel Head Scar and Armathwaite – they "took on the world". The new routes flowed: *The Gates of Delirium* **E4**, *Creation* **E5**, *Grand Alliance* **E3**, *Verdict* **E4**, *Supernatural* **E5**, *Saxon* **E2**, *Shadowfax* **E4**, *Edge of Eriador* **E4**, *Shere Khan* **E5** and *Misty Mountain Hop* **E3**. Additional input from Yorkshire was provided by Martin Berzins, usually accompanied by Chris Sowden, with the likes of *Ringwraith* **E6** and *Foxshooter* **E4**.

The locals were aware of a big hole in the ground – Hodge Close – however it was the Carlisle MC team which started the new route rush initially with *Stiff Little Fingers* (now fallen down), *Behind the Lines* **HVS** and *Main Event* **E5** – before Matheson and Cleasby came on the scene, while the Carlisle lads were in Pembroke, with the likes of *Ten Years After* **E4**. Slate had arrived!

In the past many lines had been called "The Last Great Problem", with new approaches and better gear **E5** was becoming the established grade on which to base future developments. The Last Great Problems began to be solved and the new routes began to flow – *Fear and Fascination* **E5**, *Fast and Furious* **E5**, *The Almighty* **E5**, *Rudolf Nureyev* **E5** ... then *Incantations* **E6** and *Borderline* **E6** ... then *The Siege Perilous* **E7** and *Vlad the Impailer* **E7** and *First and Last and Always* **E7** in 1990 – what a change over just 20 years!

The '90s saw another Birkett appear on the scene – Dave Birkett. Dave singlehandedly moved Lakeland climbing up a few notches. In 1991 *Dawes Rides a Shovel Head* **E8** was the culmination of attempts over 40 years to free the central wall of Raven Crag Buttress. The year after he really pulled the stops out with *If 6 was 9* **E9** – it was 15 years before it received a second ascent by Dave McLeod – his account is somewhat sobering! Towards the end of the '90s Birkett looked for *New Horizons* **E9** on the East Buttress followed by *Talbot Horizon* **E9** before a powerful trio of routes starting with *Welcome to the Cruel World* **E9** and later *Return of the King* **E9**. Many lonely days were spent going up to Scafell in preparation for all these routes – but worth all the effort when he ended up with a route like *Another Lonely Day* **E8** which he described as "simply the best route in the country".

Enchainements are an interesting concept of linking a number of climbs or mountains together to give a good day out. In the fellrunning world the 'Bob Graham' links 42 peaks in a continuous round. In climbing there is an infinite variety such as doing routes on different crags round a valley or linking a theme (Peascod's Ladies). Classic Rock and Hard Rock are two iconic books listing some of the best routes in Britain at a particular grade range. Nick Wharton and Brian Davison did the Lake District Classic Rock routes in a day which they felt comparable with a 'Bob Graham' day and it is believed that the Hard Rock routes have also been done in a day – what about Extreme Rock. To cap all these however James McHaffie had a day out assisted by his school pal Adam Hocking and others. Starting at 2.55am on *Central Buttress*, climbing with a head torch, he soloed 100 extremes finishing with *Angels Highway* at 10.15pm.

There have been many other climbers who have helped knit this story together however unfortunately space does not allow these to be included in this brief history.

The end result is a huge collection of routes of all grades awaiting out there to test and enjoy.

Ron Kenyon

EDEN ROCK™
Carlisle
01228 522 127
www.edenrockclimbing.com
The largest bouldering wall in the North of England

LANGDALE

Langdale is without doubt one of the finest of the Lakeland valleys, where the climber is immersed in some of England's most magnificent mountain scenery.

Langdale is an all-year climbing venue with a large proportion of the crags facing south. Plus, there is a spread from roadside to high mountain climbing options. Despite sporting some extreme and improbable challenges, the climber operating in the grades below **E3** will find brilliant value in this superb Lakeland valley.

Langdale's popularity with walkers and climbers goes back a very long time. Situated close to motorway and rail links on the southern side of the Lake District, it is easily accessible from the south and this puts significant pressure on the limited parking facilities. On sunny days it usually pays to arrive early. Together all these factors have sustained the popularity of the valley. However, if you are faced with a queue an equally good alternative will probably be close by. For those willing to walk a little further for a quieter day there are some sparkling gems hidden here.

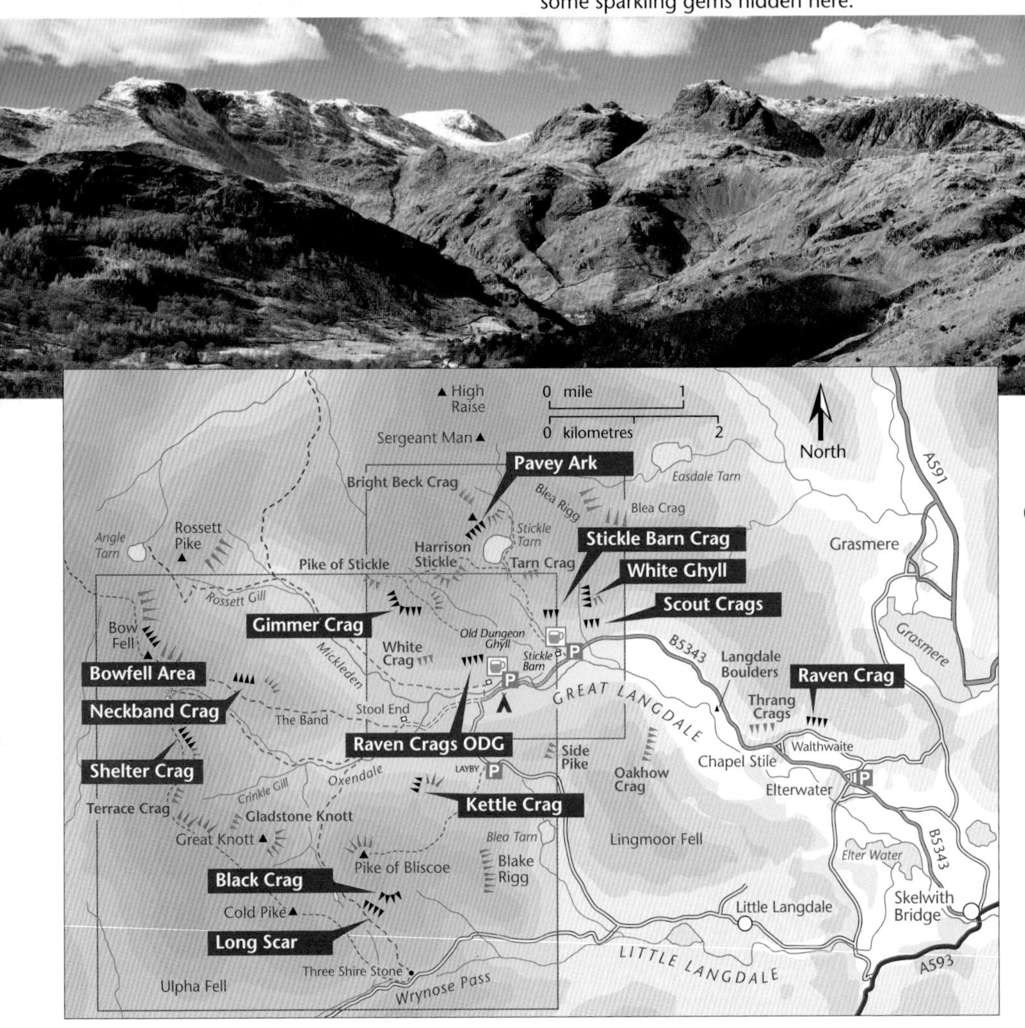

☐ *Flat Iron Wall,* Flat Crags E1 (page 97) Susan Jensen — MAX BIDEN

RAVEN CRAG WALTHWAITE

OS Grid Ref: NY 325 057
Altitude: 180m

A popular venue for an evening, a short day or poor weather alternative with generally sound and quick-drying rock. Care is needed as various scars indicate the rock can have a propensity to shear. Belays can be sparse at the top of the crag, and may have to be sought well back.

Approach: Diagonally up the hillside from the small parking layby, P NY 324 055.

Descent: Easily round either side of the crag.

Main Buttress

1 Route 1 22m S ★★
Pleasant climbing but with sparse protection. Start by belaying in the large holly beneath the slab. Move up to a ledge and follow the well marked way, first left then slightly right.
Pre 1950

2 Enterprize 22m VS 4b ★★★
Excellent climbing up the fine arête. From the holly, climb the groove right of the arête and gain its crest. Pull over a slight bulge onto the broader upper section which leads direct to the top.
N Gough - Sep 1963

3 Hardup Wall 22m VS 4b ★
Climb the parallel groove right of *Enterprize* to a good ledge. An awkward move guards entry to the recess above and easier ground.
1950s

4 Route 2 37m HS 4b ★★★
A gem with interesting and varied climbing. Start at the toe of the crag.
1 10m Climb the groove, move left onto the rib and up to a spacious ledge.
2 27m 4b The shallow square-cut groove leads to two horizontal bands of good pockets. Traverse right for 3m (crux), then leftwards into a corner. Swing onto the overhanging rib and finish up the awkward groove.
Pre 1950

⑤ Tritus-Protus 27m HVS 5a ★★★

An excellent steep and very direct combination with a fine exposed finish. Start behind the upper of two large hollies. Climb straight up the bulging wall on juggy holds to a resting place beneath twin grooves. Step left and climb the larger left-hand groove and the wall above to the final slanting roof. A small clean-cut groove slices through the left side of this to give a direct and spectacular finish; easier than it looks.

Start RM Biden, KW Forsythe - c1977;
Finish DC Birch, AR Dolphin - Jun 1947

⑥ Walthwaite Gully 27m VS 4c ★★

Not a gully but a fine corner flake giving exciting climbing in a sheltered setting. Don't be put off by the trees, they are quite benign but night definitely approaches more quickly here. Start by a small hawthorn tree below the main corner.

1 10m 4c The corner crack leads to the large ledge. Easy for gritstoners!

2 17m 4c Follow the fierce-looking flake-crack up the corner and rightwards round the roof to finish through the not-too-prickly holly tree.

JA Austin, JM Ruffe May - 1957

Right-Hand Buttress

The short wall right of Walthwaite Gully provides a number of steep pitches with a somewhat serious feel to them.

7 Persephone 23m HVS 5a ★
Good climbing around the central bulges.
M Scrowston, D Till - Jun 2008

8 Swing to the Left 22m E1 5b
An even bolder start than its sibling.
I Williamson, J White - Jun 1987

9 Swing to the Right 22m E1 5b ★★
Interesting climbing with a bold start.
I Williamson, J Billingham - Jun 1987

10 Party Animal 22m E1 5b ★★
This feels less serious if you spot the crucial nut-slot before you start.
I Williamson, J White - Jun 1987

11 Proportional Representation 20m HVS 5a ★
A fair pitch up the groove starting from the highest block behind the ash tree.
J White, G Hussey - Jun 1987

12 Militant Tendency 20m HVS 5a ★
Short grooves and knobbly black rock lead to a bulging wall. The finish rightwards is quite bold, but a left-hand escape is possible.
J White, I Williamson - Jun 1987

Swing to the Right E1 Peter Sterling — Laetitia Sterling

SCOUT CRAGS

OS Grid Ref: NY 298 069
Altitude: 210m to 275m

10 mn

Lower Scout Crag

Short steep routes, popular with groups. The rock has become highly polished by generations of feet, and the uncertain beginner should resist being put off by the resulting air of insecurity – things can only get better.

Approach: Take a track on the right side of a road-side barn, some 200m east of the Stickle Barn/New Dungeon Ghyll car parks P NY 294 063. This leads to each crag in turn.

Descent: By the path left of the crag.

Stickle Barn Cra
Page 48
P Stickle Barn
MB

1 Cub's Arête 11m S ★
A groove and small overlap just left of the arête. Avoid the large overhang by an airy traverse right.

2 Cub's Groove 13m VD ★
An excellent short introduction to climbing. A right-slanting line of polished holds leads first to ledges below the holly, then back left to finish.

3 Cub's Crack 13m HS 4b ★
The steep crack to the holly gives a good but slippery introduction to jamming. Passing the prominent nose is awkward.
J Summermatter - Oct 1927

4 Cub's Wall 13m VD ★
The shallow left-facing groove is climbed with minimal protection until forced left to join the ledge system and corner above.

5 The Slab 12m MVS ★
An especially polished route up the attractive but unprotected slab. Rightwards to the arête, then up and back left into the triangular niche where an insecure, tricky move gains easier ground.
J Summermatter - Oct 1927

Upper Scout Crag

The larger buttress with some lovely open pitches of rough, generally easy angled rock.

Approach: Follow the track above Lower Scout Crag, over a stile and past Middle Scout Crag.

Descent: From the highest point of the crag, an exposed but well worn path scrambles across and down leftwards (facing in), ending in a short crack down glaciated slabs into the easy descent gully.

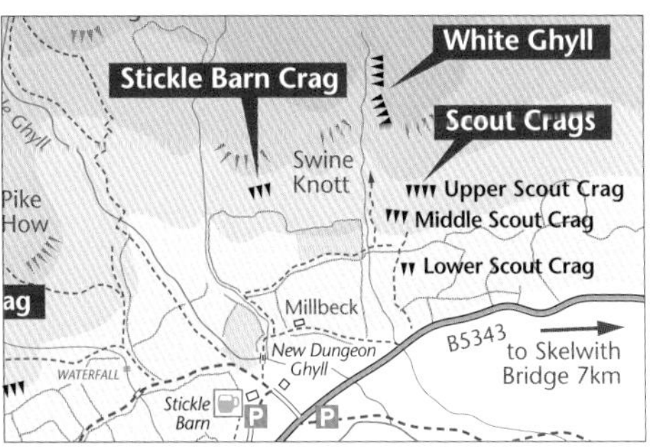

6 Route 2 55m VD ★★

Start at a detached spur of rock.

1 10m A 6m stepped groove is best entered from the right and leads to a terrace.
2 13m The polished crack leads to a short corner from which an awkward move rightwards gains a ledge with a fine oak tree belay.
3 13m Traverse 3m right and make some interesting moves up and just left of the overhangs to belay in the groove above.
4 19m Step back left and climb the easy-angled rib.
F Graham - Oct 1922

7 Route 1.5 43m VD ★

After a wet start, this route improves with height.

1 13m Climb into the mossy V-groove. Exit right after 4m and ascend to the belay of *Route 1*.
2 11m Traverse left beneath the overhangs until an awkward move joins *Route 2*.
3 19m Finish more easily up the slabs above.
RA Ewin, JR Files - Oct 1947

(8) Route 1 50m VD ★★★

An excellent route up the central rib. Adequate protection is available for the careful leader with a good range of nuts. Start left of a yew tree and below a large holly.

1 14m A short left-slanting ramp and pocketed, slabby grooves above lead to a block belay.
2 36m Climb onto the block and traverse right to the arête. Ascend this on wonderful pocketed rock in a delightfully exposed position to a ledge. Continue past flakes and easier slabs to nut and chipped flake belays.
F Graham - Oct 1922

(9) Route 1.75 46m D ★★

The easiest way up the centre of the crag provides pleasant open climbing.

1 14m As *Route 1*.
2 32m From the belay block, climb up into the bottom of the main corner. Follow good holds diagonally leftwards above the overhangs and wander up the slabs just to the right of *Route 1.5*.

(10) The Ramsbottom Variation 46m VD ★★

An excellent variation taking the prominent central corner in the upper half of the crag.

1 14m As *Route 1*.
2 32m Climb above the belay block into the main corner and climb its right-hand side until the corner bulges. Surmount this with a step up left and continue up the slabs above.
RA Brayshore, NKT Froggatt - Easter 1957

(11) Zero Route 50m VD ★

A pleasant route with a good second pitch. Start at a steep little wall just right of the yew tree.

1 14m Climb the wall past a small halfway ledge, then slabs to a flake belay. This pitch is often wet but can be bypassed on its right.
2 36m The wall on the left is split by a right-slanting shallow groove. Climb this, over a small bulge, to a junction with *Route 1*. Nail-worn rock is the best guide that you are on route.
S Thompson, J Diamond - Apr 1939

WHITE GHYLL

½ hr

OS Grid Ref: NY 298 072
Altitude: 400m

White Ghyll Crag is a fine and compelling sight as the morning sun comes round, highlighting walls and flying arêtes, the red rock glowing warmly, whilst the ominous bulges of the upper crag still lurk in the shadows. Its many fine routes weave their way through serried ranks of overhangs or up striking corners and provide memorable climbing.

Approach: See photo on page 34. From the Stickle Barn National Trust car park P NY 294 063, walk across the pub front terrace and out through the entrance opposite. Across the road, and between a cottage and the car park for the New Dungeon Ghyll Hotel, a gated track leads out towards the fell. Take the wooden bridge immediately ahead and continue over a small slate bridge to a wide track. After 50m up this, turn right onto a path traversing the fellside above a wall and follow this into the gill itself (usually dry just here). Pick your way up the gill depending on how its bed has been rearranged by winter storms and arrive at a large sycamore tree beneath the Lower Crag. See map page 28 and 62.

Descent: A couple of small cairns mark the initial gully. This is steep and somewhat loose and care is required to avoid dislodging scree as the fall-line is over routes on the Lower Crag. After 30m, scramble up past two arrows scratched on rock ramps further right (facing out) to another cairn where a rocky rake leads down left (facing in) to the foot of the Upper Crag. Do not miss the arrows, as the scree below is a dead end above the Lower Crag.

For routes right of *Feet of Clay*, either scramble from the right until ledges lead left to the top of Easy Rake, or walk down the hillside away from the crag edge until a cairn on the grassy slope below marks the start of a traverse back right (facing out) into the gill. Beware of trying to gain the gill too soon as the ground becomes steep, loose and broken.

For routes on the slabs, traverse the hillside north to the top of the scree trough and pick your way down with care.

Lower Crag

The Lower Crag comprises a series of sharply-defined corners and arêtes.

Approach: For routes right of *Slip Knot* scramble carefully up rightwards from the bed of the gill to the sycamore tree.

1 Russet Groove 28m S ★

The right-hand of the bigger grooves leads to a crimson corner higher up. The easy cracked slab leads up to the right to a ledge in the groove. Ascend the groove to a ledge and finish up a short steep wall on the left.

AR Dolphin, K Heaton - Sep 1949

2 Ethics of Heather 25m VS 4c ★★

The steep hanging groove with a fine slab for its right-hand wall (**Heather Groove** S) is slowly being reclaimed by its name-sake but this variation is excellent. Climb the corner above the large block to gain the right edge of the slab and follow this to the top.

RJ Birkett, L Muscroft - Aug 1947, E Cleasby - Jul 1977

3 Feet of Clay 25m E1 5b ★★

Essentially a right-hand start and finish to *Man of Straw*, with more good climbing. Start below the big corner right of *Man of Straw*. A short crack in the left wall leads to the ledge on *Man of Straw*. Teeter up the groove to the roof and pull out right onto the steep wall. After a couple of committing moves up this, the difficulty eases.

MG Mortimer, S Foster, MG Allen - Jun 1978

4 Man of Straw 28m E1 5b ★★★

A delightful climb, sustained but never desperate unless confidence in your feet starts to evaporate. It climbs the slim square-cut groove in the fine arête beneath the finish of *Laugh Not*. Start below the groove at a boot-wide crack which is climbed to a small ledge. Teeter up the groove until a short traverse left round two small ribs beneath the roof gains the *Laugh Not* slab. A delightful two-step move back right above the roof leads to the arête.

JA Austin, DG Roberts - Apr 1965

5 Sahara 30m E2 6a ★★

An interesting climb with a technical but well protected crux. Belay as for *Laugh Not*. Climb up into the niche/groove on the right of the slab then right again into the continuation groove above which leads to a junction with *Man of Straw* at

a thin crack in the slab. Climb the crack with difficulty into the cave of *Laugh Not* and pull out rightwards through the roof to finish.
S Howe, C Dale, D Kay - Aug 1981

6 Laugh Not 35m HVS 5b ★★★
A fine challenge, worthy of its progenitor. Start at a belay some 5m below where the striking clean-cut pink corner steepens. Well protected climbing up the gradually widening crack leads to a smooth crux section to gain and pass an overlap at 20m and onwards into the cave beneath the capping roof. (Runners but beware of rope drag.) Either step back down and traverse the slab to gain the ledge on the rib and good nut belays or, more easily but spectacularly, reach out right to the prominent flat hold on the overhang lip from where big jugs lead to the belay ledge. Go on, commit yourself – it's not as hard or as far as it looks!
J Brown, R Moseley, T Waghorn - Oct 1953

7 Waste Not, Want Not 32m E1 5b ★★★
Neat climbing across on the left wall of *Laugh Not*. Climb the initial thin crack of *Laugh Not* until a tricky traverse left across the wall using a 'non-ledge' leads into a thin left-facing fault line. Move up and use pockets to traverse left again around a rib into a groove. Steady climbing up the groove and/or its left wall gains the top.
W Lounds, P Sanson - Jun 1977

8 Do Not Direct 46m E1 5b ★★
A first-class route with varied climbing and a superbly positioned second pitch. Start below a broken groove in the rib left of *Laugh Not*.
1 25m 5b Climb the groove to a ledge and large spike below a fine crack in the impending wall. The crack is tricky to start but gobbles protection as you proceed to the big belay ledge.
2 21m 5a The square-cut groove above the right edge of the ledge leads to an overhang. Traverse steeply up and left across the wall on large handholds, until an awkward move round the nose leads to a ledge and easier climbing.
P1: L Brown, P Muscroft - Oct 1960;
P2: RJ Birkett, L Muscroft - Jun 1949

9 Slip Knot 41m VS 4b ★★★
A justifiably popular route taking an excellent line up the big slab and left round the large triangular roof above. A good introduction to the **VS** grade. Start at the foot of the corner.
1 21m 4a Climb the corner until a traverse onto the right wall gains a crack which leads on excellent holds to a spacious belay.
2 20m 4b Traverse left into the corner and make a thought-provoking move across the left wall to gain the rib. Exhilarating moves up bulging rock gain a niche on the left. Easier climbing up the steep wall leads to belay well back.
RJ Birkett, L Muscroft - May 1947

10 The Palestinians 37m E1 5b ★★
A good line up the big undercut rib left of the *Slip Knot* slab. Interesting with reasonably protection. Start as for *Moss Wall*. From the rock ramp, gain a large sloping foothold at 3m either direct or by the mossy groove on the left. Move up to the slanting overhangs and pull over leftwards onto the wall above and step right below the next overlap. Climb this by the big crack in its centre to gain the rib above and finish as for *Slip Knot*.
A Hewison, C Robinson - Aug 1981

11 Moss Wall 43m VS 4c ★★
A good route and considerably better than appearances suggest. Start at the foot of a ramp that runs leftwards from the *Slip Knot* corner.
1 13m Easily up the ramp-line to the foot of a shallow square-cut groove.
2 30m 4c Climb this groove for 4m until a traverse right across the mossy wall gains better holds leading into the short, right-facing groove above. Step left to avoid the small capping overhang, then more easily up and rightwards to the top. Belay well back.
G Oliver, D Laws - Aug 1959

12 Titus Groan 40m E1 5b ★
Good climbing, with a short strenuous hard section, which accepts the challenge of the big corner left of *Slip Knot*.
1 13m As for *Moss Wall*.
2 27m 5b The square-cut groove leads to a poor resting place above its roof (good runners). Good holds in the short overhanging groove above enable an exit left onto the rib which leads more easily to the heather terrace.
R Sager, J Hartley - Aug 1975

13 Hollin Groove 82m HS 4b ★★
A pleasant and varied route. Some 20m above the sycamore, a rib runs up into a big open-book corner. Start at a crooked crack in a short corner/niche on the right side of the rib.
1 23m 4b The crack has a mind of its own but can be persuaded to lead you to a ledge above. The rib on the left leads via another groove to a battered holly beneath the main corner.
2 24m Climb the fine right-angled corner to the Great Shelf. Walk 13m back and belay on Easy Rake below a prominent rib.
3 35m The steep rib leads to a spike and onwards pleasantly to the top.
RJ Birkett, L Muscroft - Aug 1945

Laugh Not HVS Keith Sanders — PETER STERLING

Cairn
Scratched arrows
Easy Rake descent
A
1 Russet Groove S
2 Ethics of Heather VS 4c
3 Feet of Clay E1 5b
4 Man of Straw E1 5b
5 Sahara E2 6a
6 Laugh Not HVS 5b
7 Waste Not, Want Not E1 5b
8 Do Not Direct E1 5b
9 Slip Knot VS 4b
10 The Palestinians E1 5b
11 Moss Wall VS 4c
12 Titus Groan E1 5b
13 Hollin Groove HS 4b
14 Slack Knot/Rope Not MVS/HVS 5a
15 Hitcher VS 5a
MB

10
9
8
7
3
4
5
6
3
3
2
1
4
5
7
6
8
2
1
Inferno MVS
Approach
Approach

Upper Crag

Upper Crag develops leftwards into an aggressively impressive face, protected by formidable bands of overhangs; an incredible piece of rock architecture. It is defined on its left by the beetling fissure of White Ghyll Chimney, whose left wall forms a fine sweep of steep smooth slabs.

Descent: Descend the grassy ground above the crag to pick up the top of Easy Rake.

⑭ Slack Knot/ Rope Not 35m MVS/HVS 5a ★★

A good first pitch accesses the fine wall of *Rope Not*. Start at the top of the lower section of the descent route, beneath an undercut crack in a small flying buttress.

1 15m 4b The steep cracked wall leads to a rock platform. Move up rightwards and swing around the arête. A delicate move up the left edge of the slab leads to a ledge and two thread belays at the foot of the fine wall, split by a finger crack.

2 17m 5a The crack gives pleasant, sustained climbing, technical but well protected from the moment one leaves the ground. A gem of a pitch – if only there was more. The alternative of continuing leftwards up the fault-line ramp keeps the overall grade to **MVS 4b**.

P1 RM Biden, L Gray, I Gray - Mar 2009; P2 1960s

⑮ Hitcher 44m VS 5a ★★

Varied and interesting climbing with a cracking crux. Start towards the top of the first section of Easy Rake below the prominent hanging, right-facing ramp.

1 20m 4a Gain the ramp and climb the wall above, first slightly right, then straight up to the bilberry terrace. Belay 5m higher below the mossy corner on the left.

2 24m 5a Make a rising traverse across the slab on the right and climb up to the overlap and slanting crack. The arête up on the right is tantalisingly close but requires a frustrating degree of commitment (probably **HVD** to a gritstoner!) Follow the arête to the top.

N Drasdo, FP Jenkinson - 1960

⑯ The Veil 63m HVS 5a ★★

Interesting varied climbing picking a good line up the right-hand side the Upper Crag. There may be a little loose rock on p1. Start 6m up Easy Rake, beneath a prominent metre-wide overhang at 7m, split by a slanting crack.

1 24m 5a Climb to the overhang and pull through its central break with difficulty. Climb up right to enter a short leftward-slanting ramp. At its top, move back right to a ledge and then direct to belay on the detached block under the overlap.

2 23m 5a Just left of the block, there is a small left-facing fault on the lip of the overhang. Using the edge of this fault, make a poorly protected pull onto the slab above to reach good sharp holds. Step left and climb a short flake crack until a traverse rightwards leads to the foot of the main corner. Climb the corner to the overhang and traverse left to a ledge. Pull up over the overhangs to gain a larger ledge and a selection of small belays.

3 16m 4c From the left end of the ledge, move up the wall and step right. Continue directly to the top.

GL Swainbank, C Read - Jun 1998

⑰ White Ghyll Wall 68m VS 4c ★★★

A magnificent outing, weaving its way around the right-hand side of the armoury of overhangs. Low in its grade, it is an excellent introduction to the buttress and '**VS** work'. Start at the foot of the prominent rib running up right of an ash tree.

1 25m Climb the rib and short wide crack to a ledge beneath the overhangs and traverse right for 8m to a block belay beneath an undercut, left-facing scoop.

2 15m 4c Climb the scoop and the problematic overlap above (by either side) to the foot of a large open corner. Move leftwards onto the steep wall and climb direct for 6m to an overhung ledge. Belay 2m down to the left in a slanting groove.

3 28m 4b From below the belay, traverse delicately left for 2m out onto the slabs. Now climb diagonally up left to the second of two prominent ledges at 12m and 19m. Finish up the wall above the right side of this ledge.

RJ Birkett, L Muscroft, T Hill - May 1946

⑱ Perhaps Not 63m HVS 5a ★★

An audacious line that is character building and a tribute to the boldness of its first ascentionists. The technical difficulties are confined to the notorious 'chimney' pitch but the traverse to it is serious and exposed, with a little suspect rock.

1 17m As for p1, *White Ghyll Wall* to belay on the ledge above the wide crack.

2 16m 4b A couple of spooky-feeling moves gain a line of large holds under the roof. Gambol along these out into space to a hanging belay on a variety of cams and other attachments beneath a short, capped, chimney-groove.

3 9m 5a Technical climbing into the chimney and rightwards out of it leads to a stance and belay. Faith in what may be above is required when the holds disappear.

4 21m 4b The vague crack on the left leads to a ledge; finish directly up the wall above.
RJ Birkett, L Muscroft - May 1949

⓳ Eliminot 64m E2 5c ★★
A nicely named intimidating and demanding route.
1 23m 5c From 9m up *The Gordian Knot*, traverse right to a ledge beneath a break in the barrier of overhangs. Pull through this (crux) to a resting place. Continue steeply but more easily on widely spaced holds to the hanging stance beneath the chimney-groove of *Perhaps Not*.
2 20m 5b Traverse right for 5m to a bulging break in the roof. Make an awkward, strenuous pull round this onto the left extremity of the next sandwich slab. Pull up more bulging rock leftwards and get established on the slabby wall of the left facing groove. A few metres more lead to a stance on the left.
3 21m 4b Step right and climb the wall for 7m, when moves right round the rib lead to a junction with *White Ghyll Wall*.
P1: J Brown, J Smith - 1957; P2: J A Austin, I Roper - Aug 1966

⓴ The Gordian Knot 56m VS 4c ★★★
A climb of great character following a natural line up the narrow slabby wall and hanging corner to its right. Sustained and not too well protected on the crux corner. Start at the foot of the slab which forms the right-hand side of a prominent rib running up to the overhangs.
1 20m 4b Climb the slab first slightly rightwards, then left and up to a cave with an anvil-flake belay.
2 14m 4c A teasing pitch. Traverse easily right for 4m to an exposed ledge below the corner. Bridge through the bulge above via a small ledge on the right wall and move back leftwards into a recess. Continue direct to a ledge and belay just below the top of the corner.
3 22m 4b Up the wide corner crack and exit right onto a ledge. Climb the steep wall above the left side of the ledge to finish.
JW Haggas, E Bull - Sep 1940

㉑ White Ghyll Eliminate 62m E2 5c ★★
An exhilarating climb up the compellingly steep crack springing from the belay cave of *The Gordian Knot*.
1 20m 4b As for p1, *The Gordian Knot*.
2 15m 5c Step right and survey the crack above. Translating desire into action, pull up steeply into the crack and climb it to an optional stance in the 'coffin' groove on the *Haste Not* traverse (good for keeping an eye on one's second). Debilitatingly well protected, and possibly **E3 6a** for those of a more modest stature.
3 27m 5b A short steep crack in the same line splits the roof above. Tricky climbing up this leads to a bilberry ramp. Finish pleasantly up the thin crackline in the white slabby wall above.
A Evans, D Parker, G Miller - May 1971

㉒ Haste Not Direct 56m E3 5c ★★
Varied climbing and a sensationally placed crux crack give a big feel to this route. Start in the deep left-facing corner left of *The Gordian Knot*.
1 21m 4c Climb the corner to its top roof and exit right onto the rib. Move right again to belay.
2 23m 5c Move up left through the overhangs to enter a slim groove. After a few feet, pull out left to a resting place and continue steeply to reach the *Haste Not* traverse. The notorious bulging flake crack above is tricky to start, wildly spectacular to continue and strenuous throughout, but thoroughly worth the effort. Belay on the bilberry ramp above.
3 12m 4b Finish pleasantly up the thin crackline in the white slabby wall above.
JA Austin, RValentine - May 1971

㉓ Haste Not 59m VS 4c ★★★
An impertinent excursion for its grade, probing the monumental barrier of overhangs. Its exposed and enthralling traverse will live on in the memory. Start in the right-facing corner of the big alcove left of *Gordian Knot* and just right of a broad hanging rib.
1 22m 4b Climb the slab to the roof. Cross the left wall with difficulty to gain a groove in the slab on the front. Up this to a large ledge and upstanding flake belay.
2 15m 4c Traverse easily rightwards for 5m to where a steep wall leads to the big roofs. A delicate step right gains a cramped gangway system running rightwards under the overhangs. Shuffle along this and descend a bottomless coffin-like groove to a resting place in a short left-facing corner. Step up the corner, swing right onto the rib and traverse right to belay in the next corner as for *The Gordian Knot* p2.
3 22m 4b Step back left and climb awkwardly into a short groove at the right-hand end of the overlap. Pull out left, up and finish up the narrow rib just right of a bilberry ramp. For an attractive finish, cross the bilberry ramp and climb a thin crack in the immaculate rough white wall.
RJ Birkett, L Muscroft - May 1948

Descent
13 Hollin Groove HS 4b
14 Slack Knot/Rope Not MVS/HVS 5a
15 Hitcher VS 5a
16 The Veil HVS 5a
17 White Ghyll Wall VS 4c
18 Perhaps Not HVS 5a
19 Eliminot E2 5c
20 The Gordian Knot VS 4c
21 White Ghyll Eliminate E2 5c
22 Haste Not Direct E3 5c
23 Haste Not VS 4c
27 Forget-Me-Not E1 5b
28 The Slabs, Route 1 S
29 The Slabs, Route 2 S
MB

16
15
14
13
Slack Knot MVS
Approach
14
15
Cairns and
scratched arrows
Easy Rake descent
16

24 Paladin 49m E3 5c ★★★

Climbs the biggest hanging groove in the overhangs directly above the first stance of *Haste Not*. Definitely 'out there', giving sustained, strenuous and exposed climbing.

1 15m As for p1 *White Ghyll Chimney*.

2 34m 5c The steep, fingery wall above the belay leads rightwards into a corner. Step left and climb a slab and bulging wall moving into the corner below the roof. The ominous-looking block leads rightwards into the main groove. Move up with difficulty and exit left into comparative calm. Climb the wall above, passing another awkward move, to a ledge and easier groove to finish.

R Matheson - Mar 1971

25 Chimney Variant 50m E1 5b ★★

A cheeky route with interesting and very exposed climbing in a superb position. Its essence lies along the obvious slash of the undercut gangway leading rightwards from *White Ghyll Chimney*.

1 14m As for p1 *White Ghyll Chimney*.

2 28m 5b Continue up the chimney to the overhang. Pull over this, gain the gangway and shimmy rightwards to the base of the square-cut groove (runners but beware of rope drag.) Tricky moves up this lead to a step out right onto the rib. Belay just above.

3 9m Finish up the easier groove.

JA Austin, I Roper, D Miller - Apr 1966

26 White Ghyll Chimney 56m S 4a ★★

Not to be missed by aficionados of this traditional genre. The junction of the central overhanging section and the slabs forms an impressive cleft. Start at the groove leading up to the cleft.

1 14m Easily up the groove to the large ledge and upstanding flake belay.

2 30m 4a The chimney becomes a cave which leads with difficulty to sloping holds on the left. Delicately reach small handholds, thence more easily up a steep diagonal groove to a ledge. Good belay 6m higher.

3 12m Return 3m from the belay. Climb the wall above for 5m, then a delicate traverse right leads back into the chimney for a fitting finish.

HB Lyon, J Herbert, HP Cain - Aug 1923

27 Forget-Me-Not 62m E1 5b ★★

Some bold climbing starting 5m right of *The Slabs Route 1* at short twin cracks forming a large thumbnail flake at about 18m.

1 23m 5a Straight up to gain and climb the twin cracks. Stand on the flake, pull over a slight bulge via a small spike and continue diagonally left to a good spike belay. Or continue into p2.

2 15m 5b Step right to follow a faint right-leaning flake crack at first, then trend right across a mossy streak to finish at a good ledge.

3 24m Scramble off leftwards or climb pleasantly up the steep rib above as for *The Slabs Route 1*.

P 1: M Sinker, R Isherwood - Sep 1963;
P2: R Graham, A Hyslop, TW Birkett - Apr 1980

28 The Slabs, Route 1 66m S ★★★

A really enjoyable excursion which has some interesting moves. Start at the lowest point of the slabs.

1 13m Climb to a ledge with a belay at its left end.

2 29m A fine rising traverse left across the wall leads to a small ledge. Up the steep groove to the foot of a smooth wall at the left end of a ledge (optional, spike belay 3m further right). After an awkward start, climb the middle one of three grooves to a ledge. A further groove leads up rightwards to ledges below a fine-looking rib.

4 24m Starting on its right, the rib leads pleasantly to the top.

G Barker, AT Hargreaves - Sep 1930

29 The Slabs, Route 2 43m S ★★

Start by a large flake at the left side of the slabs.

1 11m Climb steep cracks to a stance on a small ledge; flake belay.

2 21m Traverse left to the far edge and pull onto the small slab. Climb this rightwards and then the crack running back left until a ridge leads to a stance and belay.

3 11m Follow the ridge on the right of the grassy scoop. 25m of scrambling leads to the top.

S Cross, E Fallowfield, C Tatham - 1933

Descent: Scramble up and off left into the scree-filled gully.
28
26
25
24
29
25
24
29
28
27
26
23
MB

STICKLE BARN CRAG

OS Grid Ref: NY 295 069
Altitude: 220m

15 mn

A clean, sunny and quick drying outcrop of good quality rock; ideal for an evening or short day. The main wall of the crag is a huge flake with deep chimneys on either side.

Approach: P NY 294 063 See photo page 34. As for White Ghyll but after passing through the gate to contour the hillside, strike directly up the fell to the crag. See map page 28 and 62.

1 **Right-Hand Chimney** 12m VD

2 **Main Wall Scoop** 12m VS 4b ★
The scoop is entered from the right (crux), thence more easily to the top.

3 **Main Wall Crack** 12m VS 4c ★★★
The thin crack in the middle of the wall.

4 **Main Wall Rib** 12m E2 5b ★★
Gain the ledge at 4m, trend left up a shallow groove to a ledge. Step up and move right onto the front of the rib which leads to the top.

5 **Main Wall Left-Hand** 12m HVS 5a ★
At *Left Chimney*, pull right onto the undercut wall and climb it directly, passing a tricky overlap.

6 **Left Chimney** 10m S

7 **The Pillar** 12m E3 5c ★
Delicate and bold for 5m to a good handhold on the right. Continue more easily (peg). Pass the first overhang on the left and the second on the right.

8 **Heather Groove** 12m VS 4b ★★
The groove just left of the chimney. Climb the left wall of the corner to a ledge. Enter the final groove from the left.

9 **Left Wall** 12m VD ★
8m left of *Left Chimney* a rising traverse rightwards towards the ledge of *Heather Groove*, then back diagonally up leftwards.

10 **Left Wall Direct** 10m VS 4b ★
Starting a metre left of *Left Wall*, a vague crack-line with marginal protection leads directly to the top.
M Scrowston, J Loxham - Dec 2008

11 **Stickleback** 10m HVS 5a
Climb a series of short, stepped-grooves.
J Loxham, M Scrowston - Dec 2008

12 **Stickler** 10m VS 5a
Start at the foot of an overhung corner. Climb the slabby left wall around the bulge until moves right.
M Scrowston, J Loxham - Dec 2008

PAVEY ARK

OS Grid Ref: NY 286 079
Altitude: 540m

The quality of its routes, combined with the superb position overlooking Stickle Tarn and the lower reaches of Great Langdale to Windermere and beyond make this a delightful place to climb. There are routes to suit most tastes, from the very easiest to amongst the very hardest.

Pavey Ark forms part of the Langdale Pikes skyline and can be seen to the right of Harrison Stickle when driving up the valley. It enjoys the sun from first light to mid-afternoon, something best appreciated on a sunny February day. The crag comprises areas of tiered slabs and walls above terraced ledges, together with sterner buttress of unrelenting steepness. By combining climbs on the lower and upper tiers, routes of over 160m can be made to the summit.

The rocks are of splendid gripping quality; rough as a cow's tongue, Haskett Smith 1894.

Approach: Stickle Ghyll provides the line of the main path to Stickle Tarn. From the National Trust car park P NY 294 063 at the Stickle Barn, keep to the west side of the gill until a bridge is reached. Paths climb both sides of the gill to rejoin shortly before the small dam at Stickle Tarn. The crag dominates the view; the shorter and drier route is clockwise round the tarn. See map page 28 and 62.

Descent: Jack's Rake, or East Gully.

Climbs below Jack's Rake

The ground below the middle section of Jack's Rake rears up as a series of walls and slabs, access to which is protected by an undercut strata of rock. Any of these routes when combined with one above Jack's Rake will give a memorable day's climbing.

Approach: A path branches left from the main track just below the foot of Jack's Rake and runs beneath the lower tier, arriving in 100m below the undercut arête of *Cruel Sister*.

Descent: Jack's Rake.

1 Cruel Sister 73m E3 5c ★★★
The undercut rib which forms the right edge of the upper *Arcturus* wall gives a brilliant and serious climb with spaced protection.
1 30m 5b Follow *Arcturus* to the juggy foothold, move rightwards to a good ledge. Climb the obvious shallow groove to a ledge under the overhang and move right to belay.
2 25m 5c Pull onto the wall and traverse right to get established on the wall above the overhang. Step up, traverse right to a block on the edge and then up to a good foothold. Climb the wall trending slightly left to a small overlap, above which a steep crack leads to the final belay of *Arcturus*.
3 18m 5a Reverse the *Arcturus* traverse for 3m and pull over the overlap above on widely spaced holds. Step left and climb the corner to grass ledges. Continue to higher ledges for a belay.
R Matheson, S Colvin - Apr 1972

2 Arcturus 81m E2 5b ★★★
This tremendous route gives fine open climbing in excellent situations, finding the easiest way up the impressive two-tier wall which dominates this part of the crag. Sustained at **HVS** with a committing crux slab that is not well protected. Start directly below a holly bush that grows in a faultline above the initial slabs.
1 33m 5b Climb the smooth slab to the holly. 2m left, an undercut rib leads left to a jammed flake (thread). Pull right to reach and stand on a juggy foothold (old peg). A few delicate moves up the slab bring better holds to hand. Now work across leftwards into a thin crack that leads to a shallow niche and stance with holly tree belay.
2 32m 5a Move right and pull over the small overlap to climb a shallow groove then a thin crack to ledges beneath the prominent overlap. Traverse right beneath this, cross a delicate and exposed little slab, step down to belay on the large ledge below.
3 16m 4c After a tricky start, the rib on the right soon leads to easier ground.
JA Austin, E Metcalf - Apr 1962

3 Capella 70m E1 5b ★★★
Well protected and interesting climbing on good rock. Start below the birch tree growing out of the base of the initial overhang.
1 32m 5b Climb to the overhung ledge on the right side of the tree. Using holds on the left, bridge up to gain the lip of the overhang and follow the pocketed crack-line for 4m. Traverse left for 2m, then straight up past a good flake and continue to beneath a steepening wall. Move right to climb the right side of this wall and pull up left to ledges and holly tree belay.
2 38m 5b The left rib of the shallow groove gains the steep wall above. Move rightwards into a short left-facing corner and climb it to a good ledge on the right. Go up left to another ledge. Move up rightwards and climb a fingery wall to a large flake. From its top, enter and climb the shallow corner. Step left to belay on nuts and a peg.
GL Swainbank, C Read - Aug 1997

4 Venus/Crescent Direct 87m E1 5b ★★
A good combination with varied climbing which is better than it looks. The first pitch is often wet but can still be climbed. Start as for *Crescent Slabs*.
1 25m 5a *Venus* - Follow *Crescent Slabs* to the foot of the shallow groove. Move right onto the black wall and climb this on good edges and pockets, finally trending left to belay.
2 30m 5b From below the belay block, climb out diagonally right to a small jammed flake under a bulging overlap. Use the flake to step left through the overlap, then follow faint cracks through the next bulge. Easier but run-out climbing up the bluish streak leads to the right end of the *Crescent Climb* traverse.
3 22m 4c *Crescent Direct* - After an awkward start, climb the groove to where it is possible to traverse horizontally left and up onto a grass ledge on the front of the buttress.
4 12m 4b Steep slabs starting from the left lead to easy ground and Jack's Rake.
P1: M Bagness, I Almond, S Keenor -May 2005;
P2: M Bagness, S Ashworth - Apr 2005
P3&4 JA Austin, DG Roberts - May 1969

5 Crescent Slabs 60m S ★★
This climb follows a line up the clean open slabs on the right of the moss. Start at a weakness at the right end of the slabs where a black groove cuts through the bulging overhangs.
1 36m Follow a rising gangway leftwards (usually wet) to the foot of a shallow groove. Up this for a couple of metres before working left over easier slabs to a terrace. Continue up steep slabs to belay below a large block at the right-hand

end of the next terrace.
2 24m Climb onto the block and make a difficult move up into a small scoop. Climb this for a couple of metres and move left to a small ledge. Pleasant slabs now lead to a belay at the right end of the *Crescent Climb* traverse. Scramble up *Crescent Climb* to finish.
GS Bower, AW Wakefield - Jun 1920

6 Crescent Climb 100m M ★★
A good mountaineering route, especially if combined with *Gwynne's Chimney*. Its alpine aspirations are reflected in the suspect rock encountered; care is required. Start at the foot of a dirty gully. The broken arête leads in 55m to the left end of the Crescent. Stances and doubtful belays en route. Follow the pleasant crescent-shaped traverse rightwards for 15m on large holds beneath the overhang. Scramble up slabby rock, steep grass and ledges to Jack's Rake. *Gwynne's Chimney* lies some 12m to the right.
F Botterill, WE Palmer - Apr 1907

7 Great Gully 100m HVD ★★
This is the right-hand and longer of the two deep gullies towards the western end of the crag and it gives one of the few good gully climbs in the valley. Not to be treated lightly; a solo tour de force in 1882.
1 45m Easy rocks for 12m, then scramble to a cave beneath a large chockstone.
2 10m Climb the wall on the right, or enter the cave and leave by a window.
3 18m Scramble up to another cave and climb through or over it.
4 20m The Brant and Slape pitch gives a pleasant slab pitch in the dry.
5 7m An easy through route emerges in the middle of a grass ledge. Alternatively, there is a grassy exit on the right, or a difficult scoop on the left (S). These all lead eventually to Jack's Rake. Continue to the summit via the grassy gully on the right.
WP Haskett Smith - 1882

Arcturus E2 Peter Sterling — DAVID SIMMONITE

Climbs below Jack's Rake

1	**Cruel Sister**	E3 5c
2	**Arcturus**	E2 5b
3	**Capella**	E1 5b
4	**Venus/Crescent Direct**	E1 5b
5	**Crescent Slabs**	S
6	**Crescent Climb**	M
7	**Great Gully**	HVD

Climbs above Jack's Rake

8	**Stoat's Crack**	HS
9	**The Bracken-clock**	E2 5c
10	**Rake End Wall/Rib Pitch**	HVS 5a
11	**Rake End Chimney**	D
12	**Cook's Tour**	VD
13	**Rectangular Rib**	HVS 5a
14	**Rectangular Slab**	VS 5a
15	**Coati**	VS 4b
16	**Aardvark**	E1 5c
17	**Gwynne's Chimney**	D
18	**Stalag**	VS 4c
19	**Poker Face**	E1 5b
20	**Golden Slipper**	HVS 5a

Climbs above Jack's Rake

Above Jack's Rake a series of steep butresses are split by the narrow defile of *Rake End Chimney*. Leftwards up the Rake, the crag becomes more complex with walls and slabby buttresses rising amongst more vegetated areas to provide remarkably clean and attractive pitches on Pavey's renowned rough knobbly rock.

Approach: Scramble up Jack's Rake.

Descent: From the summit either traverse south to Jack's Rake and descend this, or head north to the scree filled depression of North Gully which leads down until East Gully can be seen on the right. This contains an awkward scramble down a boulder choke.

8 Stoat's Crack 112m HS ★★

A pleasant route finding the easiest way up a big area of steep rock. Bold and exposed in places. Start below a prominent left slanting, right-facing corner crack that begins 16m up the crag.

1 16m Blocks and ledges right to the corner.
2 20m Climb the crack for about 8m, break out left and ascend to a stance on the corner.
3 26m Traverse left into a groove. Follow this and the open corner above to a large overhung ledge.
4 24m Left along the grass terrace and climb an open groove, finishing to the right. Left along another ledge to a bilberry-filled groove. This leads up and right to a ledge beneath a sweep of slabs.
5 26m The pleasant slabs are delicate at first, then a short wall and slabs lead leftwards to a huge detached block. 30m of scrambling remains.

BR Record, JR Jenkins - Jun 1933

9 The Bracken-clock 102m E2 5c ★★★

Excellent climbing up the smooth walls left of *Stoat's Crack*. Start 20m up Jack's Rake below a shallow groove at a smooth slab split by a quartz vein.

1 18m 5a The shallow groove leads past a difficult bulge to the right end of a ledge.
2 14m 5c From the left end of the ledge, climb directly up the smooth slab to a good jug. Difficult moves straight up lead to a narrow ledge.
3 20m 5b Traverse right below the bulging wall for about 4m to a tiny platform on the edge. Climb directly over an awkward bulge, then right into an open groove overlooking *Stoat's Crack*, which leads to a ledge below a smooth scoop.
4 24m 4a Go up the scoop as for *Stoat's Crack* and, from the right end of the ledge above, climb slabs and ledges trending right to the ledge below the final pitch of *Stoat's Crack*.
5 26m The rib on the left gives a pleasant finish.

JA Austin, NJ Soper, A Faller - Jun 1970

10 Rake End Wall/ Rib Pitch 82m HVS 5a ★★★

A splendid route seeking the easiest way up the right rib of *Rake End Chimney*. Enjoyable climbing on excellent rock, with a well maintained standard and some thought-provoking moves. Start below a rib 5m right of the *Rake End Chimney*.

1 21m 4b Climb past a wedged flake and up an ill-defined crack until steepening rock necessitates moves rightwards round the corner. A diagonal crack leads to a huge block beneath the overhanging corner crack.
2 25m 4c Attack the imposing corner crack. The ledge above leads left to a slab. Climb this to a small groove on the right of a slight overhang. A couple of metres up this groove move awkwardly left onto the arête and follow it to the large terrace in *Rake End Chimney*.
3 36m 5a *Rib Pitch* - The left-hand rib of the chimney stands boldly in isolation and gives a superb pitch. Traverse left onto the rib and climb it via a line of slim grooves. The shorter right-hand rib, with a detour right to avoid its steepest section is **VS 4c**.

HA Carsten, EH Phillips - Aug 1945/JA Austin, JM Ruffe - Jun 1958

11 Rake End Chimney 70m D ★★★

An excellent classic of its kind up the deep cleft located some 40m up Jack's Rake. Climb the chimney to ledges, then over a chockstone to where it opens out after 30m. Walk up the gully for 20m and climb up to and through a window, then up the right wall to a small cave which is passed on the left to finish easily.

CW Barton - Oct 1898

12 Cook's Tour 88m VD ★★

A good mountaineering route with a fine finish. Start at a short leftward-facing chimney-crack, opposite a large rowan.

1 16m The chimney-crack leads to a pinnacle platform. Climb the steep slabby corner behind, moving round to the right onto the top of a flake pinnacle.
2 12m Easy climbing on the left is followed by a short trek up steep vegetation to a flake belay beneath the imposing Rectangular Slab.
3 22m Gain a grass ledge 8m left, walk along it to a flake belay in an easy-angled V-groove.
4 11m Climb the groove for some 6m to below a wedged flake. Step out right onto a grass ledge with a large flake at its far right-hand end. Traverse the outside of this flake, then up to a good ledge beneath a short right-facing corner
5 27m Ascend the corner-crack, then up left to a corner. Continue up the steep slab to a good ledge and finish up the wall above, first slightly right, then straight up.

J Cook, GB Elliott - Mar 1943

13 Rectangular Rib 78m HVS 5a ★★
The left-hand rib of Rectangular Slab is not well protected. Start below a steep shallow right-facing corner with a juniper at its base, 15m beyond the large rowan tree.
1 40m 5a Climb the corner and pleasant slabs above to the foot of the Rectangular Slab.
2 24m 5a Climb up left of the rib then move right boldly where the angle eases. Now follow the left edge to a good ledge and belay below a niche.
3 14m 4c Enter the niche, step left and follow short walls and slabs to the top.
B Swales, D Cobley - 1984; MG Mortimer, MG Allen - 1974

14 Rectangular Slab 83m VS 5a ★★
The objective is the large right-facing slab high up the cliff. Avoid pitch 3 to keep the grade at 4c.
1 45m 4c Take the easiest way up the wall one metre left of the corner, eventually moving rightwards to reach an obvious projecting block. Ascend the left-hand of two grooves, finishing up the steep left wall for the last couple of metres to reach the big terrace at 25m (optional belay). Walk 20m to the right to belay at the foot of the main slab. Climbing p1 of *Rectangular Rib* is as good and less serious.
2 28m 4b Climb the corner on the right to a holly. A delicate traverse leads left across the slab to gain a thin crack which slants back up to the right, steepening towards the finish.
3 10m 5a The sting in the tail. Escape right or, tackle the steep little crack in the right wall of the corner above, stepping right at the top.
JA Austin, E Metcalf - May 1960

15 Coati 61m VS 4b ★★★
A delightful way up the crag; with varied and continually interesting climbing on superb rock. It does not suffer from seepage and dries quickly. Start some 12m right of *Gwynne's Chimney* and just right of the quartz glacis of *Aardvark*.
1 18m 4b Scramble right to a block ledge at the foot of a steep groove. Climb this on ample holds; exit rightwards onto the rib at the top. Step up and move back left to a small ledge.
2 22m 4b Climb a narrow slab rightwards to a ledge at the right-hand end of the impending wall. A bold and awkward move gains the short right-facing corner. Pull immediately round left into a parallel corner. Step up and pull round left again into the next parallel groove which fades into a crack-line and finishes as a spike which is used to swing rightwards around the rib. Belay on the large jammed flake in the ramp-like groove.
3 21m 4b Step off the jammed flake to enter the right-facing corner. Bridge the corner to reach flakes that lead right where a left-facing corner leads to the belays. Easy scrambling gains the top.
P1 RM Biden, C Harrod - Aug 2011
P2 & 3 RM Biden, N Harvey, P Reader - Apr 2011

16 Aardvark 55m E1 5c ★★
An excellent exposed route. Start 6m right of *Gwynne's Chimney* on a small quartz glacis.
1 33m 5c Straight up strenuously to a small overhang (peg). Up and left with difficulty to gain a sloping ledge. Traverse delicately up and right across the wall to a small spike on the arête. Follow this to a ledge and spike belay.
2 22m 4a Up a short wall on the right and gain a line of flakes further right; finish up *Coati*.
P Long, DJ Harding - Sep 1972

17 Gwynne's Chimney 30m D ★★
A pleasant chimney just right of a large rowan, and some 12m below the tricky step at the left end of the first level section in Jack's Rake. Climb the chimney for 17m. Continue directly or, more pleasantly, step right to the arête and climb it to a ledge above. Scrambling up the fault-line or its slabby right-hand ridge now leads to the summit.
HA Gwynne and party - Apr 1892

18 Stalag 66m VS 4c ★
Masterly route finding up impressive terrain. Start just left of *Gwynne's Chimney*.
1 35m 4c Climb past the rowan to the big ledge above on the left. Slabs lead to a steep wall which is climbed for 5m when an awkward move gains an obvious traverse leading left into the corner.
2 15m 4b Traverse the sharp edged flake back across the steep right wall and pull into a comfortable niche. Continue traversing to a small ledge, where a short wall leads to a stance.
3 16m 4b Climb the steep little slab on the left to a small exposed ledge. Continue to a pile of blocks, then swing round the rib on the left and follow it to the top.
JA Austin, RB Evans - Jun 1958

19 Poker Face 67m E1 5b ★★
Excellent climbing up the slim, wishbone-shaped groove splitting the arête right of *Golden Slipper*. The sense of exposure in the groove is offset by the superb protection. Start just right of the tricky step in Jack's Rake.
1 25m 4b Easily up to a ledge on the left. Climb the line of the slabby corner, past a holly, until a traverse left leads to the *Golden Slipper* belay.
2 24m 5b Right to gain the thin groove on the edge of the buttress. Follow this until it steepens about 3m below the top. Make a difficult move left onto *Golden Slipper* and follow this to a ledge; direct is 5c.
3 18m 4c The right-hand rib above the stance.
JA Austin, K Wood - Jul 1966

20 Golden Slipper 60m HVS 5a ★★★
This splendid climb ascends the centre of the elegant pillar of perfect rock. Start just left of the top of the tricky step in the level section of Jack's Rake, at a gangway slanting right to a line of overhangs at 6m.
1 18m 4c Easily up the gangway to the overhang and step right to a grassy ledge. Climb the steep wall directly to a ledge and juniper belays.
2 24m 5a Climb the shallow left-facing corner in the steepening slab on superbly rough rock. At its top where the slab becomes a wall, traverse rightwards to the rib and ascend to a large ledge.
3 18m 4a Traverse left and climb the rib to the top.
JA Austin, RB Evans - Jul 1958

Pavey Ark Integrales

These two suggestions are perhaps the best combinations of routes above and below Jack's Rake. However there are many possibilities — so get out there and create your own Pavey Ark link-up adventures...

1. 5 Crescent Slabs : 17 Gwynne's Chimney S
2. 3 Capella : 20 Golden Slipper E1

The Picco-Harrison Integrale 430m AD–

A grand enchainment takes in routes on lower and upper Scout Crag, moving on to lower and upper White Ghyll, Pavey (Tarn Crag optional), followed by contouring round to the west face of Harrison Stickle and a route to the summit in the evening sun. This gives over 430m of **VD/S** rock to the final summit with very little descent en route – Allez!

Langdale Pikes — Max Biden

Coati VS (page 55) Jeanie Macfarlane — DAVID SIMMONITE

The East Wall

The East Wall is impressively steep with some fine lines and formidable pitches. The wall is divided into two parts by a right-to-left vegetated break (*Hobson's Choice* **VS 4b**). Above and right of the break, the crag is immaculately rough and sound and hosts a series of fine groove lines. There is some drainage here and routes can take a while to dry out.

Approach: Scramble up East Gully. The first three routes all start here by climbing the intial section of *Hobson's Choice* for 30m: diagonally left up the slabs to a large flake where a long step left gains a grassy groove and ledge just above. A steep and awkward little wall (**4b**) accesses the slab above and a stance below an impressive corner.

Descent: Continue towards the summit of the crag heading northwards into the scree filled depression of North Gully which leads down and round right into East Gully. This contains an awkward section scrambling down a boulder choke. Or abseil.

21 Impact Day 33m E8 6c ★★

An audacious route up the headwall left of the slim hanging groove of *Sixpence*. It provides very sustained and tenuous climbing. Start left of the main corner where a mossy streak drops down from the half-way horizontal crack. Climb the vague rib left of the mossy streak to an obvious hole, then dynamically rightwards and back left (peg). The left edge of the moss streak now leads to the horizontal break where the angle changes from merely vertical to impending. Move 1m left and make powerful moves on sloping holds and undercuts (crux) up and rightwards to gain good edges (peg). Climb, via a desperate pull from a one-finger pocket to gain another sloping hold, which facilitates entry into the short shallow scoop above.
D Birkett - May 1999

22 Sixpence 33m E6 6b ★★★

A magnificently sustained and strenuous route up the impending wall and hanging groove that beckons high on the headwall. Start in the corner. Climb the flake crack to a ledge on the right. Step up into the groove above, traverse left onto the wall and climb direct to a good jug in the horizontal break. Pull up and enter the groove with difficulty. Further progress is not easy but eventually leads to a small ledge on the right, followed shortly by the top, strength permitting.
A Atkinson, KW Forsythe, RO Graham, TW Birkett - Jul 1981

23 Astra 60m E2 5c ★★★

A fabulous route gaining the slim groove in the rib by way of some exposed wall climbing, initially strenuous then delicate. Start in the corner.
1 21m 5c Cross the narrow easy-angled slab to its right side. Make an exposed step round the rib and pull onto the steep undercut wall (useful hidden finger pocket out right) to gain the prominent flake on the right and good runners. Climb up and left delicately to where the angle eases. Move up and right to a thin crack and make a long reach right round the rib for a hidden pocket; swing round onto a slab and small stance.
2 34m 5a Climb the narrowing slab right of the groove above on superb rock and continue in the same line to a ledge. The awkward, blind, V-groove ahead is climbed to another ledge and belay on the left.
3 5m Finish via a short crack. Scrambling remains.
JA Austin, E Metcalf, DG Roberts - May 1960

24 Fallen Angel 46m E4 6a ★★★

A superb and technically demanding climb up the impressive right-slanting pea-pod groove. Start by traversing in from the gully along grass ledges, above the initial sweep of slabs, to a good ledge below the groove. The wide crack leads into the pod which is climbed until the groove opens out and the slab on the right can be gained. Climb this rightwards to a crack and good foothold. Follow the thin crack above for 6m, then step right to another crack leading right to a bollard on the arête. The groove on the left leads to the top.
E Grindley, I Roper - Oct 1972

25 Cascade 70m HVS 5a ★★★

The original route on this part of the crag gives an excellent climb. Start in the parallel side gully.
1 21m 4c Pull round onto the belt of slabs and climb the right-hand side of these to ledges below a 3-metre corner.
2 21m 5a Climb the 3m corner to a good ledge below the main slab line. Climb the slabby corner almost to a rock ledge, where steepening rock forces a few moves right and up onto a glacis.
3 28m 5a Climb the short wall left of the crack-line above, moving rightwards toward the top to gain a grassy bollard-ledge. The chimney-crack above contains a huge cigar-shaped rock. The cracks on either side of the cigar lead to the top.
JA Austin, RB Evans - May 1957

A
21
22
23
24
25
Cascade Direct E3
Hobson's Choice VS
Mother Courage E4
21
22
23
24
25
North Buttress
East Gully
AP

Sixpence E6 (page 58) Hazel Findlay — DAVID SIMMONITE

RAVEN CRAGS

Sunny, roadside, year-round climbing. Raven Crags is the collective name for the line of buttresses and outcrops that stretch eastwards across the fellside directly above the Old Dungeon Ghyll Hotel.

Approach: Behind the Old Dungeon Ghyll Hotel P NY 286 061 and through the gate a vague path leads into a stand of spruce trees. A better defined track zig-zags up to an engineered path leading to the foot of Raven Crag. Middlefell Buttress is just up to the left.

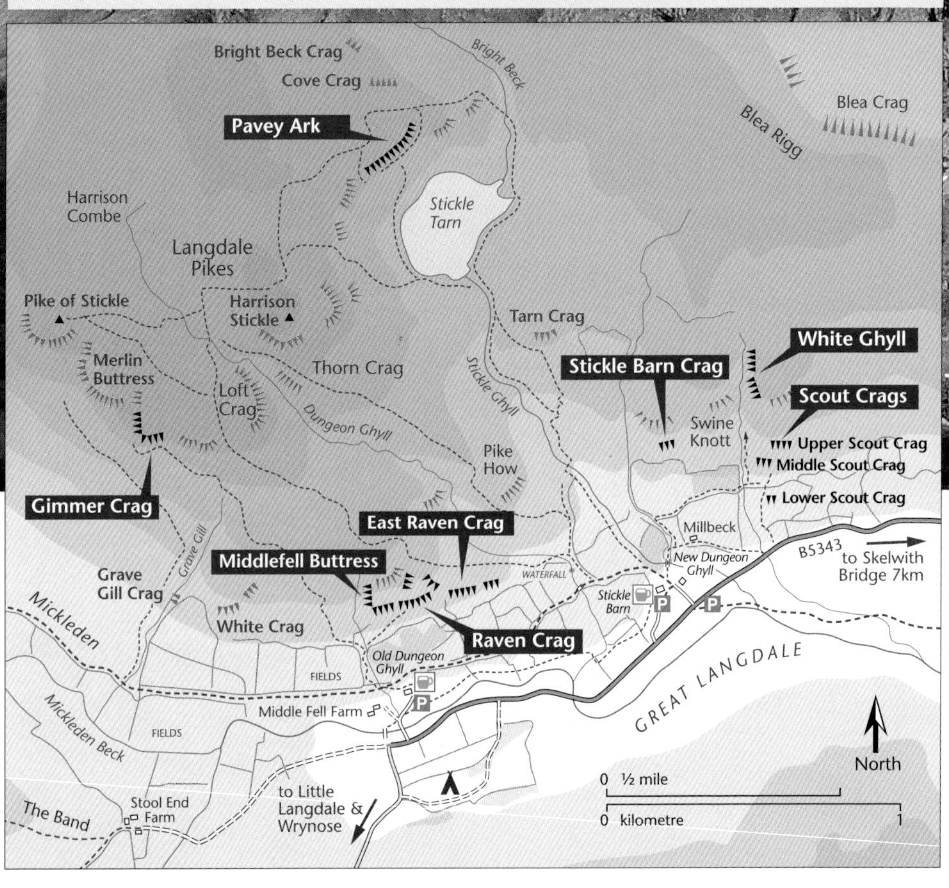

MIDDLEFELL BUTTRESS

15 mn

OS Grid Ref: NY 285 064
Altitude: 200m

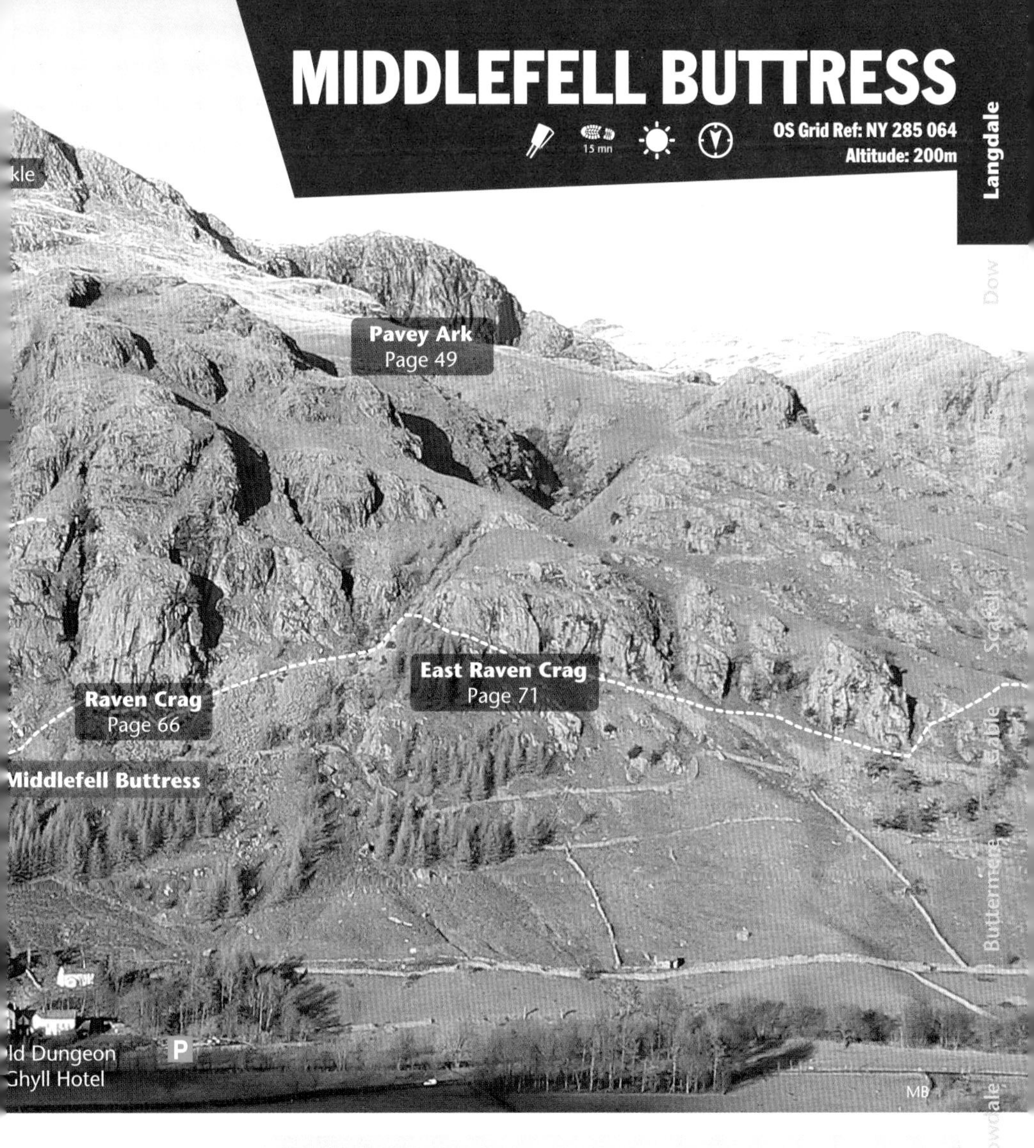

Middlefell Buttress

The conspicuous rounded rib gives a classic outing. The wall to its right gives exposed steep juggy climbing.

Descents: From the top of *Middlefell Buttress*, traverse left and cross the gully to an exposed and eroded path. This leads out to and down a broad shoulder, entering the gully near the bottom. For routes on Mendes Wall, continue up p3 of *Middlefell Buttress* or use the *in-situ* abseil slings on the tree above the side gully.

1
A
2
3
Raven Crag
Gully
Middlefell
Gully
2
3
1

1 Middlefell Buttress 80m D ★★★

A climb for all conditions. The route has the polish of ages and provides the traditional mountaineering way to Gimmer. Start at the lowest point of the crag below a steep wall split by a crack-line. The original start up the chimneys is best avoided as they are now very unstable.

1 20m Climb the crack on juggy holds for 10m and scramble up left to the belay.

2 45m Follow the well worn trail up the rib to belay just below a large terrace. A particularly polished ramp at around 8m is awkwardly delicate.

3 15m Move up to the wall behind the terrace and re-belay. Start the wall by traversing in from either right (original) or left (harder) to gain cracks and the final corner. Climb this exiting right.

J Laycock, SW Herford, AR Thomson - Sep 1911

2 Prometheus 40m HVS 5a ★★

A good and varied route with a well protected crux. Start one metre left of the large pinnacle reached by scrambling from left or right.

1 30m 5a Ascend the wall passing a blunt spike and step right to the foot of a black groove. Strenuous moves up this lead to an exit right onto the rib, whence delicate climbing leads to easier ground and a large terrace.

2 10m 4a Climb the juggy wall at the left end of the terrace.

M Scrowston, PC Bennett - Nov 2011

3 Mendes 48m VS 4c ★★

A terrific route, with some excellent positions, up the centre of the intimidating wall. Start on slabby rock below the long overhang.

1 38m 4c Climb easily leftwards beneath and beyond the overhang until almost above the large pinnacle. Make a short ascent then traverse back right to a shallow groove. Step up and continue right for a couple of metres, until good small holds lead straight up. A final pull up left gains easier angled rock. Continue to a grassy terrace beneath a short steep wall.

2 10m 4a Climb the short crack in the centre of the wall.

P Woods, J Sutherland - Feb 1953

RAVEN CRAG

OS Grid Ref: NY 285 064
Altitude: 200m

15 mn

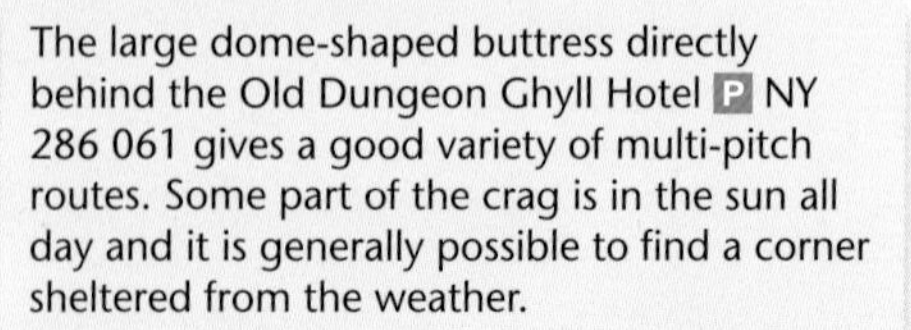

The large dome-shaped buttress directly behind the Old Dungeon Ghyll Hotel P NY 286 061 gives a good variety of multi-pitch routes. Some part of the crag is in the sun all day and it is generally possible to find a corner sheltered from the weather.

Descent: ⚠ Care; rightwards towards the trees. Down through some large split blocks and behind a final block to a grassy terrace. Do not follow the terrace leading up right from the top of the climbs as it leads into a dead-end gully.

1 Evening Wall 47m S ★★
Interesting and varied climbing, best in the afternoon. Start about 6m left *Holly Tree Traverse*.
1 11m Ascend for 4m then move right into a shallow corner. Step right and climb to a small stance.
2 15m Climb 4m to a ledge. Traverse easily left for 4m to where a short steep groove leads to a good ledge on the left.
3 21m Make some strenuously delicate moves up and right onto the exposed arête; good holds lead to the top.
A Gregory, JW Tucker, J Woods - Oct 1947

2 Holly Tree Traverse 49m VD ★★
This exposed traverse is the easiest line across the crag. Start in the gully below a prominent pinnacle.
1 6m Scramble up to belay behind the pinnacle.
2 26m Climb the groove above, or its left-hand rib, for 3m until it is possible to make an awkward traverse right (crux) to a sentry box. Continue traversing up and right heading for an oak tree.
3 17m Climb up rightwards and traverse round to a ledge below a right-angled corner which leads to the top on good holds.
A Gregory, CH Peckett, J Woods - Oct 1949

3 Oak Tree Wall 45m S ★★
Good climbing. Start below the large oak tree.
1 14 m Ascend the short corner-crack, move out right onto the wall and up to a large ledge with a pinnacle belay on the left.
2 31 m Climb the rib and groove behind the pinnacle to a bulging wall. An awkward move gains an overhung gangway which leads right to a small ledge. Step up left over the overlap and then follow holds rightwards to turn the final bulge by a shallow scoop on its left.
A Gregory, J Woods - Jul 1947

4 The Original Route 55m S ★★★
An excellent route taking a clean line of natural weakness. Start at the lowest point of the buttress, 5m right of a large holly.
1 12m Well-worn rock leads leftwards to a ledge. A quartzy wall leads to a good ledge.
2 23m Climb the narrow pillar to a long narrow ledge. Move left along this for some 6m to where a line of holds leads up the steep wall and rightwards to a group of ledges.
3 20m Go straight up for 4m, then move left to a ledge under a bulge. Step up left over the overlap and continue directly up a steep section which gradually eases.
S Watson, D Usher, R Holmes, W Cowen, N Middleton - Aug 1930

5 Holly Tree Direct 70m HVS 4c ★★★
A super route taking the best line on the crag and requiring a delicate touch on its sustained second pitch. Don't look for the holly – it's not there!
1 26m 4c Climb the wall and shallow right-facing corner to a ledge below a much larger corner; climb this to a pinnacle belay on the left.
2 21m 4c Avoid the undercut start to the groove by climbing a parallel groove on the left for 6m to good runners. Downclimb 3m and step right onto a small wall just above the initial overhang. A good foothold in the main groove is gained by a long step right, a resting place is further up on the right. Climb the groove, steep and delicate at first, to a hanging belay some 6m below an oak tree, or continue…
3 23m 4c Step out left and follow the rib to the top.
H Drasdo, E Mallinson - Jul 1952

6 Pluto 73m HVS 5a ★★★

A super route; sustained with varied and interesting climbing of increasing difficulty. Start below a steep left-facing corner-crack right of the toe of the buttress.

1 20m 4c Climb the fine corner-crack to a good ledge and block belay.

2 27m 4c Traverse rightwards beneath the overlap until an awkward move across a groove leads to a good ledge and block belays.

3 26m 5a Step back down and gain the rib on the left. Small holds trending rightwards lead up the wall to a junction with *Bilberry Buttress*. Follow this leftwards.

AL Atkinson, JR Warner - summer 1958

7 Bilberry Buttress 73m VS 4c ★★★

A classic climb with plenty of varied interest and a fine airy finish. Start at the lowest point of the right side of the crag below a curving hand-jam crack.

1 20m 4b Gain and climb the crack to a ledge.

2 18m 4c Climb the thin crack in the steep wall to a magnificent finishing hold on the right. Follow the ridge to the bottom of a sloping terrace.

3 35m 4b Up the terrace for some 8m to where a crack-line leads to the base of a large pinnacle/block. Now traverse the wall leftwards to a corner and cross this to an easy finish.

CF Rolland, JF Renwick - Jun 1941

8 Savernake 59m MS ★

A pleasant route weaving the easiest way up this part of the crag. Start just right of *Bilberry Buttress*.

1 20m Scramble up to a large V-crack which leads to a good ledge.

2 21m Walk down left until broken rocks lead up to a fine corner. This steepens to an exposed finish; thread belays.

3 18m Walk up the sloping terrace to its upper right end. Climb a broken corner for 2m and step left into a scoop. Climb past the pinnacle/block and rightwards to reach a ledge and tree belays. Scramble off rightwards.

JEQ Barford, MP Ward - Sep 1943

9 Elevation 43m HS 4a ★★

A good route, sustained and well protected. Start as for *Revelation* and after 5m, step left and climb the rough slab and the steepening above to a ledge. Step left beneath the overlap and climb the crack and wall above on good holds, eventually finishing rightwards.

M Scrowston, F Scrowston - Jun 2012

10 Revelation 43m HS 4a ★★★

A splendid gem on good clean rock and especially attractive in the early morning sun. Start at a small polished scoop.

1 12m Climb the scoop and continue rightwards until a short crack leads to a good ledge below an overhanging wall.

2 31m 4a Exciting moves up the short overhanging wall and strenuous crack (crux) leads to a small ledge on the left. Climb up to the overlap, traverse right and up the right-hand side of a small projecting nose. Continue straight up bulging rocks.

A Gregory, B Black, J Woods - Mar 1948

11 Kneewrecker Chimney 38m HVS 5a ★★

An interesting and aptly-named route, strenuous but well protected. Start below the prominent hanging flake crack leading to the trees and just left of a broken tree stump.

1 27m 4b Climb the wall and open scoop to a sloping ledge. Step right and climb the strenuous flake crack to the trees.

2 11m 5a Attack the overhanging V-chimney behind the oak. The use of at least one knee to gain a tiny ledge at 4m is probably compulsory unless double-jointed or of much smaller build. Step up, move left round the corner and more easily to the top.

AR Dolphin, J Bloor - Jun 1949

12 Centipede 90m S ★★

An excellent route on the triangular buttress above the decent.

1 18m A steep rib and short traverse left to the wide crack and a good ledge. Flake belay.

2 15m Step off the flake rightwards and up to a mantleshelf. Above traverse left under the overhang to a stance below a diagonal crack.

3 15m The crack leads rightwards to a small ledge on the arête. Follow this to a ledge; belay well back.

4 42m Climb onto the rickety flake and on up a series of slabs and trickier steps.

A Gregory, CPeckett - Jul 1948

1 Evening Wall S
2 Holly Tree Traverse VD
3 Oak Tree Wall S
4 The Original Route S
5 Holly Tree Direct HVS 4c
6 Pluto HVS 5a
7 Bilberry Buttress VS 4c
8 Savernake MS
12 Centipede S
MB

Trilogy E5
Dawes Rides a Shovelhead E8
R'n'S Special & Edge Finish E5
6
7
8
12

6 Pluto HVS 5a
7 Bilberry Buttress VS 4c
8 Savernake MS
9 Elevation HS 4a
10 Revelation HS 4a
11 Kneewrecker Chimney HVS 5a
MB

EAST RAVEN CRAG

OS Grid Ref: NY 287 065
Altitude: 240m

A short outcrop of steeper, generally compact rock with a collection of interesting pitches.

Approach: From Raven Crag Buttress, (P NY 286 061) continue diagonally across the scree.

Descent: Left of the crag.

1 Mamba 18m S ★★
Climb the pleasant tapering slabby rib to where a tricky move left gains a ledge.
AR Dolphin, J Bloor - May 1950

2 Ophidia 18m VS 4c ★★
The capped V-groove and wall above. Finish rightwards up the impending wall.
RM Biden, I Gray - Jul 1994

3 By Jingo 18m E1 5a ★★
Fine wall climbing with just adequate protection up the vague raggedy crack and bold wall above to finish with *Ophidia*.
SJH Reid, C Read, C Jones, A MacDonald - Apr 2000

4 Jingo 18m VS 4b ★
This pleasant wall climb is a little thin on protection. Start as for *Speckled Band* and climb into the right-hand of two short grooves. At its top, pull up leftwards and direct to finish.

5 Speckled Band 20m VD ★
Good climbing but poor protection up the obvious right-slanting gangway until shelving rock leads leftwards.
J Bloor, P Tuke, J Renwick - May 1950

6 Rowan Tree Groove 36m HVS 4c ★★
Not technically hard, but committing and not too well protected. Start at a shallow flaky groove which gives steep climbing to a blunt spike. Left onto the slab; then the hanging groove and rowan tree. Right at the overhang and up the rib.
JA Austin, JM Ruffe, R Jackson - May 1957

7 Ramrod 30m HVS 4c ★★
The slim hanging groove right of *Rowan Tree Groove*. Care with protection at the start. Up and left to a blunt spike; then the rib to a ledge below the overhangs. Pull directly over and ascend the slim groove.
JA Austin, I Roper, T Parker - Sep 1966

8 The Chopper 30m HVS 5a ★★
A steep and interesting pitch that requires some commitment for success. Start below a smooth wall and climb rightwards to a ledge. Ascend the left-slanting crack then more cracks in the wall above. Finish up the pillar right of the oak trees.
I Williamson, P Cornforth - 1983

9 Baskerville 30m VS 4c ★★
The steep left rib of the deep holly-filled gully gives a delightful but fingery pitch on clean rock. A shallow groove is accessed from the right and leads to a ledge. Step right and climb the left wall of the rib which eases after a short bulging section.
AR Dolphin, J Bloor - Apr 1949

GIMMER CRAG

OS Grid Ref: NY 277 070
Altitude: 525m

Hugely enjoyable, sunny, quick drying with immaculate rock, Gimmer Crag is the jewel in Langdale's climbing crown.

Bracket and Slab Climb S (page 79) — STEPHEN REID

The crag is a massive barrel-shaped sweep of grey rock whose faces have contrasting characters and a fine situation high above the valley floor. The quality of its climbs assures its popularity. As Haskett Smith recorded in 1894 in his Climbing in the British Isles, "… there are times even in the Lake District when the rain ceases and the sun shines, and it is then that the climber should gambol upon this crag". Its exposed position has implications and the sunny South-East Face may belie chillier conditions on a breezy North-West Face. The crag topography may appear simple but getting around it can be complex.

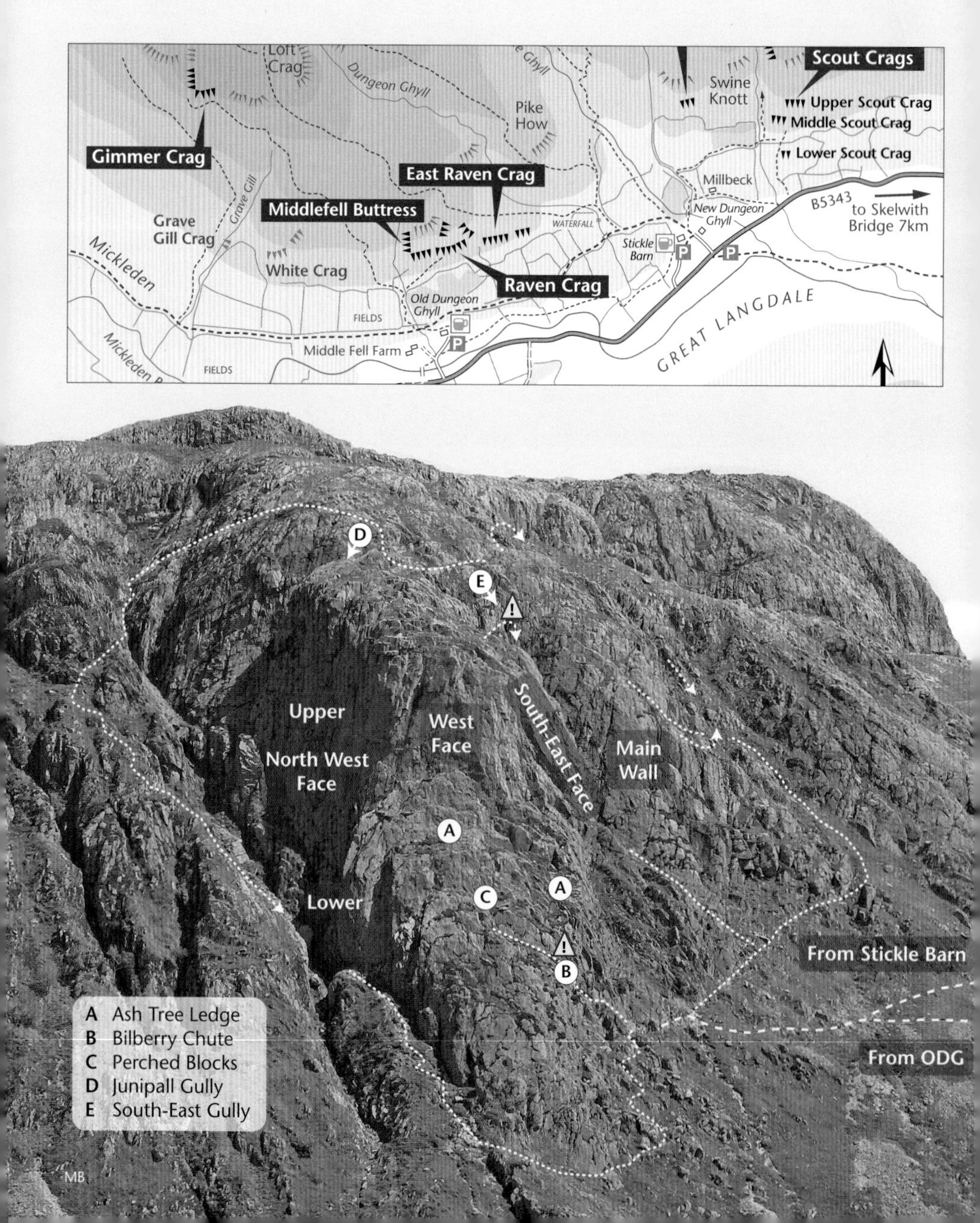

Approach, from Stickle Barn: From the National Trust car park P NY 294 063 take the main path for Dungeon Ghyll and the Langdale Pikes. After 500m go over a stile, cross the gill and follow the path for about another kilometre until it emerges onto an open plateau. Continue west heading straight for the crag, the top of which soon comes into view. At a large cairn when the main path starts to rise more steeply take a faint track leftwards, descending slightly at the end, to meet the crag at the main gearing-up point below the South-East Face.

Approach, from ODG: Take the path behind the hotel P NY 286 061 along Mickleden until past twin gates. An arduous path leads up the slope on the west side of Grave Gill, eventually heading left to the crag.

Descents: To return to the normal gearing up point below Main Wall descend the steep and exposed South East Gully which is normally gained from the higher of two ledges. Initially narrow, this gully holds some precarious blocks, below the blocks cross the rib dividing the gully and scramble down short walls to finish down the far left-hand corner below Main Wall. The gully may be avoided by traversing ledges rightwards from behind the summit block, above Main Wall and down as for *Availed of Tears*.

To return to the base of North West Face the North West Gully is descended. This is reached by scrambling up for some 15m from behind the summit block, then trend left along a faint path on ledges above the upper part of North West Face. These gradually descend into the open upper reaches of the gully. After scrambling down a short loose section, leave the gully for the heathery spur on the right (facing out) where a path winds down to the open scree opposite *The Crack*.

Above the middle of the West Face a 50m abseil leads back to Ash Tree Ledges. The line of the abseil crosses very popular routes, take great care to avoid endangering others.

Main Wall and South-East Face

The right side of the crag is split by South-East Gully, a principal descent route. The right wall of this extends across the fellside and provides some pleasant sunny routes.

Approach: For the first 5 routes scramble up rightwards from the gearing-up point to the bottom of South-East Gully.

Descent: The first 3 routes have individual descents. South-East Gully serves the rest.

1 Availed of Tiers 100m HS 4a ★

Pleasant, interesting climbing with a distinct crux. 60m right from the foot of the gully is a prominent undercut buttress. Start in the corner at the right side of this.

1 20m Traverse left along the lip to a ledge. Gain the crest of the buttress which leads to a wide terrace. Belay in the corner at the back of this.

2 35m 4a Walk 6m to the left, an easy angled rib of clean rock leads to an abrupt steepening. Move right and climb a small corner in the wall for 5m until the angle eases slightly. An excellent finger jug allows a short, slightly downward, traverse left to gain a series of easier grooves leading to the next terrace. Scramble up to belay a few metres left of a prominent right-facing corner line.

3 25m The walls left of the prominent corner are climbed by a series of grooves and cracks trending rightwards at first. Belay below a final easy-angled ridge.

4 20m Pick any way up easy rock to the top.

Descent: Rightwards and down into an area of broken ground. Scramble down the far side of this to join the approach path.

RM Biden, I Gray - May 2012

2 The Purple Edge 48m VS 4c ★★

An eliminate providing a fine, clean and direct route. Scramble up South-East Gully to an embedded flake. Start one metre right of this. Climb up the left side of a rib to a scoop. Move up and diagonally left into a corner. Up this for 2m, then rightwards towards a shallow groove in the arête. Climb this and its steeper continuation. Finish by moving left to easier ground and the top.

Descent: Carefully rightwards down slabby rocks and terraces until steep grass leads to the approach path.

BJ Clarke - Oct 2007

1 Availed of Tiers HS 4a
2 The Purple Edge VS 4c
3 Main Wall Climb VD
4 Bachelor Crack MVS 4b
5 Chimney Buttress S 4a
6 Gimmer Chimney VD
7 Remembrance HVS 5a
8 Crow's Nest Direct HVS 5a
9 Bracket Direct HVS 5a
10 Bracket and Slab Climb S
11 'B' Route S
12 'A' Route MS
13 'C' Route S
17 'F' Route VS 4c
Dipthong HVS
Oliverson's Traverse and Lyon's Crawl VD
Ash Tree Ledges
ABCE Wall
Perched Blocks
Ash Tree Ledges
Bilberry Chute Approach
MB

South-East Gully
Three Tiers Climb VS
1
2
3
4
5
7
A Amen Corner
B The Bracket
C Green Chimney
F Forty-foot Corner
G The Gangway
L Lichen Chimney
N The Crow's Nest
T Thompson's Ledge
S Neat Bit

3 Main Wall Climb 49m VD ★★
An excellent route on lovely rock. Start at the left side of the embedded flake.
1 18m Pleasant climbing leads rightwards and up to a ledge and small belays.
2 18m Move diagonally left to a ledge, step right and continue straight up to a good belay.
3 13m Starting on the left, climb direct to the top. Descend rightwards.
GS Bower, F Graham - Mar 1921

4 Bachelor Crack 54m MVS 4b ★★
Varied climbing up the right edge of the face. Start at a corner crack in a sloping recess, at the highest accessible point on the left wall of the gully.
1 18m 4b Climb the corner to a small ledge. Move left to surmount the bulge as for *Chimney Buttress*, traverse delicately back right to the far rib, then to a small ledge.
2 36m Pleasant climbing up the walls and slabs passing several grass ledges.
RJ Birkett, V Veevers, J Craven - Aug 1941

5 Chimney Buttress 64m S 4a ★★
Agreeable climbing with a short dynamic crux. Start 2m below the corner *Bachelor Crack*.
1 13m Climb a short crack and scramble up leftwards to a spacious ledge below a chimney.
2 27m 4a Climb diagonally rightwards to a small ledge overlooking the gully then back left to another ledge. 'Piano play' your way over the bulging wall, after which enjoyable slabs trending slightly rightwards lead to a good ledge.
3 24m Finish pleasantly up more slabs.
HB Lyon, G Ackerley, J Herbert - Sep 1923

6 Gimmer Chimney 80m VD ★★★
A classic route up the striking twin-cracks. Start at a broken rib under the main line.
1 32m Climb the rib and easy chimney to an awkward steep section at 23m. Easy climbing then leads to a good stance on the right.
2 17m Traverse left for 3m into a tricky groove, which leads into a sentry box. Climb the deep crack by good holds on its right rib to a stance beneath a narrow chimney.
3 11m Ignore the narrow chimney and traverse 5m right into a parallel chimney. This leads amenably to a belay.
4 20m Quit the gully bed for the rib on the right and finish up this.
E Rigby, J Sandison, AS Thomson - Nov 1902

7 Remembrance 105m HVS 5a ★★
A varied route with a distinct crux. Large cams useful. Start at the foot of a clean slab split by a slanting diagonal crack about 15m above the gearing-up point.
1 35m 4b The crack leads over the overlap and up into a groove which soon leads into another groove/crack-line running back diagonally right. Follow this until it steepens, then traverse delicately right to a rib and belay just above.
2 20m 5a Climb the short rib by its right edge to a good ledge. Step right and climb the overhanging groove to a belay below the right-hand twin chimney.
3 35m 4b Traverse rightwards along a fault to a ledge under a bulging wall. Pull over and follow the flake crack leftwards to a smooth slab which leads via a short crack in a steepening buttress to a narrow heather ledge.
4 15m Climb the short crack and buttress above.
SJH Reid, JR Grinbergs - Mar 1990

8 Crow's Nest Direct 91m HVS 5a ★★
Good climbing that stretches most people. Start as *Remembrance*.
1 26m 4b Climb the crack passing an overlap at 9m and move leftwards onto a grass bank. Belay at the back beneath an overhanging V-groove/niche.
2 14m 5a Climb the V-groove and leave by problematic moves pulling left into the hanging groove in the left wall. Climb this to a large ledge.
3 17m 5a Climb the difficult bulging wall using a small pedestal just right of a flake crack. A narrow layback crack then leads to the Gangway and a belay beneath a thin crack in the overhanging wall.
4 10m 4c A sensational, rising, semi-hand traverse across the overhanging wall on the right leads to a small ledge above the overhang. Move up left to a good belay above the traverse.
5 24m Climb leftwards to the arête and follow it to the Crow's Nest. Move left and climb a corner to the finishing slabs.
P2: I Waller, J Longland - Apr 1931
P3-5: S Thompson, P White, A Mullan, V Bolton, J Ashton - 1940

9 Bracket Direct 96m HVS 5a ★★

A pleasant series of eliminate pitches with several short difficult sections. Start as for *Bracket and Slab Climb*.

1 31m 5a Follow *Bracket and Slab Climb* to the good spike and traverse horizontally rightwards to make an awkward pull up into a small niche. Continue up the slab and rib above, taking an overlap at its left-hand end, and belay on the terrace above.

2 31m 5a Above is the Bracket. Gain the left end of this directly and follow the thin crack above to a steep exit. Climb up to a bay and continue directly via a heathery crack to emerge on Thompson's Ledge at a blunt nose left of Amen Corner. A long reach up the right side of the nose and an awkward mantelshelf leads rightwards onto the Gangway.

3 10m 4c Climb the thin crack splitting the impending pink wall to a good belay.

4 24m 4b Step up right and climb the steep wall to a bilberry ledge. Move left a metre or so and climb the slab to the top.

C King, SJH Reid - Oct 2003. P4: SJH Reid, J Roberts - May 2004

10 Bracket and Slab Climb 97m S ★★★

An excellent, long and varied route. Start at a slabby rib leading up to a large flake.

1 31m Climb the easy-angled rib to its top. Step left into a groove and follow this into a grassy bay, passing several awkward steps. Belay on the large blocks.

2 12m The Bracket is the large block stuck on the wall up and right of the belay. Starting behind the belay blocks, climb up until a devious traverse horizontally rightwards to and across the Bracket gains the groove beyond. This leads up and leftwards to an alcove stance.

3 26m Climb out rightwards and continue traversing diagonally over easy ground (well below the overhanging Amen Corner) towards the left edge overlooking Gimmer Chimney. Here, a leftwards-rising ramp (the Neat Bit) up the steep wall leads to the obvious sloping Gangway. Traverse this easily rightwards to the foot of the narrow Amen Chimney.

4 9m The chimney is **MVS 4b** – slightly overhanging, strenuous but better protected than it appears. Best suited to thin masochists; normally avoided by the easier chimney round to the right.

5 19m Traverse onto the left rib of the gully and follow it, moving left just below the top.

HB Lyon, J Herbert - Aug 1923

Gimmer String E1 (page 88) James Kinnaird — STEPHEN REID

'D' Route S (page 82) — 📷 Sean Kelly

West Face

This fine shield of rock gets the best of the sun and provides a range of classic routes on immaculate quick drying rock. The routes start from a series of ledges running across the face known collectively as Ash Tree Ledges.

Approach: ⚠ The ledges can only be accessed by climbing or exposed scrambling. The simplest way is from the gearing-up point below the South-East Face via the Bilberry Chute. Follow ledges behind a block level with the top of a spindly rowan tree, until a short exposed scramble up an rounded and polished rib leads onto a grassy terrace on the front of the crag. After 15m scramble up to some large flat perched blocks, where further exposed scrambling leads either up or left to the foot of the face itself.

Descent: Abseil or take South East Gully. See page 75.

⑪ 'B' Route 69m S ★★★

An entertaining and ever popular climb, p3 will give you a run for your money. Start left of the letters ABCE scratched on a short wall.

1 18m Scramble up then right to gain a spacious platform after 9m. Belay 9m further right.

2 10m Climb a polished flake crack to Thompson's Ledge. Easily rightwards for 6m to the foot of the formidable impending corner.

3 5m 4c Amen Corner. Short and sharp.

4 9m Up the Gangway to a good ledge.

5 12m Continue the corner (Green Chimney) until a short traverse right to a ledge, the Crow's Nest.

6 15m Step right and follow pleasant slabs to the top.

HB Lyon, J Stables, AS Thomson - Jul 1907

⑫ 'A' Route 75m MS ★★★

A great climb up an excellent line of weakness. Start as for *'B' Route*.

1 18m p1 *'B' Route*.

2 14m Climb the initial crack of *'B' Route* to gain Thompson's Ledge. Traverse left along it to the foot of the Forty Foot Corner.

3 18m The delightful corner leads to a good spike. Traverse left and slightly up to a ledge below an open groove - Lichen Chimney.

4 11m Climb the groove.

5 14m The rock staircase on the left leads to a steep finishing corner crack.

E Rigby, D Leighton, J Sandison - Apr 1903

⑬ 'C' Route 62m S ★★★

Another classic with fine climbing in good positions. Start as for *'B' Route*.

1 18m p1 *'B' Route*.

2 27m Climb a short steep wall 3m left of the belay to a recess and thence with difficulty to Thompson's Ledge. The groove above is entered by the flake on the right and climbed to belay at a good small ledge below a prominent square-cut overhang.

3 17m Pull round left beneath the overhang to a ledge. Climb the groove above, moving right at a flaky spike to a direct and exposed finish.

AP Wilson, CH Jackson, A Brundritt - Aug 1918

⑭ 'D' Route 30m S ★★★

A superb pitch, with character despite its brevity. Start 5m right of smooth slabs, on a small terrace some 20m above the main Ash Tree Ledge. Easily up, then traverse 5m left to the right-slanting groove. Climb this and the fine crack above to finish up as for *'A' Route*.

GS Bower, PR Masson - May 1919

⑮ Springbank 38m E2 5c ★★★

This brilliant "non-line" can have your toes and finger tips screaming – a superb well protected pitch. Start at the bottom right-hand corner of the smooth slabs. climb the rib, then the tenuous crack-line to the middle of the roof. Arrange yourself around the lip, pull over on small holds and continue triumphant to the top.

MG Mortimer, E Cleasby, MG Allen, M Lynch, J Lamb - Jun 1979

⑯ Whit's End Direct 38m E1 5b ★★★

Fine slab climbing with a neat section through the roof. Start at an obvious left-slanting flake-crack cleaving the slab. Ascend the crack and continue directly up the line of thin cracks to a resting point a few of metres below the overlap. Step right and move up to reach left to the end of the overlap. Enter the hanging corner and make an exhilarating move right onto the slab; finish more easily.

JA Austin, R Valentine - Oct 1972

⑰ 'F' Route 40m VS 4c ★★★

'F' for fantastic, especially as described here with the Whit's End start. A terrific pitch with its crux fittingly near the top. The flake-crack feels very insecure but soon leads to small ledges. Use a good flake to move leftwards and onto a small ledge under the overhangs. Step up right and climb the corner to a bold finish.

RJ Birkett, V Veevers - May 1941

20
19
18
17
16
15
14
12
11
A
13
19
18
16
20
'E' Route HS
Dipthong HVS
14
17
15
20
11
Oliverson's Traverse and
Lyon's Crawl VD
26
24
13
Ash Tree Ledges
11
12
ABCE Wall
13
Perched
Blocks
MB

18 Eastern Hammer 38m E3 6a ★★
A masterpiece of excellent, fingery climbing up the front of the bulging wall. Scramble leftwards up ledges from the foot of the left-slanting flake-crack and belay under the overhang. Pull over onto the steep wall and climb past a peg, follow the crack to a good hold beneath the final bulges. Step up, move to the left end of the bulge and pull across it rightwards to a small ledge. Finish more easily up *Kipling Groove*.
P Livesey, A Manson - May 1974

19 Equus 40m E2 5c ★★★
Another excellent and sustained pitch with a difficult initial overhang, some technical bridging and a bold finish. Start as for *Eastern Hammer*. Traverse leftwards to the centre of the overlap. Pull over this and continue up the groove to a junction with *Kipling Groove*. Up this a short way to a resting place beneath a bulge. Swing left to a small ledge and climb the groove and exposed wall on the right to the final horizontal crack; traverse left to finish.
E Cleasby - Apr 1976; Finish: MG Mortimer, MG Allen - May 1976

20 Kipling Groove 52m HVS 5a ★★★
A magnificent and popular classic taking an impressive and 'Rudyard' line up the buttress. Start at the foot of the left-slanting flake-crack of *Whit's End Direct*.
1 10m Scramble easily up leftwards to the ledge below the overhang.
2 11m 4c Move up to and traverse the photogenic undercling leftwards to a crack which leads to an overhung recess. Clipping both ropes into protection placed in the crack beyond the roof should avoid them jamming.
3 31m 5a Climb the right wall of the recess, past a dubious block, until forced out right onto the edge. Follow the crack to a good resting place beneath the bulge. Pull up and reach strenuously rightwards to a diagonal crack. Finger or toe traverse a horizontal crack right to a ledge. Ascend a crack to easier ground.
AR Dolphin, JB Lockwood - May 1948

Gimmer Integrales

These great combinations marry classic routes on the lower and upper sections of Gimmer providing memorable and long adventures.

1. **24 Ash Tree Slabs : 12 'A' Route** MS
2. **27 Aterisk : 14 'D' Route** MVS
3. **26 North-West Arête : 17 'F' Route** VS
4. **25 Intern : 16 Whit's End Direct** E1
5. **23 Crystal : 20 Kipling Groove** E1

North-West Arête VS (page 86) Sean Bell — NEIL CARNEGIE

North-West Face (Lower Section)

The Lower North-West Face offers a series of well known routes which provide access to Ash Tree Ledges. Excellent rock but it can be chilly before the sun comes round, finally hitting the *Asterisk* wall mid-afternoon.

Approach: Follow the track up the edge of the crag to arrive at a large rocky ledge just beyond *Ash Tree Slabs*, where the path starts to traverse towards the huge boulder chockstone blocking the gully.

Descent: ⚠ Scramble off rightwards down the Billberry Chute.

21 Herdwick Buttress 27m VD ★★
A pleasant route which gives the easiest way onto the front face. Start as for *Ash Tree Slabs* by scrambling up into the bay.
1 12m Scramble rightwards into the open corner. Climb this on good holds, pulling out right onto the rib which leads to a ledge.
2 15m Climb a left-facing flake and thin twin cracks above to the terraces and belays. Scrambling leads to Ash Tree Ledge.
F Graham - Mar 1925

22 Introduction 32m MVS 4b ★★
A delightful slab up an elegant slim groove. Easy ground to the foot of the groove. Climb the left edge of this overlooking *Ash Tree Slabs*, crossing an awkward bulge.
DJ Cameron, AB Durrant - Apr 1948

23 Crystal 38m E1 5b ★★
An excellent sustained pitch up the steep wall overlooking *Ash Tree Slabs*. Climb the very steep crack in the wall and move left to below a vague groove-line. Bulges in this are negotiated in turn by stepping left then climbing up, until a more direct line leads to easier ground.
TW Birkett, A Atkinson, D Lyle - Jun 1981

24 Ash Tree Slabs 48m VD ★★★
This great and ever popular little climb takes the handsome sweep of slabs rising across the wall at the top of the approach path. Scramble to a small bay at the foot of the slabs.
1 16m Climb 3m up the corner then diagonally left on good holds to the edge of the slab. Follow this to a ledge.
2 32m Climb 3m up left to a platform and take the groove leading right until it eases. Continue up slabs to finish on a ledge above the main Ash Tree Ledge.
GS Bower, AW Wakefield - Jun 1920

25 Intern 48m E1 5b ★★★
The compelling succession of ramps across the wall, beckoning for an ascent; excellent, sustained and varied. Combined with *Whit's End Direct* it provides a superb way up the crag. Start at a right-slanting crack below the first ramp.
1 18m 5b Climb the crack and step left to gain the tapering, left-slanting slab. Holds on the slab above permit moves leftwards to the edge, then pull up into a short groove which leads to a left-slanting gangway.
2 30m 5a Climb the gangway and up the wall on the right and pull over the bulge above. Move left onto the rib (*North-West Arête*) and follow it to the top.
P1: P Fearnehough, J Oliver, J Hesmondhalgh - May 1963
P2: J A Austin, I Roper - Mar 1966

26 North-West Arête 42m VS 4b ★★★
A beautifully exposed route on good rock and generally excellent holds. Start at the left end of an obvious very thin quartz ledge in the gully by the large jammed boulder. Easily up right to gain the base of the wall. Ascend to a small overlap, traverse right and follow cracks to the left side of the overhangs. Pull through these on good holds and move right to the arête. Climb this, treating the final thin flake crack in the crest with care.
RJ Birkett, V Veevers - Sep 1940

27 Asterisk 38m MVS 4b ★★★
A splendid wall pitch, mostly on jugs. Modern protection has taken much of the 'risk' out of the name. Start at a rock ledge slanting up right, a short way up the left side of the wall. From the right end of the ledge, climb rightwards into a groove which gives good holds to the obvious crescent-shaped ledge at 7m. Climb diagonally right for 6m to a small niche in the centre of the wall, then follow the crack-line which becomes intermittent towards the top.
HS Gross, G Basterfield, B Tyson - May 1928

28 Detour 36m VS 4c ★★
A direct version of *Asterisk* with pleasant climbing and good protection. Climb the wide crack direct to the crescent ledge, then its continuation into a right-slanting scoop. Negotiate the small roof at the top by an exhilarating move left on excellent holds and finish up a thin crack.
SJH Reid, N Timmins - Jun 1995

29 Samaritan Corner 38m VS 4c ★★
A contrasting companion to *Asterisk* with good and well protected climbing up the obvious corner to its left.
AR Dolphin, JB Lockwood, J Bloor - May 1948

29
28
27
26
25
24
23
22
21
25
29
28
27
23
26
24
22
21
25
MB

North-West Face (Upper Section)

Approach: Follow faint scree tracks and billberry ledges left below the Lower Section skirting the base of the crag.

Descent: The North West Gully is used initially and then the heathery spur on the right, see page 75.

30 Gimmer String 78m E1 5b ★★★
A brilliant combination of pitches, strung together to provide varied and enjoyable climbing in exposed situations.
1 26m 4c p1 of *The Crack.*
2 25m 4c Traverse right and up to the top of a pinnacle spike below a wide crack. Step right and pull awkwardly into it, then continue to join *Kipling Groove.*
3 27m 5b Climb up to some dubious blocks and traverse left to a niche-like ledge on the rib. Follow a thin crack on the right until a difficult pull leads round the rib to overlook *The Crack.* Climb the arête to a thin crack leading up a short problematic wall until forced out right to an abrupt finish.
JA Austin, E Metcalf, D Miller - Jul 1963

31 The Crack 74m VS 4c ★★★
The obvious great corner cleaving the crag from top to bottom. A combination of a fine natural line with exposed and sustained climbing on excellent rock make this one of Lakeland's grandest crack climbs. Start at the foot of the corner which rises to a beautiful hand-jam crack.
1 26m 4c Climb the corner and clean-cut crack until a delicate traverse across the left wall leads into a short groove. Up this to a ledge and pedestal belay.
2 26m 4c Gain the horizontal break above (the Mantelshelf) which leads left to a large ledge. A hard pull up the steep ridge leads to better holds and an easy traverse back right into the crack where a strenuous pull out of the Sentry Box leads to a good ledge – The Bower.
3 22m 4c The deep corner-crack provides a sustained pitch, with a problematic overhang en-route.
AB Reynolds, GG Macphee - May 1928

32 Outside Tokyo/Dight 68m E1 5b ★★★
An excellent historical hybrid taking the best line up the slabby wall immediately left of *The Crack.* Interesting, technical climbing with good protection.
1 21m 5b Easily up the corner and left to the foot of a slim groove comprising a series of slanting steps leading to a pedestal belay.
2 31m 5b Mantelshelf as for *The Crack* and step right to a thin crack. Up this to ledges below overlaps. Pull over the first one with difficulty, stepping right into the thin crack above. Follow this past a second smaller overhang, then more easily leftwards into a sentry box. The crack on the left leads to more overhangs and a step right to a small stance.
3 16m 5a Climb the corner above before pulling up strenuously round a small rib into the groove on the right. Ascend this to easier ground.
Various - 1953, 1963, 1979

33 Hiatus 100m VS 4b ★★
An historical tour-de-force. A somewhat tedious introduction relieved by a final superbly exposed traverse left on slabs sandwiched between overhangs. Start 2m left of *The Crack.*
1 32m Up the steep wall to a terrace at 7m then easily up left for 4m to a deep corner. Move right around the rib into an awkward scoop, where the ridge on its left leads towards the pedestal belay of *The Crack.* From below this, step left across the corner to a slab leading to a belay below the grassy corner-gully. (The deep corner is **4c** if climbed direct.)
2 32m Climb the gully for 9m, then left along a ledge and back right into the gully. Up this until forced left across a mossy wall to some ledges.
3 21m 4b Climb into the corner under the big roofs and traverse left under them into a more open corner. Head up and left, then traverse under a bulging rib to where a second rib leads into a good niche.
4 15m 4b Up the left wall of the niche into a short awkward scoop leading to easier climbing.
GS Bower, AB Reynolds, AW Wakefield, GG Macphee - Jul 1927

34 Inertia 103m HVS 5a ★★
Two good pitches up the slabs left of *Outside Tokyo/Dight.* Start as for *Hiatus.*
1 32m As for *Hiatus* p1.
1 20m *Hiatus* p2 to the foot of a prominent groove.
2 27m 5a Climb up rightwards into a cave and pull round the overhang into the main corner. Ascend a short way, then traverse right to the arête. A difficult move up this allows access to the sentry box up and right. Climb the main crack out of this and step right to a small stance.
3 24m 5a Climb a long narrow slab and crack leftwards under a line of overhangs until another groove slanting off rightwards leads to the top.
P3: L Brown, RG Wilson, CEM Yates - Aug 1959
P4: E Metcalf and JA Austin - May 1963

35 Grooves Traverse 98m HVS 5a ★★

A harder finish to *Hiatus*, turning the overhangs by a long traverse to the right. Start as for *Hiatus*.

1 64m As for *Hiatus* p1 and p2.

2 17m 4c Climb until level with a large block. Pull up and make a strenuous traverse right across the steep right wall into a groove which leads to a small stance below a scoop.

3 17m 5a Climb the scoop for 3m and make a dainty traverse right beneath a small overhang. Continue rightwards to finish up a slanting groove.

RVM Barry, EG Harper - Sep 1936

36 Grand Finale 68m E1 5b ★★

A splendid route of steadily increasing difficulty. Though short and very well protected, the crux provides plenty of food for thought. Start below a smooth wall split by a groove-line and standing at the top of a grass terrace parallel to the gully floor.

1 26m 4c Climb the groove-line, finishing up the left side of the arête beyond.

2 12m 5a Attack the left side of the steep clean rib above, step right and continue direct to a chockstone belay and tiny stance.

3 30m 5b Climb the left edge of the slab to the overhang. Stride left along the *Hiatus* traverse into the open corner-groove. Ascend this to the biggest roof and make an exposed and committing move right to reach an obvious downward pointing spike. Use this to gain good hidden holds beyond, leading to a small ledge. The steep but straightforward groove above leads to the top.

C Read, GL Swainbank - Oct 1997

37 Carpetbagger 75m VS 4b ★★

A slightly harder companion to *Hiatus*, initially vegetated but improving with height. Start as for *Godiva Groove*.

1 27m 4b Starting below the right rib of *Godiva Groove*, climb cracks and grooves diagonally rightwards up the edge of the slabs to a ledge at 16m. Traverse horizontally right under a dubious flake and belay below the large overhang.

2 27m 4b Make a long ascending traverse left below the line of overhangs almost to the far edge. Now pull up onto a little slab, climb an awkward groove above to the niche stance of *Hiatus*.

3 21m 4b Make a short semi-hand traverse across the right wall, pull up and finish more easily.

N Allinson, NJ Soper - Jun 1968

38 Godiva Groove 57m VS 4c ★

A good natural line up the most prominent left-facing corner-groove which culminates as a much deeper V-groove. Start in the grassy bay left of *Grand Finale* and below the corner.

1 38m 4c Scramble easily up left for 5m and make a rising traverse into the groove. Climb this for 10m, then move left to a ledge and loose block. Avoiding this, follow the rib, then the groove again, to belay a little below the final deep V-groove.

2 19m 4b Climb the groove for a short way and move onto the left wall, which leads to overhangs. Avoid these by moving left into another mossy groove and finish up a steep broken wall.

CMG Smith, LJ Griffin - Jan 1950

14	**'D' Route**	S
15	**Springbank**	E2 5c
16	**Whit's End Direct**	E1 5b
18	**Eastern Hammer**	E3 6a
19	**Equus**	E2 5c
20	**Kipling Groove**	HVS 5a

Junipall Gully
38
33
37
36
Pallid Slabs
32
35
34
33
38
37
36
MB

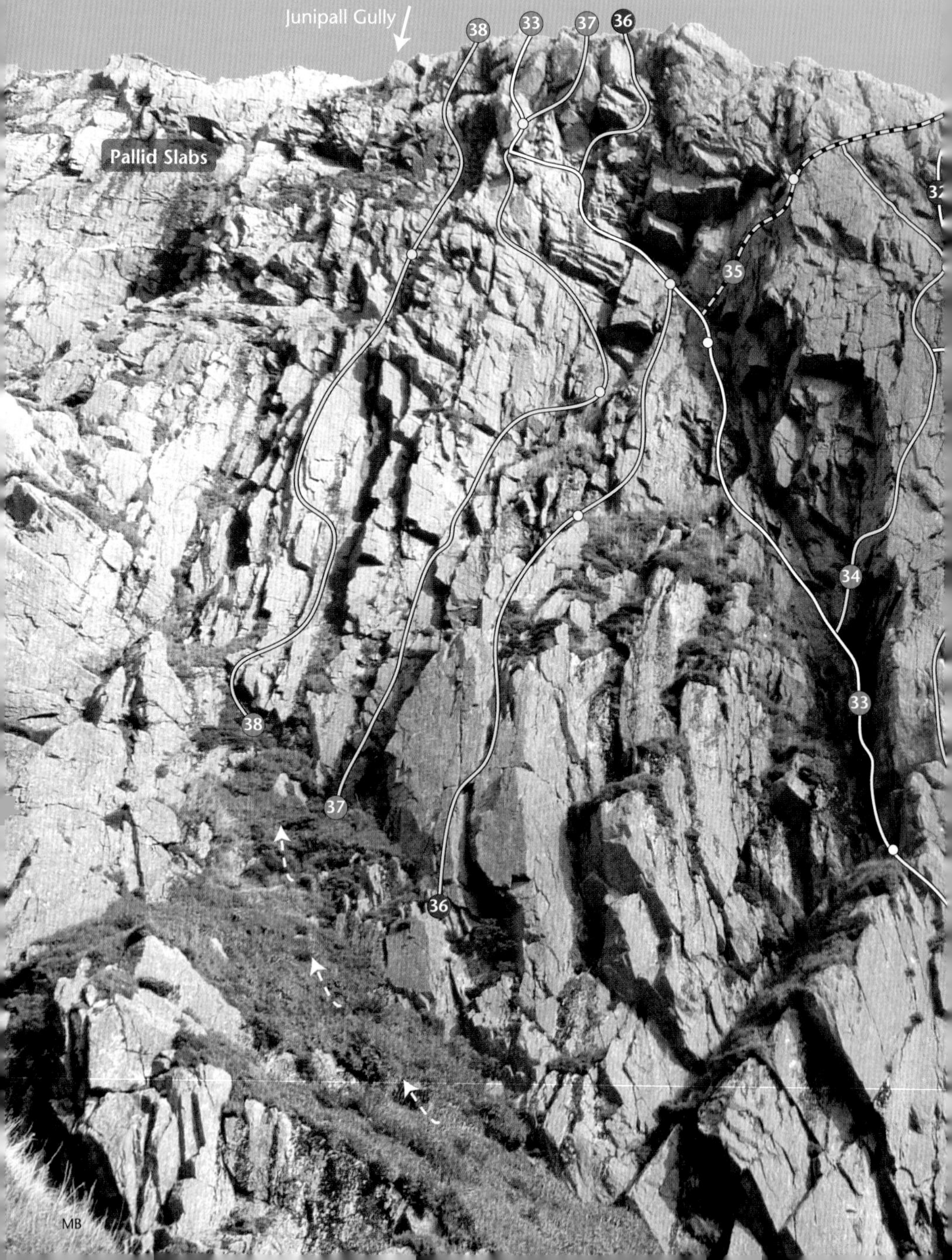

30	**Gimmer String**	E1 5b
31	**The Crack**	VS 4c
32	**Outside Tokyo/Dight**	E1 5b
33	**Hiatus**	VS 4b
34	**Inertia**	HVS 5a
35	**Grooves Traverse**	HVS 5a
36	**Grand Finale**	E1 5b
37	**Carpetbagger**	VS 4b
38	**Godiva Groove**	VS 4c

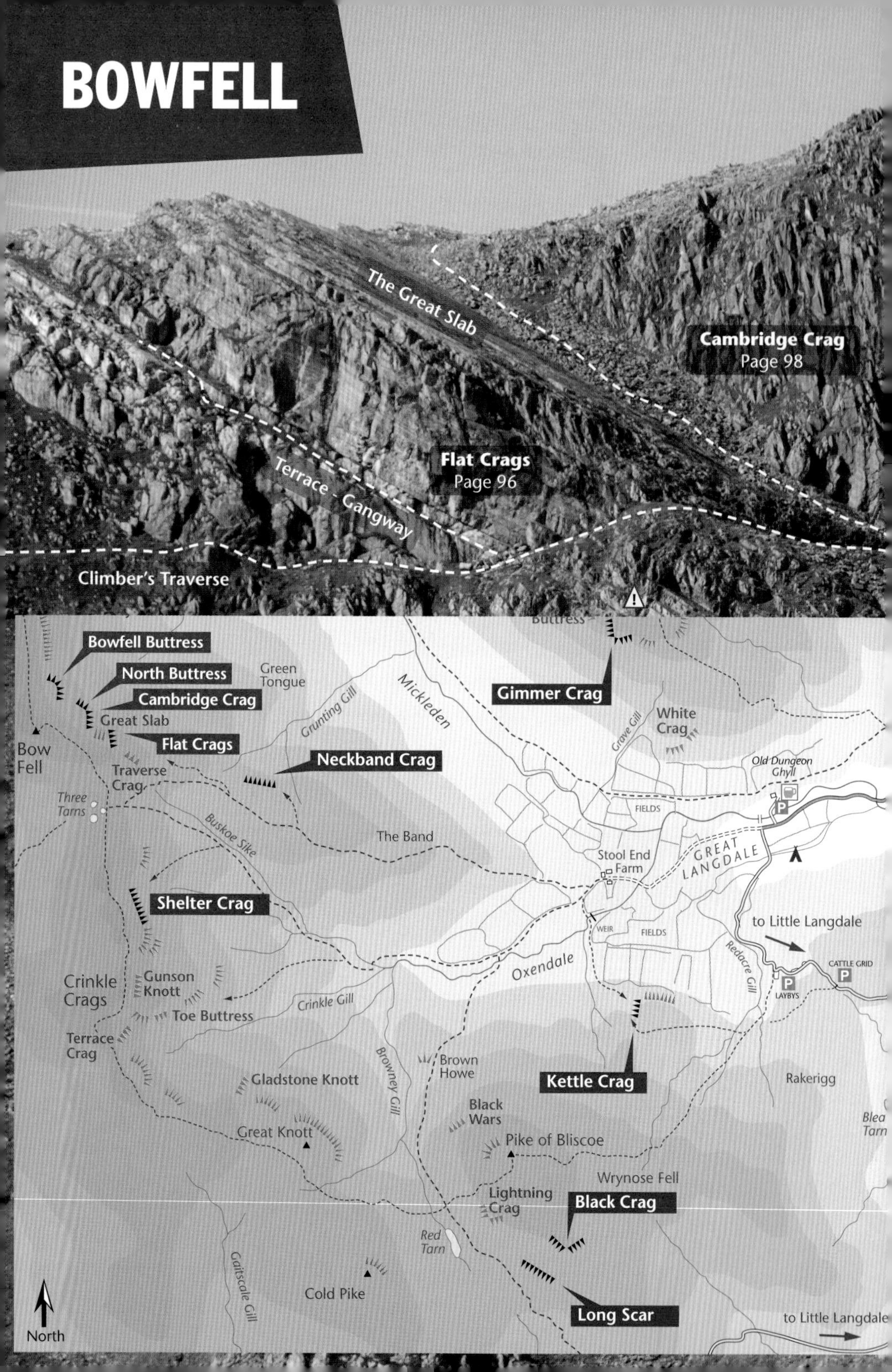
BOWFELL
The Great Slab
Cambridge Crag
Page 98
Flat Crags
Page 96
Terrace - Gangway
Climber's Traverse
Buttress
Bowfell Buttress
North Buttress
Cambridge Crag
Great Slab
Flat Crags
Green Tongue
Gimmer Crag
Grunting Gill
Mickleden
White Crag
Grave Gill
Bow Fell
Neckband Crag
Traverse Crag
Old Dungeon Ghyll
Three Tarns
FIELDS
Buskoe Sike
The Band
Stool End Farm
GREAT LANGDALE
Shelter Crag
WEIR
FIELDS
to Little Langdale
Redacre Gill
CATTLE GRID
Oxendale
Crinkle Crags
Gunson Knott
LAYBYS
Crinkle Gill
Toe Buttress
Terrace Crag
Browney Gill
Brown Howe
Kettle Crag
Gladstone Knott
Rakerigg
Black Wars
Blea Tarn
Great Knott
Pike of Bliscoe
Wrynose Fell
Lightning Crag
Black Crag
Red Tarn
Gaitscale Gill
Cold Pike
Long Scar
North
to Little Langdale

Bowfell Summit

Bowfell is the highest summit of the Langdale Horseshoe and its crags offer some excellent climbing in a wonderful mountain setting. Its long approach (by Lakeland standards) is well worth the effort. Most of the crags are in the sunshine from early morning to around midday. The rock is generally very good with superb friction. Being so high, routes can suffer from drainage and areas take a while to dry out but a well chosen day here will reap rewards.

Approach: From the Old Dungeon Ghyll National Trust car park P NY 286 061. Take the road to Stool End Farm (no parking allowed here) and up the long ridge of The Band. The track levels out and splits, the main route heading round left to the Three Tarns col. A vague path on the right leads towards the summit ridge, soon improving and culminating with the undulating Climbers' Traverse to the foot of Flat Crags. Keeping close to the foot of the crag, the path soon arrives at an ever-flowing spring, The Waterspout, at the base of Cambridge Crag and North Buttress. Bowfell Buttress lies across the wide scree fan to the right.

NECKBAND CRAG

OS Grid Ref: NY 256 062
Altitude: 550m

1 ¼ hr

This superb compact crag has an outcrop atmosphere. Tucked away on the north-facing side of The Band in a cove overlooking Grunting Gill, it is quiet with a fine outlook. The left side of the crag hosts a concentration of immaculate pitches up inspiring corners and cracks on rough, solid rock. It does take a few days to dry out, particularly at the beginning of the season; but it is a cool haven on a hot summer's day.

Approach: P NY 286 061 Old Dungeon Ghyll Hotel. Up The Band for about an hour until the path levels off just before some "stepping stone" rocks across a damp area. A vague path branches off right, going anticlockwise around the summit knoll and descends steeply towards the left end of the crag. If the ridge rising up to Bowfell summit and the Climbers' Traverse is reached, you have over-shot the turning so drop down northwards and traverse the fellside back eastwards to the crag, which will be seen as a rock ridge.

Descent: Leftwards until a scramble, first up, then down steep ground, leads back to the foot of the crag.

1 Cravat 35m VS 4c ★★
An excellent route up the steep east wall, initially steep and fingery. Start in a short right-facing corner. Climb this and the crack above until a line of holds lead rightwards to a scoop in the arête. Move up this to a ledge, go round the rib on the right, then diagonally right up a thin crack in the slab. Finish up a good crack 2m left of the corner.
H Drasdo, N Drasdo - 1950

2 Gandalf's Groove Direct 36m E2 5b ★★★
A magnificent outing on beautiful rock with delicate climbing requiring steadiness on the upper section. Climb the corner for about 16m, until a descending traverse leads easily out left to a very shallow right-facing corner. Climb this and step left onto the rib. Now, fortified by a runner in the diagonal crack, continue boldly up the right-hand side of the rib, which eases slowly towards the top.
JA Austin, FP Jenkinson - Jul 1964;
Direct Finish: I Williamson, J White - Jul 1983

3 Mithrandir 33m HVS 5a ★★★
A classic line up the first large left-facing corner. Much harder if damp.
J Hartley, R Sagar - Aug 1972

4 Glorfindel 35m HVS 5a ★★★
Splendid varied climbing and low in the grade which links parts of other routes to give the easiest way up the central area of the crag. Climb *Mithrandir* until it is possible to gain ledges on the right wall at half height. From the top one of these, traverse right to the arête. The slanting crack round the corner is awkward to enter but soon leads to the top.

5 Gillette Direct 35m E2 5c ★★★
Surely one of the best single pitch climbs in the Lake District. A brilliant, well protected route up the compelling line of narrow, hanging grooves in the right wall of *Mithrandir*. Climb *Razor Crack* to the overhang. Traverse left onto the slab and enter the groove with difficulty. Continue up the steepening groove to good finishing cracks in the final bulge.
K Wood, JA Austin - Jul 1968
Direct Finish: W Lounds and party - 1969

6 Tracheotomy 35m E2 5c ★★★
Another excellent combination accessing the superb crack in the wall left of *Razor Crack*. Climb *Gillette Direct* until it is possible to move right onto a ledge/niche below the upper crack, this gives finger tip climbing to the top. The original start, *Cut Throat* **E3 6a**, climbs the hanging groove immediately left of *Gillette Direct*, entered by some finger-searing moves.
M Berzins, B Berzins - May 1978

7 Razor Crack 35m E1 5a ★★★
A classic pitch climbing the superb crack up the middle of the clean wall with good protection and resting places is strenuous and sustained. Start at a ragged undercut crack running up to a band of overhangs at 5m. The crack is immediately strenuous. Traverse right beneath the overhangs until a thin crack facilitates a pull over and moves back left into the main crack. This leads over several overlaps and the odd jammed flake to the top, where you can sink thankfully amongst the bilberries.
JA Austin, K Wood - Aug 1966

1
3
5
4
2
7
4
6
1
5
6
7
2
3
4
MB

FLAT CRAGS

OS Grid Ref: NY 249 065
Altitude: 750m

A dramatically steep crag that appears less so due to the sloping nature of the rock strata, which is solid and compact. The climbing is excellent, technical and demanding – proper climbing, where finesse and an awareness of body position pay dividends. The crag catches the sun till late morning.

Approach: As for Bowfell (P NY 286 061) until the end of the Climbers' Traverse, where the crag rears up overhead. See map page 92.

Descents: Either scramble rightwards down the Great Slab to the Climbers' Traverse, or go up and scramble down leftwards onto the upper reaches of the rock terrace and reverse this, taking care at the break in the middle.

1 Flat Crags Climb 43m S ★★

A cheeky excursion probing the upper reaches of the crag to ascend a fine hidden corner. Start at the slabs immediately right of a short hanging corner above a huge block.

1 16m Climb direct up the excellent slab for 7m when a short traverse left gains a ledge. Traverse diagonally rightwards and up past another ledge to reach the large grassy terrace.

2 27m Walk up the terrace to where it steepens and re-belay. Teeter left along a sloping ledge beneath the steep wall out to the edge of the crag in an exposed position. Move delicately round the rib to discover a fine deep crack. Climb this and the corner above and belay. The ridge on the left gives a pleasant scramble to an obvious summit.

2 Exposure 33m E5 6a ★★★

A sustained and well protected route up the forbidding overhung curving groove-line. Start at the bottom of the rock ramp. The short wall leads to a slab, step left and climb a slim groove to the big overhang. Step right and follow the groove to the top overhang. Move right on small holds to a ledge, gain the slabs above then more easily to the grass terrace.

B Berzins, M Berzins - May 1980

3 Ataxia 46m E5 6b ★★★
An incredibly sustained pitch up a vague crack/groove-line. Start about 5m up the rock ramp below a gritstone-like roof crack.
1 23m 6b Attack the roof and crack to gain a ledge on the right. Step back left and follow the steepening crack to a narrow ledge below a short groove. Pull into the groove where hard moves eventually gain good holds at its top. Move up to a small ledge and belay.
2 23m 4c The slabs above trending leftwards.
M Berzins, B Berzins - Jul 1979

4 Remains of the Day 45m E6 6b ★★
The large niche left of *Ataxia* provides sustained and interesting climbing. Start below a groove through the initial overlap. Climb up (peg), move right into the groove and follow this over a bulge into the niche and a possible no-hands rest. Climb up to the roof where some long moves out right gain a small ledge and tiny belays. 25m of easier rock lead to the top.
M Berzins - May 1990

5 Redundancy of Courage 45m E5 6b ★★
Probably the easiest of the main wall routes taking the hanging groove left of *Remains of the Day*. Start at a recess left of the line of the groove.
1 20m 6b Climb the thin crack almost to the break. Traverse right to an obvious sloping hold below the groove. Pull into it and climb to a belay.
2 25m 4c Easier slabs to the top.
M Berzins, CP Smith - 1992

6 Fastburn 36m E2 5b ★★★
A superb pitch directly up the *Flat Iron Wall* providing a contrasting combination of strenuous and delicate climbing. Start at a hanging crack right of *Flat Iron Wall*. Ascend the crack and hollow flake to a good ledge. Delicately up the wall, trending left to join and climb a line of thin slanting cracks, moving right at the top to a good ledge. Move immediately back left and climb the wall to easier ground.
E Cleasby, I Greenwood - Jun 1979

7 Flat Iron Wall 43m E1 5b ★★
An excellent first pitch finding the easiest way up the undercut wrinkled wall so prominently visible from the approach walk. The wall looks holdless but is just off-vertical and covered in little edges. Protection is better than might be expected – sufficient to allow one to savour the excursion. Start in the corner.
1 22m 5a A rising traverse rightwards leads to a small ledge. Step right and climb trending slightly rightwards up the wall, over the left-hand of two slight bulges near the top, to a ledge on the right arête. Belay on the larger ledge above.
2 21m 5b On the left is a succession of three little corners, which prove disproportionately awkward for their size.
JA Austin, F Wilkinson - Jul 1971

8 Slowburn 33m E2 5b ★★
A good route, steeper than it looks. Start below the toe of the slab leading into the huge corner. Climb the left wall easily to a small pocket. Pull out left to a cracked spike and follow a ramp rightwards. At the top, traverse delicately up and leftwards to a ledge on the arête. Pull up and follow the edge of the wall up and right in an exposed position until a steep move gives access to easy slabs leading to the top.
B Berzins, M Berzins - Jul 1979

9 Moon Shadow 35m E1 5b ★
Start in the corner where the crag turns left above a rock step. Climb the crack which splits the right edge of the corner. Reach and/or the right size of hands are useful for the difficult start. At the roof, pull round into the groove-line and follow the left side of this to a ledge. Continue directly up the centre of the bubbly slab and short wall to the top.
D Armstrong, J Williams - Jun 1988

10 Mary Ann 42m VD ★★
A good route on immaculate rock. Start just right of a large flake some 6m right of a mossy cave.
1 22m Climb cracks leading to a line of overhangs. Traverse left below these and go up into a slabby bay.
2 20m A short crack on the left leads to a rising traverse leftwards across the slabby wall. Finish steeply on good holds.
J Umpleby, P Grindley, J Slockett - summer 1971

11 St Luke 32m HVS 4c (5.8) ★
Accepts the challenge of the deep parallel-sided chimney and gives two contrasting pitches. Not overly well protected. Start at the mossy cave.
1 12m 4c Climb the right wall of the cave and articulate oneself into the chimney. Classic off-width chimney technique or a more humid, squirming style leads to a comfortable platform and belay.
2 20m 4c Step right and climb the shelving gangway for 2m whence a break in the left wall allows escape onto the slabby rib leading more easily to the top.
P1: BJ Clarke - Oct 2007; P2: I Gray, RM Biden - Aug 2010

CAMBRIDGE CRAG

OS Grid Ref: NY 246 066
Altitude: 775m

Under the summit of Bowfell the crags fold round into each other, separated only by a more vegetated area. The crag is a mass of jumbled pinnacles, short walls and ribs building in height as it rises up to the right. The rock is typical of Bowfell with wonderful friction. The high mountain nature and more northerly aspect of some routes delays them coming into condition and can be a bit grubby.

Approach: Follow the Climbers' Traverse to The Waterspout. *The Cambridge Climb* lies 10m left and the North Buttress routes are reached by a scramble rightwards up steep grass and outcrops close the foot of the crag. See map page 92 (P NY 286 061).

Descent: Either over to the left and down the path by the side of the Great Slab, or head rightwards to the top of the rough open gully/scree chute and pick a way down this.

1 The Cambridge Climb 77m VD ★★
A very good climb, a classic of its era and genre, with some excellent positions. The grade increases exponentially in the wet, except in nailed boots. Start 10m left of The Waterspout at a right-slanting slab.
1 11m Climb the slab to a corner.
2 9m Step round the right rib and climb to a good ledge with an overhanging block belay.
3 14m Traverse left to the second of two grassy niches, above which a sharp jutting flake is climbed to another grassy corner.
4 15m Climb the pleasant flake chimney to a ledge on the right.
5 11m Step back left and climb the chimney to a large terrace.
6 17m A giant's three-step staircase leads up and rightwards with increasing difficulty to an exit onto the ridge. Easy scrambling remains.
WT Elmslie, A de St C Walsh - Sep 1922

2 Riboletto 43m E4 6a ★★★
A brilliant pitch; an excellent line on perfect rock. Graded for its bold start. A fine arête rising to its own summit stands above the central vegetated area. Scramble up this to the foot of a smooth groove on the right side of the rib.
1 33m 6a Climb the groove for 5m to a grassy incut hold (skyhook); make some delicate moves left to gain the narrow hanging slab below the rib. This leads left round the corner to a thin groove and crack. Climb the left side of the rib (crux - useful hidden hold right of the rib) to reach a good ledge. Now follow the right side of the rib past another small ledge and belay below a short wall.
2 10m 4c Easily up the wall. The summit of the mountain lies just behind and an effort should be made to visit it.
P Rigby, A Greig - Jun 1988

3 Siamese Chimneys 82m E1 5b (5.10a)  ★★
A very unusual route for the Lake District and a "must" for anyone intent on sampling Yosemite-style offwidth cracks. Start below an initial pillar, split by a chimney/crack, which lies about 100m right of The Waterspout.
1 18m 4a Steep easy rocks into the hanging chimney. Avoid the large overhang by stepping right onto a slab, then up to a sloping ledge.
2 26m 4c The triangular corner on the right is exited via the left-hand crack. Easy rocks rightwards to belay below a deep chimney-crack splitting the left wall of the corner above. If the corner is wet, climb its right rib and traverse back left to the belay.
3 20m 5b Enter the slim chimney and ascend with a combination of dignity, despair and no small display of energy. The chimney gradually widens and the left rib is gained, then easier climbing. (Beware of rock debris in the chimney for the final few metres.)
4 18m Climb the buttress moving right to a ledge at 9m. A small crack above leads to the top.
D Hopkin, AR Dolphin, PJ Greenwood - Aug 1952

4 The Gnomon 63m E1 5b ★★
A good main pitch up the left-hand of three big grooves. Start on a grassy platform with large spike belay, gained by scrambling in from the right.
1 40m 5b Climb the corner crack into a niche. Step left and up to a larger niche. Left again to a small ledge on the rib. Swing back right and climb to a good ledge, then the steep groove until scrambling leads to a final tower.
2 23m 4b Move up to gain a line of holds leading rightwards to the edge, then directly to the top.
L Brown, G Lund - Apr 1960

5 Sword of Damocles 56m E1 5b ★★★
This classic route of the 1950s climbs the right-hand and largest of the three grooves. Start from a ledge beneath a prominent, overhung curved crack, actually the base of a huge pinnacle.
1 23m 4c Climb the curving crack into the groove. Easily to the foot of a groove behind the pinnacle and climb it until a long stride right gains a ledge on the edge. Up a little to where a semi-hand traverse leftwards leads to a stance on the left wall of the main groove.
2 33m 5b Climb the groove passing to the left of an awkward bulging nose. Continue up the impressive flake crack to a resting place, then on until a move right leads to easier climbing.
PJ Greenwood, AR Dolphin, D Hopkin - Aug 1952

6 The Scabbard 61m VS 4c ★
Some good positions and a crack pitch of esoteric qualities. Start at a thin crack in a short wall about 12m right of *Sword of Damocles*.
1 22m 4c Climb the thin crack to a grass ledge at 7m. Scramble up to belay below the line of the main crack.
3 13m 4c Climb steeply for a couple of metres, then make an awkward move to gain a shallow scoop near the left-hand rib. Follow this to a stance and high thread.
3 26m 4c Climb the widening crack with interest to finish up broken grooves.
JA Austin, E Metcalf - May 1960

BOWFELL BUTTRESS

OS Grid Ref: NY 246 067
Altitude: 750m

2 hr

This bold triangular buttress stands proud and independent of the fellside. Its routes feel more like expeditions; all lead to its summit and create a real mountain atmosphere with exposed views down the length of Langdale. It gets sun until at least midday and the rock is generally immaculate.

Approach: From The Waterspout traverse the fellside and scree chute rightwards to the foot of the buttress. See map page 92 (P NY 286 061).

Descents: Walk over the summit of the buttress (Low Man) down into the col and descend the loose cleft on the left, keeping to the right (facing out) towards the bottom. For those seeking the mountain summit itself, climb up the other side of the col.

1 **Silent Witness** 95m HVS 5a ★

Interesting climbing with good positions winding its way around the central overhangs. It needs a week of dry weather to be in good condition. Start at a short rib 6m left of *The Central Route*.

1 40m 5a Climb the rib, over a perched block at 3m, move right and continue close to the fault-line which forms the higher corner. After 20m, enter and climb the corner itself. When it steepens, traverse left along a flake and climb the short corner crack beyond. Move left and follow a left-slanting gangway to an overlap. Make a committing pull over this, then leftwards up a short slab to an obvious spike. Belay on the right by a large pinnacle.

2 30m 5a Surmount the pinnacle and gain the base of a right-facing ramp. Step up left to a good ledge and climb directly to beneath an overhang. Go diagonally right to twin cracks, move up and pull out right onto the steep clean wall which is climbed directly to a grass ledge and embedded block belay.

3 25m 4a Climb the crack in the wall behind and continue to a large ledge; scramble to the top.

C Read, G L Swainbank - Sep 1998

2 **Bowfell Buttress** 106m HS ★★★

A classic mountain route taking the easiest way up the front of the buttress. Book early to avoid the queues. Generally **D** except for the notorious crack on p4 which becomes even harder in the wet. Start at a small ridge 3m left of *The Central Route*.

1 23m Climb the ridge then the short smooth chimney to easy ground.

2 12m Climb the steep wall diagonally leftwards to a sentry box in a chimney.

3 18m Follow the chimney for about 12m and continue up easy ledges to a large terrace. Follow this down right for about 7m and belay below a crack in the steep wall.

4 17m The crack is very steep, polished and awkward (**4a**). Slabby rock above leads back left to a pinnacle belay.

5 18m Move left and ascend a groove to a chimney. Go up to a slab and continue up the wall above until a short traverse left across the corner leads to a platform.

6 18m Step back right and follow a groove and its left-hand branch to finish.

T Shaw, GH Craig, GR West, C Hargreaves, LJ Oppenheimer - May 1902

3 **The Central Route** 93m VS 4c ★★

Start at a groove near the left edge of the smooth wall forming the foot of the crag.

1 13m The groove leads pleasantly to a good belay.

2 16m 4c Attack the left-facing chimney-corner. When it impends, use good holds on jammed flakes to step out right onto the arête. Climb this to regain the corner and continue easily to block belays.

3 20m 4b Traverse a few metres left until it is possible to climb up and back right onto a slabby rib. Follow this to a block belay below a long thin groove-line.

4 27m Climb the groove with increasing difficulty to an awkward finish into a recess. The steep right corner and rib then leads to a crevassed ledge; step back left and up another rib to grass shelves.

5 17m Traverse left to finish up a rough slab and a short wall.

HM Kelly, B Eden-Smith - May 1931

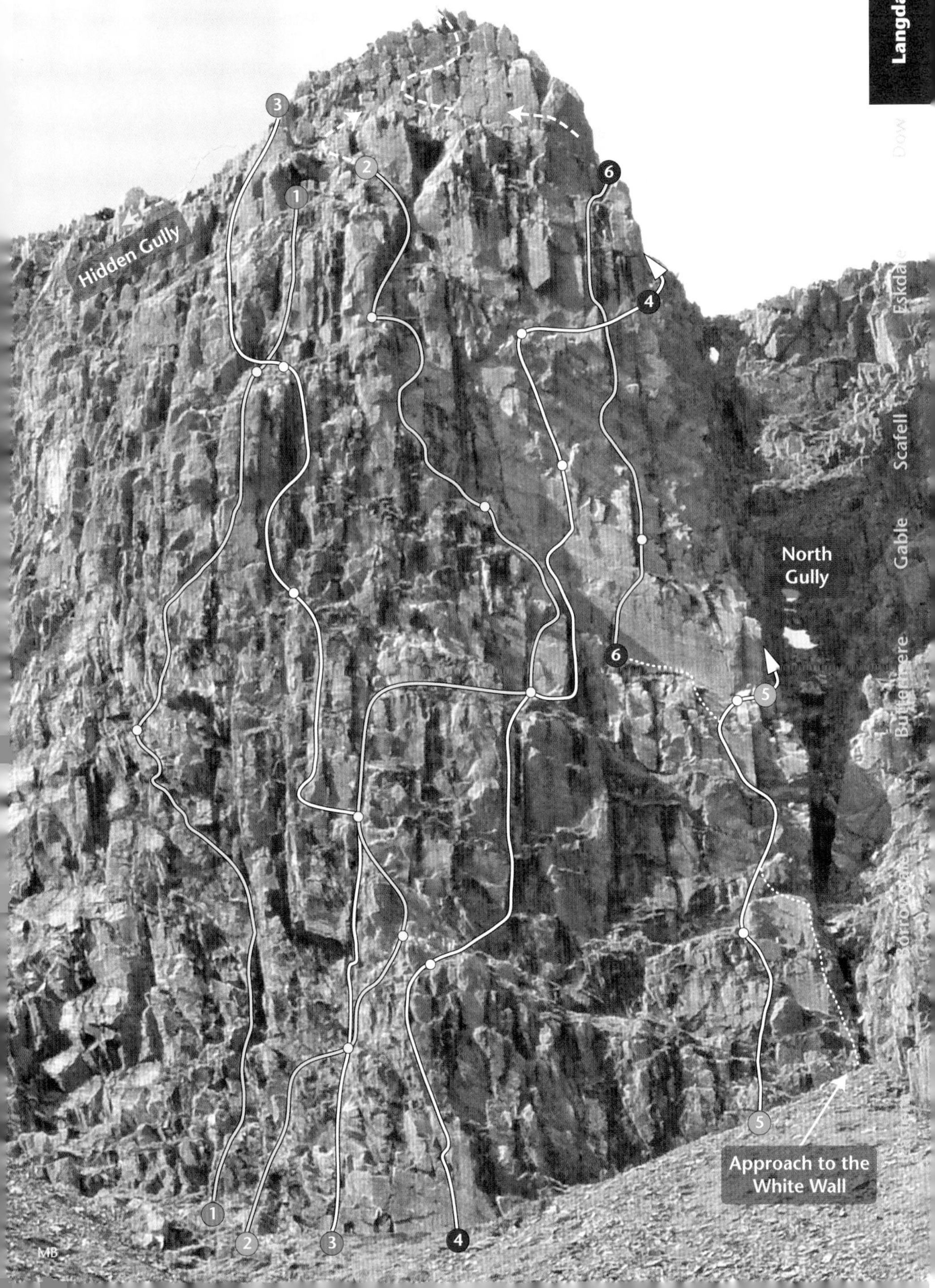
Hidden Gully
North Gully
Approach to the White Wall
1
2
3
4
5
6
MB

❹ Bowfell Buttress Eliminate 108m E2 5b ★★

A good route that probes the intimidating White Wall. Low in its grade but with some bold climbing. Start below the right-hand of the cracks splitting the smooth wall at the foot of the crag.

1 25m 5b The crack is deceptively hard with no protection until the difficulties ease at a niche after 5m. Step right and continue more easily to a grassy ledge.

2 25m 4c Move 5m right and climb a long slim groove to a terrace.

3 23m 4c Step down right and climb the deep V-groove to a ledge below the steep White Wall. Up the corner on the left for 3m, then swing right onto the wall and climb easier rock to a small niche on the left.

4 12m 5b Climb boldly up the wall heading for a short thin left-slanting crack which leads to a fine narrow ledge.

5 23m 5b Traverse right and upwards and, with a few delicate moves, gain the far edge of the buttress. Round the corner is a steep crack which leads to easier ground.

JA Austin, DG Roberts - Jun 1964

❺ Ledge and Groove 102m HVD ★★

A fine mountaineering route which attempts the fine arête. Start 20m right Bowfell Buttress Eliminate and some 4m left of the gully.

1 17m Climb a short wall and groove to a large ledge at 5m, then a rib to another ledge.

2 21m A short wall is followed by a rightwards staircase to a ledge at 9m. Follow the line of good holds leftwards up the wall above for 4m, then go right to a ledge overlooking the chockstone in North Gully.

3 12m Step up and traverse right to a short groove which leads to a sloping ledge. Move left along this and climb the ridge to a stance.

4 15m Crux. Make a delicate traverse right across the wall into a chimney/corner and climb it to a ledge and large belay.

5 20m A shallow groove on the right has an awkward landing onto a small grass ledge at 7m. Traverse left for 6m to a steep corner-crack. Up this for 2m, make an awkward move left onto a small ledge, then more awkward moves past a projecting boulder guarding entry to a large terrace.

6 17m Go left along the terrace and climb a crack to a ledge, then the short wall above.

RD Stevens, G Stoneley - May 1945

❻ Air on a Bowstring 50m E3 5c ★★★

A magnificent route up the centre of the White Wall. Varied climbing, bold in its middle section and having a well positioned crux at the top will make this a memorable trip. Start on a grass ledge below a right leaning crack easily reached from *Ledge and Groove*.

1 15m 5c The crack is very stubborn for a couple of metres. Its continuation or the groove on its right both lead to a block belay.

2 35m 5c Climb the short corner to ledges below an impending wall guarding entry to a continuation corner. Move 2m left then work up right boldly to gain the foot of this corner and climb to its top. Step left round a neat triangular rib into a slim groove and from its top, use a small upside down spike on the left to pull onto the final headwall.

J Cooper, T Walkington - Jun 1992

❼ Woolly Jumper 60m E1 5b ★★★

An excellent minor classic up the right arête of the White Wall. Modest protection makes the exposure well felt. Start at the right-hand end of the long terrace below the White Wall, reached by scrambling up North Gully for 25m, then out left onto the ridge to below a short groove with a heavily undercut right wall.

1 30m 5a Use an obvious layaway hold on the lip of the overhang to pull round onto the slab. Continue more easily up left to the next groove in the arête. Up this to a ledge below the main arête.

2 30m 5b Starting on the left side of the arête, make an awkward move round it to gain a niche in the right wall. Delicate moves up its right rib gain a ledge above. Step left and climb to a small quartz ledge. Now follow a shallow flake rightwards to a narrow ledge. Step back left and layaway up the arête on superbly rough rock and with great exposure until the angle eases below a wide crack. Climb this to a large ledge and belay. Scramble off to the left.

P1: RM Biden, G Halliwell - mid 1990s; P2: J Cooper - Aug 1990

7
4
6
5
2
5
Right Wall Eliminate E1
6
5
2
4
7
North Gully checkstone
5
MB

SHELTER CRAG

OS Grid Ref: NY 250 056
Altitude: 720m

An easily accessible crag, yet quiet and hidden from the thousands of walkers traversing the Crinkles just behind. The rock is generally very good, with the reassuring limpet-like frictional qualities one almost expects of the higher crags in Langdale. The sun shines on the crag all morning and on the gearing-up terrace at its top all day. The routes dry relatively quickly for a high crag and a day spent here is well worth the walk.

Approach: From the Old Dungeon Ghyll Hotel P NY 286 061, take the track to Stool End Farm and up the Band all the way to the Three Tarns col. Now follow the main ridge path south for 15 minutes, passing west of a small but distinct rocky tower until, after a series of slabs, the summit of the highest Crinckle comes into view in the distance. Branch off diagonally left immediately and scramble across rocks and down onto a prominent terrace set at a lower level. A collection of flat boulders at its higher southern end make a good base. See map page 92.

Buscoe Buttress

Approach: To get to the start of the routes, a steep descent eastwards down a rocky grass slope leads to the top of a rock ramp on the left, marking the edge of the crag. Descend the ramp under the first buttress and zig-zag down steep grass to the central Buscoe Buttress.

❶ Baker San 58m E1 5b ★
Varied climbing up the long slab and steeper ground above. Start directly below the slab. Good spike belays.
1 35m 5b Climb a thin crack-line up the centre of the steep wall and move left onto the clean slab. Near the top move rightwards into a small recess where the rock steepens into a wall. Gain a slabby ramp on the left leading to a short, steep, wide crack. Climb the crack until a move out right leads up to a stance just right of the overhang. The final mossy area looks unappealing but the greenery does not actually affect the climbing too much.
2 23m 5a Traverse left below the overhang and

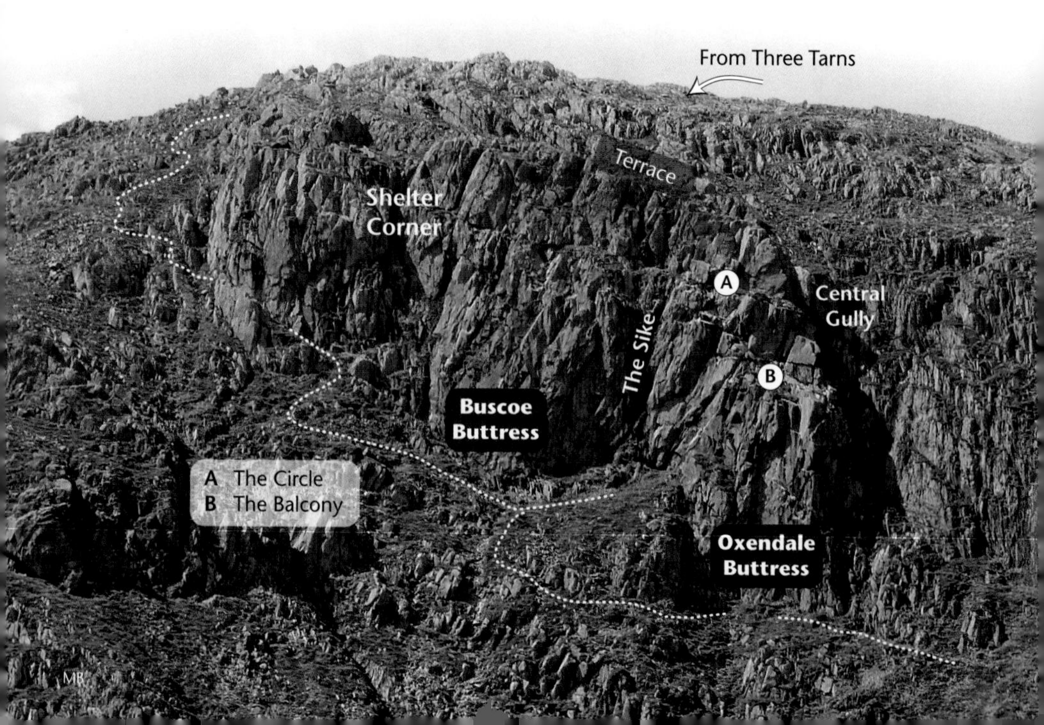

climb the wide hanging crack which is awkward to enter.
C Read, GL Swainbank - Jun 1999

2 Lone Star 60m HVS 5a ★
Pleasant climbing up the slab leads to a stiff crux starting p2. Start as for *Baker San.*
1 25m 4a Climb steeply up the wall trending right, then step back left to gain the main groove-line which leads to a recess stance where the crag steepens.
2 35m 5a Move up left and ascend the steep, shallow and awkward groove-line to a ledge. Move up right, past a large perched block, and pull up left to enter another groove. Climb this until a short slab leads up left to the top.
GL Swainbank , C Read - Apr 1999

3 Panjandrum 63m E1 5b ★★★
Takes a neat line up the crest of the buttress, overlooking the big corner of *Moonstruck*, giving very good, steep and well protected climbing in a fine position. Start at the lowest point of the buttress.
1 20m 5b Climb direct to the bottom of a shallow hanging groove. Enter and climb this, then continue up the fault-line on the edge to a stance and spike belays.
2 23m 5b Continue strenuously right up the line of grooves overlooking *Moonstruck* for 12m. Step left onto a rib and follow it to block belays.
3 20m 5a. Climb the steep headwall using the crack near the right edge, stepping left and up to reach the top.
C Read, GL Swainbank - Jul 1999

4 Moonstruck 60m E1 5b ★★
A brilliant exercise in sustained and intricate bridging with good protection; much better than it looks! Start in the grass bay below the corner.
1 40m 5b Climb up leftwards into the corner and follow it as it arches rightwards, with a final swing right round a blunt rib before entering the groove above. Climb this and the line of short grooves above to the terrace.
2 20m 5a As for p3 *Panjandrum.*
C Read, GL Swainbank - May 1999

5 Diplodocus 60m HVS 5b ★
Strenuous climbing weaving its way up the steep right wall of the big corner. Start just right of *Moonstruck* at a rightward-slanting open groove.
1 40m 5b Climb the groove until a pull up and left gains a second rightward slanting groove. Climb this to an overhang and make a committing pull out left into a niche (crux). Climb straight up almost to the groove above the arch, then move out right onto the arête and up to a short groove. Finish up the wall above, trending left to block belays.
2 20m The narrow rib right of the headwall leads to the top.
C Read, GL Swainbank - Jul 1999

Oxendale Buttress

Approach: The left-hand routes are approached as for Buscoe Buttress. For those on the right, descend steep grass below the toe of Buscoe Buttress, then leftwards (facing out) to the clean pillar-like lower wall.

6 Island of Dreams 46m E2 5c ★★
An excellent main pitch picking a way up the bulging upper buttress. Start 2m left of a small hidden cave, right of The Sike.
1 33m 5c Climb straight up to beneath a small bulge and step right. Continue up until the foot of a short steep hanging groove, left of the main overhang, can be gained. Difficult moves up this gain a poor resting place. Continue up the crack above and pull out right at its top. Climb the rightward-slanting fault to a ledge, move left into a short capped groove and pull up out left onto a sloping ledge, finishing more easily.
2 13m 4b From the top of the large block, climb the vertical fault-line and finish up a short crack above the ledge.
C Read, GL Swainbank - Jul 1999

7 Pleasure Zone 46m E1 5b ★★★
Excellent climbing up the right-facing open corner defining the right-hand side of the bulging upper buttress. Start beneath a small square-cut overhang, immediately right of the hidden cave.
1 30m 5b Climb past the left side of the overhang to a spike runner. Move up, then pull out left to gain a sloping ledge. Ascend towards the overhangs, where a step right leads to the obvious rightward-slanting corner/groove. Follow this to horizontal ledges beneath a short steep wall and climb this to The Circle. Thread belay in the left corner.
2 16m 5a Step out left and up onto the large slab. Finish up the steep narrow crack ahead.
C Read, GL Swainbank - Jun 1999

1
2
4
3
5
The Sike
1
2
4
5
3
MB

8 Cloud Walker 48m E1 5b ★★

1 30m 5b Climb past the right side of the overhang and step left onto a narrow slab leading to a hanging block. Use this to surmount the bulge leftwards. Move up and right, then follow thin twin cracks up the slabby wall to a horizontal ledge. Step right, ascend a short groove to slabby blocks and move up left to an open, right-trending corner. Climb this to The Circle.
2 18m 4b Climb the short rib on the left to a sloping ledge, then the pleasant wall on the right to finish using holds on the arête.
GL Swainbank , C Read - Jun 1999

9 Footlights 60m VD ★★

A good mountaineering route with interesting climbing. Start at a right-slanting gangway, 2m right of the hidden cave.
1 22m Step across right to gain and climb a series of gangways leading right until, near the top, moves right gain belays at the top of the Balcony.
2 21m Climb leftwards along slabs and ledges until stopped in a corner. Move out left and up to The Circle. Thread belay in the corner.
3 17m Ascend the corner and the crack up the wall above, until a step up left gains a short groove leading to the top.
GL Swainbank , C Read - Apr 1999

10 Arcanum 68m VS 4c ★

Super route finding and varied climbing. Start some 7m up steep grass ledges left of the main corner-line of the buttress, beneath a short steep pillar with a crack in its left side.
1 7m 4b Ascend the left edge of the pillar until a pull right gains a small ledge. Move up and left to a large ledge.
2 30m 4a From the ledge, move up and swing right into a recess. Right again onto the arête and follow it to a platform. Continue up, passing right of a prominent (hollow) blade of rock, then go out right and continue up to The Balcony. Belay below the wide crack.
3 17m 4c Climb the right wall of the crack to a ledge, move up left and make a steep pull up the short wall to gain The Circle. If the final moves are wet, move further right and then up.
4 14m 4c Some bold moves up the left side of the sharp arête above gain the crest and the crack emerging from the chimney behind. Follow the broad rib leftwards to the top.
GL Swainbank , C Read - Jul 1999

11 Showtime 76m E1 5b ★★★

Good climbing of sustained interest following the prominent central right-facing corner line, overhung at the top.
1 44m 5a Climb the wall to a thin crack, where a pull up and left leads onto a large slab. From the top of the slab move left and climb the main corner until a move right leads to beneath a large hollow flake (beware). Bypass the hollow flake by moving right onto the steep wall and climbing direct to the foot of the final groove. Block belays above on the left.
2 15m 5b Climb over blocks onto a slab in an overhung recess. Pull up and right onto the steep wall. Traverse right onto the front and up to enter an open groove. Ascend it to The Circle.
3 17m 4c At the left side of the headwall is a short steep corner topped by an overhang. Climb the corner, pulling out left into the groove.
GL Swainbank , C Read - May 1999

12 Thespian 72m VS 5a ★

A direct line of sustained interest and well protected. Start below a corner at the right side of the smooth wall.
1 12m 4a Climb the corner to a recess. Step onto the left wall and ascend to the foot of the prominent ramp.
2 30m 4c Move up and right to gain and ascend a groove. Move up left and climb an obvious hanging groove. Step left, then trend right up the wall above until the right-hand of two prominent grooves can be climbed to The Balcony. Scramble up and belay beneath a wide crack.
3 16m 5a Climb the leaning groove left of the wide crack to a ledge; then a steep pull up the short wall immediately above to gain The Circle.
4 14m 4c Climb the crack immediately right of and behind the sharp arete.
C Read, GL Swainbank - May 1999

13 Oxendale Arête 77m VS 4c ★

Interest is maintained throughout with each pitch having its moment. Start just right of *Thespian*.
1 23m 4c Climb the rib right of the corner to a resting place beneath a steep impending wall. Step right, go up and make an awkward move up rightwards. Ascend to a ledge and step left to belay on the arête.
2 19m 4c From the sentry box on the left, pull up awkwardly. Pull immediately right and up to regain the arête. Continue up a right-slanting groove, then leftwards onto an easy-angled slab.
3 21m 4c Climb a groove in the right end of the wall above to a glacis. Swing left and climb into a niche and then onto an easy-angled slab. Trend right across the slab and pull over overlaps onto The Circle. Belay at the foot of the open chimney.
4 14m 4c Climb the right side of the open chimney and exit right to gain a ledge. Finish up the easy-angled arête.
C Read, GL Swainbank - Apr 1999

6
7
9
11
8
10
12
13
A
B
A The Circle
B The Balcony
The Sike
6
7
8
9
Cave
10
11
12
13
MB

PIKE OF BLISCO

Pike of Blisco is an attractively rugged mountain whose slopes host a series of easily accessible outcrops. The rocks are beautifully rough, provide many interesting and varied features and are a delight to climb. They lend themselves to bouldering and an excellent range of problems and circuits has been developed. Comprehensive details of which can be found in the Lakes bouldering website, www.LakesBloc.com

LONG SCAR

OS Grid Ref: NY 273 036
Altitude: 550m

This friendly outcrop complements Black Crag providing a selection of pleasant routes of more modest grade on equally good rock, well suited for both tyro and mellow expert. It has a marvellous outlook across Langdale's western skyline and is a great place to get in some footage at the beginning of the year or relax in the autumn afternoon sun.

Approach: P NY 277 027 then follow the Red Tarn track for about 1km to where a well-marked trail at the top of a small rise leads off rightwards towards the centre of the crag. See map page 109.

Descent: Either down one of the two rakes splitting the crag, or round either end.

Right Side

1 **Billy's Climb** 17m MS ★
Pleasantly up the crack in the slabs.
A McCaig, P Brown - Aug 2002

2 **Islay** 17m VD
The left-facing corner for 5m. Break out right up a crack/groove and wall above.
PC Bennett - Jul 2006

3 **Twin Cracks Right** 14m VS 4c
The right-hand of two wall cracks, with a long reach to enter the upper section.
D Oddy - 1982

4 **Rizla Rib** 20m VD
Climb the line of the rounded rib on small holds.
G Robertson, K Taylor, I Harrison - Jul 2009

5 **Old Holborn** 23m M ★★
The prominent ramp, moving right at the top onto broken rock. The direct start is **D**.
D Worrall - 1982

6 **Intruder's Corner** 18m VD ★★
The line of weakness trending slightly rightwards, finishing up the fine corner.
D Worrall, R Linton - 1982

7 **Platt Gang Groove** 16m VD ★★
Climb the right-slanting, groove-line in the centre of the wall.
D Worrall, R Linton - 1982

8 **Llywndyrys** 17m MVS 4b ★
The hanging flake-groove in the middle of the wall, gained from *Sam's Saunter*.
D Davies, A Maughan - Oct 2002

9 **Sam's Saunter** 15m HS 4b ★
The groove on small holds and wall directly above
R Linton, D Worrall - 1982

10 **Forrudd** 18m MVS 4b ★
Step right from the end of the rock ledge to climb the awkward crack.
D Oddy - 1982

11 **Something Stupid** 18m HVS 5a ★★
Thin wall crack above the middle of the rock ledge.
D Oddy, D Potter - 1982

12 **Step to the Right** 20m MVS 4b ★
A flaky crack towards a perched block, then rightwards to mantelshelf into a groove.
J Cooper, J Kelly - 1992

13 **Katie's Dilemma** 20m MVS 4b ★★
The prominent corner above the perched block contains a tricky move.
R Linton, D Worrall - 1982

14 **Heart of the Matter** 20m VS 4b ★
The right-leaning groove to a mantelshelf move.
J Cooper, J Kelly - 1992

15 **The Opportunist** 20m MVS 4b ★
The short steep wall (crux), then trending rightwards to finish up a rib.
RM Biden, I Gray - 2005

16 **Tornado Alley** 18m HVS 5a
The zig-zag crack line starting off an embedded block.
R Whitham, T Walkington - May 2009

17 **Longy Chewed** 18m HS ★
Pull up left onto the arête. Follow it and the delicate wall above.
BJ Clarke - Jun 2008

Left Side

18 Green Treacle 28m HS 4a ★★
The cracked weakness in the wall to the descent rake and continuation crack-line above.
J Green, W King - Apr 2009

19 Trigger 18m S ★
Starting at the steep arête, a short traverse right gains the clean wall and grooves.
J Cooper, B Charlton - Jul 1998

20 Roundup 20m HS 4a ★
Climb left beneath the overhangs, then up and back right into the groove above.
J Cooper, S Harth - Aug 1996

21 Cowgirl 18m VS 4c
Series of grooves below and above the rock ledge.
T Walkington, R Whitham - May 2009

22 The Singing Cowboy 20m VS 4c ★★
A good crack-line direct to the right-facing hanging corner. Up this, exit left, then continue direct.
J Cooper, S Harth - Aug 1996

23 Monster in a T-Shirt 20m HVS 5a ★★
The left-hand cracks in the wall to a ledge. The striking impending crack rightwards (crux) to gain the horizontal ledge (serious if you cannot reach the crucial runner placement).
J Cooper, B Charlton - Jul 1998

24 Long Scar Groove 22m S ★
The obvious groove-line is entered by an awkward move. Good holds lead rightwards to finish.
R Whitham, T Walkington - Apr 2009

25 Great White 22m VS 4c ★
The line of the rounded, white, shield-like arête, finishing up a thin crack in a steep wall.
BJ Clarke - Jun 2008

26 Lucy 25m VD
A crack leads rightwards to the corner. Continue up the blocky wall above the descent rake.
J Cooper, T Walkington - Apr 2009

27 Roxy 25m D
The rib just right of the descent rake.
J Cooper - Apr 2009

28 Dot's Delight 30m VD ★★
A belt of slabby rock leads rightwards then more directly to the top. Nice, but a little harder, continue rightwards to climb a fine, striated rib.
D Wood - Aug 1996

29 Glen Miller 22m HS 4b
Prominent central twin cracks in a steep wall, then the crack-line in the slab above.
T Walkington, J Cooper - Apr 2009

30 Big Band 22m VS 4c ★
Climb over the huge block and into the slanting groove. Exit via twin cracks in its steep left wall.
T Walkington, TW Birkett - Apr 2009

31 Nightshift 22m VD ★
The rib left of the block to the grooved arête.
A McCaig, P Brown - Aug 2002

32 Dayshift 22m MVS 4b
A corner leads to a difficult move into a niche, then grooves to the top.
R Whitham, T Walkington - Apr 2009

33 Brass Band 23m D ★
Take a direct line up a rib of good continuous rock.
T Walkington - Apr 2009

34 Trombone 22m HVS 5b
A short right-facing overhanging corner above a bilberry ledge is reached starting up an initial V-groove/niche. A couple of strenuous moves gain better holds. Finish pleasantly up a steep wall.
T Walkington, TW Birkett - Apr 2009

35 Long Stand 22m VS 4c
The vegetated groove-line is better than it looks, starting up the rib to its right.
R Whitham, T Walkington - Apr 2009

36 Trumpet 22m HVS 5a ★
The slabby rib leading to the corner through the overhangs. Finish up a thin crack-line.
T Walkington, R Whitham - Mar 2009

37 Flake Crack 22m HVS 5a ★
Tackles the central crack.
T Walkington, R Whitham - Mar 2009

38 Edge Crack 22m HVS 5a
Left edge of the undercut buttress split by a crack.
T Walkington, R Whitham - Apr 2009

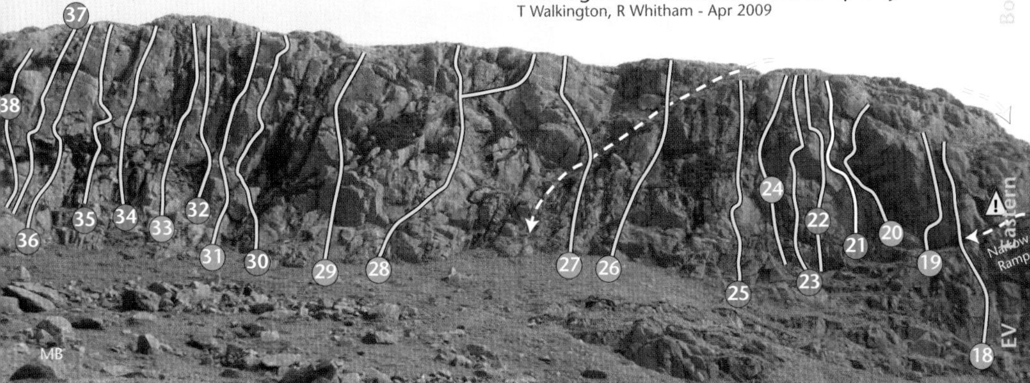

BLACK CRAG

OS Grid Ref: NY 274 037
Altitude: 580m

A marvellous outcrop of excellent clean rock. The routes may be short but they receive the sun from early morning until sunset and dry very quickly. With the bonus of easy access, they can provide a delightful day or evening's climbing; try a windless sunny winter day...

Approach: Follow the path north-west from the top of Wrynose Pass P NY 277 027 for about 750m when a vague track strikes off rightwards just beyond a small rocky stream. Pass a fenced-off boulder and head generally in the direction of the mountain summit towards the crag.

Descents: Numerous easy scrambles. All the routes on the West Face end on a terrace leading leftwards.

West Face

1. **Pocket Crack** 10m E3 6a ★★
2. **Sleep on my Pillow** 10m E1 5b ★
3. **Nod Off** 10m S ★
4. **Noddy** 10m E1 5c ★
   The problem arête.
5. **Three** 16m VS 4c ★
6. **Blind** 16m VS 5a ★
7. **Mice** 16m VS 4c ★
8. **The Real World** 16m E5 6a ★
   Protectionless pocketed wall to a circular hole.
9. **Slipshod** 16m HVS 5a ★★
   The fine crack above the triangular niche.
10. **Yellow Fever** 16m E2 5b ★★★
    Superb climbing; thin cracks in the smooth wall.
11. **The First Touch** 16m E1 5b ★★★
12. **Hold On** 10m HS ★★
13. **Stop Showing Off** 10m HVS 5a ★
14. **Mind of No Fixed Abode** 10m E1 5a ★★
15. **An Evening with Friends** 7m E1 5c ★
16. **The Needle** 12m VD ★★
17. **Needle Arête** 12m E3 6a ★★
    South-west arête using holds on either side.

Glass Slipper Buttress

Located 100m right of the West Face.

18 **Not so Jolly** 16m D ★
The left arête to the easy-angled slab and arête.

19 **Jolly Roger** 16m VS 4b ★
Slanting cracks feel steeper than they appear from below, followed by an easier slab.

20 **Jolly Corner** 16m D ★
The corner line.

21 **Fun Run** 16m S ★
Leftwards to a ledge at 3m. Directly up the wall, avoiding a perched flake by a move right.

22 **Ann's Agony** 16m HVS 5b ★★
Gain the crack by an awkward undercut start and follow it direct.

23 **Glass Slipper** 16m E2 5b ★★★
Deliciously delicate climbing up the slab, starting in the corner. Low in its technical grade but with minimal protection.

24 **Pumpkin Corner** 15m VD
The corner direct.

25 **Sharp as Glass** 16m S ★★
Float up the right-hand side of the arête.

26 **Glass Clogs** 14m MVS 4b ★
The centre of the knobbly slab.

KETTLE CRAG

OS Grid Ref: NY 278 049
Altitude: 300m

½ hr

This hidden venue of quick-drying Gimmer-like rock basks in the afternoon sun with a beautiful outlook across Bowfell, hosting a good range of lower to middle grade routes.

Approach: The main Pike of Blisco path leaves the road P NY 285 054 some 400m above the cattle grid along Redacre Gill. After 800m and level with the top of Kettle Crag on your right, traverse horizontally rightwards across the hillside heading for a col in the summit crest. Once through this, a wire fence leads down into a steep grass gully and the routes. See map page 109.

Descent: ⚠ A slanting rock terrace and a tree-filled corner lower down both provide descents. For routes finishing above the terrace, continue to the top of the crag and walk round into the gully.

① **Earl Grey** 20m VS 4c ★★
A vague crack (crux) leads to the roof. Jugs over this gain the finishing slab.

② **Rose Puchong** 20m MVS 4b ★
The right-hand crack system past the overhang to finish up the knobbly slab.

③ **Singing Kettle** 20m VS 4b ★★
The left-hand crack system to a heather ledge. Good holds over the overhang in the rib and continue delicately up the left edge of the slab.

④ **Minor Slab** 30m VS 4b ★★
Delightfully up the right side of the slab to the break then the rib on the right.

⑤ **Minor Melodic** 25m VS 4b ★★
The left side of the initial slab to the break, then leftwards and finish up a slab.

⑥ **Red Slab** 18m S ★★★
A gem of a pitch up the side wall of the main slab, starting from a small cave.

⑦ **Serendipity** 30m S ★★★
Start below the right-hand side of the slabby wall. Easily up, then slightly right to a blunt rib. A good crack leads to an exposed arête to finish.

⑧ **Major Slab** 30m VD ★
Climbs the central crack-line in the slabby wall.

⑨ **Heather the Weather** 30m S ★
The left side of the slabby wall, starting steeply.

⑩ **Orange Pekoe** 20m VS 4c ★
Start at a deep crack 15m down from the slab and vegetated corner. Pull left onto the wall and climb it. Follow the bulging arête above.

⑪ **Semerikod** 22m VS 4c ★
Start below the corner 5m left of *Orange Pekoe*. Climb left over ledges. An overhanging crack leads to the overhangs, right into a niche and another. With hands over the top, move left to exit.

⑫ **Tea Time Arête** 25m MVS 4a ★★
Climb the arête to a ledge, good holds but poor protection. Avoid the heather by stepping airily on to the front face.

MB

From Blea Tarn Road
5
3
1
2
4
6
4
9
8
7
10
11
12

DOW, COPPERMINES & SLATE

The area around the busy village of Coniston with its shops, cafes, pubs, hostels and an outdoor shop, offers a superb mountain crag, an interesting valley with outcrops, bouldering and fascinating archaeological sites and the bold technical climbs on the slate quarries near Tilberthwaite.

www.conistontic.org/info.shtml

FRCC Guides

Doe Crag (1922) by George S Bower was the first in a series of bound guides published by the FRCC. The Editor, RST Chorley, envisaged a uniform series providing lucid and accurate descriptions spanning Lakeland, although he recognised that the style adopted by the authors would be individual. Bower's writing is thorough and entertaining in stark contrast to HM Kelly's terse **Pillar Rock** (1923). By 1926 the series was completed.

Bower commented on the unlikelihood of any route being possible on the Great Gully Wall of 'A' Buttress, so if you do climb Sidewalk you are 'of a race of climbers fitted with suctorial digits'.

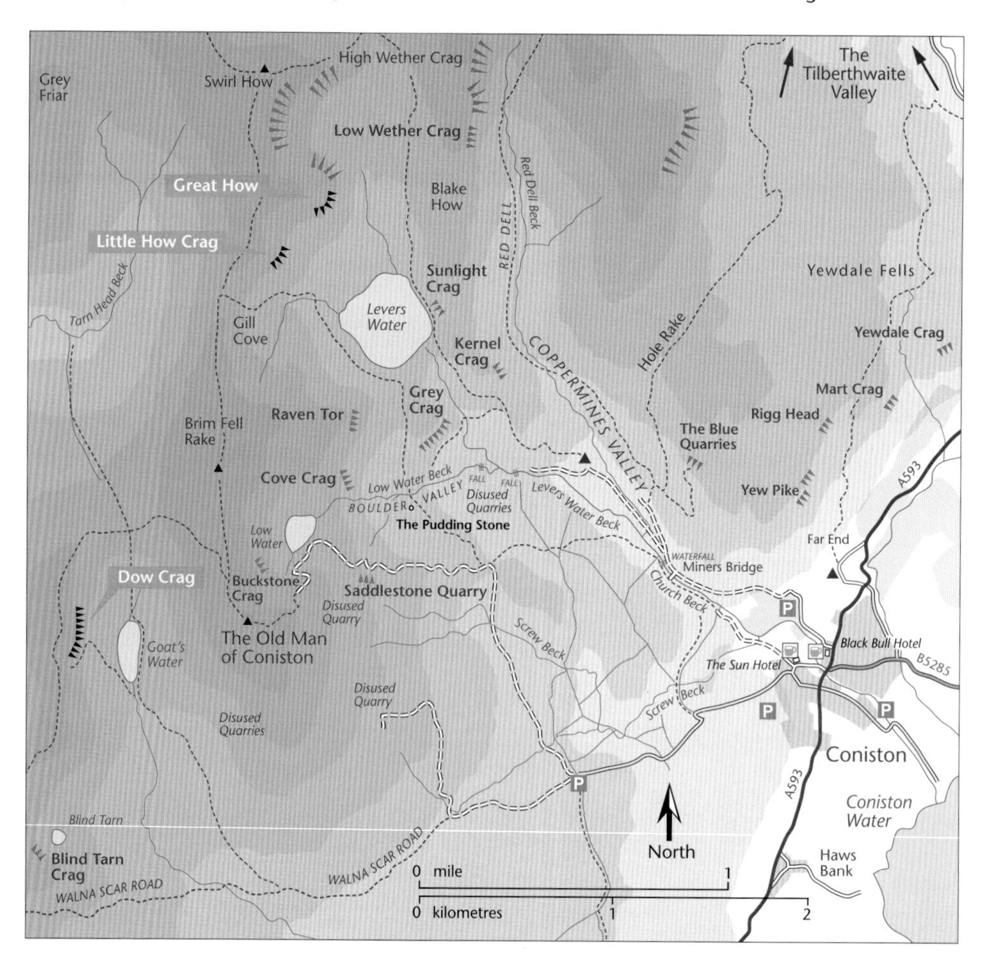

☐ *Balrog*, Dow Crag E2 (page 121) John Lynch — JOHN HOLDEN

DOW CRAG

OS Grid Ref: NY 264 977
Altitude: 610m

1 hr

First class climbing throughout the year and right across the grading spectrum; the sound rock, a superb setting and ease of approach make Dow the equal of any high mountain crag in the Lakes.

Conditions: Start early; the crag is a sun trap even in winter. On summer afternoons, with a sea breeze and shade, things can become distinctly chilly. Good friction when dry, can resemble verglas in the wet.

Approach: Park at the end of the metalled road P SD 32169 99881. Follow the Walna Scar road to a cairn, go right towards Goats Water.

Nimrod E1 (page 123) Cal Reid — PADDY CAVE

A Buttress

Descent: Follow the summit ridge south and descend South Rake, or left down a terrace into Easy Gully.

① Arête, Chimney and Crack 96m MS ★★★
Traditional and very popular. Start early or book your place in the queue.
1 27m Enjoy the clean arête then climb steeply up and slightly right, to an exposed crack.
2 21m The broken groove leads rightwards past large flakes passing left of a prominent pinnacle to a recess.
3 15m A flake crack below the bulge leads right to a short hand traverse into an open chimney. Land on a ledge above the chockstone.
4 10m Its not that far but its an exposed traverse right to a crack cleaving the face above.
5 24m The crack; easy ground and scrambling to the ridge.
TC Ormiston-Chant, THG Parker, SH Gordon - Sep 1910

② Gordon and Craig's Route 101m MS ★★
The most exposed climb of its standard in England. Deservedly popular.
1 22m The clean delicate scoop and steep crack; if that's occupied use a flake line to the right.
2 21m P2 of *Arête, Chimney and Crack.*
3 15m P3 of *Arête, Chimney and Crack.*
4 13m Exposed rightwards traversing to a ramp.
5 18m Romp right up the ramp (crux) round a corner. Continue up to a ledge of dubious blocks overlooking Great Gully. Exit left from the exposed and awkward corner above onto welcoming ledges.
6 12m 6m easily left; a slab on the right ends on the narrow neck at the top of the buttress. Scrambling remains to the summit ridge.
SH Gordon, A Craig, JP and R Rogers, J Hanks, R Gregson - Sep 1909

1	Arête, Chimney and Crack	MS
7	Eliminate 'A'	VS 4c
10	Giant's Crawl	D
14	Tumble	E4 5c
18	Leopard's Crawl	HVS 5a
21	Murray's Route	S
33	C' Ordinary Route	D
36	Intermediate Gully	MVS 4b
37	'D' Ordinary	VD
43	Hopkinson's Crack	HS

3 The Balrog 55m E2 5c ★★

A monster!

1 18m 5a Climb the corner to exit left below the overhangs.

2 25m 5c Reaching the main groove-line is taxing on the arms.

L Brown, K Jackson - Oct 1965 FFA J Eastham, M Lynch - Jun 1975

4 Abraxas 85m E3 5c ★★★

A relentlessly steep route that takes a lot of scalps!

1 18m 5c A steep wall followed by a hard mossy slab are bold with little protection.

2 25m 5c A resting place is on the right. From an undercut flake an exhilarating move right leads into a groove above the steepest section. Under the roof go right to *Eliminate 'A'*.

3 42m 5b Aiming to the left of a hanging arête at 20m, find the easiest direct line up the grooves walls and bulges.

R Matheson, JR Martindale - Jun 1975

	Route	Grade
1	**Arête, Chimney and Crack**	MS
2	**Gordon and Craig's Route**	MS
3	**The Balrog**	E2 5c
4	**Abraxas**	E3 5c
5	**Isengard/Samba Pa Ti**	E2 5b
6	**'A' Ordinary**	E7 6c
7	**Eliminate 'A'**	VS 4c
8	**Side Walk**	E2 5b
10	**Giant's Crawl**	D

AP

5 Isengard/Samba Pa Ti 102m E2 5b ★★★
An amazingly enjoyable bipolar masterpiece. Technical and well protected becomes bold and strenuous.
1 9m 4b The right facing corner.
2 39m 5b Sweep diagonally left crossing a long horizontal ledge to a steep crack leading through the overhang; cross the slab into the large cave.
3 30m 5b Excellent holds get you through the bulge onto the steep wall. Skirt the next bulge on the right before moving left on easier ground.
4 24m 4b A fault line 9m right of the main crack leads to a narrow neck at the top.
Isengard can be climbed to the cave finishing up *Eliminate 'A'* - **107m HVS 5b** ★★★.
Isengard: L Brown, A McHardy - Apr 1962.
Samba Pa Ti: A Hyslop, RO Graham - Aug 1977

6 'A' Ordinary 55m E7 6c ★★
Far from ordinary... Start 2m right of *Isengard*.
1 25m 5c Climb directly up the short wall to ledges. Weave right then left between the bulges on the blunt rib below the giant detached flake.
2 10m 6c Explode from the flake to reach the ledge.
3 20m 6c Follow *Samba Pa Ti* to the roof. Pull over this and traverse leftwards (peg). Powerful and technical climbing above (peg) leads to sanctuary over the bulge. Climb the wall moving slightly rightwards over a bulge into a short finishing corner.
C Matheson, R Matheson - Aug 1999

7 Eliminate 'A' 116m VS 4c ★★★
One of England's great routes; cunningly conceived, of absorbing interest and with a superb atmosphere.
1 19m 4b Traverse delicately rightwards, round the edge, onto a steep wall overlooking Great Gully. A short groove leads to a grass ledge.
2 23m 4b After a steep wall mantleshelf onto a little ledge at 6m. The groove above leads left into the Raven's Nest. Now traverse right round the exposed corner and up a wide crack to a sloping ledge.
3 15m 4c Diagonally left across the exposed wall to a delicate step down and round the rib (thread); easily leftwards to a large cave.
4 16m 4b Left beneath the roof on the impressive diagonal flake until an exposed bulge at the far end leads to a recess. Block belay above.
5 18m 4c Rightwards across the slab to a bold and very exposed section up into a groove reaching the traverse of *Gordon and Craig's Route*.
6 25m 4b Climb a steep shallow corner 3m left and traverse right to a rib just left of a wide crack. Pull leftwards over the overhang; into a clean shallow groove.
HS Gross, G Basterfield - Jun 1923

8 Side Walk 91m E2 5b ★★★
A magnificent exposed expedition.
1 16m 5b From below the first chockstone the top of the pillar is reached up a crack. Commit left to a small ledge; now tackle the wall.
2 9m 5a A short and sustained corner.
3 12m 5b Traverse right beneath an impressive steep wall overlooking the gully. Over a small overhang into a corner containing a thin crack. Climb to another overhang, pulling out rightwards.
4 27m 4b Climb slightly right to some perched blocks. Go above these, trending first left, then right until a large triangular grass ledge is reached. Climb up to the right for 3m to some blocks.
5 27m 5a A large bulging groove leads to the top; an overhang at 12m is turned on the left by an awkward crack. Doubtful blocks.
L Brown, B Stevens - Apr 1960

B Buttress Upper

9 Broadrick's Direct 43m VS 4c ★★
A satisfying line of grooves.
1 21m From the gully, 5m below the chockstone, take a steep wall on the right, a slab and a groove.
2 10m 4b Follow the groove.
3 12m 4c Take the right-hand groove, cross into the left-hand groove and follow this steeply.
4 21m Diagonally right over easy ground to a final wall.
R Matheson - May 1980

10 Giant's Crawl 115m D ★★★
An excellent, inescapable route. In poor conditions it is desperate!
Section 1 67m Follow the slabby-gangway taking belays as and when...
Easy Terrace is easily gained from here by scrambling down to the right.
Section 2 48m Go left to an awkward corner crack leading to a large ledge on the edge of the buttress. Round to the left take the crack up a groove and exit right to easier ground.
ETW and OT Addyman Stobart, TC Ormiston-Chant - Apr 1909

11 Nimrod 84m E1 5c ★★★
Satisfying and sustained. One of the best routes in the Lakes.
1 30m 5a Steeply up and right to pull over the left-hand side of a small overhang. Traverse right to small ledges beneath a bulging wall. Climb down these.
2 15m 5b Regain the ledges and climb the steep wall on the right; an awkward traverse left leads to a groove. Exit left from a small spike on large finishing holds.
3 26m 5c Climb a light-coloured crack in the left wall of the open, left-facing corner. Trend

delicately left across the steep wall and up to a prominent small blocky ledge on the arête with awesome exposure. Turn the bulge on the right.
4 13m A short wall up and rightwards.
D Miller, D Kirby - Jun 1962

⓬ Holocaust 72m E4 6a ★★★
Simply a great climb requiring confidence and impetus on the crux.
1 36m 6a Follow a shallow groove to reach a diagonal crack, move right here to a good hold then continue up a steep bold slab. A delicate traverse left rounds things off nicely.
2 21m 5b After a groove make for a quartz-riddled slabby gangway round the rib to the left.
3 15m 5b The steep crack rising from the left end of the ledge.
R Matheson, G Fleming, J Poole - Jul 1971 FFA R Matheson - Aug 1975

⓭ Another Fine Mess 72m E4 6a ★★★
A rising traverse of the steep *Tumble* wall linking together some of the best sections of existing routes. Warm up on *Nimrod*. Climb *Holocaust* past the crux and continue rightwards joining *Pandora's Box*. Follow this through the big roof, traverse right and pull through the final bulges to finish.
A Phizacklea, S Wood - Jun 1990

⓮ Tumble 36m E4 5c ★★★
Another very fine climb providing sustained, rather than technically exacting climbing accepting the challenge of the slim groove in the steep wall right of *Holocaust*. Climb the groove to a bulge, step left, continue directly to the left of the diagonal roof.
P Livesey, J Lawrence - Jun 1975

⓯ Pandora's Box 37m E5 6b ★★★
A brilliant route up the shallow groove 2m right of *Tumble*. Start at a thin flake pressed against the face and make very bold moves to a jug at the bottom of the groove. Continue up this (2 pegs) to a step left into the top of the groove of *Tumble*. Move up and traverse right below the bulges to reach a sloping niche. Pull back left immediately and mantleshelf onto a fine rock ledge, just below the line of large overhangs. Climb round the large roof to a good hold in the headwall and then climb through the final bulges to reach *Giant's Crawl*.
A Phizacklea, JL Holden, R Knight, D Kells - May 1990

⓰ Catacomb 60m E1 5b ★★
Enjoyable, varied and high in the grade.
1 36m 5a From the right-hand end of the terrace climb up and commit to a rising traverse line below the overhangs to a belay up and right.
2 12m 5b Cross to the right-hand end of a grass ledge using the pumpy flake on the left.
3 12m 5b Step up right to testing moves across the overhang to enter a groove. Broken cracks right lead to a grass terrace.
R Matheson, MR Matheson - Apr 1972

B Buttress Lower

⓱ Pink Panther 40m E2 5c ★★★
An excellent diagonal line up the immaculate *Leopard's Crawl* wall, with fingery climbing and adequate protection. The first target, a slight depression in the middle of the face, is followed by steeper rock to reach a groove over on the right. Pass the right-hand end of a roof to easier ground.
R Matheson, MR Matheson - Jun 1973

⑱ Leopard's Crawl 48m HVS 5a ★★★
A masterpiece; superb open climbing on perfect rock - and a big tick.
1 28m 5a Step off the huge propped block and traverse right across a brown crinkly wall to the base of a scoop. Climb this to a ledge.
2 20m 4c A flake system leads right to a shallow groove in the wall above and easier ground.
RJ Birkett, L Muscroft, T Hill - Sep 1947

⓳ Tarkus 53m E1 5b ★★
Delicate, strenuous and exposed.
1 33m 5b Getting to a flake in a shallow groove is bold; its uncomfortable here, so move quickly up to the break. Go right to a crack and wall.
2 20m 4c The flake line of *Leopard's Crawl*.
R Matheson, MR Matheson - Apr 1972

⑳ Murray's Direct 48m VS 4c ★★★
Excellent - another justifiably popular climb.
1 22m 4c Tiger Traverse. The outward shelving slab leads delicately rightwards.
2 10m 4b The Link Pitch. Climb the wall to a hand-traverse left.
3 26m 4c Keep moving right up the final steep corner to an exit can up cracks.
Strung together between1922 and1945 by EH Pryor, JB Meldrum, GH Mackereth, B Tyson, AH Griffin, JA Mullan

㉑ Murray's Route 74m S ★★★
A classic, threading a way up an impressive area of rock with delightful situations.
1 23m At the top of the 'V' chimney you get forced onto a polished slab on the left (crux), the line continues under bulging rock, round a corner and up to a large ledge.
2 12m To avoid the wall of the 'Direct' head rightwards across the detached flake to the arête. Stepping right a short chimney leads to a comfortable stance in Abraham's Cave.
3 21m Exit leftwards; cross the steep final corner of *Murray's Direct* to a chimney in the left wall. Swing along the exposed flake line, descending slightly to a stance below a chunky flake.
4 18m The awkward wide crack above the flake leads to a ledge and Easy Terrace.
DG Murray, WJ Borrowman, BL Martin - Apr 1918

12
9
16
10
Dow
13
11
15
13
16
11
15
14
12
13
9
17
10
11
AP

11
10
12
14
15
21
17
11
17
18
19
10 Giant's Crawl D
11 Nimrod E1 5c
12 Holocaust E4 6a
14 Tumble E4 5c
15 Pandora's Box E5 6b
17 Pink Panther E2 5c
18 Leopard's Crawl HVS 5a
19 Tarkus E1 5b
20 Murray's Direct VS 4c
21 Murray's Route S
22 Abraham's Route S 4b
23 Abraham's Covenant E7 6c
24 Eliminate 'B' HVS 5a
26 Woodhouse's Route VD
27 Critical E6 6c

18
20
22
24
26
Dow
21
23
27
26
21
22
24
AP
Stretcher Box

22 Abraham's Route 62m S 4b ★
A fine classic route of increasing interest. Start at the first easy break right of the stretcher box.
1 13m The rightwards trending open groove crosses ledges to a recess.
2 12m From a rock ledge on the right stride left across the recess; continue leftwards to a long grassy ledge.
3 13m Climb the very shallow open groove on the left side of the steep wall above. Easier rocks lead to a grass terrace.
4 24m 4b Grooves and walls lead to a ledge below a blocky spike, at the left end of the overhangs. Standing on the slab to the left is tricky but good small holds lead to a gangway running rightwards to the crest.
GD and AP Abraham, FT Phillipson - Mar 1903

23 Abraham's Covenant 30m E7 6c ★★
Apes across the huge roof above the cave to some good jugs (protection). Desperately hard climbing leads onto the wall above.
J McHaffie, S Wood - Apr 2011

24 Eliminate 'B' 95m HVS 5a ★
Explores the right edge of B Buttress saving its best until last. Start behind an embedded flat-topped block.
1 21m 5a Climb the thin crack behind the block. Continue up the groove to an arête, climb directly to a good rock ledge.
2 20m 4c Climb the thin crack above to the detached blocks. Climb the rib immediately left of the large overhang until a step right can be made onto an exposed slab. Cross this to an easier groove which leads up to a ledge.
3 16m Walk left and then climb easily right up the slab (Pilgrim's Progress). Belay on the left of a block below the impending wall.
4 18m 4c Giant Grim. Step off the block and climb the steep wall to easy ground. Traverse right to belay below a crack forming the left side of a pillar.
5 20m 5a Round the rib is a ledge with a loose block. Step down onto a blunt spike below an overlap and pull up rightwards, with difficulty, to gain footholds above. Step right into the shallow corner and climb this, moving right at the top to easier ground. Continue leftwards to the top.
HS Gross, RST Chorley, G Basterfield - Oct 1922

25 Woodhouse's Arête E6 6b ★★★
Follow the arête above Woodhouse's Pinnacle.
K Phizacklea, R Matheson - May 1998

26 Woodhouse's Route 57m VD ★
A good old-fashioned route. Scramble to a well worn platform below a wide groove with a block at its base.
1 20m A steep crack up on the left leads to the crevasse behind the pinnacle (stance). The slanting chimney is entered awkwardly and climbed to a ledge and belays. The ledge system is followed leftwards to a deep recess.
2 22m Climb the wall and then the arête on the left to a large terrace and scrambling.
GF and AJ Woodhouse - Aug 1905

27 Critical 22m E6 6c ★★★
A brilliant route following the hideously overhanging crack above Woodhouse's Pinnacle.
G Sutcliffe - Jun 1992

28 Close To Critical 39m E4 6b ★★★
Needs a cool head and deserves respect.
1 27m 6b Step off the pinnacle to a good flake on the steep left wall (blind runner out right). Climb the groove precariously (pegs), to reach an easing of the angle. Exit out of the upper left-hand corner to a belay on the capstan block.
2 12m 5c Step off the right hand side of the block onto the bulging wall and climb directly to ledges.
E Cleasby, R Matheson - Jul 1982

29 The Shining Path 40m E5 6b ★★★
Superb climbing! Natural protection is available; pegs replaced 2012. (Low peg) Bridge up the right edge of the pinnacle to get established on the wall. Climb to reach a pocket. Finish leftwards up the short corner below the headwall.
A Hyslop, D Kells - Jun 1992

30 Paths of Victory 59m E6 6c ★★★
The extension to *The Shining Path* ramps up the difficulty. From 'the pocket' a desperately difficult sequence right and up over the bulge brings the right-hand pocket into play to get established on the featureless wall above. Traverse right to holds near the arête overlooking Central Chimney (peg). A final hard move leads to a diagonal ramp and some respite! Step right onto the upper slab (peg), then continue directly up the centre, crossing an overlap.
S Wood, D Kells - Sep 1993

31 Central Chimney 43m HS ★
An old classic. Start by scrambling up easy ground to a large ledge on the right of Woodhouse's Pinnacle.
1 25m Climb the crack, with an awkward smooth section at 9m. Belay in a recess above some wedged blocks.
2 10m Follow the rib on the right wall, then back left into a conspicuous cave; care - loose rock.
3 18m Exit awkwardly leftwards to ledges above. Follow grass leftwards to belays. Easy Terrace is reached by scrambling up and left.
OG Jones, G Ellis - Apr 1897

Arete, Chimney and Crack MS (page 120) — Donal Griffin

C Buttress

32 Sirius 57m HVS 5a ★★

An enjoyable climb with exposed positions. Start at the quartz splashed slabs.

1 24m 5a Climb the quartz wall direct, just right of a quartz stalactite, to easier slabs above. Continue straight up, parallel to Central Chimney to a line of overhangs. Pull into a hanging groove above the centre of these and then step left to a belay.

2 13m 5a Entering the groove on the left requires a bold and aggressive approach. Continue more easily to sloping ledges beneath an overhanging wall.

3 20m 5a A delightfully airy pitch. Traverse to the right beneath an overhang, at first slightly upwards, then delicately downwards to reach a small ledge. Step right and climb the wall just left of the black moss, to grassy ledges above Central Chimney. Care needed to protect the second.

Easy Terrace is easily reached up to the left.

p2 D Miller, D Kirby - Aug 1963 p3 AW Gough, D Jewel - 1965, p1 A Phizacklea, JL Holden - Aug 1991

33 'C' Ordinary Route 100m D ★★★

A classic route of outstanding quality. Start just left of the lowest point of the buttress. Follow the flake crack up to a protruding block and then pass just left of three small triangular overhangs up the crest of the buttress to the top of a long flake. The slab on the left provides a pleasant variation. Follow the slabby scoop, leading to easier ground. Scrambling leads to a big ledge, with a fallen flake lying on it, below a steep wall. From the left end of the ledge follow a scoop up right to a ledge, or the steep wall can be climbed direct but is harder. Trend back left across the slabs to reach a ledge on the edge of the buttress. Follow this directly to another large ledge. Step onto a large slab above which leads rightwards to ledges. Continue right to a ledge with spectacular views into *Intermediate Gully*. The flake system in the steeper wall on the left is obvious.This leads leftwards to a large unsympathetic flake in an exposed position. Fight your way to its top. A stance and belay will be found up and right. Move right along the slabs to a good ledge. Follow a gangway rightwards round a bulge to another ledge. Pull up to the left and traverse horizontally left until easy rocks lead to easy terrace.

GF and AJ Woodhouse - Aug 1904

34 Charmer 52m HVS 5a ★★

A fine open route taking the steep arête just left of *Intermediate Gully*. Start 10m up the bed of the gully where a series of curving scoops lie on the left wall.

1 16m 4b Climb the scooped slab to a short right facing corner overlooking the gully, which leads to a grass ledge.

2 24m 5a Traverse right to reach the foot of the arête. Climb this direct, bold and on good holds, to reach a ledge on the arête at 12m. Move up to a grass ledge and follow the easier rib above to a belay.

3 12m 5a Directly above is a steep hanging corner, just to the right of a large nose of rock. Climb this past some awkward shelving holds to reach a ledge on the *Ordinary Route*. Scramble up to Easy Terrace.

A Phizacklea, JL Holden - Jun 1992

35 Eliminate 'C' 46m VS 4c ★★

A very enjoyable route, providing delicate climbing in an exposed position high on the left of *Intermediate Gully*. Start from the large ledge at the top of p1 of the Gully.

1 14m 4c Climb the slab leftwards, using a diagonal (often greasy) crack beneath an overlap to start. Step left onto the wall to reach a small ledge. An awkward traverse left leads to an exposed ledge on the arête. Climb a crack above to reach a grass ledge.

2 12m 4a A shallow groove on the right leads up the wall above and around the arête on the right. Follow this easily to reach a large ledge.

3 20m 4c Move into the steep corner on the right. Traverse delicately right across the rough wall to reach an obvious and slightly loose spike on the arête overlooking *Intermediate Gully* - a very exposed position! Climb up the arête to a gangway which runs back left towards easier ground and ledges.

Scramble up the *Ordinary Route* to Easy Terrace.

H S Gross, G Basterfield - Jul 1922

36 Intermediate Gully 52m MVS 4b ★★★

The deep cut crack separating C and D Buttresses is one of the greatest of classic struggles in the Lakes. Begin by scrambling about 30m up the lower section of the gully to a cave.

1 9m Climb the awkward crack and the right wall of a short chimney to a large ledge.

2 8m The troublesome chockstone above is climbed direct. Continue more easily to a ledge and a belay on the right.

3 21m 4a The wide crack leads strenuously to easier ground. When it steepens again, climb the left wall to a recess below a jammed chockstone.

4 5m 4b Another unsympathetic chockstone leads with considerable difficulty to a deep cave.

5 9m From a small ledge on the right, stride left into a groove. Follow a crack to Easy Terrace.

For the complete mountain experience, continue to the summit.

EA and JH Hopkinson Campbell - Apr 1895

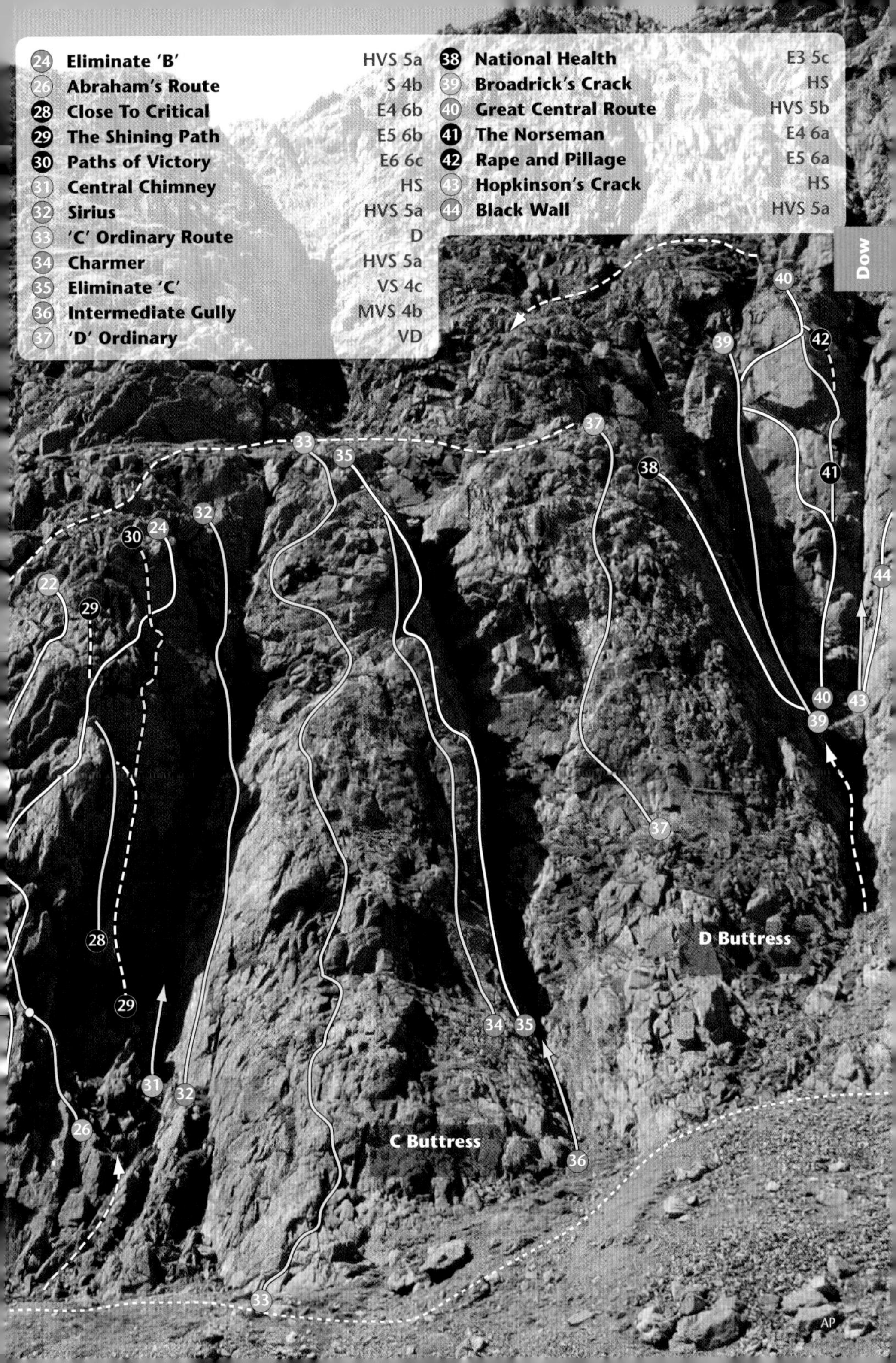
24 Eliminate 'B' HVS 5a
26 Abraham's Route S 4b
28 Close To Critical E4 6b
29 The Shining Path E5 6b
30 Paths of Victory E6 6c
31 Central Chimney HS
32 Sirius HVS 5a
33 'C' Ordinary Route D
34 Charmer HVS 5a
35 Eliminate 'C' VS 4c
36 Intermediate Gully MVS 4b
37 'D' Ordinary VD
38 National Health E3 5c
39 Broadrick's Crack HS
40 Great Central Route HVS 5b
41 The Norseman E4 6a
42 Rape and Pillage E5 6a
43 Hopkinson's Crack HS
44 Black Wall HVS 5a
Dow
C Buttress
D Buttress
AP

D Buttress

37 'D' Ordinary 52m VD ★
A good buttress climb, open and clean. Scramble to a grass shelf in the centre of the buttress, below some steep slabs. Excellent flake belay.
1 10m Climb the steep slab on the left, moving further left to belay behind a large detached block.
2 20m Step off the large block with difficulty and continue up the right side of the arête to a ledge. Climb the slab above, and move right to ledges and belays a few metres higher in a recess.
3 12m Climb a shallow groove on good holds for 7m, then traverse horizontally right along ledges and up to a stance overlooking Easter Gully.
4 10m Scramble up and left to Easy Terrace.
G F and A J Woodhouse - Aug 1904

The Amphitheatre

38 National Health 40m E4 5c ★★
A fine challenging climb up the steep wall left of Broadrick's Crack which requires a high degree of confidence as there is ground fall potential. Start 10m up *Broadrick's Crack* in a grassy bay.
1 28m 5c Climb the wall left of the lower groove of *Broadrick's Crack* to a small groove and a poor spike. Move up and right to a good hold and make a hard move past the quartz splashes to a ledge. Continue up a slim light-coloured groove to a good ledge.
2 12m 4c Climb the crack to below an overhang. Move right and follow a groove to the top.
I Greenwood, A Phizacklea - May 1980

39 Broadrick's Crack 60m HS
Takes the left hand corner using small stances.

40 Great Central Route 60m HVS 5b ★★
A superb blend of strenuous and delicate climbing in a position of great exposure give this climb great character. A major breakthrough for its time, even with the use of combined tactics, a method still occasionally employed today. It follows the imposing pillar in the centre of the Amphitheatre. Start at the foot of the pillar.
1 24m 4c Climb the nose and follow the pleasant slabs rightwards to a ledge below a steep crack. The infamous South America Crack. Climb it and exit left onto The Bandstand Ledge.
2 24m 5b As delicate as the previous pitch was strenuous. Step from the sloping left edge of the ledge, just left of a slight nose, onto the thin crinkly wall to reach slightly better holds, move right (nut), and up to a good little ledge (crux). Follow the crackline above to the large diagonal overhang. Traverse left under this, across the mossy slab to join *Broadrick's Crack*. Up this for a couple of metres, then step right onto a ledge on the front face of the pillar.
3 12m 4b Traverse rightwards along the ledge and move round the grossly exposed corner. Finish up the pleasant slabs above.
JI Roper, GS Bower, G Jackson, AP Wilson - Sep 1919

41 The Norseman 57m E4 6a ★★
Difficult climbing in a fine situation up the arête at the top of the central pillar. Start as for *Great Central Route*.
1 24m 5a P1 of *Great Central Route*.
2 33m 6a A thin crack leads to the diagonal overhang. Pull over this rightwards to a rock ledge. The committing wall above (peg) leads to a step left around the arête. Climb the crack on the left side to easier ground.
I Greenwood, P McVey - Jun 1979

42 Rape and Pillage 30m E5 6a ★★
A stunning pitch. Where *The Norseman* escapes left move right; a brilliant rockover (crux) follows. Finish straight up.
S Wood, J Burrell - Jun 1998

43 Hopkinson's Crack 45m HS ★★★
A superb old-fashioned crack climb taking the big corner crack on the right of the Amphitheatre.
1 15m The crack is climbed directly to a good ledge on the left, below the South America Crack. Thread belay.
2 12m Step back into the crack and climb with greater difficulty, exiting left onto the Bandstand ledge (phew!).
3 18m Follow the wider crack directly to easier ground.
C Hopkinson, O Koecher - Apr 1895

44 Black Wall 30m HVS 5a ★★
An enjoyable wall climb well-protected on the crux, yet requires a steady head on the lower section. Takes the steep right-hand side of the wall to the right of *Hopkinson's Route*. Climb the steep little buttress on well-spaced holds crossing a rock ledge to beneath the overhang. Pull round the left side onto the wall above then continue directly to ledges.
JI Roper, G Basterfield - Jun 1920

COPPERMINES VALLEY

The Coppermines Valley abounds with crags and offers plenty of variety on good rock, particularly for those who enjoy classic routes in a remote setting. The two major climbing areas are Boulder Valley and Levers Water.

Approach: From Coniston drive up to the first gate on the Walna Scar road and park P SD 32169 99881. Walk up the right fork in the road - easy and very pleasant. Or drive up the road between The Black Bull and the CO-OP; park P SD 30145 97798 on the roadside before the unmetalled road is reached. Walk up the Church Beck track.

Bouldering

The fellsides and valleys around Levers Water and Low Water are strewn with boulders of all sizes. The best known of these is the Pudding Stone, situated in Boulder Valley below Low Waterfall and close to the beck - Grid Ref: NY 281 984.

See www.LakesBloc.com

Coniston — Jon Allison

LITTLE HOW CRAG

OS Grid Ref: NY 274 996
Altitude: 550m

1 hr

Thunderclap VS Alan Dickinson — Ron Kenyon

Beautifully positioned with some lovely routes high above the north-western shore of Levers Water. All the routes can be recommended being on rough sound rock which catches the sun for most of the day.

Approach: From the Walna Scar gate.

Descent: Down a gully well to the left.

1 Black Moss Route 32m HS 4a ★

The slabs to the left of *Black Moss Crack* give peasant climbing.

W J Borrowman - 11 May 1919

2 Black Moss Crack 39m HS 4a ★

The obvious curving line.

3 Greased Lightning 31m VS 4c ★

A good route, left of *Thunderclap* and bounded on its left by the curving corner.

A Phizacklea, JL Holden - 17 Oct 1992

4 Thunderclap 30m VS 4c ★

Sustained interest taking a direct line up the centre of the slabs.

R Matheson - Jul 1983

5 Thunder Slab 42m HS ★

An enjoyable open climb, taking the easiest line up the right side of the slab.

1 30m 4a From the chockstone, climb the corner for a couple of metres and move left across the slab using a thin diagonal crack to reach a small grass ledge. A few moves back right lead to the base of a short shallow corner, 3m left of the main corner. Climb it, exiting left and move up to the line of bulges. These are avoided on the right by following the main corner to grass ledges.

2 12m Follow the easy line leftwards to the top. The left-hand crack in the steep wall above is an entertaining alternative.

G S Bower, WJ Borrowman, T C Ormiston-Chant - 11 May 1919

6 Sunshine Arête 41m VD ★

Very enjoyable - the easiest line up the arête starting from the corner on the left.

GS Bower, WJ Borrowman, TC Ormiston-Chant - 11 May 1919

7 Trouble and Strife 41m S ★

Start down and right of *Sunshine Arête* at a wide left-slanting crack at ground level: this is just right of the arête.

2005

JH

Langdale
Copper
Eskdale
Scafell
Gable
Buttermere
Borrowdale
Eastern

GREAT HOW

OS Grid Ref: NY 277 998
Altitude: 540m

Well worth a visit; the climbing is on rough sound rock with excellent positions. The longer routes have a real mountaineering feel to them. The main feature of the crag is a prominent rocky ridge which separates the easier slabby climbs on the left from the steeper routes on the right.

Approach: From Walna Scar or, longer, from Coniston.

Descend: To the right, down a grassy rake and turning right by a low dry-stone wall and down the gully. The descent in wet conditions is desperate and needs extreme care.

1 Original Route 60m S ★★

An interesting route following the sharply defined ridge with a distinct mountaineering feel and a definite crux. Start from the lowest point of the crag.

1 15m Starting from the foot of the ridge, climb its left side to a ledge. Move round to the right and back through a window to a large block ledge.

2 6m There are now four choices:
i) Step onto the wall from the top of the block on the left and make a difficult rising traverse up to the right to a grass ledge.
ii) Step off the higher block on the right and make a gymnastic move to get established on the wall.
iii) Climb straight up from the ledge starting just right of the higher block.
iv) Escape leftwards and climb easily back up and right to the big block belay.

3 12m Climb the slab, behind the block at the back of the ledge, to the foot of the steep crack. Ascend the crack with difficulty and continue to a grass ledge above.

4 10m Ascend the big flake and descend to a block bridge in the gap beyond.

5 12m Climb the broken groove up and left to a grass and bilberry ledge. Step left and climb up to the left to another ledge. Ascend the grooves above to large grass ledges.

D Copley, WL Barnes, IR Currie - Sep 1961

2 Copper Dragon 91m E1 5b ★★

A big mountaineering route with considerable variety and interest. A classic of the valley. Start 8m

JH

left of *Original Route*, at the second crack system.
1 18m 4b Climb easily to the foot of the steeper wall, where a fine crack leads up and left to the blocky ledge.
2 14m 4c From the shorter block at the left side of the ledge, pull up into a short steep groove to reach a large ledge. Block belay further back.
3 18m 5a Step right onto the slab to reach a small horizontal break. Climb delicately up and right using the edge of the slab to gain a dank corner. Swing left onto the front face and climb straight up to the crest of an arête. Move up this to a block belay. If the corner is wet step right onto the slab to reach a small horizontal break. Traverse horizontally to the right, round an awkward bulge, to the foot of a wide crack. This eases in angle and leads to large grass ledges.
4 12m Easily along the ridge and over a pinnacle to belay in the gap (as for *Original Route*).
5 28m 5b Pull up right to a ledge and block below a smooth steep corner. Climb this to a difficult exit onto a slab on the right, then continue to a grass ledge system. Using a short vertical crack in the headwall, pull right into a recessed scoop and follow this to the top.
Al Phizacklea, JL Holden - Apr 2011

3 Misty Slabs 60m VD ★★
A enjoyable climb. Start at the foot of a slab running up to the right, 80m left of *Original Route*.
1 40m Traverse diagonally right across the slab for about 15m, to steeper clean rock. Climb up to the easier-angled slab above and go up leftwards to a stance and belay at the foot of a crack. Or (**MVS**) climb either of two breaks which cut the steep wall above the slab. The right-hand break leads to the stance at the top of p1; the left one leads to a grass ledge at the foot of the buttress on p2.
2 30m Climb the crack to the easier slabs above. Continue up the arête on the right edge of the slabs.
AW Gough, H McDonald, H Turner - Oct 1961

4 Play Misty for Me 36m VS 4c ★
A good pitch up the shallow groove above the belay of Misty Slabs. Move up the mossy slab to the foot of the groove. Climb up for 4m to a steepening. Climb diagonally up and right with difficulty. Move up the easier angled rock leftwards to a grass ledge. Climb the rib to a stance below a corner and continue up *Misty Slabs*.
2011

5 Falcon Crest 66m VS 4c ★
An exciting route starting at the same point as *Misty Slabs*.
1 17m 4b Boldly follow the leftwards slanting slab, stepping out to the left arête where necessary, then surmount the top wall near a rightward slanting break. Belay immediately over the top.
2 17m 4c Adjust your cap and make a long step left across the cleft. Follow the crest of the buttress leftwards via an open corner.
3 32m Ascend slabby rock direct to the top.
E Davies, T Sainsbury - Jun 1986

HODGE CLOSE

OS Grid Ref: NY 316 017
Altitude: 170m

First Night Nerves E5 (page 140) Caroline Ciavaldini — David Simmonite

Climbing at Hodge Close is an adventure. Originally carved out by quarry workers Hodge has become the focal point of Lake District slate climbing. It offers a wide variety of climbing styles for the extreme leader, from unpopular unprotected run-outs, to well bolted routes for those who want to ensure they survive for future outings. The quality of the rock varies too; generally it is very solid with reasonable friction (for slate) with fewer of the friable edges found in other slate areas. Ease of access, low altitude and sunny, quick drying rock have ensured that Hodge Close has become a favourite venue for local climbers. It is also very popular with divers, abseilers and tourists.

⚠ Slate is not the safest of rock to climb on. Several areas of the quarry are unstable.

The quarry is a huge hole in the ground, with a 32m deep, green pool at one end. It is directly connected to Parrock Quarry by a large archway supported by a pillar of slate, the location of The All Weather Gym. The Main Wall, extending the full length of the east side of the quarry opposite the car park, contains some of the best slate routes in the country.

Approach: P NY 31587 01686, walk with care down the spoil heap at the southern end of the quarry, or alternatively abseil.

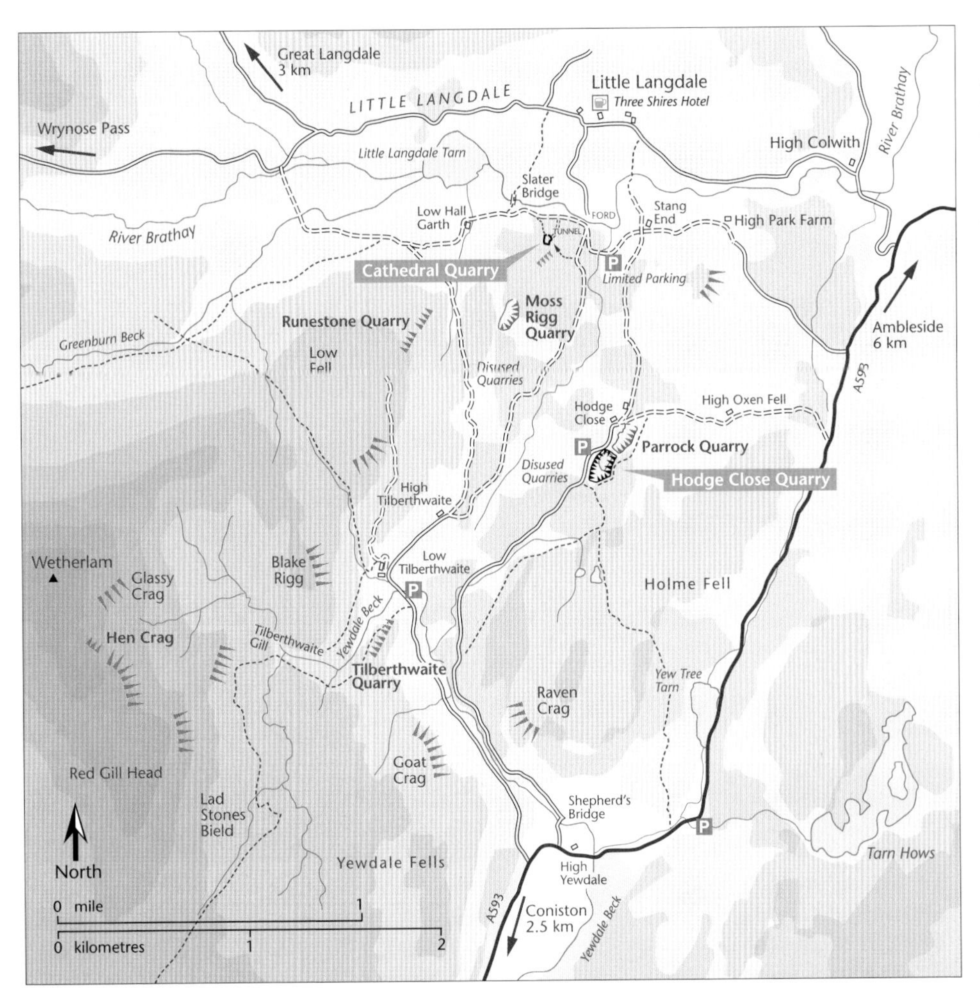

The Main Wall

This impressive wall extends the full length of the east side of the quarry.

❶ Joie de Vivre 57m F6b+ ★★★

A Towse, J Hool, S Harvey - Sep 2009

To the right of *Joie de Vivre* is a large, clean rock scar capped by an overhang. The shallow crease line at the right-hand side of this is the substance of the following route.

❷ Second Coming 55m E4 6a ★★★

A superb, ingenious climb, requiring a cool and competent approach. Start about 10m right of the highest point of the scree, below a little alcove sporting an iron spike at shoulder height.

1 46m 6a Stand on the spike (bolt) then climb up the two sloping niches on the left to gain a traverse line below the steeper rock. Move left into a hanging groove (nuts and Friend 2) then step left again onto a speckly slab using doubtful holds to reach a tiny shattered ledge below the blankness (wires). Climb up and right (bolt) to reach the shallow crease line, which is followed until a long stride right can be made (bolt) onto a good flake ledge. Boldly climb onto a good hold above (bolt), where an acrobatic sequence leads out right into the large bottomless groove. Follow this steadily to reach a large sloping ledge and a bolt belay a mere 8m below the top.

2 9m 5b Traverse left from the belay to a nut slot, and climb directly up the wall via two slim, stepped grooves.

E Cleasby, P Short, JL Holden, A Towse - Jul 1992

❸ First Night Nerves 55m E5 6b ★★★

An excellent route which provides sustained, well protected climbing up the steep black wall right of the rockfall scar, before taking a bold direct line up the left side of the Main Wall. Start as for *Second Coming*.

1 48m 6b Follow *Second Coming* to the hanging groove, then step up and right (twin bolts). Climb up and right precariously across a quartzy band (bolts) to reach a good hold below an undercut flake. Climb the flake (wires) then (bolt) further delicate climbing leads directly to a junction with *Stage Fright* at a blunt spike, above and left of its crucial groove. Continue directly (bolt), then traverse left to reach a large sloping ledge and bolt belay in the groove of *Second Coming*.

2 7m 5a Continue up the corner to the top.

RO Graham, A Phizacklea - Sep 1987

4 The Main Event 70m E5 6a ★★

An impressive route, which lacks popularity due to its wandering nature, poor protection and difficulty! Start below the overhanging wall, a few metres right of *Second Coming*, at the foot of a steep thin crack.

1 28m 6a Climb the crack, using a sloping ledge out left to reach a traverse line below the overhanging wall. Traverse right, following the flake to reach a large ledge.

2 45m 6a Traverse back leftwards, along a ramp below the steep wall for 4m, pull up right, then back left to gain the upper wall (peg). Follow the thin flake up and left then rightwards to good ledges, then climb the shallow groove on the left to a ledge (bolts). Climb up for a couple of metres before stepping right to finish more or less directly.

The short open corner above the belay (to the left of the big flake) can be followed (peg), thin moves above lead to a junction with the main pitch at the good ledge, reducing the grade to **E4 6a**.

P2 P Whillance, R Parker, P Botterill, D Armstrong, A Murray - Mar 1980 P1 Whillance, Parker - Apr 1980

The Upper Main Wall

Approach: Abseil to the ledge system which runs across the foot of the Main Wall, about 20m above the pool.

5 Stage Fright 50m E6 6b ★★★

A superb, sparsely protected and intimidating route, which climbs the narrow, tapering groove on the left-hand side of the wall. An extra rope is required to reach a belay. Start from a large flake on the left-hand side of the ledge.Traverse leftwards across a short ramp below the steep wall for 4m. Pull up right, then back left to gain the upper wall (peg). Traverse delicately left across the slab to a rib (peg). Step left, using a hidden foothold, into the slim leftwards leaning groove then climb it with difficulty to a poor resting place (peg). Move left and up to a good ledge then climb the wall trending rightwards for 10m until a thin flake leads directly to the top.

P Whillance, D Armstrong

6 Ten Years After 45m E5 5c ★★★

Once one of the star attractions of the quarry, sadly the initial flake has dropped away. Sustained elegant climbing with well spaced gear. Start off the left-hand ledge, at the foot of a tapering flake groove. Climb the large flake and enter the groove for protection (thin tape slot in the rib) before pulling out leftwards onto the undercut wall. Step delicately left then climb up to better holds (peg and wire); rock over leftwards to reach some ledges (good wires). Step right from here, and use a hollow flake to reach and climb a shallow stepped groove (peg). Continue directly up the wall to a small groove, cimb this (good wire) to an awkward finish.

R Matheson, E Cleasby - Easter 1980

7 Wicked Willie 45m E5 6b ★★★

A superb route with good but widely spaced protection. Start as for *Ten Years After*. Climb the large flake and enter the groove for protection (thin tape slot in the rib) before pulling out leftwards onto the undercut wall. Step delicately left then climb up to better holds (peg and wire). Make a hard move up and right (peg) then climb easier ground (bolt). The thin flake above is climbed (Friend ½) until a final wild move rightwards leads to a friendly ledge. Climb the wall above, first on the right (wire) before moving left to a good hold directly below the fir tree at the top.

A Phizacklea, G Cornforth, P Cornforth - May 1987

8 Sky 47m F6b+ ★★★

Good climbing. Belay on the right-hand side of the ledge, below the left-hand end of the big roof. Climb up to a ledge below a thin flake crack; follow this strenuously to where it peters out level with the big roof. Make a hard move left into a short corner and out again to join a grooveline. Step back right onto the headwall, and traverse rightwards across the ledge system above the big roof to reach a shallow groove. Climb this to the top.

E Cleasby, R Matheson - Easter 1980

9 Great Expectations 42m F7b ★★★

A very technical exercise up the vague rib and roof right of *Sky*. Start as for *Sky*. Climb up and rightwards to a prominent overlap, then traverse out right to the rib. Hard climbing up the rib leads directly to a good side hold, where a move left enables a flake to be reached, this is followed to the roof (wires). Hand traverse the lip of the roof rightwards to a little flake, and pull over the roof to reach the upper traverse of *Sky*. Climb directly up the wall to finish with a long reach.

A Phizacklea, J L Holden, B McKinley - Jul 1990

The Central Wall

⑩ Big Mirror 64m E2 5b ★★

Start on the large terrace below a steep flake crack, towards the left end of the ledge.

1 34m 5b The flake leads strenuously to a ramp system. Follow this, past a bolt belay and climb the continuation groove to a bollard and bolt belay.

2 30m 5b Traverse the wall on the left for 8m, then climb up to a ring bolt. Continue leftwards (bolt), then step down and traverse delicately left onto the arête which is followed directly to the top.

P1 P Whillance, R Parker - Mar 1980
P2 E Cleasby, A Phizacklea, R Matheson - Apr 1980

⑪ Limited Edition 33m F6c ★★★

An excellent route which climbs the left side of the wall. Usually reached by abseil. From the lower left point of the ramp, step across left to gain a shallow right-facing scoop and climb this delicately to an excellent hold. Traverse diagonally left across the wall to reach a flake then up and slightly right to better holds below a slight steepening of the headwall. A hard move on quartz holds leads to a tiny right-facing flake to finish.

P Carling, P Noble - May 1986

⑫ Behind the Lines 33m HVS 5a ★★★

A classic up the prominent slabby corner which forms the angle between the Central Wall and the arête of *Malice in Wonderland*. Start by a large pine tree growing at the right end of the ledge. Not all the holds can be trusted. Delicately left from the tree to reach a short corner. A few bold moves up this enables the main corner line to be entered. Follow this, with good protection, and the odd dubious hold to the bulge. Traverse right to finish.

R Parker, A Murray, P Whillance - Mar 1980

⑬ Malice in Wonderland 43m E3 5c ★★★

A beautiful route requiring a bold, graceful approach. Start at the pine tree, as for *Behind the Lines*. Climb the slab on the right to a rib and follow it to the overhang. Step right (bolt) and pull directly through the overhang on good, but widely spaced holds, to land on the slab above. Traverse back left, just above the roof to reach the main arête. Climb the left side of this, passing a good diagonal crack, to a tree on its right flank. Step back onto the arête and climb it with conviction, past a thin crack on the left (RP), to a delicate and gripping finish.

P Whillance, R Parker, E Cleasby - Apr 1980

CATHEDRAL QUARRY

OS Grid Ref: NY 314 028
Altitude: 150m

This impressive hole of high quality slate contains some spectacular climbing in a sunny location pleasantly sheltered from the wind (midges). The quarry is heavily used by groups for abseiling, and at such times it is usually better to climb elsewhere.

Approach: From the A593 Coniston to Ambleside road, ½ kilometre south of the Little Langdale turning, follow a minor road (signed High Park). Take the right fork alongside the woods, through two farmyards, and drop down to the river and a ford. Parking is very limited P NY 316 029. The ford can also be reached in 5 minutes from the Three Shires pub in Little Langdale. 100m west of the pub take the narrow lane on the left. No parking is available down this lane.

From the ford, follow the lane upstream for 100m where a steep little path leads to a flat-topped spoil heap. At the far end of this, either walk around the top to find the descent route, or enter through the flooded tunnel using half-submerged stepping stones. This tunnel leads into the main underground chamber, complete with a resplendent column of slate, which gives the quarry its name.

See map page 138.

The routes start in the open part of the quarry by the large cave 'window'.

1 Orifice Fish 40m E4 5c ★★
Not to be missed – the unique V-chimney above and left of the cave! Start at a protruding arête just right of the cave.
1 23m 5b Climb the arête to the steeper rock at 9m (bolt). Move left and swing round a bulge to enter a smooth grooveline (bolt). Climb the prominent crack on the left until a standing position can be attained on the short arête to its left. A descending traverse left, across the polished slab above the lip of the cave, leads to a bolt belay in the groove.
2 17m 5c Climb left around the bulges to enter the holdless bottomless and merciless V-chimney. Sustained back and foot floundering leads precariously to an awkward exit up the right-hand groove.
K Stephens, P Morris - Jun 1988

2 More Banana Related Japery 32m E4 6b (F7a) ★★
The soaring arête provides a technical challenge of incredible exposure above the yawning chasm! Step left and climb the arête to a good finger slot. Continue over the bulge with difficulty, where thin climbing leads to the final groove of *Orifice Fish.*
A Hyslop, I Williamson - Jun 1989

3 Night of the Hot Pies 30m E1 5b ★★
An excellent route. This follows the straight crack-line on the right of the hanging slab. Climb the arête to steeper rock at 9m (bolt). Move left and swing round a bulge to enter a smooth groove-line (bolt). Climb the prominent crack on the left, which runs directly up the side of the slab to the top (wires).
R Brookes, M Dale - Jul 1987

4 An Alabuse 32m E2 5c ★★
A superb route. Follow *Night of the Hot Pies* to the smooth grooveline, then continue rightwards to a prominent hanging flake (bolt). Layback around this to stand on a good hold on the rib. Continue directly, passing a spike, to finish delicately up the top slab (bolt).
R Brookes, S Alden, N Toledo, A Warrington - Jul 1987

5 Going Underground 40m F6b ★★
The original route in this quarry which follows the diagonal fault across the wall. Now well bolted and well worth doing. Start up *Night of the Hot Pies*. Step right and follow the ramp line rightwards through some awkward bulges to enter the final groove. Climb this with difficulty.
P Clarke, R Brookes - Aug 1981

6 Darklands 38m F6b ★★★
A spectacular route which forces an improbable line straight through the overhangs. Climb the slab to the overhang at 6m, move up a V-notch (bolt) into a scoop (Friend 1½ in shot-hole). Cross the red wall on the right to reach a large bollard on a ledge at 10m. Take the slab on the left to below the large roof, then pull up right into a bottomless V-groove (bolt). Step right airily (bolt) to below a second large jagged overhang (hidden pocket) (bolt). Make a wild pull over the roof onto a hanging slab, then follow the groove up right to a narrow slot. Climb past this and continue up a shallow groove to a sapling, finishing either left or direct – but watch that rope drag!
M Dale, R Kirby - Aug 1988

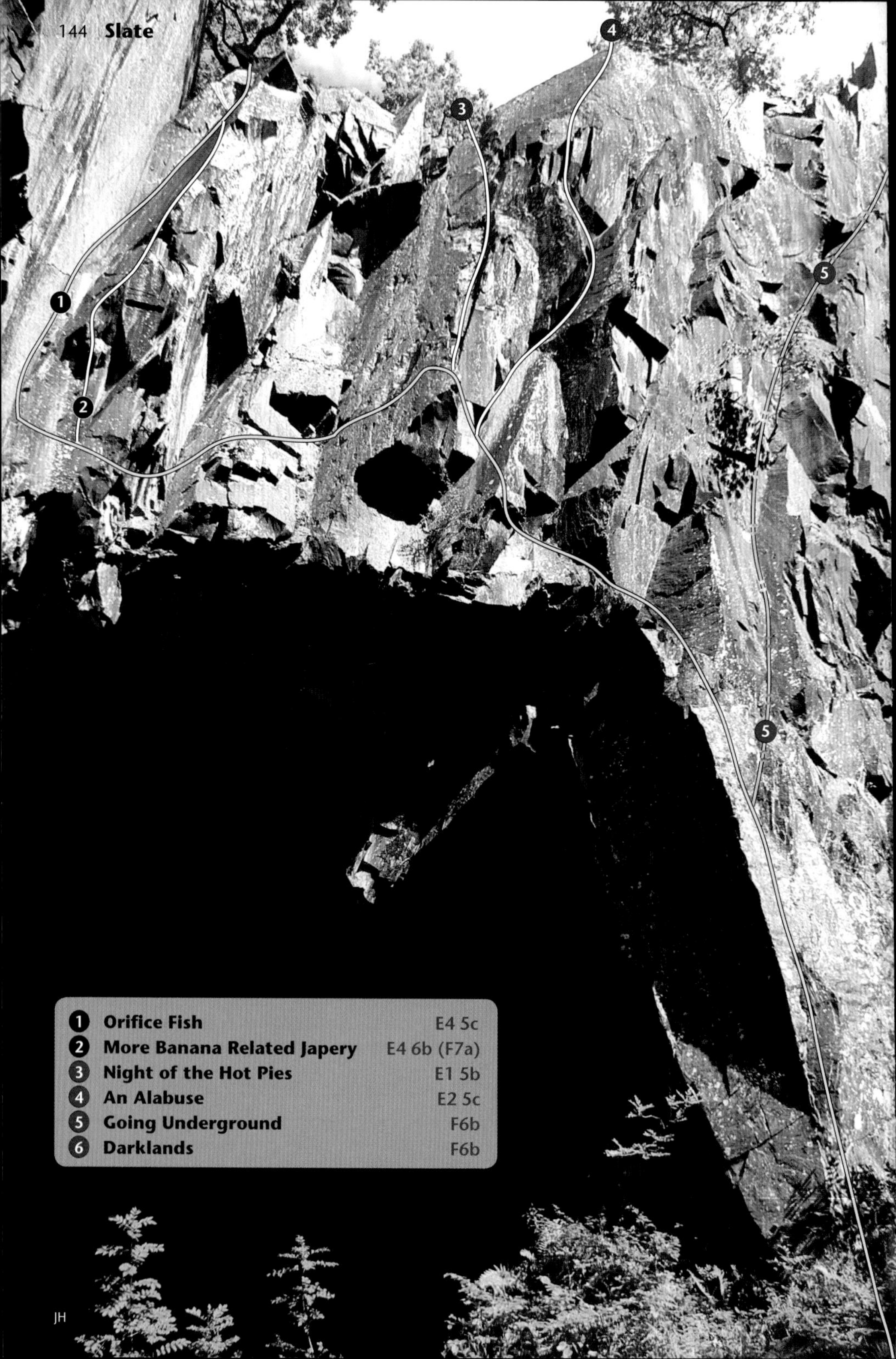
1
2
3
4
5
5
1 Orifice Fish E4 5c
2 More Banana Related Japery E4 6b (F7a)
3 Night of the Hot Pies E1 5b
4 An Alabuse E2 5c
5 Going Underground F6b
6 Darklands F6b
JH

5
6
6
5
JH

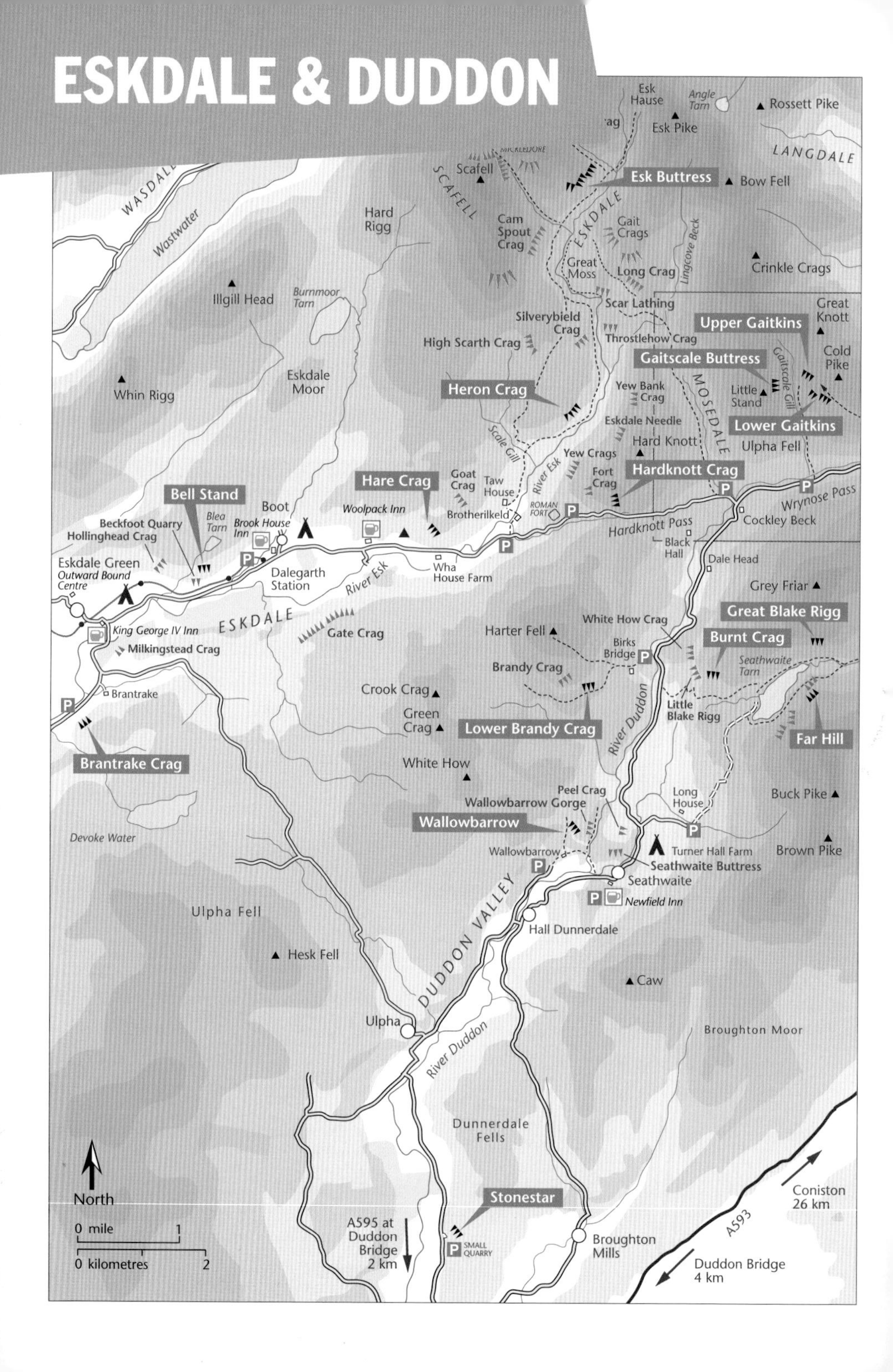
ESKDALE & DUDDON
Esk Hause
Angle Tarn
Rossett Pike
Esk Pike
LANGDALE
Scafell
SCAFELL
Esk Buttress
Bow Fell
WASDALE
Wastwater
Hard Rigg
Cam Spout Crag
ESKDALE
Gait Crags
Lingcove Beck
Great Moss
Long Crag
Crinkle Crags
Illgill Head
Burnmoor Tarn
Scar Lathing
Great Knott
Silverybield Crag
Upper Gaitkins
High Scarth Crag
Throstlehow Crag
Cold Pike
Gaitscale Buttress
Gaitscale Gill
Whin Rigg
Eskdale Moor
Heron Crag
Yew Bank Crag
MOSEDALE
Little Stand
Lower Gaitkins
Eskdale Needle
Hard Knott
Ulpha Fell
Scale Gill
Yew Crags
River Esk
Fort Crag
Hardknott Crag
Hare Crag
Goat Crag
Taw House
Bell Stand
Boot
Woolpack Inn
Brotherilkeld
ROMAN FORT
Wrynose Pass
Cockley Beck
Beckfoot Quarry
Hollinghead Crag
Blea Tarn
Brook House Inn
Hardknott Pass
Black Hall
Eskdale Green
Outward Bound Centre
Dalegarth Station
River Esk
Wha House Farm
Dale Head
Grey Friar
ESKDALE
King George IV Inn
Milkingstead Crag
Gate Crag
Harter Fell
White How Crag
Great Blake Rigg
Burnt Crag
Birks Bridge
Brandy Crag
Seathwaite Tarn
Brantrake
Crook Crag
Little Blake Rigg
Green Crag
Lower Brandy Crag
River Duddon
Far Hill
Brantrake Crag
White How
Peel Crag
Long House
Buck Pike
Wallowbarrow Gorge
Wallowbarrow
Devoke Water
Wallowbarrow
Turner Hall Farm
Brown Pike
Seathwaite Buttress
Seathwaite
Newfield Inn
Ulpha Fell
DUDDON VALLEY
Hall Dunnerdale
Hesk Fell
Caw
Ulpha
River Duddon
Broughton Moor
Dunnerdale Fells
North
Stonestar
Coniston 26 km
0 mile 1
0 kilometres 2
A595 at Duddon Bridge 2 km
SMALL QUARRY
A593
Broughton Mills
Duddon Bridge 4 km

☐ *Central Pillar*, Esk Buttress E2 (page 164) Shaw Brown — Loz Monckton

ESKDALE

A beautiful valley with two distinctive sections of differing character. Its upper reaches are remote and tree-less dominated by the wild Great Moss and one of the most imposing buttresses in the District – Esk Buttress; here you will find routes to rival any in the country. In contrast Sampson's Stones - meteoric boulders thrown from the sky, lie in such an idyllic setting on the Great Moss the walk-in is well worthwhile. The lower valley is equally beautiful, for different reasons; it has a shady tree-lined lane, a burbling beck and popular tourist attractions and amenities. Despite this bustle, the crags are secluded, hidden behind the dry-stone walls above the woods and bracken.

Lower Eskdale – the valley offers a wide variety of climbing and bouldering, easy to get to and viable year-round. These low-lying crags, composed of rough granite offering excellent friction, are delightfully secluded, yet only a short walk from the road. With a shop, pubs, campsites, a Youth Hostel and the added attraction of a castle, working mill and the narrow gauge railway, t' la'al ratty – Eskdale makes a great venue for a family: www.eskdale.info

Eskdale Enchainments

The Lakes is a fine place to enjoy big enchainment days, linking routes creating a rock climbing way from the valley floor on to the summits. Eskdale is no exception and provides plenty of opportunity with loads of variation possible.

Heron Crag: *Gormenghast* **E1** or *Bellerophon* **VS** continue to the Great Moss for bouldering on Sampsons Stones. From here eye up a line on **Esk Buttress:** *Bridge's Route* **HS** or *Square Chimney/Medusa Wall* **VS**. This takes you from a valley setting into the high mountains. If it hasn't been enough of a day, the crags of Scafell are just over on the Wasdale side of Mickledore and will be in the sun until last light, so continue up *Botterill's Slab* **VS** a perfect evening climb during summer.

Great Moss, Esk Buttress and Scafell — Jon Allison

BELL STAND

OS Grid Ref: NY 164 007
Altitude: 210m

A sunny, quick-drying 15m face of rough granite, which bears a close resemblance to a gritstone edge with everything that entails. Bell Stand is a pleasant venue for a short visit for anyone operating at VS and above –the grades are outcrop stiff.

Approach: Limited off-road parking P NY 16800 00400 opposite Stanley Ghyll House. Walking west along the road, passing Beckfoot Quarry (P NY 16416 00295) on the right to reach an old railway hut. From here a sketchy path leads alongside a wall to the quarry.

See map page 146.

Descent: To the right facing the crag.

1. **Incey Wincey** HS
2. **Spider Wall** VS 4c
3. **Arachnid** HVS 5a
4. **The Seams** HVS 4c
5. **Terminator** E3 6a ★
6. **Innocuous Corner** HVS 5a ★
7. **The Nose** E2 6a
8. **Sideslip** E2 5c ★
9. **Ladies Day** HS ★
10. **Anniversary Waltz** E2 6a ★
11. **The Birthday Present** E5 6a ★
12. **Plumbline** VS 4c ★★
13. **Hollow Flakes** MVS 4b ★
14. **Tipsy Crack** HVS 5b ★
15. **The Puzzle Book** E2 5c ★★
16. **Enigma Wall** E5 6b ★★
17. **Black Dancer** E1 5c

HARE CRAG

OS Grid Ref: NY 200 013
Altitude: 170m

A collection of steep clean buttresses and blank slabs formed of rough granite. The routes are clean, fast drying and sunny, allowing a pleasurable afternoon's climbing at any grade. The crack lines are frequently shallow, rounded or flared, offering only limited protection. The crag is prominent on the fell side behind the Youth Hostel as one drives up the valley.

Approach: Park P NY 19979 00944 directly opposite Wha House Farm, from where an easy walk over a low hill leads to the crags.

See map page 146.

Descent: Well to the left.

Alternator Buttress (15m)

1. **Magnetron** E2 5c ★
2. **Alternator** E3 6a ★★

The Upper Wall (18m)

This lies directly above The Central Slabs.

3. **Left-Hand Route** MVS 4a
4. **Route 1** VS ★
5. **Right-Hand Route** VS 4c

The Central Slabs (25 to 30m)

These magnificent smooth slabs are an obvious feature and are easily identified by a steep lower wall formed by a pronounced knuckling of the rock.

6 **Jugged Hare** VS 4b ★
7 **Hareless Heart** E1 5b ★
8 **Butterballs 2** E5 ★
9 **Slit Wall** E1 5b ★
10 **Birthday Boy** E1 ★
11 **Short Back and Sides** HVS ★
12 **Slab Route** S ★

The Lower Buttress (20m)

This is the steep wall capped by a slab, rising above a blocky bay about 40m left of the Right-Hand Slab; the most obvious feature on this section of the crag is *The Groove*.

13 **Fireball XL5** VS 4b ★
14 **The Groove** E1 5b ★★
15 **International Rescue** E3 6a ★
16 **Gangway** MVS 4b

Right-Hand Slab (25m)

A clean open slab on the right.

17 **The Rib** D ★
18 **Easy Slab** VD
19 **Pleasant Slab** S

Langdale
Duddon
Eskdale
Wasdale
Gable
Buttermere
Borrowdale
Eastern
EV

HERON CRAG

OS Grid Ref: NY 222 030
Altitude: 250m

The biggest low-level crag in Eskdale - dries quickly, is steep, and offers impressive, strenuous routes. Despite the dirty appearance, many of the routes are clean.

The focal point of the crag is the central pillar containing the classic *Gormenghast*. Its comfortable belay ledge has for some years now been chosen as the annual nesting site for a pair of peregrines.

Approach: Park by the roadside at Brotherilkeld (bottom of Hardknott Pass), P NY 21274 01089. Cross the river Esk and go via Taw House and Scale Beck Bridge. A narrow path contours along the hillside to the crag.

See map page 146.

Descent: Traverse leftwards to a wide scree gully.

1 Sidetrack 55 m VS 4b ★★

A popular route with an enjoyable main pitch, which makes an ascending traverse beneath the overhangs.

1 8m 4b Climb a stepped groove and slabs rightwards to a belay.

2 35m 4c Gain a ledge, above on the left, and make an ascending leftward traverse until beneath a steep wall, which leads to a groove beneath the overhangs. Continue delicately up left to a sloping ledge and second groove; follow this over a small overhang and pass a second overhang on the right. An easy wall leads to an oak tree.

3 12 m 4a Climb the rib above.

RB Evans, IF Howell - Aug 1960

2 Gormenghast 53 m E1 5a ★★★

A classic climb of great character. The rock is delightfully clean and solid and the protection good, except at the start of p2.

1 10m 4c Climb the steep clean grey wall directly to a ledge below the main crack.

2 18m 5a Power up flat holds on the steep wall, a couple of metres left of the main crack, to a slight easing, then traverse right to a niche. Or climb the crack to the niche at a well-protected **5b**. From the niche, move up then step left into a groove which leads to a flake belay 6m below the holly tree.

3 25m 5a From the tree step right and climb up on good holds past a prominent block. Cracks lead directly up the headwall until better holds lead right to a good ledge and tree. Climb straight up to the top.

L Brown, AL Atkinson - Mar 1960; p3 DD Whillans - c 1960

3 Iago/Titus Combination 51 m E3 6a ★

This exacting climb takes a direct line up the crag, starting 6m right of *Gormenghast*.

1 12m 5b Climb the obvious clean groove between *Gormenghast* and *Bellerophon*, until a crack near the top of the groove allows a large hold to be reached. Move up to a large grass ledge.

2 21m 6a Climb the very steep wall boldly to an overhang below a slim groove (peg) then climb the crack in the groove with difficulty, to reach good holds before moving up to a ledge. Follow the obvious crack first right, then left, to the top of the needle.

3 18m 5c Stand on a 'musical' (very fragile) flake on the right and step up to obvious undercuts, where a long reach above the overhang reveals a good flake. Step left and climb directly to a tree, finishing as for *Gormenghast*.

I Singleton, A Jackman - Jul 1965; P3 A Phizacklea, DR Lampard - May 1989

4 Bellerophon 57 m VS 5a ★★

An excellent route with good positive holds, good protection and an inescapable line. It looks extremely mossy and is frequently wet, although the holds are always clean. Start at the toe of the arête.

1 10m 4b Climb the shallow groove in the arête, left of a square-cut chimney, to a large grass ledge.

2 12m 4c Make a delicate move to the right and climb the steep crack to a large grass ledge.

3 13m 4c Climb the groove to a step left and belay on the pinnacle at its top.

4 22m 5a Either step off the top of the pinnacle, or move round a nose on the right and work up a crack to a strenuous pull on good holds. Easier climbing leads to a ledge. Finish up an overhanging crack on small holds and pull out right at the top. Or avoid this on the left.

ORD Pritchard, BS Schofield - May 1953

5 Spec Crack 58 m E1 5a ★
An interesting route which breaks through the overhangs right of *Bellerophon*.
1 22 m 5a Climb the wall, pull strenuously through the overhang and follow the crack past heather patches to a holly.
2 12 m 4b The crack on the right leads to a small stance below an overhanging crack.
3 24 m 5a Climb the crack until it is choked with rock; break onto the left wall and ascend to a small ledge. Follow the crack above.
JA Austin, E Metcalf - Aug 1961

6 Mean Feat 54 m E4 5c ★★
An excellent route of absorbing technical interest.
1 26 m 5c Climb to a ledge at 6m; awkward moves lead into a scoop above on the left (peg). Traverse the undercut wall leftwards to the edge, then steeply up to easier moves and a junction with *Spec Crack*. Follow the thinner, left-hand crack directly above the holly tree to a peg belay below a long roof.
2 28 m 5c Ascend the wall just left of the belay, moving slightly right to a short bulging section (poor RP). Bold moves lead to a resting place. Step right, and climb the wall above directly to the centre of a long square overhang; pull over this and continue more easily to the top.
P1 TW Birkett, RO Graham - May 1977; P2 E Cleasby, A Phizacklea - May 1982

BRANTRAKE CRAG

OS Grid Ref: SD 145 984
Altitude: 90m

A fine collection of granite crags situated close to the road.

Approach: Follow the road towards Birker Fell, passing the King George IV en route, and turn right down the narrow Bootle road for 500m – parking area on the right, P SD 145 986. Opposite a small boggy path leads steeply uphill to the crag.

See map page 146.

Descent: Either side of the crags.

The Lower Crag

This is rather broken and vegetated in appearance and around 15m high. All routes are on good clean rock.

1. **The Mantelshelves** VS 4c
2. **The Crack** VS 4b
3. **Lady Fingers** HVS 5b ★
4. **Nail File** HVS 5b ★
5. **Diagonal Route** VD ★
6. **Cuckoo Pillar** VS 4c
7. **Lingbeck Pillar** HVS 4c

The Main Wall

This is easily identified, being a clean and impressive piece of rock, split by three distinct crack-lines.

8 **Left Edge** 33m VS 4a ★

9 **Tunnel Vision** 30m E2 5c

10 **Left-Hand Crack** 18m E1 5c ★

11 **Central Crack** 20m VS 5a ★

12 **Art for Art's Sake** 20m E5 6b ★★

13 **Right-Hand Crack** 15m HVS 5b ★★

14 **Abstract Arête** 12m E3 5c ★★

The Upper Crag

This 10m high face lies just above and right of The Main Face. It offers a fine open aspect and comes complete with a large flat grassy base.

15 **Open Groove** D
16 **Closed Season** HS
17 **Open Season** MS
18 **Block and Tackle Left-hand** VD
19 **Block and Tackle Right-hand** VD
20 **Face Route** VS 4c ★
21 **Direct Start** E1 5c
22 **Terrace Crack** VD
23 **Slim Line Tonic** VS 4c ★
24 **The Middle Way** S ★
25 **Dog Leg Crack** VD ★
26 **Edge Hog** D

Fun Link-up Cragging

Tortoise Crag (NY 206 017), **Hare Crag** (NY 200 013), and **Goat Crag** (NY 204 017)

No more than about 10 minutes apart and never far from the road, all enjoy a secluded feel. You follow the sun starting out on short routes on a south-east facing crag, progressing to multi-pitch routes at Goat Crag enjoying late afternoon sun. None of these crags offers good protection, so they are not places to push your grade. Having said that, due to the slabby nature of many of the routes, grades can feel on the soft side. Only Hare Crag is featured in this guide; grid references for the other crags and route information is available on the FRCC website: www.frcc.co.uk

International Rescue, Hare Crag E3 (page 151) Ben Scroggs — JOHN HOLDEN

ESK BUTTRESS

OS Grid Ref: NY 223 065
Altitude: 490m

Hydra E2 (page 161) Steve Hubbard — NICK WHARTON

Approach: P NY 21274 01089 bottom of Hardknott Pass. From Brotherilkeld in Eskdale, follow the River Esk to arrive at the outlet of the Great Moss. Cam Spout is now directly ahead with Esk Buttress ½ km to the right. Alternatively, cross the river Esk and go via Taw House Farm to Scale Beck Bridge, just beyond which a good path rises up the hillside, then levels out before arriving at the Great Moss directly under Cam Spout, Esk Buttress is a further 15 minutes beyond.

For those based in the South Lakes, drive to Cockley Beck P NY 242 017. Walk up Mosedale and over to Lingcove Beck. Beyond a narrow path contours under Long Crag and Gait Crag before descending to the Great Moss. Esk Buttress is seen on the far side with Cam Spout ½ km to the left.

See map page 146.

Descent: The best descent from all routes is to scramble beyond the top of the cliff a short distance, then gradually descend broken ground towards the left side of the crag (true right) using a sketchy path. A short wall is descended to reach a small stream.

Without doubt one of the finest and most impressive crags in the district. The situation is idyllic; with large open walls looking out over the wild expanse of Upper Eskdale. Despite its apparent remoteness the crag can be reached fairly painlessly by a variety of scenic routes. It receives the sun until mid-afternoon and dries quickly. The sunny aspect coupled with excellent solid rock makes it a pleasant place to climb. It is a place where any climber, whatever their standard, can enjoy exceptional wall climbing of the highest calibre.

The crag is a series of steep walls, gradually rising in size from the left to culminate in the inspiring Central Pillar. Defining the right side of the Central Pillar is the deep groove of *Trespasser Groove*. Below the crag steep broken ground with easy scrambling leads to the starts of the climbs.

From The Great Moss

The Gargoyle Wall

This is the steep clean wall at the left-hand side of the main crag. It is easily identified by The Gargoyle, a curious protruding block sitting atop the left side. There is a large expanse of steep, broken ground below, which must be negotiated to reach most of the routes. The usual approach is to follow the first pitch of Gargoyle Direct, or by scrambling up from either end of the ledge. Another way to reach the foot of the wall is to climb a route on the main crag and then walk down to the top of the wall, to fix abseil.

Descent: Abseil from a thread found at the top of Gargoyle Groove, 60m ropes needed. Alternatively, scramble well back to traverse left over broken grassy terrain and down to the stream. Follow the streambed until just before a steepening, exit right to find a good path down to the base.

1 Gargoyle Groove 55 m VS 5a ★

A good route with a brilliant top pitch. Better and harder than its apparently broken appearance would suggest, although the initial climbing is dirty. Start directly below the groove, at a triangular wedged block.

1 19m 4a The broken buttress and a scruffy scramble to the foot of the main groove.

2 18m 5a Climb just right of the groove until forced left under the nose by a tricky and reachy move. Strenuous and balancy climbing leads up and shortly back right above the nose. Easy climbing to the upper groove and a good nut belay.

3 18m 4c Step right and follow the delightful wall just right of the main groove, aiming just left of The Gargoyle.

AR Dolphin, LJ Griffin - Aug 1947

2 Alehouse Rock 42m E4 6a ★★

Sumptiously steep technical wall climbing. A small overhang at 5m is reached via a shallow groove. Undercut right and up to a spike; now left and up the wall, fingery, to an easing at the arete. Traverse a narrow rock ledge right 5m to the groove and superb thin crack splitting the headwall.

A Phizacklea - Aug 1988

3 Gargoyle Direct 81 m HVS 5a ★★

Delightful, open wall climbing with good protection. Start well down to the right of *Gargoyle Groove* at a narrow rock rib directly beneath The Gargoyle. This is the only continuous line of rock leading to the foot of the wall.

1 42m 4a Climb easily up the clean rib to grass and heather ledges. Steep scrambling, passing a rock crevasse, leads to a spike belay directly below The Gargoyle.

2 39m 5a Climb the wall, trending left slightly to reach a large spike at 8m, then move back right to a sloping ledge. Follow a strenuous crack in a shallow groove for 5m, move left to a rest. Continue left to a rib and follow it to a ledge beneath The Gargoyle. A short crack on the left leads to a block belay.

DW English, M McKenzie, K Brannon - Jun 1962

4 Wild Bunch Left-Hand 38m E3 5c ★

An outstanding steep pitch that appears to have evolved. Climb the thin crack left of *Wild Bunch* for 9m to a small ledge and groove. Soon quit the groove left for a ramp, follow this to a roof. An arduous crack leads to a large ledge, step left to finish up the nose.

5 Wild Bunch 37m E3 5c ★

The bi-polar thin cracks seaming the wall are friendly enough at first, then they steepen, close and offer little respite until the ledge is reached.

R Fawcett, J Hesletine - Spring 1975

6 Grand Slam 39 m E1 5b ★★

An excellent pitch up the wall right of *Wild Bunch*, with a strenuous fingery crux. Where *Wild Bunch* steepens follow a rising line right to a spike. The wall above leads to a stiff pull to pass the left side of a square-cut overhang and thankfully gain a ledge. The wall on the right leads to the top.

W Young, I Singleton - Aug 1973; FFA J Lamb, J Adams - Mar 1974

The Red Edge Area

7 Desperately Sea King 40 m E6 6b ★

An excellent, sustained route culminating in a desperate overhanging crack. Abseil approach recommended. Climb the awkward corner to its top, then swing boldly left to enter a bottomless recessed scoop (peg). Step left to reach a thin crack and climb this, avoiding a suspect block, to an outrageous finish.

N Foster, M Berzins - May 1991 - the pair discovered part of a rotor blade from a Sea King helicopter on the ledge.

8 The Red Edge 60 m E1 5a ★★★

One of the great routes of the Lakes with continuous exposure and sustained, though not excessive, difficulty. Start at the foot of the chimney.

1 39m 5a After 5m a thin flake on the right wall leads to the rib. Follow the rib until a shallow groove on the left can be entered. Climb the steep groove to an overhang, turned on the right; an easier groove above leads to a belay on the right.

2 21m 4c Move back left and follow a crack and then large flakes, slightly leftwards, towards the top.

JA Austin, NJ Soper, E Metcalf pa - Jun 1962

9 Hydra 54m E2 5c ★★

A route that should get more attention with a well-deserved reputation for difficulty. Ignore the moss as it isn't climbed.

1 33m 5c Climb diagonally left to the arete and up to a good ledge. Traverse right to climb the corner by technical bridging (RP) as soon as it gets dirty pull right onto a footledge and up to a ledge on the left. Abseil or ...

2 21m 4c A short corner and wall to finish.

RJ Isherwood, CH Taylor - 1967

10 Humdrum 38 m E3 5c ★★★

Tremendous wall climbing boasting the best pitch of its standard on the cliff. Scramble up to the belay on *Hydra*. Climb steeply up towards some stepped grooves and follow these, with several bold moves, to a resting position. Go diagonally up leftwards to the top of the groove on *Hydra*. Move up then traverse right to a flat hold in the middle of the wall. Follow a thin crack above into a groove, pull directly over the square-cut overhang above to finish at a grass ledge.

R H Berzins, M Berzins - Aug 1977

11 GTI 42 m E4 6a ★

A quality pitch squeezed onto this immaculate pillar. Climb the wall to a shallow groove right of an overhang. Climb the groove before committing left to moves up the crinkly brown wall. Head rightwards past a rockscar to a final pull through a bulge. Abseil off.

I Turnbull, J Robinson, S Miller - Sep 1993

12 Black Sunday 63 m HVS 5a ★★

Beaten to The Central Pillar the Lakes team created this justifiably popular climb up the steep groove/crack system. The lower sections need time to dry out after rain. Scramble up to a small tree beneath the main pitch.

1 33m 5a Move up to a prominent mossy crack and climb it to a slab on the right. Regain the crack and follow it for a couple of metres to where it fades; step left to a thin slanting crack. Follow this to a resting place beneath an overhang. Traverse right, back into the main crackline, and pull rightwards round an overhang, and ascend a short wall to a ledge.

2 17m 5a Climb the corner crack above until more broken rocks lead to a belay on the left.

3 13m 4b The wall to the left of a mossy scoop is climbed; belay well back.

JA Austin, E Metcalf, NJ Soper - Jun 1962

The Central Pillar

The unmistakable towering wall in the centre of the crag. Bounded on the left by a mossy groove-line; the lower part forms a square-cut chimney, the starting point for the next route.

13 Square Chimney Route/Medusa Wall 79 m VS 4c ★★★

An excellent combination finishing in an awesome position above the main headwall. Start by scrambling with care up broken rocks to a ledge below the chimney.

1 15m 4c Climb the chimney to a sloping ledge on the left.

2 15m 4b Cross a mossy slab on the left to enter a groove with a crack in the back; follow this to a small stance.

3 9m 4c Continue up the groove to a sloping ledge on the left; or if the groove is wet, climb the left rib to the same point. Belay on a second ledge slightly higher.

4 13m 4c Climb the shallow groove up the left side of the wall, directly above the belay, to the top of a pinnacle. Traverse right to an exposed stance on the edge.

5 16m 4b Take the groove above for 5m followed by a traverse right to the very edge overlooking the central pillar. Continue in an amazing position to a ledge. Scrambling remains.

RJ Birkett L Muscroft - Aug 1947; AR Dolphin, LJ Griffin - Aug 1947

14 The Long Good Friday 95m E3 5c ★★

A good, sustained eliminate stringing together a number of excellent pitches. Start at the base of *Square Chimney*.

1 33m 5b Move up to a good spike at the very base of the *Square Chimney*, then step right on a heathery ledge to an incut hold on the steep wall. Pull up to gain a thin crack-line in the front of the pillar, which is followed delicately to the top of a large flake. Climb the thin crack just right of the flake corner to a stance just right of a pinnacle.

2 38m 5c Follow the thin crack which leads directly to the junction between the slab and the headwall. Move rightwards, passing an awkward overhang, and continue up into a delicate scoop. Move right across a slab to belay in a corner.

3 25m 5c Start up the thin crack in the wall directly above the belay to a good hold at 4m, then pull rightwards across a fingery wall (poor Rock 2 in a horizontal crack) and lurch for the "doubtful block" on *Central Pillar*. Pull onto the higher ledge, as for *Central Pillar*, then reach a higher ledge, which is hand-traversed left to a point directly above the initial crack. Finish straight up.

A Phizacklea, J Holden - Apr 2003

1 Gargoyle Groove VS 5a
2 Alehouse Rock E4 6a
3 Gargoyle Direct HVS 5a
4 Wild Bunch Left-Hand E3 5c
5 Wild Bunch E3 5c
6 Grand Slam E1 5b
7 Desperately Sea King E6 6b
8 The Red Edge E1 5a
9 Hydra E2 5c
10 Humdrum E3 5c
11 GTI E4 6a
12 Black Sunday HVS 5a
13 Square Chimney Route/ Medusa Wall VS 4c
14 The Long Good Friday E3 5c
15 Bridge's Route HS
16 First and Last and Always E7 6b
17 The Central Pillar E2 5b
18 The Cumbrian E5 6a
19 Trespasser Groove HVS 5a
A

12
10
A
11
12
13
14
16
17
14
18
18
13
15
14
17
19
19
AP

⑮ Bridge's Route 71 m HS ★★★

One of the classic mountaineering outings of the district. The route takes a direct line up the lower part of the pillar before losing its resolve, traversing leftwards across the crag to finish above *The Red Edge*. Rope up and scramble over grass ledges and short rock walls to a cleaned ledge.

1 21m Move slightly right from the belay, and follow steep rocks passing an awkward pinnacle to gain a very shallow cracked corner which leads to a grass ledge. Climb a crack above to a good flake which leads leftwards to a ledge overlooking *Square Chimney*.

2 13m Climb a steep groove above the left-hand side of the ledge and continue directly to a spike.

3 12m Traverse delicately left to a mossy ledge below an open chimney. A groove on the left leads to a block belay.

4 9m Continue traversing left along the sloping shelves to a small stance by a pile of flakes on the edge of the buttress.

5 16m Climb a mossy groove to a large grass shelf; belay well back.

AW Bridge, AB Hargreaves, M Linnell, WS Dyson - Jul 1932

⑯ First and Last and Always 45 m E7 6b ★★★

A committing breathtaking challenge tackling the wall below and left of *The Cumbrian*. Only the very best will succeed, whilst those who only think they're the best will at least receive good Hospital treatment! Start, if you wish, from the top of p2 of *Bridge's Route*. Climb directly to the top of a shallow groove. Exit left then pull steeply up and right to reach the right-hand end of the largest and most obvious roof. (Avoid a dubious undercut flake.) (peg; Rock 1 and poor Flex. Friend 1½ on the right). Make very steep moves on the wall above (Flex. Friend ½ on the left). Powerful undercut moves lead up rightwards to join *The Cumbrian* at a point half-way up its main groove.

D Pegg, M Smith - May 1990

⑰ The Central Pillar 98 m E2 5b ★★★

A superb climb; cunningly side-stepping the beetling headwall adds to its character.

1 21m P1 of *The Cumbrian* or *Bridge's Route*.

2 13m P2 of *The Cumbrian* or *Bridge's Route*.

3 21m 5a Climb the wall above for a couple of metres, until a traverse, on small holds, leads diagonally rightwards across the wall to a narrow ledge. Move up left, then step airily right around a nose to a hanging stance on a small ledge on the light-coloured rib.

4 13m 5b A good pitch to second. A shallow groove is climbed to a small ledge on the right. Go up left, over a small overhang, onto a slab and follow this rightwards to a small ledge below an open corner.

5 21m 5b Traverse delicately across the exposed wall on the right and pull up to a small ledge (peg). Climb up the steep wall on the left past a doubtful block to a higher ledge, then move right and climb up to reach a grassy bay on the right.

6 9m 4c Climb the undercut flake crack on the right of the bay or, alternatively, the easier wide crack on the left.

P Crew, M Owen - Jun 1962

⑱ The Cumbrian 89 m E5 6a ★★★

Awe-inspiring. Its main pitch takes the sensationally positioned, left-slanting corner, high on the front face. Technically sustained and strenuous on the crux, protection is good.

1 40m 5a Follow p1 of *Bridge's Route* to the top of the flake crack. Climb a thin crack directly up the wall for 9m and step left to a continuation crack; follow this to a narrow ledge.

2 16m 5a Continue up the slab above, in the same line, to join the traverse on p3 of *The Central Pillar*; this pitch is followed rightwards to a small ledge on the rib.

3 33m 6a Traverse left from the belay towards the steep wall (wires). Step left onto the impending wall to reach a shallow groove. Move up and left again with increasing difficulty, to enter the base of the slim corner. Climb the corner, surmounting a bulge near the top, and follow a slabby groove rightwards to a final bulge. Overcome this with difficulty.

R Valentine, P Braithwaite - May 1974; FFA M and R Berzins - Aug 1977

⑲ Trespasser Groove 121 m HVS 5a ★★★

A deservedly popular route which offers thuggy, well protected climbing in the deep corner.

1 30m Climb clean slabs to finish onto heather on the right.

2 20m Make for the foot of the main corner.

3 27m 4c Ascend a slab then move left to climb the main corner to a tiny ledge and spike belay.

4 10m 5a Climb onto a ledge on the right wall of the corner; continue up a thin crack in the wall above to a large flake. Move up right to a good ledge.

5 10m 5a A corner on the left is followed to an overhang; pull awkwardly up to the right and step across rightwards to better holds. Climb directly to The Waiting Room.

6 24 m 5a Frankland's Crack leads with difficulty onto a slab, finish up a steep crack out of the top left hand corner.

AR Dolphin, D Hopkins - Sep 1952

HARDKNOTT CRAG

5 mn

OS Grid Ref: NY 228 016
Altitude: 440m

An imposing and impressive crag that lies conveniently close to the top of Hardknott Pass P NY 22899 01489. It faces west, dries quickly, and offers excellent steep strenuous climbing. There is good roadside cragging to be had at the far right extremity of the crag as it turns to face the road.

See map page 146.

Descent: To the right.

1 Caesar 30 m E4 6a ★★

An excellent route up the slim corner. Good protection relies on the skilled use of small wires. Climb the wide initial corner using the narrow flared V-slot to reach a ledge. The slim corner is followed with escalating difficulty, and only relents once a good flake is reached. Finish up the groove above.

E Rogers, RO Graham - Sep 1989

2 Earl Boethar 33 m E2 5c ★★

A very strenuous route for its grade, but the good protection makes this an excellent test of a climber's fitness – or lack of it! It takes the largest of the square-cut grooves in the centre of the crag.

E Cleasby, M Lynch - May 1982

3 Powerglide 30 m E3 6a ★★

A superb, sustained pitch directly up the left side of the steep wall. Start below a slim bottomless groove 6m above the ground. Climb the wall on the right for a couple of metres (wire), then step left to a sloping ledge below the groove. Enter the groove with difficulty and continue boldly to gain a good hold out left. Climb directly up the wall, passing a good spike to where a long reach gains an obvious undercut below a left-facing flake. Step left to a thin crack and follow this to better holds by the left arête, finishing easily above.

E Cleasby, K Gibson - Jun 1982

4 Copenhagen 27 m E2 5c ★★

The original line up the centre of the wall - excellent climbing. Climb a short wall for a couple of metres then follow a shallow groove that slants slightly right to good holds in the centre of the wall. Continue into the shallow inverted 'V' directly above then struggle onto a sloping ledge and second niche above. Step right to a small rib, go up then back left boldly over the roof, finishing slightly leftwards.

R Matheson - Jul 1976

DUDDON

With an array of small crags set amongst the woods and fellsides west of the Coniston range this valley is a hidden gem. Turner Hall campsite is in a superb setting and the Newfield Inn offers great food and proper ale. The valley has other draws; Wallowbarrow gorge is one of the most fearsome whitewater passages in the Lakes. On warm days bridges are freely jumped at Birks and Ulpha. On a road bike any circular route involves climbing Hard Knott or Wrynose and with the best single-track in the Lakes it's also a great spot to ride off-road.

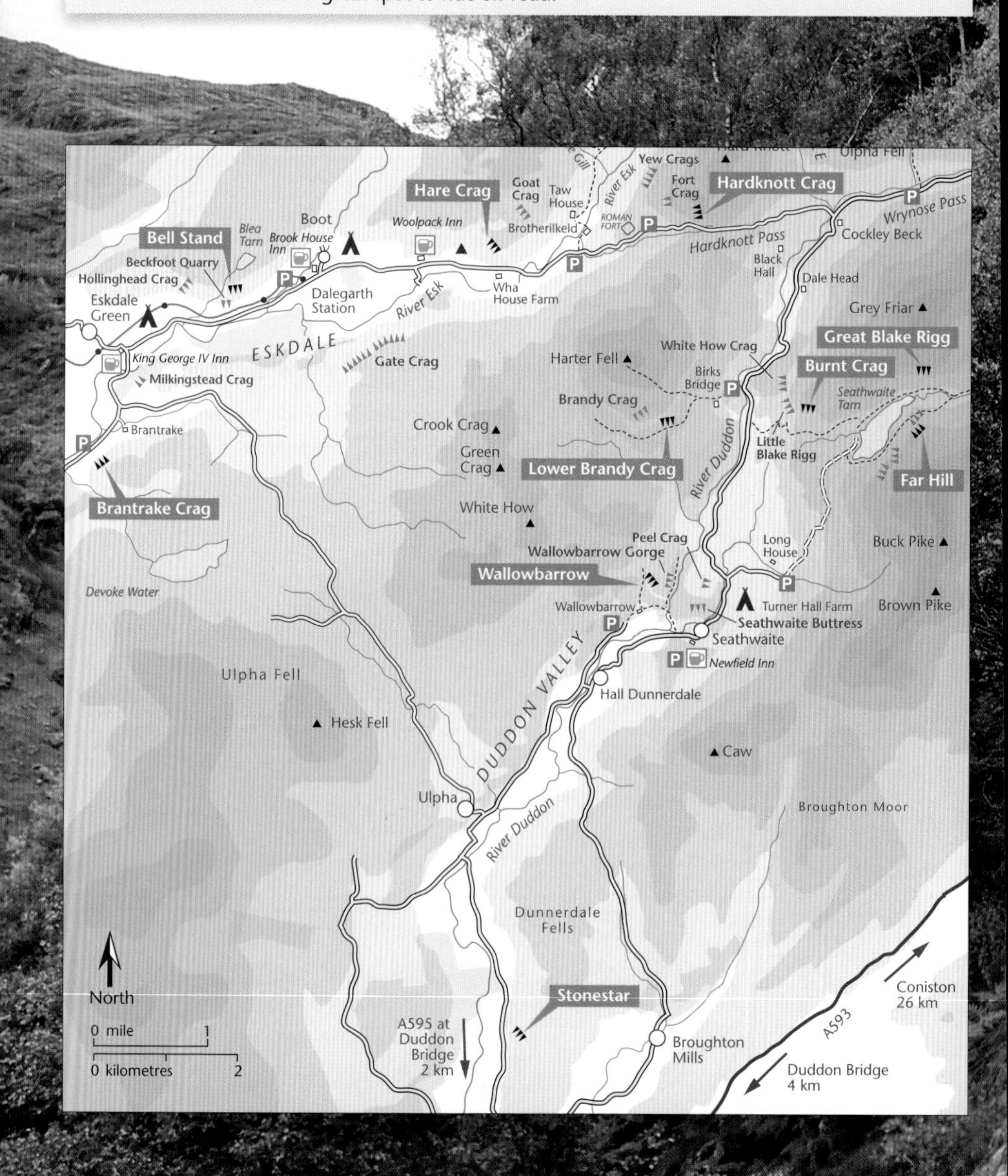

Digitation, Wallowbarrow MVS (page 172) — JOHN HOLDEN

STONESTAR

OS Grid Ref: SD 203 907
Altitude: 150m

❶ **Last Chance Saloon** 23m MVS 4b ★
From beneath the right end of a square cut overhang climb onto a fin of rock and continue up a crack. A tricky move gives access to the right trending crack.

❷ **Venezuela** 24m HVS 5a ★
Pleasant open climbing, slightly lichenous in parts. The rounded rib leads past a little nook to a block runner at 9m. Traverse left to gain and follow a crackline diagonally rightwards.

❸ **Columbia** 27m E1 5b ★★
A superb wall climb with good protection from small wires, the difficulty increases in proportion to the height.

❹ **The Challenger** 30m E2.8 5c ★★
Pull over a small overhang to stand in diagonal slots. Delicately move rightwards to a good crack below the main overlap, follow this with difficulty diagonally leftwards. Take a direct line up the wall past a small flat topped flake.

❺ **The Breech** 27m E2.3 5c ★★
A strenuous route breeching the obvious overlap. From directly below its right-hand side pull over rightwards and move boldly up the diagonal crack until it eases; take a direct line to the top.

❻ **Anchor Handling** 27m E2.1 5c ★
Starts at the same point as The Breech and takes a counter-diagonal line above the overlap. 3m up, from a good slot below the lower overhangs, go right past a sapling to reach good holds. Move onto the headwall then traverse left to gain a crack (*The Breech*). Continue leftwards, above the overlap, to a good hold and directly to the top.

An excellent crag for a short day or evening, sunny and quick drying.

Approach: From a small open quarry, 400m past the cattle grid, directly below the crag. P SD 2005 9070 Keep right of the scree.

See map page 166.

Descent: Easily to the right.

Western Wall VS, Wallowbarrow (page 171) — JOHN HOLDEN

PSSST! WANNA CLIMB?

In 1990 Al Phizacklea produced an iconic guide to the valley headlined - PSSST! WANNA CLIMB? HAVE A DEKKO AT THIS!

THE DUDDON VALLEY CRAG GUIDE was hand drawn by Al and although it claimed to be Britain's Crappest Guidebook, it was priceless. One unique innovation was the decimalisation of **E** grades – to entertain you, some are reproduced here…

Olive – Far Hill Crag	E1.2
Anchor Handling - Stonestar	E2.1
The Breech – Stonestar	E2.3
Breaker – Burnt Crag	E2.4
Drum Roll – Far Hill Crag	E2.4
Just Good Friends – Stonestar	E2.5
Laypincher – Upper Great Blake Rigg	E2.6
S.P.C. - Burnt Crag	E2.7
The Challenger - Stonestar	E2.8
Double Trouble - Burnt Crag	E3.1
Tirfor Rib - Upper Great Blake Rigg	E3.2
Lagonda – Far Hill Crag	E3.3
Shifter - Burnt Crag	E3.4
Double Gravity – Far Hill Crag	E3.5
Innocenti - Burnt Crag	E3.6
Sparkle in the Rain – Far Hill Crag	E3.8
Bowel Howl - Upper Great Blake Rigg	E4.2
Satyriasis – Far Hill Crag	E4.4
The Burnt Ones - Burnt Crag	E4.5
The Lutine Bell - Upper Great Blake Rigg	E4.7
First of Class – Far Hill Crag	E4.7
Machiavellian Paragon – Far Hill Crag	E4.9
Kleptomaniacs - Upper Great Blake Rigg	E5.0
Burning Desire - Burnt Crag	E5.2
The School of Hard Knocks - Upper Great Blake Rigg	E5.5

WALLOWBARROW CRAG

OS Grid Ref: SD 222 967
Altitude: 210m

Wallowbarrow defines the traditional crag with a selection of good routes in the **VD** to **VS** range. Fast-drying wall climbing on clean and solid rhyolite and a popular refuge for climbers when the higher crags are wet.

Approach: From the bridge over the River Duddon, about 1.5km south of Seathwaite, take the single-track road to High Wallowbarrow Farm. Very generously the farmer allows parking P SD 21830 96173 in return for a charitable donation, the honesty box is on the gate to the farmyard. Walk up a winding track on the wooded hillside.

Alternately, from Seathwaite a footpath near the church leads to High Wallowbarrow Farm.

See map page 166.

West Buttress

The rock is generally good though belays prove scarce near the top.

Descent: To the left.

1 Western Wall 33 m VS 4b ★★

A little gem, exposed and satisfying. It climbs the grey wall on the buttress front on a rising diagonal ramp-line. Start 5m below and right of a large flake, beside a detached-looking block.

LG Sullivan, PE Wilson, J Jenkinson - May 1963

The next three climbs share a common first pitch.

2 Malediction Direct 49 m VS 4c ★★
A fine little climb with some steep moves, following the distinct incut groove of pale coloured rock to the right of *Western Wall*. Start below the middle of the buttress where a broken rib points towards a dry-stone wall.
1 24m Climb the rib to a niche.
2 15m 4c Climb the bulge to the left of the small roof, pulling into the open grooveline and following it steeply, trending left at the top up impending rock.
AJ Simpkin, AH Greenbank - Mar 1959

3 The Plumb 51 m VS ★★
An uncompromising line with a difficult finish.
1 24m Climb the rib to a niche.
2 27m 4c Climb right to the obvious chimney crack surmounting the hanging flake with difficulty.
CJS Bonnington, D Farley - 1964, Direct Finish D Miller, JAA Austin - Jun 1967

4 Bryanston 53 m MVS 4b ★★
A good climb of increasing difficulty with an exhilarating finale.
1 24m Climb the rib of *Malediction Direct*.
2 16m Go 9m diagonally right, following an obvious weakness. Traverse horizontally right and up to a small stance next to a detached block.
3 13m 4b Entering the crack is awkward. Reach a recess, step left and climb the wall directly. Belay well back.
J Smith - Apr1956

5 Thomas 57 m S ★★
Fine climbing and deservedly popular. Start 3m left of the large oak at a well worn patch on the ground.
1 21m Take the crackline steeply up to the right. Move up and then right below perched blocks and up to a ledge and belay.
2 18m The steep cracked wall on the right leads to a large ledge at the top of the pillar.
3 18m An awkward move right onto the wall, then up the exposed and shallow grooves above, well endowed with good holds. Belay well back.
WF Dowlen, D Stroud - Jun 1955

A cracking rightwards girdle, **West Buttress Girdle** MVS ★★, strings together the best pitches starting up *Western Wall* **MVS**.

East Buttress

Good routes on sound rock, if mossy in places.

Descent: To the right, to the gearing-up site below *Wall and Corner*.

6 Nameless 76m MS ★★
A very good climb, exposed and satisfying.
1 32m Climb the prominent groove to a decidedly awkward final section; sparse protection. From the large ledge move up and left a few metres before climbing directly to easy rocks and a stance.
2 18m Climb the shallow groove on the right, passing 2m to the left of a large grass ledge. Climb directly to a good ledge with a flake belay.
3 26m From the higher rock ledge on the right, climb the ramp leftwards for 4m; climb diagonally right to a lovely finish.
WF Dowlen, J Hollin - Jun 1956

7 Digitation 48 m MVS 4b ★★
One of the most popular routes on the crag. Start from the three poised blocks below a clean slab.
1 30m 4b Step off the topmost block climb and to the overlap. Pull boldly over leftwards and continue to a ledge.
2 18m 4b Climb a thin crack in the centre of the steep wall behind the ledge to the horizontal flake. Pleasant walls lead to the top.
DG Heap, JR Amatt, CB Greenhalgh - Apr 1963

8 Agitation 48 m VS 4c ★
A worthwhile companion route to *Digitation*, climbing the wall to the right and breaching the overlap.
C Childs, G Saxon - Aug 1973

9 Trinity Slabs 60 m VD ★★
An excellent climb, high in its grade and offering a couple of 'boulder problems' en route. 12m right of *Agitation* is a stepped buttress. Start left of a flake capped with an overhang.
1 18m The wall and a short shallow corner.
2 12m The bouldery wall on the left leads to a leaning block. Step off this onto a short wall leading to a large ledge - belays over to the right.
3 15m The grooveline on the right is awkward and leads to the next ledge system.
4 15m Make a difficult pull into an incipient groove above, then step right onto the final arête.
1951

(10) Wall and Corner 58 m VD ★

An absorbing climb for its grade and of no mean difficulty in its first 30m. This wall of clean rock, distinguished by a massive flake/overhang in the approximate shape of a blunt handgun, is an attraction in itself. Begin up a short smooth wall near the right-hand end of the crag.

1 10m Climb onto a small rock ledge and continue up the centre of the wall on small polished holds to a large ledge below the 'handgun'.

2 15m Climb the shallow groove and crack (crux) past the left side of the overhang, until easier rocks lead leftwards to a large flake.

3 12m The wall above the flake is climbed for 5m until a short traverse left arrives at a dry-stone wall. Climb past this to a belay by a bridged block.

4 21m Step left off the block, up the steep wall, and bridge back right across the corner to a grassy recess. Follow the right-hand wall of the large corner above to the top.

1951

BRANDY CRAG

OS Grid Ref: SD 226 980
Altitude: 450m

A fantastic crag for confident climbers.

Approach: From the Birks Bridge car park P SD 23530 99548 walk up the forest track taking the bridleway opposite Birks Homestead towards Harter Fell. After 100m, take the left junction, and after a further 250m thrash across to the crag.

See map page 166.

Descent: Either side of the crag, or abseil.

1 **Courvoisier** 12m VD
Climbs the first piece of decent rock.
E Rogers - Oct 2004

2 **Cognac** 12m S ★
Straight up to a grass ledge.
E Rogers, K Forsythe - Oct 2004

3 **Three Barrels** 12m VS 4b
Direct to a crack on the right.
E Rogers, K Forsythe - Oct 2004

4 **Napoleon** 12m HVS 5a
The rib direct and slab.
E Rogers, K Forsythe - Jul 2004

5 **Brandy Snap** 12m HVS 5a ★
A sweet little climb.
E Rogers, K Forsythe - Jul 2004

6 **Don't do Football** 24m E1 5b
A left to right diagonal ramp leads to the overlap; straight through this to the crack. Cross the ledge and climb the wall to the top of the stepped ledges. Up and slightly right to the left end of the heather ledge, then follow the slab on the left.
G Wilks, B McGowan - Jun 2004

7 **Snake** 12m HVS 5a ★
The obvious line diagonally leftwards.
E Rogers, K Forsythe - Oct 2004

8 **Slim Groove** 20m E3 6a ★
Best to use the right rib - small wires. Swing left at the top.
E Rogers, K Forsythe - Jul 2004

9 Stumpy and His Friends 21m E1 5b ★
1 12m 5b Climb a broken groove with a noticeable V-slot at the top.
2 9m 4a The fine crack.
B McGowan, G Wilks - Jun 2004

10 Summer 20m E2 5b ★★★
Start 2m to the left of *The Groove*. Climb direct to finish just right of the prow. Small wires.
P Strong, G Wilks, B McGowan - Jun 2004

11 Solstice 20m E3 5c ★★★
In the centre of the main buttress below an obvious sickle shaped groove. Climb a slim groove to the sickle. Move left and finish direct. Small wires.
P Strong, B McGowan, G Wilks - Jun 2004

12 Duddon Challenge 19m E4 6a
A bold eliminate that straightens *Solstice*.
RO Graham, P Graham - Oct 2004

13 Left Rib 20m E2 5c ★
Follow the arete to finish at a layback flake.
K Forsythe, E Rogers -Jul 2004

14 The Groove 19m HVS 5a ★
B McGowan, G Wilks - Jun 2004

15 Right Wall 12m E1 5b ★★
Not as hard as the one in Wales!
E Rogers, K Forsythe -Jul 2004

16 The Rib 12m HVS 5a
The crack and rib to finish just right of *Right Wall*.
E Rogers, K Forsythe - Oct 2004

17 The Slab on the Right 12m S
E Rogers, K Forsythe - May 2007

Upper Crag

Combine the upper pitches for long routes; or split, with a belay on the halfway ledge.

18 Leaning Tower E1 5b
Some steep pulls up a leaning wall.
E Rogers, K Forsythe - Oct 2004

19 Brandy Sour E1 5b ★
A wall leads to a slim groove which is quite delicate and not without interest!
K Forsythe, E Rogers - Jul 2004

20 Brandy Bitter E1 5b
K Forsythe, E Rogers - Jul 2004

BURNT CRAG

OS Grid Ref: SD 243 991
Altitude: 350m

Definitely the best crag in the valley for the hard climber. Fine lines on steep, compact rock and being south facing it dries quickly.

Burning Desire E5 (page 178) Jon Stevens — Laetitia Sterling

Approach: From the cattle grid P SD 2345 9836 south of Troutal follow the track along the wall through several gates then strike rightwards up the hillside, aiming for a gate in the wall which is hidden behind a small knoll. The crag lies diagonally leftwards up the fellside.

See map page 166.

Descent: Easily on either side.

1 Breaker 24m E2.4 5c ★★
A strenuous route attacking the diagonal crack, then the wall to a chockstone below a prow of rock. Traverse right to a small cave then pull left using the large flake.
RO Graham, G Smith - Jul 1983

2 Double Trouble 27m E3.1 6a ★★
Unyielding climbing tackling the steep wall and difficult final groove.
I Greenwood, A Hyslop, A Phizacklea - Oct 1979

3 Innocenti 30m E3.6 6a ★★★
A sustained climb. Getting into the niche is awkward; the strenuous flake crack leads to a resting foothold. A slanting line leads back right above the overhang; where a good sharp flake continues through the final bulge.
RO Graham, A Hyslop - Oct 1979

4 Shifter 30m E3.4 6a ★★★
A great climb up the central rightwards-facing corner; strenuous and well protected.
I Greenwood - Sep 1979

5 S.P.C. 28m E2.7 5c ★★
A good one-move climb, but a little bold on the crux.
RO Graham, IGreenwood - Sep 1979

6 Burning Desire 30m E5.2 6b ★★★
One of the best pitches in the Lakes. Start below a steep pink groove 8m right of *Shifter.*
A Phizacklea, JL Holden - Apr1989

7 An Alien Heat 26m E5 6b ★★
A blistering route starting below the left-hand end of a sloping glacis - take lots of small wires.
M Radtke, J Cooksey - Jul1989

8 The Burnt Ones 20m E4.5 6b ★
This fine route takes the open corner above the right-hand end of the sloping glacis. Starting the corner is hard, bold and painful!
G Smith, D Hinton - Jul 1985

UPPER GREAT BLAKE RIGG

15 mn

OS Grid Ref: SD 259 996
Altitude: 590m

1. **Laypincher** E2.6 5c ★
2. **Kleptomaniacs** E5 6b ★★
3. **Just Good Friends** E2.5 5c ★★
4. **The Lutine Bell** E4.7 6b ★★
5. **Bowel Howl** E4.2 6a ★★
6. **The School of Hard Knocks** E5.5 6b ★★★
7. **Tirfor Rib** E3.2 5c ★

A hard man's dream - steep, clean, fast drying, sunny, beautifully situated, with some great climbing…

Approach: From the bottom of the Walna Scar track P SD 23975 96818 head towards Grey Friar cross the Seathwaite Tarn dam and steeply up and then right at the 600m contour.

See map page 166.

Descent: Easily to the right facing the crag.

FAR HILL CRAG

OS Grid Ref: SD 259 989
Altitude: 450m

A brilliant crag of superb clean rock. The second best crag in the valley. Well worth a visit. All routes are excellent on perfect and quick drying rock.

Approach: From the bottom of the Walna Scar track P SD 23975 96818 head towards Seathwaite Tarn dam.

See map page 166.

Descent: To the left facing the crag.

1 Olive 22m E1.2 5b ★
The fine jamming crack.
RE Wightman, M Lynch, I Wall - Sep 1987

2 Drum Roll 30m E2.4 5c ★★
A very good pitch.
E Cleasby, R Matheson - Jul 1983

3 Double Gravity 25m E3.5 6a
The sandwiched wall has a stiff start.
A Phizacklea, JL Holden, A Rowell – Apr 1990

4 Sparkle in the Rain 25m E3.8 6a ★★
The steep capped corner can be stubborn. Avoid the wet part by starting up a short groove on the left.
RE Wightman, A Phizacklea - May 1988

5 First of Class 26m E4.7 6a ★★★
A first class climb too! Camalot 2/Friend 2½ needed.
A Phizacklea, A Rowell, JL Holden - Apr 1990

6 Machiavellian Paragon 26m E4.9 6a ★
A bold route up the shallow scoop. Friend 2 low down. The peg is reached with mounting trepidation, after which the difficulties ease.
RE Wightman, A Phizacklea - May 1988

7 Lagonda 25m E3.3 5c ★★
A marvellous pitch up the Y-shaped crack in the centre of the slightly mossy right wall; the final move being the hardest!
E Cleasby, R Matheson - Jul 1983

8 Satyriasis 25m E4.4 6a ★
Good; though poorly protected.
A Phizacklea, B McKinley - Aug 1988

GAITSCALE BUTTRESS

40 mn

OS Grid Ref: NY 253 034
Altitude: 670m

This prominent granite pillar overlooks the head of Gaitscale Gill 2 kms north east of Cockley Beck Farm. The rock is rough and solid, although mossy in some areas.

Approach: Park near the cattle grid P NY 25809 02089; ford the river and a sketchy track is followed northwards alongside the gill.

See map page 182.

Descent: Either end of the crag.

1 Slim Slow Slider 35m S ★

The grooveline improves with height. Start in the grassy recess. Climb steeply onto the lowest rib then trend left and up, keeping left of a short V-groove to reach the base of the main groove. Follow this pleasantly. Where it curves left and peters out into moss, step right to join *Gaitscale Buttress.*

JL Holden, A Phizacklea - May 1993

2 Gaitscale Buttress 33m E1 5b ★

Pleasant and delicate with a few strenuous moves thrown in. Start on a ledge 3m above and right of the grassy recess. Up and left to climb a short groove and the slab above to the steep nose. Follow the prominent crack strenuously through the bulge to a good hold; gain the rib on the left. Climb this to a grass ledge and good belays.

A Phizacklea, JL Holden - May 1993

3 The Masterplan 34m E4 5c ★★

The seemingly blank wall left of *Crack of Dawn* gives a superb, intricate route. Start as for *Crack of Dawn.*

1 26m 5c Using the quartz pocket, climb up and left on good holds to a shallow nut runner in the vague green groove (thin sling on a small spike). Traverse leftwards delicately into the centre of the wall to reach a flake (peg and nut). Pull up to an incut hold (skyhook), then move right to gain a tiny shallow groove; a fingery traverse left leads to a good hold. Pull up onto the large shelf, and a flake belay below the upper rounded pillar.

2 12m 5b Climb the thin crack line directly up the nose and over a bulge, then continue to the top.

A Phizacklea, A Rowell - Aug 1993

4 Crack of Dawn 32m HVS 5a ★

An excellent route which finishes up the rounded pillar above the steep wall. Start 4m left of the dirty corner, below the right-hand of two short green cracks high on the wall. Flake holds give entry to a short groove; climb directly, past the quartz to reach the crack. Follow this to just below the grass, then step right and continue up to a heathery crack. Climb the rounded slab above (sparse protection) to gain a niche, finish directly above.

A Rowell, A Phizacklea - Aug 1993

GAITKINS

OS Grid Ref: NY 257 035
Altitude: 640m

These open clean outcrops arranged in a series of steps above Gaitscale Gill are really worth exploring offering great fun for a sunny day.

Approach: From the summit of Wrynose P NY 27612 02663 follow a path under Long Scar, cut across wet ground to contour round the south flank of Cold Pike.

Plaque Slab (7 to 14m)

1	**Brass Plaque Vandals**	VS 4b
2	**Plaque Attack Direct**	VS
3	**Trench Town Rock**	MS
4	**Reluctant Snowmen**	S
5	**Plaque Wall**	VS 4c
6	**Plaque Arête**	MS
7	**Corner**	VD
8	**Blowing in the Wind**	HVS 5a
9	**Plaque Groove**	VS 4c

Smooth Slabs (10 to15m)

10	**The Mountain Ringlet**	E2 5c
11	**Seriously Smooth**	E3 6a
12	**Smoothly Severe**	S
13	**The Scoop**	S
14	**Nick's Route**	VD
15	**Runny Nose**	D
16	**Snecklifter**	MVS 4b

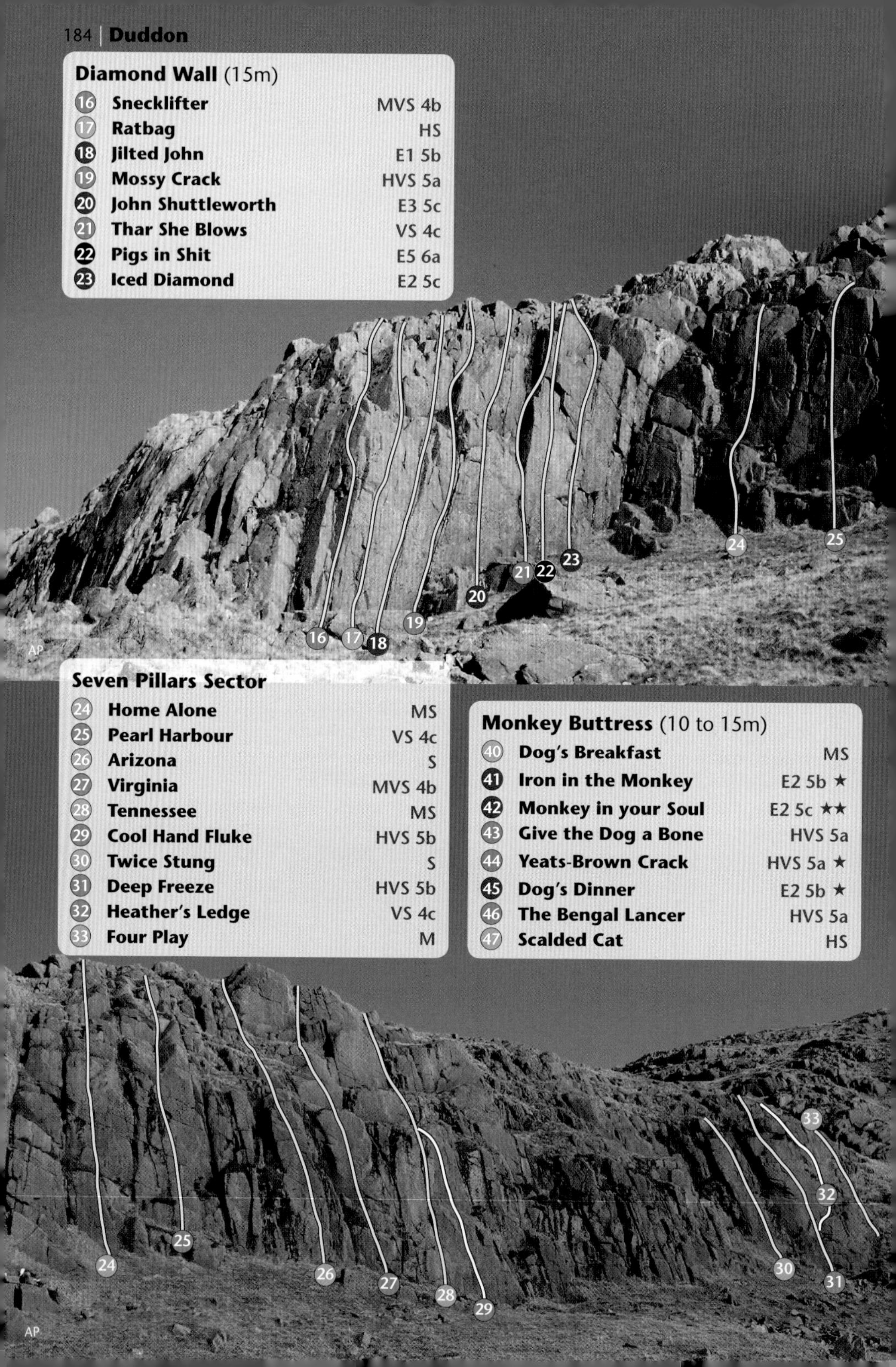

Diamond Wall (15m)

16	**Snecklifter**	MVS 4b
17	**Ratbag**	HS
18	**Jilted John**	E1 5b
19	**Mossy Crack**	HVS 5a
20	**John Shuttleworth**	E3 5c
21	**Thar She Blows**	VS 4c
22	**Pigs in Shit**	E5 6a
23	**Iced Diamond**	E2 5c

Seven Pillars Sector

24	**Home Alone**	MS
25	**Pearl Harbour**	VS 4c
26	**Arizona**	S
27	**Virginia**	MVS 4b
28	**Tennessee**	MS
29	**Cool Hand Fluke**	HVS 5b
30	**Twice Stung**	S
31	**Deep Freeze**	HVS 5b
32	**Heather's Ledge**	VS 4c
33	**Four Play**	M

Monkey Buttress (10 to 15m)

40	**Dog's Breakfast**	MS
41	**Iron in the Monkey**	E2 5b ★
42	**Monkey in your Soul**	E2 5c ★★
43	**Give the Dog a Bone**	HVS 5a
44	**Yeats-Brown Crack**	HVS 5a ★
45	**Dog's Dinner**	E2 5b ★
46	**The Bengal Lancer**	HVS 5a
47	**Scalded Cat**	HS

Monkey Buttress

Purple Slab
48 Lambing Ring MVS 4a
49 Tuppin' Harness HVS 5a
50 Chewing the Cud VS 4c
51 Clean Stepped Arête S ★
48
49
50
51
SH
Winter Sun Amphitheatre (10 to 25m)
52 Plaything E2 5c
53 Winter Sun HS 4a ★
52
53
SH

Furrowed Brow Area
54 Easy Edge VD ★
55 Direct Start VS
56 Faulty Tower HVS 5a ★
57 Tup's Purse E1 5b
58 Furrowed Brow E1 5b
59 Take Three (RPs) E3 6a
60 Lost Generation E2 5c
61 Nicked E2 5c
62 Hand Job VS 4c ★
Half of Call Girl Corner then left to Nicked.
63 Call Girl Corner S
64 Right Wall HVS 5a
54
55
56
57
58
59
60
61
63
64
JH
Duddon
Dream Buttress (10 to 20m)
65 Crinkle Cracks VD
66 Gale Force S
67 Paul I S ★
68 Solo Slab VD ★
69 Gearless VD ★
70 Picasso's Nose HVS ★
71 Paul II MVS ★
72 Thin Horizontal E1 5b ★★
65
66
67
68
69
70
71
72
JH

SCAFELL & WASDALE

Scafell is the spiritual home of traditional climbing in Britain and offers some of the best, boldest and most beautiful climbing to be found in these Islands. Dark, foreboding, complex Scafell Crag holds some of the most historic routes. In contrast, the magnificent barrel-shaped East Buttress is home to the best mountain rock-climbing above **VS** in England; and also some of the hardest, with the technically-demanding *Welcome to the Cruel World* and the heart-stopping *Talbot Horizon* **E9** setting the upper limit at present.

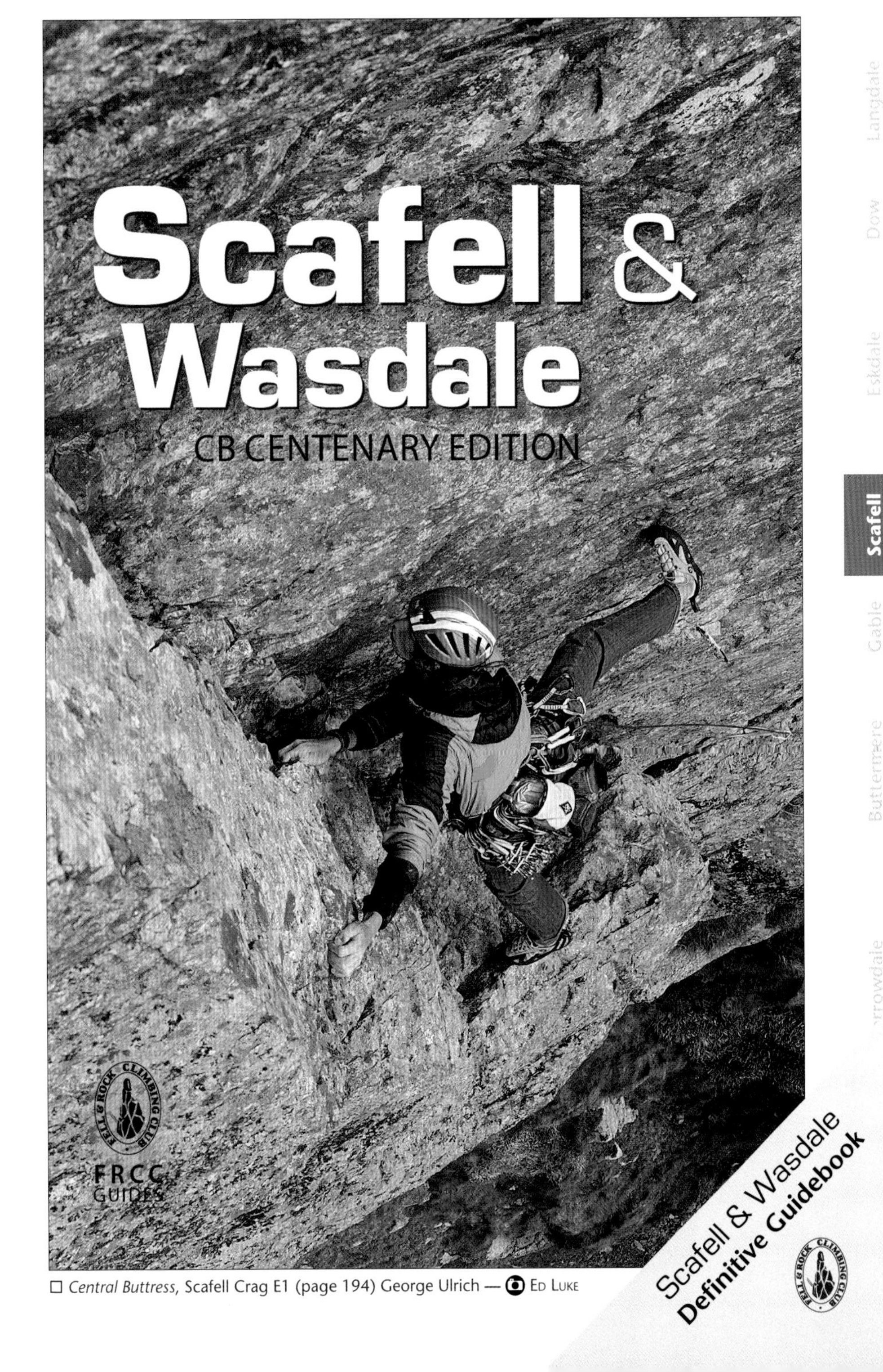

☐ *Central Buttress*, Scafell Crag E1 (page 194) George Ulrich — Ed Luke

SCAFELL CRAG

OS Grid Ref: NY 209 068
Altitude: 790m

"There's nobbut a fleein' thing cud get up theer!"
Will Ritson – the world's greatest liar…

A magnificent crag for climbers of all grades, with a long and illustrious history enhancing an already impressive setting.

Pisgah Buttress Direct S (page 197) Peter Metcalfe — CATH SULLIVAN

Scafell lies close to the hub of the district and may be reasonably accessed walking from any of the nearby valleys for a day's climbing, yet Wasdale remains overwhelmingly the most popular base. The head of this remote valley offers a hotel, outdoor shop, toilets, and campsites.

Camping: Wild camping options at Hollow Stones or on the grassy flat area just beyond the Woolworth Boulder (water). Also directly below *May Day Direct* on the East Buttress, or the flat grassy spur directly opposite the crag.

Approach: From the NT car park and campsite at the head of Wastwater P NY 182 076, 1km south-west of Wasdale Head.

See maps page 188 and 204.

Descent: Leftwards to reach Mickledore by abseil is safest. From the top of the crag, walk across and down leftwards until a large shelving platform on the right (looking out) can be reached. Go left (looking out) to a large perched block 10m directly above the crest of Mickledore; abseil (thread). See page 204.

Central Buttress

This large, clean face is the highlight of Scafell Crag. The rock is generally sound and reliable on the trade routes, loose material will be found on the ledges, the aspect and some seepage produces areas of lichen or moss.

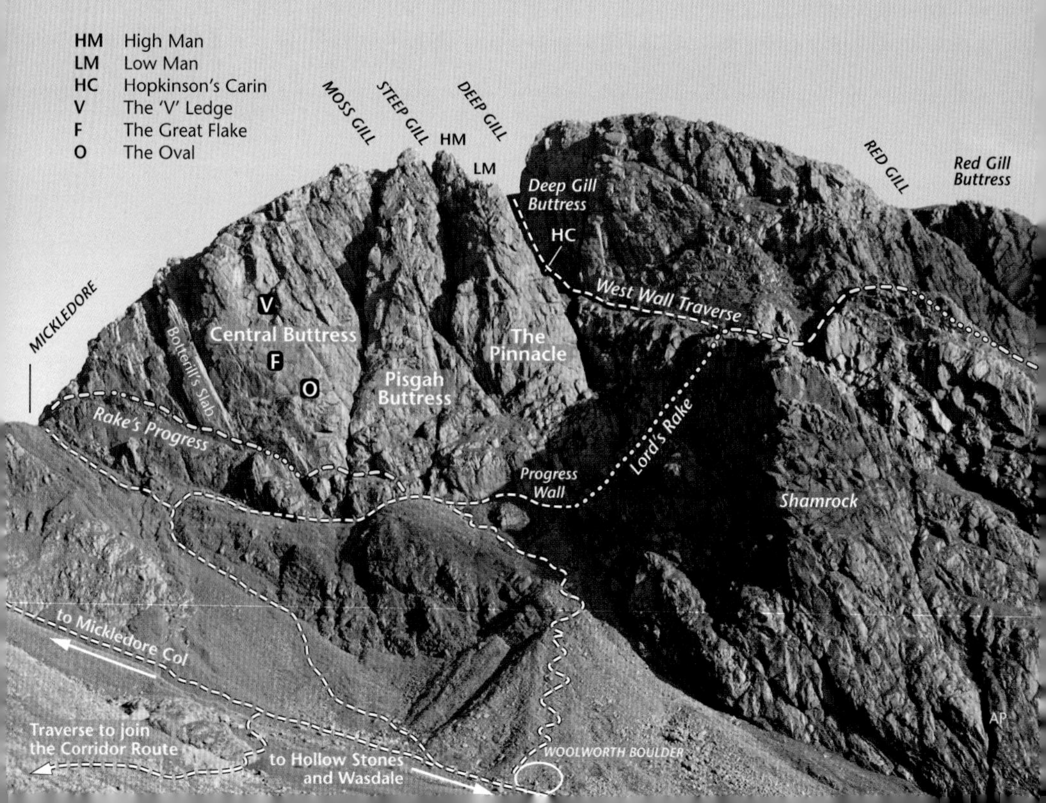

1 Mephisto 30m E4 6a ★★
A devilish route up the thin cracklines between *Shadowfax* and the left arête.
M Berzins, C Sowden - Aug 1983

2 Black Rider 38m E5 6b ★★
An excellent face climb.
A Mitchell, N Pike - Jul 2013

3 Shadowfax 42m E4 6a ★★
A sustained wall climb with the crux near the top.
P Botterill, S Clegg - Jul 1976

4 Botterill's Slab 87m VS 4c ★★★
A compelling line of huge historical significance – outstanding. The route dries quickly and is deservedly popular.
1 15m 4b Climb a short chimney and continue to the foot of the slab.
2 36m 4c Climb the slab by its left edge to a platform on the arête. Continue up a thin crack to belay in a recess on the left.
3 36m Climb the left edge of the slab above, keeping out of the gully on the right.
FW Botterill, H Williamson, JE Grant - Jun 1903

5 The White Wizard 96m E3 5c ★★★
A magical route – sustained, varied and interesting climbing, culminating in a tremendous finale.
1 15m 4b P1 of *Botterill's Slab.*
2 24m 5c *Botterill's Slab* for a few metres. Make a long step right and follow a steep crack to a ledge (peg). Climb the shallow corner on the right, until a move left and a crack lead to a ledge.
3 20m 5c Continue up the corner to an overhanging crack leading to a good ledge.
4 15m 5b From the right-hand end of the ledge, move right and up to gain the bottom of a prominent crack. Climb this to a ledge.
5 22m 5c Pull round the arête on the right (peg) and climb the dirty awkward groove on the right to a small ledge. Step up delicately round the bulge to the right to easy ground.
CJS Bonington, N Estcourt - 1971; FFA M Berzins, G Higginson - 1976

6 Ringwraith 94m E6 6b ★★★
A spectral route powering up the leaning wall and slender hanging corner to the right of *The White Wizard.* When clean it is the best route of its grade in the Lakes.
1 18m 4a P1 of *The Nazgul.*
2 30m 6b Climb the short ramp on the left to a bulge (nut), a long reach gains a series of layaway holds (peg). Climb directly up the smooth wall to a jug. Step left (runner) to a small ledge above, then continue directly on better holds to a pinnacle belay.
3 10m Easily up the ramp to belay on a ledge.
4 36m 6a Traverse right to the obvious overhanging corner and follow this strenuously to a dirty groove, follow this to a small ledge. Step up delicately round the bulge to the right to easy ground.
M Berzins, RH Berzins, C Sowden - May 1977

7 The Nazgul 84m E3 5c ★★★

This tremendous climb cleaves a direct line the full height of the crag. A superbly strenuous second pitch contrasts with the delightful, airy last pitch. Start at a short crack just right of *Botterill's Slab*.

1 18m 4a Climb the crack and ascend easily right to a flake belay below an obvious thin green crack slanting left.

2 24m 5c Step left and climb the arduous crack to a resting place in a niche. Swing out left on to a narrow slab and follow it for a few metres until it is possible to climb the wall on the right into the obvious deep corner. Belay by large flakes.

3 12m 5b Reach a flake forming a detached pinnacle. Stand on this, then step right into a surprisingly delicate scoop and climb up to a good ledge.

4 30m 5a Climb the thin crack/ramp on the left. Continue up to a bulge then pull over right to gain the higher parallel ramp line. Follow this in a superb situation to the top.

L Brown, K Jackson - Jul 1966; FFA P Botterill, S Clegg - Jun 1975

8 Central Buttress 124m E1 5a ★★★

This route can justifiably claim to be the most famous rock climb in the country. Start left of the foot of Moss Gill.

1 42m 5a Climb the corner, then the rib and go up to a large ledge below a triangular roof. Traverse left for 4m to a corner and climb this and the wall above, bearing left, to The Oval.

2 25m 5a Marr's Variation - Climb to the foot of The Great Flake and continue for 5m to a sloping ledge on the left. An exposed traverse leads left for 2m onto the front face of the flake. Step up slightly left and continue to a flat hold, then move awkwardly up before trending right to a shallow crack and the top of the flake. Follow the flake left to reach a spacious ledge - Jeffcoat's Ledge.

3 33m 4c Walk along the ledge and climb an easy ramp to a block. Descend a little and traverse delicately right past a small pinnacle into a corner. Climb the corner and traverse easily right to The V-ledge.

4 24m 5a Climb the thin crack and gangway on the left for about 5m, traverse right into an open corner. Climb the corner to its top and exit left. Alternatively, starting from the left-hand end of the ledge follow the fine top pitch of *The Nazgul*.

SW Herford, GS Sansom, CF Holland - Apr 1914
Marr's Variation: T Marr, M Tooke - Jul 1990

9 The New and Superior Start 40m VS 4b

Made during the second ascent this start was immediately adopted as the normal start, remaining so for 90 years. Start 10m left of Moss Gill at the foot of a leftwards-slanting ramp above a marked step on the Rake's Progress. Climb a narrow slanting ramp to its top. Climb up easily and traverse left to a crack which leads to the left-hand end of a large ledge (The Oval). Traverse right to a belay below the obvious flake crack.

CD Frankland, B Beetham - Aug 1921

10 The Great Flake 26m E3 5c

The original way. Attaining a layback position is an extremely strenuous and committing procedure.

11 Saxon 108m E2 5c ★★★

A magnificent climb - a modern classic with a committing and strenuous main pitch. Start as for the *Central Buttress New and Superior Start*, just right of a short rock step.

1 30m 5c Climb the ramp for 8m, move right into a shallow corner and make a steep traverse right to a corner on the left-hand side of a triangular roof. Continue up the corner and trend right to belay below a corner.

2 39m 5c Climb the corner and move 2m left (flake). Continue up the steepening wall and then climb diagonally right to the arête, and a small ledge. Tiny, stepped ledges lead left, then climb straight up to the obvious left-trending crack. Climb the crack (often wet) and the groove above to belay on the left.

3 39m 5b Climb the mossy left-facing corner-crack behind and continue to a second short corner, climb this to below an overhang and pull right. Step left onto the headwall above and climb to the arête, and the top.

J Eastham, E Cleasby - Jul 1976; p1 R Matheson, E Cleasby - Jul 1976

Moss Gill is the prominent deep gully to the right of *Central Buttress*. Scramble up the cleaner rocks on the right.

12 Anglo 78m E1 5b ★

A direct eliminate to the left of *Moss Gill Grooves* in a fine, exposed position. Start as for *Moss Gill Grooves*.

1 30m 5b Traverse left onto the arête and climb to a good ledge. Continue directly up the arête above to a stance.

2 30m 5a Move up, then left onto the face. Continue steeply in the same line to gain a ledge, then move up and slightly right to a traverse line. A short groove above leads to a large stance on *Moss Gill Grooves*.

3 18m P4 of *Moss Gill Grooves*.

RJ Kenyon, C King - Jun 1995

13 Moss Gill Grooves 79m MVS 4c ★★★

A magnificent, delicate climb following the slanting groove just right of the main face. The crucial

Foxshooter E4
Central Buttress
Original Finish VS
The V-ledge
Jeffcoat's Ledge
The Look-Out
Foxshooter E4
The Oval
Botterill's Slab
MOSS GILL
MOSS GILL

sections are short and well protected. Start from Moss Gill, about 25m above The Rake's Progress, where a slanting groove runs up to the left.

1 17m The groove leads to a good ledge at the same horizontal level as The Oval. The overhanging block on the right is climbed to a ledge below the main corner.

2 20m 4c Climb 3m up the corner and traverse delicately left to a small ledge. Ascend the arête leading back to the groove. Go up this and the narrow slab, then traverse right into the next groove, arriving at The Look-Out.

3 24m 4a Wander serenely up the slab ahead first on its right, then the left, and finally straight up to belay in a gully.

4 18m Climb the left wall of the gully for 5m and break out to a large ledge on the left. The steep wall above is delicate at its start and leads to the summit ridge.

HM Kelly, B Eden-Smith, JB Kilshaw - Jul 1926

14 Slab and Groove Route 72m VS 4c ★★

A fine route with a superb first pitch. Start up the big slab on the left side of Moss Gill, opposite Tennis Court Wall at the top of p2 of *Moss Gill.*

1 33m 4c Climb the groove on the right side of the slab for 6m, then traverse left to the foot of a thin crack which is climbed to a pocket near the arête. Follow the edge for a couple of metres and traverse left into a groove, which is climbed until level with a recess on the left. Go back right into a corner immediately above the overhangs that cap the slab.

2 39m 4a Follow the groove then easily to the top.

RJ Birkett, L Muscroft - Aug 1948

15 Central Buttress Girdle 174m HVS 5a ★★

Straps some excellent pitches together; imaginative alternatives can be found that reduce the grade to **VS**.

1 15m 4b P1 of *Botterill's Slab.*

2 27m 4b Climb p2 of *Botterill's Slab* until a very narrow ledge leads right into the chimney, and beyond to a ledge in an impending corner.

3 18m 5a Swing out and mantelshelf right on to a ledge on the arête. An awkward move leads to a narrow ledge, which is followed to join *Central Buttress* half-way along p3.

4 15m 4c Descend a little and traverse delicately right past a small pinnacle into a corner. Climb the corner and traverse easily right to The V-ledge.

5 21m 4b Continue right to a junction with *Moss Gill Grooves* p4, which is descended to a sloping stance.

6 24m 4c Descend the slab, then move right. Climb a groove in the slab until an exposed hand-traverse right can be made round the rib. Descend a groove to a stance.

7 12m 4a Descend to a junction with *Slab and Groove Route.* Follow this to its first stance.

8 18m 5a Traverse along a narrow sloping ledge on the lip of the overhang, go round a nose and continue along the fault line until it ends. Move right to easier ground – *Moss Gill.*

9 24m Take the easy slabs on the left. Then the Collie Exit to *Moss Gill.*

CJS Bonington, M Thompson - Aug 1971

16 Ring of Air 187m E2 5b ★★★

Enjoyable and exposed climbing, with a magnificent finale, covering more new ground than the original girdle.

1, 2 & 3 60m Follow the original *Central Buttress Girdle* to join *Central Buttress* half-way along p3 above the ramp.

4 9m Climb down the ramp of *Central Buttress* and across to the left side of the Great Flake.

5 24m 5b Traverse the top of the Great Flake right nearly to its end. Climb up into the obvious horizontal crack and follow this right, savouring the exposure, across the wall to *Moss Gill Grooves.* A really enjoyable pitch.

6 30m 5b Climb down *Moss Gill Grooves* for 4m to just above its first crux. Traverse right and across into the obvious wide crack at a small chock-stone. Move across to a ledge. Climb down for 2m and across a groove to the stance at the top of p1 of *Slab and Groove Route.* Follow p8 of the original Girdle into Moss Gill.

7, 8 & 9 64m 5a Climb p1, 2 & 3 of *Clockwork Orange.*

M Berzins, C Sowden - Aug 1983

17 Moss Gill 120m S ★★★

A route for all seasons; climb it in any conditions, by one of many variations. The usual start is from The Rake's Progress directly below the beetling, mossy, dripping cave, although there is a chimney/chock-stone pitch of 10m below. The first two pitches can be avoided by fairly straightforward scrambling up the clean slabs to the right, but this misses much of the fun.

1 20m Move up to a mossy chimney, and climb the wall on its left to a platform under a vile, wet cave. Avoid this by moving right to a ledge and block belay.

2 30m Climb the clean wall rising left back into the gully, and follow this to another chimney which leads to a belay below another high mossy cave.

3 8m Tennis Court Wall. Climb the impending, broken crack in the steep right wall of the gully. Belay on the right.

4 8m A delicate traverse across a slab leads left into the gill and a walk into the back of a cave.

5 17m Climb into the roof of the cave and go left through The Attic Window above the large chock-stone. A thin traverse left (The Collie Step) leads to a dirty groove. Step left and climb up into The Amphitheatre.
6 27m The Collie Exit lies up the sweep of broken slabs on the left. Start 5m left of the chimney up a blunt rib past a small pedestal to a crack that leads to large blocks at 15m. Traverse left and climb an easy chimney.
7 10m The short corner on the left.
JN Collie, G Hastings, JW Robinson - Dec 1892

(18) Clockwork Orange 64m HVS 5a ★★
Worth a special visit. Best reached by abseil.
1 23m 5a Climb the chimney until the slab on the left can be gained move up to a groove leading to a ledge (peg).
2 33m 5a Climb the left-hand of three small grooves above the belay to a ledge. Ascend the steep wall left, then go back to the right to another groove. Climb this and a gangway to a grass ledge.
3 8m 4c Climb the steep corner to the top.
MJ Burbage, W Young - May 1973

Pisgah

Good rock and interesting climbing, despite a broken and vegetated appearance.

Descent: Left and abseil to Mickledore, or right to Deep Gill and Lord's Rake.

(1) The Gripe 57m HVS 5a ★
A steep route making the best use of the excellent rock high on the left side. The difficulties are short and well-protected. Start from just below the cave at the top of p3 of *Moss Gill*.
1 12m 4a Move to a ledge on the right below a groove, climb this to a grass ledge on the right.
2 33m 5a From the right-hand end of the ledge continue up a groove for 6m, then traverse left for 3m below a small overhang. Climb directly to below the steep crack at the right-hand edge of the block. Climb the crack to the top of the crevassed block.
3 12m 5a Climb the centre of the steep wall behind the crevasse. Scrambling remains.
R Valentine, J Wilkinson, D Pogson - Sep 1971

(2) Pisgah Buttress Direct 95m S ★★
A very fine route weaving up the centre of the buttress. Start near the middle of the face at a right-facing, shallow corner.
1 18m Climb the left-hand of two corners and continue slightly left. Delicate moves up a rib on the right lead to easier walls; follow these to a ledge and flake belay on the right.
2 21m Climb the slab above, then make a short upward traverse to the right under some doubtful looking blocks. Continue up a corner, a staircase now leads to a deep crevasse on the right overlooking Steep Gill.
3 10m Traverse left along a horizontal ledge to the Fives Court and belay beneath a corner-crack.
4 19m Climb the awkward corner-crack. Easy slabs follow which lead to blocks on the edge of the buttress overlooking Steep Gill.
5 27m Starting with a difficult move to a ledge, follow the ridge above to its end. Scramble up easy-angled slabs.
OG Jones, GD Abraham, AP Abraham - Apr 1898

(3) Hilarity 83m HVS 5b ★
An interesting direct line up the steep right-hand side of the buttress. Start 7m left of *Bos'n's Buttress* at the edge of the grass ledge.
1 38m 5b Move left onto a clean slab and climb directly to a large grass ledge. A steep, fingery wall above leads to another small ledge, where a vague groove continues directly up to a belay on top of a detached pinnacle.
2 18m 5b Climb a slabby groove running up to the overhangs above. Pull round the left-hand side of these and continue directly up steep ground until a shallow groove leads to a block belay on the edge of the buttress.
3 27m P5 of *Pisgah Buttress Direct*.
M Morrison, M Fowler - Summer 1976

(4) Bos'n's Buttress 92m VS 4c ★
A good route when dry, which closely follows the right edge of Pisgah Buttress. Scramble up to the foot of an open V-groove, 3m left of a conspicuous grass chimney line, at the right-hand side of the buttress.
1 26m 4c Climb the groove and continue up the steep crack to a grassy stance.
2 12m 4a Climb the deep chimney splitting the wall on the right of the arête. At its top, a short traverse left leads to a rock ledge.
3 21m 4b Go up the edge for a short way, then traverse right to the foot of a twisting crack. Up this, then a short slab and wall to a pinnacle.
4 33m 4a Climb a short wall and continue up the arête until a move right can be made to a steep wall and a finish up the arête above. Scrambling remains.
HI Banner, LJ Griffin - Aug 1959

Collier's Chimney
MOSS GILL
STEEP GILL
Pisgah
1 The Gripe HVS 5a
2 Pisgah Buttress Direct S
3 Hilarity HVS 5b
4 Bos'n's Buttress VS 4c
Moses Trod S
Collie Step
CAVE
Tennis Court Wall
MOSS GILL
STEEP GILL
Moses Trod S
AP

Scafell Pinnacle

Magnificent rock, very clean, solid, sunny and fast drying.

Descent: The Pinnacle has two summits, High Man and Low Man. Most of the routes lead to Low Man. High Man is reached by the stunning Knife-Edge Arête (40m **M**). Descending into Jordan Gap (10m **M**), the cleft which separates High Man from the top of Pisgah Buttress, allows an easy traverse left to the top of the mountain.

Deep Gill and Lord's Rake: Take care to avoid the steep direct descent from Jordan Gap into Deep Gill (*Professor's Chimney* **D**), instead, enter the gill at its head and descend loose scree for about 80m until it opens out by an impressive chimney on the left (looking out). The small cairned hump on the true left side of the gully bed indicates the start of the West Wall Traverse. Go down this until it meets Lord's Rake. ⚠ Lord's Rake is loose and unstable - take great care especially when it is busy. Alternatively, Mickledore can be gained by trending leftwards crossing the top of the crag to pick up a faint rocky track leading down to the slabby area and abseil.

The first five routes start from the bed of Steep Gill, easily reached by scrambling up the lower rocks.

1 Slingsby's Chimney Route 97m VD ★★
The easiest way up The Pinnacle, this route has a fine, classic atmosphere and good situations. Only **VD** for a few metres at the start of p2, the rest is **M**. Start about 60m up Steep Gill, below where it steepens and narrows.
1 28m Easy rocks, ledges and slabs on the right wall of the gill lead to The Crevasse. Step awkwardly across this and climb a short slab to the foot of Slingsby's Chimney.
2 36m Climb the chimney - the undercut start soon relents. From its top scramble to the summit of Low Man.
3 33m The Knife-Edge Arête is ascended, followed by fine climbing up the crest to reach High Man.
WC Slingsby, G Hastings, E Hopkinson, WP Haskett Smith - Jul 1888

2 Leftovers 94m VS 4b ★
Start in a big corner on the lower edge of Steep Gill, to the left of and slightly below *Hopkinson's Gully*. The top pitch is distinctly awkward, and has been the scene of several epics.
1 18m 4b Climb the steep corner for 12m and continue directly to a grassy nook.
2 23m 4b Climb the groove to its top. Continue up and right to The Waiting Room on *Jones' Route Direct*.
3 19m 4b Follow the green crack and its continuation for 9m to a ledge overlooking Steep Gill. Step right, and traverse into the chimney below The Crevasse. Climb this to belay below Slingsby's Chimney.
4 34m 4a Climb the crack left of the chimney to a slab leading left, avoiding a thin, smooth slab in the wall on the right. From the top move right and scramble to the top of Low Man.
R Bennett, R Lavender - Aug 1972

3 The Left Edge 48m VS 4c ★
A worthwhile route giving steep crack climbing, but slow to dry. Start in a big corner on the lower edge of Steep Gill.
1 30m 4c Climb the steep corner for 12m, move right up a slanting corner then onto easier ground leading to the foot of an obvious corner. Follow this and move right to gain the upper edge. Easy grass ledges lead right for 5m to a small stance overlooking *Hopkinson's Gully*.
2 18m 4c Straight above is a crack at the side of a huge flake. Climb this and continue up the crack above until a line of good holds can be reached on the right, follow these diagonally left to The Waiting Room.
3 19m 4b Follow the green crack and its continuation for 9m to a ledge overlooking Steep Gill. Step right, and traverse into the chimney below The Crevasse. Climb this to belay below Slingsby's Chimney.
4 34m 4a As *Leftovers*.
LO Kendall, DW English - Whit 1960

The routes tackling the front of The Pinnacle start from The Pinnacle Terrace, a series of broken grassy ledges running across the foot of the face, easily reached by scrambling from the left.

4 Bushwhacker 90m E2 5c ★★
An interesting route on good, clean rock which eventually finishes up the rounded rib to the right of Slingsby's Chimney. Start just left of the base of *Hopkinson's Gully*.
1 26m 5c Climb awkwardly into the scoop above, then move left and climb a fine crack, continue to a ledge on the right.
2 18m 4c *The Left Edge* p2.
3 46m 5b Step right across the slab of *Hopkinson's Gully* to gain the left-hand edge of the upper slab. Climb this until level with the foot of Slingsby's Chimney, then pull up and right to break out across the headwall, above the two dark niches.
A Phizacklea, R Knight - Jul 1984

5 Hopkinson's Gully 54m MVS 4b ★★★

An excellent delicate route on good rock which follows the well-defined, shallow, open corner running up the centre of the buttress. Sustained, with spaced protection on the first section. Start from the extreme left end of the Pinnacle Terrace at the foot of a corner guarded by a 2m wall, which has a little pyramid of rock to its left.

1 24m 4b Climb the short wall into the corner. Continue with interest until this becomes a square chimney that leads to a ledge on the right.

2 21m 4a Follow the shallow bed of the gully, finishing up a wide crack which splits the slab forming the left-hand flank of the gully.

3 9m The chimney above leads to The Crevasse on *Slingsby's Chimney Route*, follow this to the summit.

SW Herford, GS Sansom - Jun 1912

6 Low Man by the Jubilee Line 104m HVS 5a ★★

Contains some thin climbing on immaculate rock. Start 6m right of *Hopkinson's Gully*.

1 25m 4c Step off the square block onto the wall, then traverse left into a short corner which leads to the rib right of *Hopkinson's Gully*. Move up and step right then follow a short groove to an easy rib which leads to the belay overlooking the groove of *Hopkinson's Gully*.

2 45m 5a Go straight up, following a thin crack to below a steepening, where a rising flake leads right to a grass ledge (runner). Traverse immediately left to reach a small rock spike just above the steepening. Continue directly to reach the detached block in the centre of the face, then step right and climb up to a small overlap. Traverse left, with difficulty, to the rib which leads to the ledge below Slingsby's Chimney.

3 34m 5a Climb the corner just left of the chimney to reach a thin, smooth slab. Climb this to an awkward finish right, then scramble to the top of Low Man.

A Phizacklea, JL Holden - May 2012

7 Jones' Route Direct from Lord's Rake 54m HS ★★

This classic line runs diagonally left from the bottom right of The Pinnacle reached by scrambling up slabs and ledges, from the Pinnacle Terrace, to some detached blocks and a good thread on the edge overlooking Deep Gill.

1 15m The Gangway. Go delicately up to stand on the slabby ramp, then follow this left and continue up a slab to a grassy niche. Care is needed to protect the second.

2 21m Go straight up, making for a rock scar at 9m. Step left into a shallow corner, climb this to a vibrating flake, then cross diagonally left to The Waiting Room.

3 9m Climb up into the cave on the right. A triangular ledge projects from its roof, the mantelshelf move onto this gives the traditional, precarious, entertaining crux. The Toe Traverse follows and leads to a wide crack. Or, avoid all the excitement by making a hand-traverse from the cave.

4 9m P3 of *Hopkinson's Gully*.

OG Jones, GT Walker - Apr 1898

8 Direct from Lord's Rake to Hopkinson's Cairn 45m S 4a ★★

A popular route which provides excellent slab climbing of a sustained nature. Start at the thread.

1 15m P1 of *Jones' Route Direct from Lord's Rake*.

2 18m Climb the shallow corner on the right, through a bulge and continue directly up a second left-facing corner where a steep move leads to some doubtful flakes. Step up and right to a good ledge - Moss Ledge.

3 12m 4a Climb the steep slab ahead, Herford's Slab, bearing left to reach Hopkinson's Cairn Ledge; belay on the left.

Continue to the top by a traverse left to The Crevasse and take *Leftovers* p4, or climb *Low Man from Hopkinson's Cairn*.

SW Herford, GS Sansom - Apr 1912

9 Moss Ledge Direct and Jones' Arête 93m VS 4c ★★★

One of the finest outings of its standard in the Lake District. Start 6m left of the edge of Deep Gill at the top of a grassy trod, at the foot of a small buttress.

1 12m The face of the small buttress is climbed to reach a grass ledge.

2 9m 4c A couple of metres to the left, a bold rib on the wall leads, with difficulty, to a stance.

3 15m 4b Follow a diagonal fault cutting up through a nose on the right and step onto slabs which are followed to Moss Ledge.

4 12m 4a Climb the steep slab ahead, Herford's Slab, bearing slightly left, then back right to Hopkinson's Cairn Ledge.

5 27m 4c The rock overlooking Deep Gill is climbed to a short shallow corner - The Bad Corner. This leads to a sloping ledge on the edge of the buttress.

6 18m 4a *Jones' Arête* is poorly protected however you approach it. Go straight up on the left to the top of Low Man.

A cast of venerable explorers 1896/1919/1925

1 Slingsby's Chimney Route VD
2 Leftovers VS 4b
3 The Left Edge VS 4c
4 Bushwhacker E2 5c
5 Hopkinson's Gully MVS 4b
6 Low Man by the Jubilee Line HVS 5a
7 Jones' Route Direct ... HS
8 Direct from Lord's Rake ... S 4a
9 Moss Ledge Direct ... VS 4c
10 Zenith VS 4c
11 Right-Hand Edge ... HVS 5a
12 Low Man ... VD
LOW MAN
DEEP GILL
Slingsby's Chimney
STEEP GILL
The Crevasse
W The Waiting Room
M Moss Ledge
H Herford's Slab
Hopkinson's Cairn
West Wall Traverse
Waiting Room frm Steep Gill VS
The Gangway
STEEP GILL
THE PINNACLE TERRACE
AP
Scafell

10 Zenith 98m VS 4c ★★

A direct route on lovely clean rock. Start at a small slab in a corner, below a right-slanting diagonal fault, 4m left of the edge of Deep Gill.

1 16m 4b Climb the slab, crossing the diagonal crack onto a higher slab. Follow its right edge to a ledge.

2 27m 4c Step right and ascend to the left-hand end of an overlap, crossing The Gangway of *Jones' Route Direct*, follow a crack line which continues past the left-hand edge of the next overlap. Pull over a bulge and ascend the left-hand of two corners to a belay.

3 12m 4c Gain a small slab on the right and follow this steeply onto the slab above. Continue to Hopkinson's Cairn Ledge.

4 18m 4c Climb the slabby wall and cracks to gain the left-hand side of a large flake/block. From its top right, move left to gain and climb a short but prominent groove to a ledge.

5 25m 4c Move up and climb directly up the rough wall to a shallow groove, continue to the top of Low Man.

GL Swainbank, C Read - May 1996

11 Right-Hand Edge and Pinnacle Face Direct 91m HVS 5a ★★

Another very fine route which gives interesting and rather intimidating climbing throughout.

1 25m 4b Climb onto The Gangway of *Jones' Route Direct*. Gain the slab above, and continue directly through a break onto the next slab. Climb this diagonally right until Deep Gill is overlooked; large cam belay.

2 20m 5a Step round right on to the wall overlooking Deep Gill and ascend diagonally right, up a series of overlaps, move left to the edge and climb up to Hopkinson's Cairn Ledge.

3 28m 4c From the left-hand end of the ledge, step up and traverse horizontally left for 12m to the large block on Sansom's Traverse. From the left-hand edge of the block, climb the grooved wall, delicately, to the edge of the platform under Slingsby's Chimney.

4 18m 5b Step down and traverse right on to a slab below two dark niches. Step up through the overhangs between the niches onto another slab. From its right-hand end, ascend very delicately to easy ground.

JJS Allison, CJF Rowbotham - May 1961

12 Low Man from Hopkinson's Cairn 51 m VD ★★

The easiest way off Hopkinson's Cairn Ledge.

1 21m Start from the centre of the ledge. Climb up a shallow groove left of the arête which trends left up to a ledge, and then follow a shallow corner above to a difficult finish onto a grass ledge on the left.

2 30m A slanting gangway to the left, followed by scrambling, leads to Low Man.

E Hopkinson, C Hopkinson, A Hopkinson, WN Tribe - Sep 1887

Scafell Pinnacle - Deep Gill

Approach: Best reached by following Lord's Rake and the West Wall Traverse to a ledge below the length of The Upper Pinnacle Slabs that overlook Deep Gill.

13 Central Route – Deep Gill Slabs 51m HS 4a ★★

Start at the base of the blunt arête where the Deep Gill wall meets the wall coming down from Old Professor's Chimney

1 18m Go diagonally left across the slab, crossing a small overlap before trending left to reach a pile of blocks.

2 18m 4a Climb straight up the slab to a niche in the overhangs at 9m. An awkward pull over leads onto a narrow slab on the face on the right, which leads to a grass ledge.

3 15m The steep overlapping slabs immediately left of the grassy groove give an interesting finish.

HM Kelly, GS Bower, REW Pritchard - Aug 1920

14 High Man by the Central Line 48m HVS 4c ★★★

A long, sustained pitch on amazing rock. Climb a short crack to a slab, climb directly up through a vague V-niche in an overlap to a second overlap. Pull over left of a moss streak and continue to a vague nose which is climbed directly to a break below an overhang. Climb directly onto the headwall and continue straight up to reach High Man.

A Phizacklea, T Moore, JL Holden - Jun 2013

15 Woodhead's Climb 45m MS ★★★

One of the best climbs of its length in the area. Start at the base of the blunt arête.

1 24m Follow the arête, delicately at first, easier on the right. Continue to a grassy recess beneath the huge overhangs.

2 21m Herford's Finish - climb into a corner on the left and cross the slabs above to the right to a small ledge. Continue straight up for a few metres, over a bulge, and trend left to turn the next overhang. Steep and exposed, but well protected. Follow easier rocks up the crest to High Man.

AG Woodhead, WL Collinson - Aug 1907

16 Thompson's Route 45m VD ★★

Short route, big impact, enhanced by pitiless exposure and worrying holds. Start at the bottom of Professor's Chimney.

1 18m Climb the chimney for 6m, then diagonally left, over bulging rock, to a recess beneath huge overhangs.

2 13m Traverse left to splintered rocks and continue traversing for a further 5m. Surmount the bulge above on excellent holds to reach grass ledges.

3 14m Climb the slabs on the right of the grassy groove to High Man.

PS Thompson, PA Thompson - Jun 1900

THE EAST BUTTRESS

OS Grid Ref: NY 214 067
Altitude: 750m

Dyad E3 (page 207) Andy Mitchell

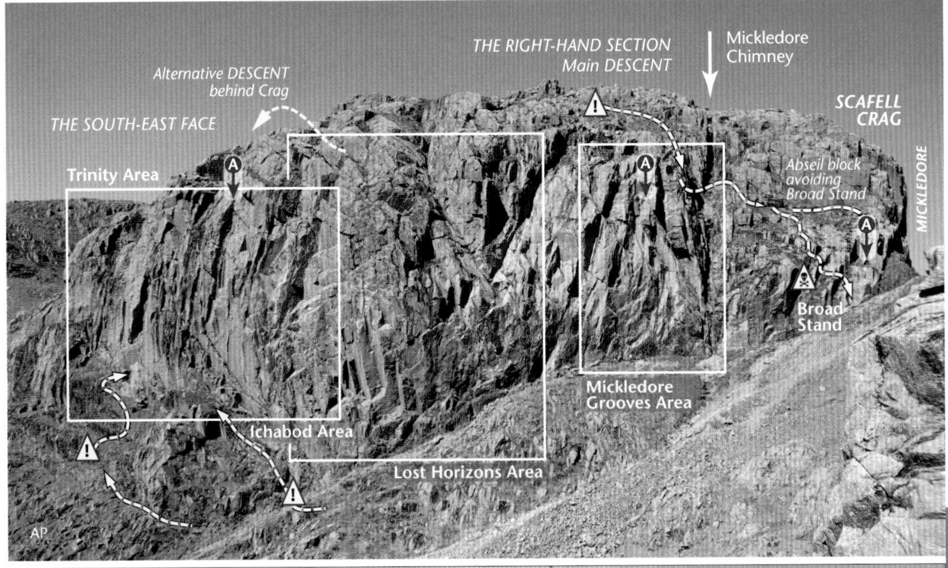

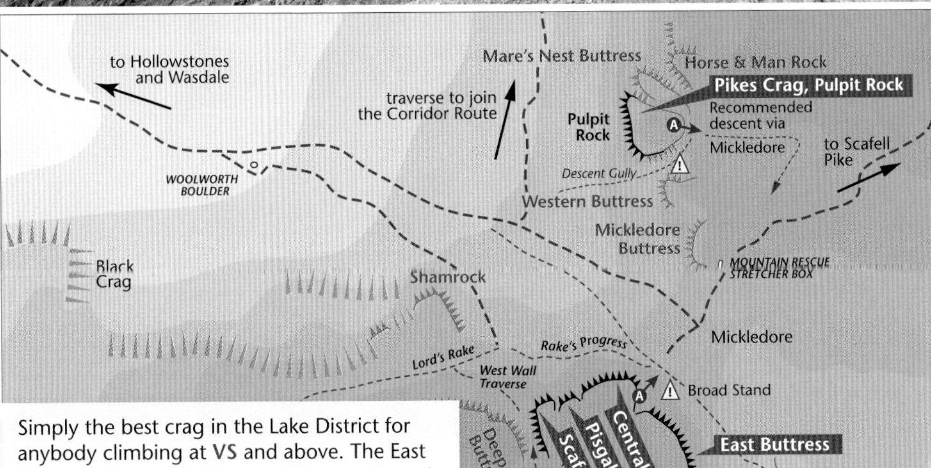

Simply the best crag in the Lake District for anybody climbing at VS and above. The East Buttress is a formidable crag, the rock is excellent, dries quickly and gets the sun into the afternoon.

Approach: From Mickledore from where the crag can be reached in two minutes. Sacks are usually left on Mickledore.

See map page 188.

Descent: Go right to a stony path and short, greasy rock chimney leading down into the upper part of Mickledore Chimney. Cross to a path leading down to the abseil. For the left-hand side of the crag trend left and descend an awkward gully, returning along a good path below the crag.

Abseil: Above *Chartreuse* (45m) and *Ichabod* (50m). Check who is below.

May Day Direct
Aquavit
Fulcrum Direct
Mickledore Arete
Strider
Pernod
Pernod Direct
MICKLEDORE CHIMNEY
Aquavit
MICKLEDORE CHIMNEY

Mickledore Grooves Area

1 Barry's Traverse 33m HVS 5a ★
A rising left-trending traverse across the upper part of the Great Slab from the foot of Mickledore Chimney.
RVM Barry, CGT Collin - Sep 1936

2 Chartreuse 54m E1 5b ★★
A serious slab and a strenuous, brutal crack.
1 27m 5a Climb easily right up a diagonal break above the gully to a ledge. A ledge leads left, make thin moves cross the slab, then climb up using flakes to a large ledge.
2 27m 5b Move right to a ledge. A diagonal crack leads right over a bulge. Step back left and climb up to a rest left of the huge block. Traverse right and climb the crack to the top. Some even claim this crack is easy!
R Smith, D Leaver - May 1957

3 Midnight Express 45m E3 6a ★★
Superb, with two contrasting pitches - a long and very committing slab followed by a short, technical groove.
1 36m 5b Follow *Chartreuse* to the grass ledge then climb the centre of the slab to an obvious triangular hold. Move awkwardly left for a couple of metres and climb up over a small overlap to a second, larger overlap. Move right and pull through the bulge at a diagonal crack above the bulge. Climb directly to a large block and step right to belay in a groove.
2 9m 6a Regain the block and climb the shallow groove above, moving left to the top of the crack on *Chartreuse*.
P Botterill, J Lamb - Jul 1979

4 The Fulcrum 54m VS 4c ★★
Pleasantly improbable. Start at the first break in the wall, below a short, open chimney.
1 15m 4c Climb up for 5m, gain a sloping ramp/groove on the right. Climb this to a small stance.
2 18m 4c Up the recessed wall on the left onto a slab (awkward). Traverse horizontally left, under an overhang, to a pair of cracks. Climb these to the base of a groove and follow this to a stance on its left rib.
3 21m 4b Continue to the overhang. Take the steep crack on the left. At the top pull right, then left and up.
K Jackson, J Adams - Jun 1968

5 Leverage 48m E1 5b ★★★
Good, steep, sustained climbing - fast-drying. Start at a steep crack 6m left of *Fulcrum*.
1 22m 5b Climb the stiff initial crack, cross the gangway and continue up the steep crack above to a slab on the right. Step left onto a bulge and follow the cracks and V-groove above to a stance.
2 26m 5a Take the groove above and move right into the corner. Climb this, traverse right under the obvious roof and climb up onto a slab. Continue to the top.
R Smith, D Leaver - May 1958

6 Mickledore Grooves 67m VS 5a ★★★
One of the best routes of its standard in the Lakes. Start at the foot of a right slanting gangway. Some climbers boulder the steep start and have the rack passed up to them.
1 25m 5a Climb the short overhanging wall to a gangway on the right. Follow this to the foot of twin grooves. Climb the left-hand groove for 5m, make an awkward step right into the right-hand groove. Climb to a ledge with a large block.
2 42m 4c Move onto a ledge on the slab to the right. Step left and follow a diagonal crack right, over a bulge, on good holds. Climb up and right to a groove, follow it until it steepens and traverse right to a sloping ledge. Move around the corner on the right and continue horizontally for 9m to a mossy opening leading to the top.
CF Kirkus, IM Waller, M Pallis - May 1930

7 Dyad 63m E3 6a ★★
A good, strenuous climb. Start 5m left of *Mickledore Grooves* at a small steep ramp.
1 21m 6a Climb the delicate ramp and pull right. Climb the crack above to a poor ledge and follow the thin crack above to a ledge on the left; belay (peg; low nuts).
2 18m 5c Follow the groove above until a step right can be made onto the rib. Climb this for 3m, step left and follow a slab to a ledge.
3 24m 4b The easy crack on the right.
K Jackson, C Read - Jun 1968; FFA J Lamb, P Botterill - Jun 1974

8 Edge of Eriador 57m E4 6a ★★★
A fine challenging route taking the soaring arête. P2 is poorly protected.
1 21m 6a P1 of *Dyad*.
2 36m 5c Climb the arête crossing a ledge.
R Matheson, E Cleasby - May 1977

11
12
19
15
14
13
16
10
Armageddon E2
Moonday E2
Shikasta E4
9
11
12
New Horizons E8
14
11
9
15
13
10
19
16
AP

May Day Area

9 Zeya 48m E6 6b ★★★
The best route on this sector. Start below the first short groove on the left of the brown wall. Scramble up a short deep groove to belay below the corner.
1 24m 6b Climb the groove to a small spike. Pull right with difficulty to a ledge (peg). Climb the intimidating wall above trending right to the foot of the serious groove of *Shere Khan*. Follow this to its stance.
2 24m 5c Step left, across the void, into the crack and climb this to a ledge. Climb the groove above to belay at the top of p2 of *Shere Khan*. Finish up this or scramble off left.
M Berzins, C Sowden - Jul 1983

10 Shere Khan 72m E5 6a ★★★
A magnificent and bold climb. Scramble up the groove below *Zeya*, and traverse a glacis left to below a steep groove with 2 old peg runners at 6m.
1 24m 6a Climb the groove and pull out right with difficulty to gain the sloping ramp (old pegs). Follow this to its end (low runner) and climb the serious groove to a move right onto a sloping ledge.
2 21m 5c Climb the obvious steep groove above and continue up a mossy crack to belay on the ledge system.
3 27m 5a Move across to the obvious mossy steep corner. Climb this and break out right at its top.
E Cleasby, R Matheson - May 1977; FFA R Fawcett - May 1977

Lost Horizons Area

11 Overhanging Wall 60m HVS 5a ★★
A strenuous start leads to pleasant climbing up the great white slab. A large boulder sits on an overhung ledge.
1 24m 5a Climb the corner to the left of the ledge to a small ledge. Move up and traverse right and up to a protruding rib; descend on its right and climb a crack to a ledge. Swing right to a crack and climb over a bulge. Climb up, step right, and up again to a ledge. Traverse left into a corner and belay above.
2 36m 4b Traverse left to the foot of the great White Slab and climb it to a large square block in its centre. Go straight up to a good ledge and climb up left from its right-hand edge.
M Linnell, AT Hargreaves - Jul 1933; FFA RJ Birkett, L Muscroft - c.1938

12 Minotaur 75m E1 5b ★★
Varied and interesting with a very exposed first pitch.
1 24m 5b Follow *Overhanging Wall* until the rib is reached. Move straight up into a scoop and follow the moss-speckled wet ramp left to its top. Pull over the bulge (crux) to another ramp and follow this to The White Slab.
2 24m 4c Climb The White Slab for 10m until a move up and right can be made onto a big wet gangway; this is followed almost to its top to a restricted stance.
3 27m 5a Continue to the end of the gangway and climb the corner to a slab on the left. Climb this and exit left onto a ledge. Go diagonally left up another slab then scramble to the top.
S Clark, G Oliver, H Loughran, G Lowes - Jun 1968

13 Lost Horizons 69m E4 6b ★★★
Superb and varied climbing in very impressive positions. Start at an opening 5m right of the lowest part of the crag.
1 17m 4c Climb up then trend right up slabs to a short wall. Up this and the slab above to the foot of the largest corner.
2 37m 6b Climb the strenuous corner to a ledge which is deceptively unbalancing. Continue up (peg) to below the narrow V-niche and traverse left to a ledge. Move right to regain the crack line above the corner and climb up to a ramp. Block belay on the right.
3 15m 5c Climb the crack which splits the overhanging wall above.
P Livesey, J Lawrence - Sep 1976; FFA RH Berzins, M Browell -Jun 1982

14 Equinox 67m E4 6a ★★
1 16m 4c Climb p1 of *Lost Horizons* but move left and belay right of the smaller corner.
2 16m 6a Climb the corner and overcome the bulge with difficulty to reach good nut belays on the slab.
3 25m 6a Gain a ledge on the right, below a hanging flake. Climb the frantic flake to a ledge and then follow flake cracks and ledges to a ramp.
4 10m 5b Climb the corner crack to a large sloping ledge on the left. Pull up into a flake crack on the steep wall on the right and climb to better holds and easy ground.
J Lamb, P Botterill - May/Jun 1978

15 The Centaur 93m HVS 5a ★★★

A magnificent climb threading an intricate line that can be difficult to read.

1 18m 4b Climb *Great Eastern Route* to the ledge on the left, then step up right to a higher ramp and follow a light-coloured, left-trending groove to a good ledge. Continue up the cracked wall to a stance.

2 14m 5a Climb the corner for 3m and move left onto the very edge of the buttress. Follow this for 5m then traverse right crossing a groove to a stance.

3 15m 5a Move right and climb a short corner parallel to the main groove onto a ledge on the left. Traverse left into the main groove and climb this to join *Great Eastern Route*. Go up the step in the slab above and belay.

4 18m 4c Traverse 5m right and climb a short groove to a ledge which runs across an impending wall above. Follow this left and upwards to a large green slab near the corner.

5 28m 4c Climb steeply up to the left and traverse behind the detached pinnacle to a ledge. Step up to the left and climb back right to two more poised pinnacles and a ledge. Layback the spectacular crack to the top.

L Brown, S Read - Jun 1960

16 Great Eastern Route 77 m VS 4c ★★

A magnificent, inescapable climb that wanders up the buttress in an impressive setting. The technical difficulty is not great; care should be taken to protect the second. Start at an opening 5m to the right of the lowest part of the crag.

1 5m Easy rocks are followed by a walk left.

2 24m 4c Ascend the cracked slab slanting up to the left to bulging rocks at 6m. Pass an overhang; a little higher is a ledge. Traverse left across the slab and climb the corner. Step left onto the face and climb up onto a good stance.

3 9m 4b The steep cracks ahead lead to a stance below a nook.

4 24m 4b Cross the slab on the right and go up the step. Up a little, on good holds and continue right to a crevasse.

5 15m 4a Climb 3m, left or right, to a shelf below a corner. Climb round the corner on the right to a ledge.

M Linnell, SH Cross - Aug 1932

17 The Yellow Slab 79m HVS 4c ★★★

Superb climbing in a magnificent situation.

1 29m 4c P1 and 2 of *Great Eastern*.

2 30m 4c The crack on the left is climbed to a ledge at the foot of The Yellow Slab. Climb this directly at first, then left until it ends. Move left and follow an exposed crack, belay on a shelf on the left.

3 20m 4c Move left round the corner, using a doubtful flake, then work diagonally left across the exposed wall, keeping a few metres below the overhangs, to a delicate finish.

M Linnell, H Pearson - Sep 1933

18 Chiron/Gold Rush 99m E1 5b ★★

1 39m 5b P1 *Chiron* then continue up *Great Eastern* to a belay below a corner line.

2 15m 4b Step down and follow sloping ledges horizontally left, then climb the black wall and cross a slab to belay.

3 30m 5b Climb the corner to join *The Yellow Slab*. Follow the crack to a belay on a shelf on the left.

4 15m 5a Continue up the crack in a short corner on the right to the overhang and move left; continue to a large ledge.

AG Cram, W Young - Jun 1969

19 Chiron 77m E3 5c ★★

An excellent route.

1 25m 5b Scramble left to reach a thin flake system in the steep wall left of the initial groove of *Great Eastern*. Follow the flake past a hollow section, then traverse left above the waterfall. Pull up to belay in a sloping recess.

2 16m 5c Move right to the apex of the slab, then pull up strenuously to reach a ledge system. Climb into a shallow recess above (Flexi Friend ½ on left), climb the wall on the left to exit precariously onto a smooth glacis. Step left and up to a belay.

3 9m 5c Above a step on the belay slab is a short steep wall. Climb this to a horizontal ledge and overcome the bulge above on the right to another large sloping slab.

4 27m 5c Walk right and gain a crack running diagonally left in the overhanging wall above. Follow this strenuously until 3m short of the corner on the left. A short steep flake and crack above leads to a grass ledge. Exit up the corner behind.

A Phizacklea, A Rowell, JL Holden - May 1990

The South-East Face

Here you get the sun until early-afternoon. The climbs start from a system of terraces above a broken mass of rock and vegetation reached by unpleasant scrambling.

20 Overhanging Grooves Direct 75m E3 5c ★★

A sensational climb taking the obvious prominent overhanging flake crack, which is the first major feature on the terrace.

1 21m 5c Climb up to the flake (thread); follow the flake and the exciting wall above (crux) to a ledge. Climb two ramp/grooves above to a belay.

2 30m 5b Climb up a ramp diagonally right to join *The Yellow Slab*, where a fine crack in a white corner can be gained (usually wet). Follow this until it steepens, whence a short traverse right can be made into a large niche.

2a 5b To avoid the wet crack follow p2 as far as the fine crack. Climb this for a short distance, traverse right into a shallow groove in the steep rounded pillar. Climb this to the large niche at the top of p2.

3 24m 5a Step left and follow the crack to a ledge. Traverse right and finish up *Centaur*.

J Adams, C Macquarrie- Jul 1975; FFA M Berzins, RH Berzins - May 1977

21 Borderline 54m E7 6c ★★★

An awe-inspiring route which provides intricate, sustained climbing using the incredible curving flake on the overhanging wall.

1 36m 6c Climb the flake (peg); step left and climb the wall with difficulty (peg and nut). Continue by moving right on improving holds then back left to a resting ledge (thread). Move up to join *Roaring Silence* to belay as for *The Yellow Slab* at the top of p2.

2 18m 6b Climb the crack which splits the overhang to the left of the niche. Desperate; you can't claim the route if you miss it!

C Sowden, M Berzins - Jun 1986

The next climbs start in a niche at the top of the easy ramp and below a line of corners in a tower. Scramble up the ramp to a stance and belay in a niche. Abseil descent: 50m.

22 Roaring Silence 54m E3 5c ★★★

Excellent, airy climbing; a fast-drying route.

1 36m 5c Follow the first pitch of *Ichabod* into the top of the shallow corner. Traverse right to a thin crack and climb it until it steepens. Step right again to a good crack and follow it and the slab above to belay.

2 18m 5c Climb the niche, which splits the right-hand side of the overhangs, to the top.

RH Berzins, J Lamb, M Berzins - Jun 1979

23 Ichabod 45m E2 5c ★★★

Excellent rock and thrilling positions – a mega-classic. Climb the right-hand of the two cracks, passing a protruding nose. Pull into a slot below a flake crack, then traverse delicately right into a corner. Follow the corner to the foot of a V-chimney. Follow this to an awkward exit left into the larger mossy main corner. Climb this more easily (often damp) and continue up a steep crack to the top.

G Oliver, G Arkless, L Willis - May 1960; FFA T Sullivan, L Brown - Sep 1964

24 Barad-dûr 55m E6 6b ☆☆☆

An eye catching line up the impressive overhanging pillar. Best belay on the ground for a grandstand view of the action. Enter the niche utilising a series of steep cracks. From the resting ledge of *Phoenix* the line up and rightwards to the fin and hanging groove, is obvious enough, the method of achieving this is not; bold, strenuous and perplexing. The reward of success is a rest further up on the right edge. Move directly to the roof and traverse leftwards, with interest, to a thin crack which splits the headwall above the left-hand end of the roof. Layback spectacularly over the bulge and climb directly on some good holds to a small jammed block. Stretch right to a jug and pull rightwards to sloping ledges on the front of the pillar. Finish up the scoop and easier angled wall.

R Matheson, C Matheson – May 2014

25 Phoenix 51 m E2 5c ★★

A superb, well-protected, exposed climb, following a strenuous groove up the front of the tower to the left of *Ichabod*.

1 27m 5b Enter the groove by the obvious jamming crack left of Ichabod, then climb the cracked corner above and pull out left with difficulty to a poor resting place. Continue up the groove and pull out left again. Climb the corner to belay on the ramp.

2 24m 5c The Arête Finish - Move down the gangway and climb the obvious crack in the rib to its top. Move right across the rib, then climb steeply up to the top.

R Moseley, DM Adcock - Aug 1957; FFA K Wood - 1967;
p2 R Matheson, E Cleasby - summer 1976

32
26
28
30
31
27
Lucius E5
Slime Chimney VD
28
Incubus E5
Talisman E2
30
32
31
29
15 The Centaur HVS 5a
16 Great Eastern Route VS 4c
17 The Yellow Slab HVS 4c
18 Chiron/Gold Rush E1 5b
19 Chiron E3 5c
20 Overhanging Grooves Direct E3 5c
21 Borderline E7 6c
22 Roaring Silence E3 5c
23 Ichabod E2 5c
24 Barad-dûr E5 6b
25 Phoenix E2 5b
26 Morning Wall MVS 4c
27 Pegasus HVS 5b
28 Chimera E1 5b
29 The Almighty E5 6b
30 Hell's Groove E1 5b
31 Bat out of Hell E2 5c
32 Trinity HVS 5b

25
24
23
A
18
20
15
19
17
Foirbidden Colours E4
22
25
17
19
18
26
16
21
Welcome to the Cruel World E9
Return of thec King E9
27
24
18
19
23
Gold Rush E1
20
AP

26 Morning Wall 72m MVS 4c ★

The easiest line diagonally left gives good climbing in an impressive situation. Start at the foot of the right-hand ramp which leads to *Ichabod*.

1 20m Climb the right-hand ramp until about 4m short of the niche, where a descent can be made onto the second ramp. Follow this left to a stance in the corner below a crack.

2 15m 4c Climb the vertical crack in the wall left of a V-corner (crux). Move up, then traverse left, over a rib, to a spike at the foot of a chimney.

3 22m 4a Follow the chimney into the amphitheatre. The sloping slab on the left leads to thread belays.

4 15m 4a Climb up a slab left to its top, then pull up and traverse right along the block to a chimney, follow this to finish.

AT Hargreaves, W Clegg, M Linnell - Aug 1933;
FFA AR Dolphin, AB Gilchrist - Aug 1945

27 Pegasus 84m HVS 5b ★

An exposed and delicate line below *Morning Wall*; when dry the moss is merely a cosmetic hindrance. Harder for the short.

1 12m 4a Follow a left slanting ramp to a belay in a corner below a small grass patch.

2 24m 5b Traverse left around the arête using a flat ledge for handholds and continue past a blunt pinnacle into the base of a steep short chimney on the left. Climb this for a couple of metres, follow a left sloping gangway until a difficult move leads into the larger open groove on the left (crux). Climb this to a poor stance.

3 12m 5a Take the corner above until a steep V-groove leads to a good ledge below an overhang.

4 21m 4b Climb a crack in the wall to the right of the overhang to ledges. Traverse the steep wall on the left to an open chimney; climb this to the left-hand end of the amphitheatre of *Morning Wall*. Thread belays.

5 15m 4a P4 of *Morning Wall*.

AR Dolphin, P Greenwood - May 1952; FFA R Miller, P Moffatt - Aug 1955

28 Chimera 75m E1 5b ★

Good climbing with an excellent final pitch.

1 12m 4a P1 of *Pegasus*.

2 27m 5b Follow p2 of *Pegasus* to the middle of the gangway, below a shallow open corner. Climb the corner.

3 12m 5a Take the corner and its continuation crack to a large ledge.

4 24m 5a Finish up the fine crack in the wall.

W Young, A G Cram - Jun 1969

29 The Almighty 18m E5 6b ★★★

The thin, fierce and overhanging crack provides a short sensational climb. Start on a large block.

P Botterill, J Lamb - Aug 1981

30 Hell's Groove 68m E1 5b ★★★

A superb climb of great character.

1 8m 5b The problematic crack leads to a belay in the groove.

2 22m 5a From the sloping ledge in the groove climb right into a crack and ascend to another sloping ledge. Continue to a further ledge with a block at its right-hand edge. A short wall and crack lead to the belay above p3 of *Pegasus*. Finish up this.

P Greenwood, AR Dolphin - May 1952

31 Bat out of Hell 64m E2 5c ★★

Good climbing, allowing access to the upper walls via a detour into the lower part of the corner avoided by *Hell's Groove*.

1 10m 5b Climb up and right, crossing an awkward overlap to a point below an overhanging nose. Step right to a belay.

2 12m 5c Climb directly up the impending corner, moving right to avoid the wet, to belay on a sloping ledge in an alcove.

3 42m 5b A difficult traverse left across the wall leads to a good hold on the arête. Climb the crack, move left and up to a decaying runner. Traverse left, climb a steep slab on sloping holds to a vague recess, climb up to a large grass ledge.

T Marr, M Tooke - Jun 1995

32 Trinity 67m HVS 5b ★★★

Interesting and enjoyable climbing.

1 30m 5a Gain and climb the groove and pass an overhang on its left to a ledge.

2 28m 5b Climb the bulge in the corner onto a slab. Follow the slab and the fine corner crack above to a resting place. Move diagonally left to the foot of a short wall and belay above on the large grass ledge.

3 9m 4c The corner.

DD Whillans, J Sutherland - Jun 1955

Shere Khan E5 (page 209) Chris Fisher — Al Phizacklea

PIKES CRAG - PULPIT ROCK

OS Grid Ref: NY 210 071
Altitude: 760m

1 ¾ hr

The large crag to the left of Mickledore has the benefit of catching the sun for most of the day, dries more quickly than Scafell and offers a grandstand view of *Central Buttress*. The rock is clean and rough on the better routes, but there are some large ledges of particular botanical interest and a number of loose blocks, neither should be disturbed.

Approach: The base of Pulpit Rock is a tier of broken rock topped by an almost continuous grass terrace from which the routes start. The right hand end of this terrace can be easily reached from the scree below Descent Gully.

Descent: From the top of Pulpit Rock a short, steep scramble down the Scafell Pike side leads to a col, but in bad weather an abseil may be preferable. The main path to Mickledore is on the far (east) side. Abseiling down the main face takes two long abseils, and you have to leave gear that might not be possible to retrieve, but if you arrange things carefully, you can grab two routes in quick succession.

1 Megalith 130m HVS 5a ★★
A long route following a series of clean protruding ribs to the right of the big corner of Slanting Groove. Good sustained climbing. Start just right of *Grooved Arête* beneath a prominent rib of rock.
1 23m 5a Climb the rib to a small overhang; step left to turn it. Move up and rightwards onto the steep slab to reach a crack in an overlap. Move up, then to the right edge and follow it to a ledge with a block.
2 42m 5a Climb directly up the slab above to reach easier ground, continue towards some large blocks on the right arete, go through them with care, onto the wall above. Step left and follow a deep crack, continue directly to ledges. Belay in a crack up on the left side of the next tier.
3 22m 4c Climb directly up the centre of the wall just right of the belay, passing some cracked blocks, continue to a ledge. Follow the line of the crack up the wall above, to a good ledge.

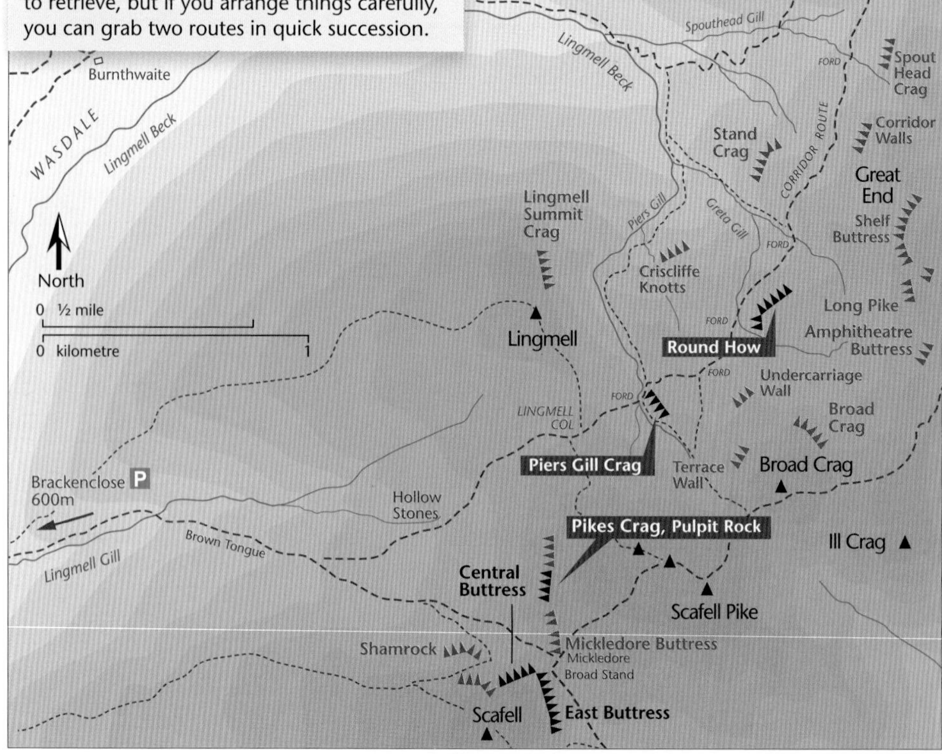

4 26m 4c From blocks up on the right, pull left onto the arete and delicately move up. Move left to a short crack, follow it and continue leftwards up an easy stepped ridge, to take a belay at the chockstone behind a megalithic block.
5 17m 5a Start just right of the chockstone. Climb directly up the steep stepped wall, turning the final step on the left, to reach the summit.
GL Swainbank, C Read - Aug 2003

2 Grooved Arête 114m VD ★★★

A good clean route with sustained and varied situations. Start from a well-worn ledge below a V-shaped hollow below a large overhang, just to the right of the arête which falls from the highest point of the crag.
1 12m Enter the easy grassy groove running back to the left and belay in the V-shaped recess at the foot of a steep crack.
2 15m The left-hand crack is climbed for 8m, then traverse to the arête on the left, climb this past the end of the overhang to a grass ledge. Belay in the chimney a little distance back.
3 24m The chimney is climbed, passing a bulge at 8m. Continue up a broken groove until grassy ledges lead rightwards into a rectangular corner.
4 20m The crack in the right-hand corner is hard to start. Continue up to a pile of blocks, pass them, and make a pleasant traverse to the right, to a prominent block on the edge of the ridge.
5 18m Climb the slab ahead, work to the left, and then cross over to a series of ledges on the edge.
6 12m Step over the corner on the left and continue up a slab to a ledge below a huge block. Climb the chimney on the left of the block.
7 13m Go along a ledge, running down to the left, on the wall above the gap, and regain the slabby front of the buttress, which is climbed direct to the summit of Pulpit Rock.
CF Holland, GR Speaker - Apr 1924

3 The Steeple to The Nave 129m HVS 5a ★

This adventurous climb runs up the sweep of slabs left of *Grooved Arête*.
Start 20m below and left of *Grooved Arête* in a grassy bay on the left of, and just above, the lowest rocks of a rib, directly below the summit block.
1 42m 4c Up and into a short groove, topped by a small overhang. Turn it on the right and continue up the left edge of a clean rib, to where it meets a mossy slab. Move up then step left; go up then right to gain a good ledge and crack (thread).
2 39m 5a A good pitch. Go left across the ledge for 5m and climb diagonally leftwards for 7m up the slabs to a black mossy streak. Move back rightwards and straight up the centre of the slabby pillar to a bold finish.
3 30m 4b The slabs, starting on the left, lead more easily to a stance.
4 30m 4b Climb the slabs and cracks above, heading for a conspicuous notch in the skyline, right of a large overhang and finish on the summit of the crag.
P1 GL Swainbank, C Read - Aug 2003; W Young, J Wilkinson - Jun 1974

4 The Sentinel 77m VS 4c ★★

This route is easily identified by the striking face crack which splits a square-cut pillar 20m up the crag. Start at the right-hand edge of the steep rib, which lies immediately to the left of a green mossy gully.
1 18m 4c Steep delicate climbing first up the rib, then trending left, leads to a grass ledge.
2 24m 4c Climb the corner above the ledge for 5m to an overhang split by a crack. Climb the striking, and bulging crack to the top of the pillar. Beware loose flakes.
3 20m Easier climbing straight up to a stance below and to the left of an obvious overhanging crack which can be seen on the skyline.
4 15m 4c Climb carefully up doubtful rock to the overhang and pull over it strenuously. Continue straight up the crack to a stance. Alternatively, the overhang may be avoided by climbing the corner above the stance, and traversing right across the clean wall above to rejoin the route.
P Fearnehough J Wright - Easter 1960

5 Juniper Buttress 75 m S ★★★

A very satisfying route which is the cleanest on the crag. Start at a detached block at the foot of the crag about 13m to the right of *Wall and Crack Climb.*
1 18m From the block a ledge is reached and a traverse made to the right into a corner below a crack. The crack is climbed and near the top it is left in favour of the arête. From the ledge so reached, climb a furrow slanting up the wall to the right to a grass ledge.
2 10m Climb a series of blocks to the left, finishing up a rather difficult crack.
3 15m Ascend rightwards to the edge of a grassy gully.
4 17m A groove, above and to the left, followed by a crack leads to a shelf with a recess at its back.
5 15m The exposed wall above is climbed by a difficult thin crack, starting at a rib just to the right. Easy scrambling to the top.
HM Kelly, REW Pritchard, NL Eden-Smith, W Eden-Smith - Apr 1924

⑥ Wall and Crack Climb 80 m VD ★★

A clean route on very good rock, with some polished problems. Follows the apparent left-hand ridge of Pulpit Rock.

1 10m Climb the ridge.

2 9m A steep wall is climbed to a ledge.

3 15m A vertical crack, or the face to the right, is climbed to a rock platform. From here, starting on the right, a staircase of rock is ascended to a terrace.

4 10m The wall above is climbed from right to left on improving holds.

5 10m Climb a zig-zag crack running up to the right in three risers.

6 11m A rock staircase leads to a ledge.

7 15m The almost vertical crack, or the wall on its left, is followed by easier rocks to the top.

1 Megalith HVS 5a
2 Grooved Arête VD
3 The Steeple to The Nave HVS 5a
4 The Sentinel VS 4c
5 Juniper Buttress S
6 Wall and Crack Climb VD
Pulpit Rock
The Steeple VS
The Pulpit VS
The Chancel VS
Slanting Groove HS
Crenation Ridge D
AP

PIERS GILL CRAG

OS Grid Ref: NY 214 078
Altitude: 730m

A small compact wall of excellent rock, reminiscent of the best Bosigran granite, found at the head of Piers Gill, just above the point where it is crossed by the Corridor Route to Scafell. Although small, it is conveniently situated for any climber returning to Sty Head from Scafell, as it catches the afternoon sun.

See map on page 216.

1 The Watchtower 22m VS 4c
Climb the crack and the slab on the right.
R McHaffie - Jul 1989

2 Mazurka 23m S 4a
Takes the rounded buttress just right of *The Watchtower*.
BJ Clark – Jul 2006

3 Verbal Abuse 23m HS
Climb the obvious crack.
R McHaffie - 10 July 1989

4 Slanting Groove 23m MS ★
A good route on solid rock up the main feature of the crag.
G Milburn D Gregory - Jun 1968

5 Pier of the Realm 23m VS 5a ★★
An excellent, well-protected route starting just right of *Slanting Groove*. Follow the triple flake crack system, finishing awkwardly up the right crack.
A Phizacklea M Lynch - Aug 1995

6 Body of Society 22m HVS 5a
Follow *Merchants of Death* to the traverse, then pull left and climb the obvious groove.
R McHaffie B Brown - Jul 1989

7 Merchants of Death 24m HVS 5a ★
Very pleasant climbing. Start on a ledge 3m right of *Slanting Groove*. Climb the steep wall on good quartz holds until a traverse right for 5m leads to a ledge. Pull left around an overhang, then swing right over a second roof to finish.
R McHaffie J Bosher - Jul 1989

8 Rock and Rolling 23m VS 4c
Start at a grassy V-groove 6m right of *Slanting Groove*. Scramble on top of the block, then climb a steep cracked wall past an ancient peg stump to a little niche. Follow a left-trending mossy break to the top.
R McHaffie B Brown - Jul 1989

9 Heatwave '95 22m E2 5b
The steep, clean wall is split by four thin crack systems. This is the second crackline. Climb onto the ledge, and follow the crack directly to the top.
A Phizacklea M Lynch 10 Aug 1995

10 Sleeping With the Stars 24m E2 5b ★
Superb climbing up the third crack. Follow *Wind Beneath My Wings* for 5m, then hand traverse left to gain the crackline. Follow this to below a small niche, where a flake leads left to finish up *Heatwave '95*.
A Phizacklea M Lynch - Aug 1995

11 Wind Beneath My Wings 23m E1 5a ★
A good sustained pitch starting just right of a spike on a ledge, 13m right of *Slanting Groove*. Climb the obvious curving right-hand crack.
R McHaffie P Turner - Summer 1989

12 Shaun & Haley 10m E2 5c ★
The superb upper wall and crack between *Sleeping with the Stars* and *Wind Beneath My Wings*. Short but good.
A Horsfield, R Newall – Jun 2003

13 Piers de Piece 23m E1 5b
Pleasantly sustained at the crux. Start 2m right of *Wind Beneath My Wings*. Climb a short wide crack for 4m, then step right onto a ledge and follow the crackline directly above to finish.
M Lynch A Phizacklea - Aug 1995

14 Darren's Route 23m MVS 4b
Start below a large pinnacle. Climb on to the top of the pinnacle, then follow the groove and crack above.
R McHaffie - Jul 1989

15 Peer Gynt 20m VS 4c
Pleasant climbing up the thin crack right of *Darren's Route*. Climb the thin crack to gain a ramp, move up to a higher ramp, follow this a short way before pulling over a slight bulge on the right to reach easier rock.
BJ Clark - Jul 2006

16 Sweat Tea 20m S
A good route starting 2m right of a ramp going up left. Climb a wall and a shallow groove, then move left on flakes below a grass ledge. Follow slabs above to finish.
R McHaffie - Jul 1989

17 Muffin Crack 20m VD
Start below a juniper-carpeted alcove at 3m. Gain the alcove and follow the crack above, step right and finish up the short wall.
BJ Clark - Jul 2006

18 Cancan 20m HS 4a
Start at a steep brown rib 4m right of *Muffin Crack*. Climb a rib to a ledge, then move up left and follow a shallow groove. Finish up the short arete on the right.
BJ Clark - Jul 2006

19 Extra Route 20m VD
Start in a shallow recess 6m right of *Muffin Crack*. Climb the recess and the steep crack above, finishing up the arête on good holds.
A Soper - Jun 1993

20 Armoanium 12m HVS 5a
Start at a flake 5m right of *Extra Route*. Climb a short layback flake to a ramp, and pull over the prominent overhang (unprotected) then move right to finish just left of the arete.
BJ Clark - Jul 2006

ROUND HOW

OS Grid Ref: NY 219 082
Altitude: 670m

A delightful crag of excellent clean rock, rough and quick-drying, situated in surprising seclusion 100m above the Corridor Route just beyond the place where the path crosses Greta Gill.

See map on page 216.

1 Zephyr Ridge/Victor 85m HVS 5a ★
The best combination of pitches.
1 45m 4b Take the slabby arête to a large grass ledge below a steeper wall. A crack in the left side of this wall leads to a ledge and crevassed block.
2 40m 5a A good pitch. Climb the shallow groove on the left of the bulging nose and move up to a right-facing scoop formed by a flake. Up this to an easier finish.

Or 40m **5a** *Zephyr Ridge* continues 4m to the right by a small pillar. Climb up to a thin crack in a steep wall. Step left to reach the upper groove. Follow this and the easier ground above to finish.
A Phizacklea, M Lynch - Aug 1995

2 Group Therapy 40m E1 5b
Start just right of the second pitch of Corridor Route on a ledge.
1 20m 5a A shallow groove leads up the wall. Climb this and the arete above turning the small overlap on the left to a large ledge.
2 20m 5b Climb the wall directly above past a loose block to a ledge below the short steep square-cut corner. Climb the corner then bend left up the middle of the slab to finish up a broken V-groove.
S Millar, P Andrews - Jul 1996

3 Cresta 60m VS 4c ★
Another fine crack climb, starting at a short V-groove above the easy lower slabs, 6m left of *Wyvern Groove*.
1 42m 4c Climb to a grass ledge, continue up the crack with an awkward finish onto a ledge. A shallow groove and cleaner rock on the right lead to a grass ledge. Climb a short right-facing corner to a larger ledge.
2 18m 4b The slight rib on the left leads to a shallow scoop which is followed to the top.
M Lynch, A Phizacklea - Aug 1995

❹ Railton Special 42m E1 5b ★

A good delicate route up the prominent V-groove in the left side of the slab. Start at the foot of *Wyvern Groove*. Traverse left for 3m to a very thin crack. Climb this to a sloping ledge and move up left to a runner, then ascend the shallow scoop which leads into the main V-groove. Climb this to its top, then pull out right and continue up a crack to belay as for *Velox*.

A Phizacklea, M Lynch - Aug 1995

❺ Velox 43m E1 5b ★★★

A very fine route up the crack and shallow groove left of *Wyvern Groove*. Step left and climb a crack, past a doubtful block and continue directly to a slim groove. Climb this, runners on the left, to an easy ramp. Follow a thin crack in the right wall to a ledge. A higher crack leads to a larger grass ledge and belay.

M Lynch, A Phizacklea - Aug 1995

⑥ Wyvern Groove 36m VS 4c

The prominent, central, right-facing corner line. Start right of the foot of the groove. Up diagonally right to a mossy crack leading to the main groove via some large flakes. Climb the groove to a large block, and continue with an awkward move past a bulge. Traverse right across the upper wall to finish.

JR Wilkinson, H Williamson, JA Wood - May 1954

⑦ Zodiac 42m VS 5a

A pleasant crack line in the centre of the mossy slab. Climb the crack to where it fades, then follow a tiny ramp rightwards (nut). Make a hard move to a good hold in a groove, then move up left to a small blocky overhang. Traverse right onto the upper section of a rounded arête to finish.

M Lynch, A Phizacklea - Aug 1995

⑧ Slab Happy 37m HVS 5a

The clean crack, 2m right of and parallel to *Zodiac*.

D Clark, J Beverage - Jul 1996

The Buckbarrow Needle VS (page 228) Paul Winstanley and Mike Gullen — Ron Kenyon

BUCKBARROW

Away from the traditional and popular crags clustered around Mickledore and Napes Needle, Wasdale offers seclusion and the opportunity to explore.

Lang
Dow
Eskdale
Wasdale
Gable
Buttermere
Borrowdale
Eastern
EV

BUCKBARROW

Buckbarrow has some excellent climbing on fast drying rock a short walk from the road. The area has a great situation holding the sun all day with a number of crags scattered over the fell.

Approach: From Gosforth follow the Wasdale road; the crags come into view from a cattle grid before Harrow Head Farm.
P NY 13681 05491.

Descent: Down grassy ramps to the right.

The easy access low level climbing on Buckbarrow is often in condition when the high crags are shrouded in mist.

Arguably the first bouldering venue in Britain – the Y-shaped boulder – is a short walk up wild and esoteric Mosedale.

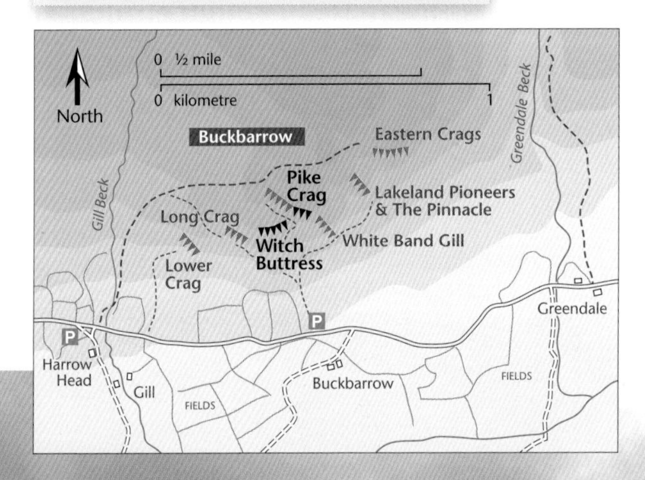

WITCH BUTTRESS

OS Grid Ref: NY 135 058
Altitude: 300m

The largest, cleanest piece of rock on the hillside is easily identified from the road by its fine central detached pillar with a pleasant grassy ledge below.

Descent: By the grass rake down right until a small path leads back left and down over a rock step to the base.

1 Gagarin 60m MS

Start at the base of a rib just above the path.

1 23m Climb the rib, bearing right to a ledge, then the short wall followed by a step up left onto a slab. The corner above leads to a stance.

2 17m Move left to the edge, then climb up, breaking right, over mossy slabs to a clean rib. Belays above at a corner stance.

3 20m The easy ridge ahead leads to an obvious crack. Climb the crack followed by a ridge and slabs above.

AH Greenbank, P Moffatt - 1957

2 The Mysteron 35m HVS 5b ★★

A very good climb with a short, technical, enigmatic crux providing a safe introduction to the harder routes on the crag. Start below a large corner left of the central detached pillar. Climb up and left to a large flake below the overhanging corner of Imagine. Traverse left below a green wall to the base of a groove. Climb this with a committing move left onto a tantalisingly high small ledge. Follow the crack up and right until a step left can be made into a crack that leads to the top.

WS Lounds, JC Eilbeck - 1960s

3 Imagine 38m E1 5b ★★★

An excellent route giving steep and sustained climbing. Start and climb to the large flake as for *The Mysteron* and pull into the steep groove on the right. Difficult moves lead to the roof (thread runner). Pull over on undercuts and good jugs into the easier continuation corner which is followed, trending right, to below an undercut

crack. Awkward moves give access to the crack which leads to the top.
A Stephenson, J Wilson - Apr 1981

4 Harmony 35m HVS 5b
Don't be fooled by the beguiling name: the wide crack on the left side of the central pillar is very strenuous with a difficult and frustrating start. Finishg up *Witch*.
WS Lounds, JC Eilbeck - 1960s

The detached central pillar contains some high quality routes with steep, hard and committing crux pitches.

5 Witch 40m VS 4c ★★★
A justifiably-popular route of traditional style taking the obvious chimney line on the right-hand side of the central pillar.
1 27m 4c Climb the chimney for 10m then move right with difficulty into a small niche. Good holds lead up the wall to regain the chimney/crack line above the overhang. Follow the crack to the top of the pillar.
2 13m 4c Step up and left into the open groove that leads to the top.
P Walsh, M Burke - Mar 1961

6 Moffatt's Route 40m VS 4c ★
A surprisingly enjoyable pitch starting at the bottom of the obvious corner 5m right of *Too Many Hands*. Climb the corner to a bulge, step left into the next corner and follow this until forced out right to the rib that leads up to a ledge. Step diagonally left to a spike then up to a ledge below a steep corner. Finish up the corner, which is difficult to start.
P Moffatt, P Hogg - 1940s

Pike Crag is the line of crags above Witch Buttress, stretching diagonally down rightward to the 'Needle area' just up and right of the Witch Buttress.

Descent: Traverse left and down below the upper part of the crag.

7 Sunset Strip 50m VS 4b ★
1 20m 4b Climb the obvious crack to a good ledge, then step left onto a steep slab which is followed with increasing difficulty to a grassy bay.
2 30m 4a Up the corners above and over a doubtful block to a crack. Climb this to the top. Descend off to the left.
WE Pattison, AW Dunn - Sep 1975

8 Last of the Summer Wine 22m E1 5b ★★
Good climbing up the steep wall just left of The Needle finishing with an intimidating crack up the overhanging wall. Climb the groove and step right onto a flake. Continue up the wall trending right until it is possible to swing across left into the base of the overhanging crack - straight up this to the top.
J Wilson, B Smith - May 1982

9 The Buckbarrow Needle 23m VS 4c ★★
An interesting climb of traditional character – to get the full experience the route should be done in one pitch! Climb one of the cracks, on either side of the pinnacle, to its top. Step onto the wall above and make a bold move up on small holds to easier ground above.
P Moffatt, P Hogg - 1947

10 Needle Front 23m E1 5b ★
Bold climbing on good rock up the left-hand side of the The Needle. Climb up the wall, then follow a line of footholds onto the right arête, and up to the top of the pinnacle. Finish up the wall above as for *The Buckbarrow Needle*.
J Earl, P Stewart - Jun 1979

11 Needless Eliminate 22m E1 5b ★★
A fine pitch climbing the groove and crack just right of The Needle. Start in the corner just right of the right-hand crack. Hand traverse diagonally left to a large spike then move up and pull onto a ledge on the right. Step back left and climb the crack, well-protected by small wires, direct to the top.
P Stewart, J Earl - Jun 1979

12 Living in Sin 15m E1 5a ★
A poorly-protected and serious line up the thin crack in the bulging wall just right of the corner of Junkie. Follow the crack to a scoop then a ledge. Step right and climb the arête to the top.
P Strong, C Daly - Apr 1984

13 Attic Stairs 1 20m MVS
Climb the arête and short wall right of *Living in Sin* to a recess, then climb the wall to the top.
WE Pattison, AW Dunn - 1974

PIKE CRAG - THE NEEDLE AREA

OS Grid Ref: NY 134 058
Altitude: 350m

GABLE & PILLAR

Historically significant as the birthplace of climbing in Britain the crags of Great Gable, overlooking the head of Wasdale are busy on fine summer days, and justifiably so, The Napes, Tophet Wall and Kern Knotts are classic venues not to be missed. On the shady side there are equally fine challenges.

In stark contrast some of the most isolated and remote crags are here; places to become completely immersed in the surroundings. To climb here requires fitness and commitment, as they all have long approaches. For those willing to make the effort the rewards of a long-day or a high-camp can be huge.

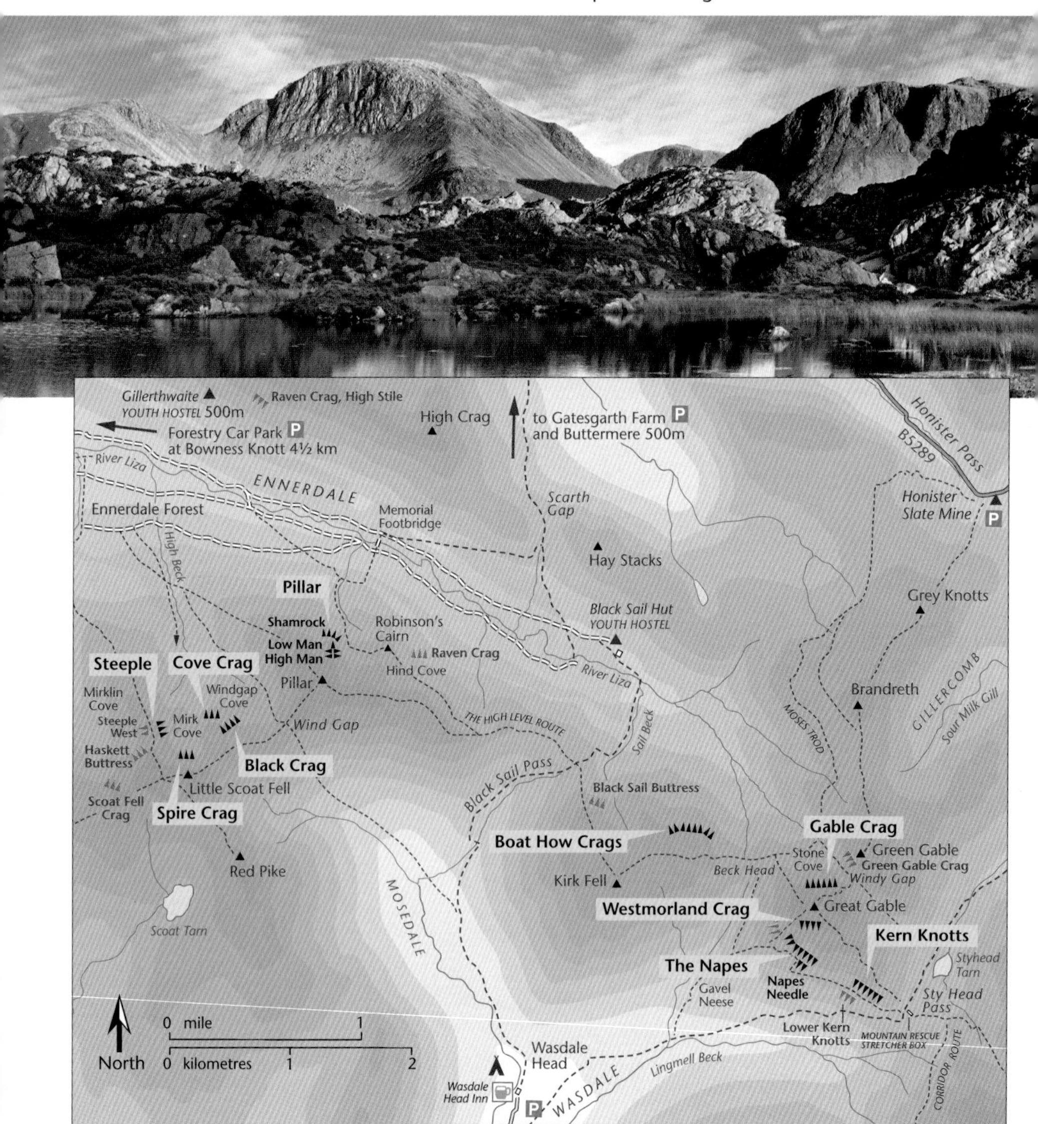

☐ *The Wasdale Roof*, Napes Needle E3 (page 246) Craig Matheson — Al Phizacklea

GREAT GABLE

Great Gable offers four superb and varied climbing areas, ranging from the sunny mountain outcrop of Kern Knotts to the dark brooding north-facing Gable Crag. All are well worth the walk and offer great adventures in superb settings.

The FRCC Great Gable summit memorial plaque

On the summit of Great Gable is a plaque commemorating 20 members of the FRCC who died in The Great War. The memorial to them is a tract of land, containing twelve majestic Lakeland mountains, purchased by the Club in 1923 to preserve our freedom to venture among these fells. The bridge over the Liza in Ennerdale is a memorial to the13 members killed in World War II.

Every November the Club holds a simple Act of Remembrance by the summit memorial plaque, lest we forget the 'freedom we have to follow our dreams...'. This section of the guidebook is dedicated to all those who gave their lives.

KERN KNOTTS

OS Grid Ref: NY 215 096
Altitude: 520m

A superb crag providing high quality climbing on steep rough rock. Sunny and quick drying. The climbs are described from left to right starting with the very clean and distinctively banded Cat Wall.

Approach: From Wasdale Head P NY 18680 08957 follow the Styhead Pass path until directly below the crag then walk straight up to it. From Seathwaite P NY 23547 12290 in Borrowdale follow the Styhead Pass path to the Mountain Rescue Box then follow the Climbers' Traverse, a gently rising track which crosses the south flank of Great Gable. The path is rather vague at first but soon becomes better defined and Kern Knotts is reached in a few minutes. See map page 230.

Descent: Easiest to the left.

1 Grimalkin 44m E4 6a ★★★
Bold climbing.
1 24m 6a Climb the thin ragged crack; make committing moves to reach the corner. Rightwards again across the bulging wall to reach a slim groove leading to a good ledge.
2 20m 5a Climb a short wall to a large glacis, then the wall right of a corner to the top.
K Telfer, J Gilhespey, P Morgan - May 1998

The next three routes share the same start just left of a blunt arête bounded by a shallow groove on the left.

2 Pussy 40m E4 6a ★★★
Traverses the banded wall on perfect rock.
1 30m 6a Climb the groove to a large spike. Step right onto the steep cracked wall and up to an obvious square-cut overhang, pull leftward to a shallow scoop. Difficult moves left reach a short hanging corner (*Grimalkin*) which leads to a small flake, continue left along the narrow ramp, until forced to make delicate moves to gain a good ledge.
2 10m 4b The rib left of the corner to the top.
A Phizacklea, PW Fox - Apr 1989

3 Moggy Traveller 20m E4 6a ★★
From the square-cut overhang, pull leftward to a shallow scoop and climb steeply following a groove.
A Phizacklea, A Rowell - May 1990

4 Sylvester 25m E3 5c ★★★
A problematic pitch requiring a cool head. From the large spike. Step right onto the steep cracked wall and climb to a small sloping ledge. Step left and follow the awkward groove to good holds.
T Furness, P Rigby - Jun 1981

5 Fat Freddie's Cat 20m E2 5c ★★
Start just left of Kern Knotts West Chimney. Gain and climb an awkward crack right of the blunt arête. From a small ledge on the left, step back right and climb the steep right-hand shallow groove to the top.
A Phizacklea, A Rowell, D Kells - May 1990

The next four routes lie between Kern Knotts West Chimney and the larger Kern Knotts Chimney.

6 Kern Knotts West Buttress 33m MVS ★★

Start at the toe of the steep buttress and follow cracks, grooves and large flakes upwards.

GS Sansom, SW Herford - Apr 1912

7 The Kraken 35m E1 5b ★★

A puzzling start and a fine finish taking the corner until good holds high up lead out to the left arête.

S Miller, T Stephenson - Apr 1974

8 The Crysalid 30m E2 5c ★★

Steep and fingery. Climb the blunt rib to a rightward diagonal crack in the steep slab, continue rightwards to reach a steep groove. Committing moves gain a good hold on a doubtful flake. Step left onto the final slab.

S Clegg, J Lamb - Oct 1976

9 Triffid 30m E2 5c ★★★

Climb the finger crack left of Kern Knotts Chimney past a pinnacle and up a short wall to reach the bulging crack on the left, followed by a narrow V-groove. Pull over the small overhang and continue to the top.

P Botterill, J Lamb - Apr1978

10 Kern Knotts Chimney 50m HS ★★

The prominent chimney on the Wasdale side; negotiating a chockstone and passing under a leaning block.

OG Jones, WH Fowler JW Robinson - Dec 1893

11 The Buttonhook Route 30m E1 5b ★★★

Very steep, with exposed blind moves. Start at the foot of the buttress at a small rock pillar. A short slab to the first overhang, pull rightwards to a jug and climb the crack to a small ledge. Good holds lead leftwards to a short groove, climb this then trend rightwards to a pinnacle on the right edge of the buttress. The shallow stepped groove above has an awkward finish.

G Balcombe, CJA Cooper - Jun 1934

The fine wall set at right-angles to the rest of the crag is split by two classic test pieces.

12 Kern Knotts Crack 22m HVS 4c ★★★

The wide left-hand crack is not always straightforward.

OG Jones, HC Bowen - Apr1897

13 Innominate Crack 20m VS 4b ★★★

The thinner right hand crack is more amenable.

GS Bower, B Beetham, JB Wilton - Apr 1921

14 Innominate/ Sepulchre Combination 35m E2 5b ★★★

The bottomless corner groove at the right-hand side of the wall is gained reasonably from *Innominate Crack*; climbing it is tougher. Take small wires and RPs.

J Lamb - 1975

A
11
12
13
14
PR
Langdale
Dow
Eskdale
Gable

THE NAPES

OS Grid Ref: NY 210 101
Altitude: 650m

Rightly considered to be the birthplace of English rock climbing. In addition to the unique Napes Needle the surrounding walls and ridges provide a superb variety of routes from Victorian masterpieces to cutting edge classics, all climbers, whatever their ability, will find something to enjoy. Most of the crag is quick drying and holds the sun late into the day.

Little Hell Gate Descent
White Napes
Sphinx Ridge Descent
Little Hell Gate
Arrowhead Gully
17
Eagle's Nest Gully
Napes West
Needle Gully
Napes Central
The Sphinx
14
16
28
20
Climber's Traverse
Napes Needle
Page 246

AP

Westmorland Crags
Page 246
29
Connecting Ridge
Great Hell Gate
Descent
1 Lucifer Ridge VD
14 Arrowhead Ridge Direct VD
16 Abbey Buttress S
17 Eagle's Nest Ordinary Route VD
20 Eagle's Nest Ridge Direct MVS 4a
28 Needle Ridge VD
29 Pinnacle Ridge M
Back Staircase
Descent
Great Hell Gate
Hell Gate
Pillar
Tophet Wall
Page 238
1
Langdale
Dow
Eskdale
Scafell
Gable
Buttermere
Borrowdale
Eastern
EV

TOPHET WALL

OS Grid Ref: NY 210 099
Altitude: 650m

Magnificent and impressively steep with an unforgettable atmosphere.

Tophet Wall HS (page 241) Paul Horsman — JON HALL

Approach: From Kern Knotts (see page 233) follow the Climber's Traverse west to arrive at the scree slope of Great Hell Gate below this stunning wall.

See map page 230.

Descent: From the top follow the ridge north until it joins a broad saddle and then descend Great Hell Gate to the base of the crag. It is faster to descend 'the back staircase', a narrow diagonal scramble from near the top of *Tophet Wall*, into Great Hell Gate.

The first two routes are reached by an easy scramble.

1 Lucifer Ridge 43m VD ★
The distinctive ridge is followed in three pitches with a step down and left at 15m.
FG Balcombe, JA Shepherd - Jun 1934

2 Lucifer Crack 30m S ★
A traverse left avoids the first 6m; pass a niche to a large ledge (belay); then take the cracked wall above.
F Graham - Oct 1925

3 Tophet Bastion 82m VD ★
Start at the bottom of a broken arête on the left side of a large diagonal ramp.
1 20m The easy arête across a grass ledge then a steep corner on the right to a rock platform.
2 17m The slab for 8m to a ledge; step left around the corner and up a steep arête.
3 12m Step right and straight up for 7m then climb the awkward groove direct (crux).
4 16m Scramble up steep grass to the Shark's Fin high on the left.
5 17m Starting from the right, climb the edge of the rib to the foot of a crack in a V-groove. Climb the crack exiting left.
HM Kelly, EH Prior, AR Thomson, E Kelly, CG Crawford - Jun 1919

4 Tophet Grooves Direct 78m E1 5b ★
The obvious diagonal groove at the left side of the crag, slow to dry.
1 18m 5b Follow the groove to a good ledge on the right.
2 18m 5b Climb the scoop above past a doubtful block to the overhang; step right and pull over the bulge.
3 24m 5b Step right and climb the mossy wall to a good ledge. Move back left into the main groove, climb the overhanging cleft through the roof, then an easier groove to a large ledge.
4 18m 4a Scramble to and climb a prominent rib.
SJH Reid, J Grinbergs - Jul 1991

5 The Vikings 57m E3 5c ★★★
An awesome archetypal Lakeland crack - determination is essential.
1 42m 5c Climb leftwards to reach a steep crack, follow it then step right into another crack and pull into the corner above. Climb the corner and exit left at the top to a good ledge. Move back right and attack the main overhanging crack through the obvious flared niche then directly to a grassy crack leading to a pedestal belay.
2 15m 4b The crack and groove above are suitably anti-climactic.
AR McHardy, P Braithwaite - Jun 1969

6 Tophet Grooves 84 m HVS 5b ★
The first route to breech the left side of this buttress. Start below a nose about 3m right of the obvious upstanding block.
1 22m 5b Climb the nose direct stepping left into a grassy groove leading to a large sloping ledge.
2 12m 4a Descend the groove then climb the crack to a large pedestal. Traverse the narrow ledge leftwards to belay below a mossy groove.
3 15m 5a Climb the groove (doubtful blocks) to the overhang, traverse right across a mossy scoop onto a rib. Move up the rib and then step left back into the groove.
4 20m 4c Step right and climb the mossy wall to a ledge, then follow the grassy crack on the right to a large pedestal belay.
5 15m 4b The crack and groove above.
RJ Birkett, V Veevers - Oct 1940

7 Incantations 87m E6 6b ★★★
A superlative test piece with two powerful pitches.
1 22m 5b P1 *Tophet Grooves*.
2 35m 6b Serious and sustained with no real rests. Difficult, bold moves lead up the overhanging wall (wires out left). Continue up the wall (wires behind expanding flakes) to reach a thin right-slanting crack in the steep slab above. Climb the crack to ledges, then move rightwards over a bulge and step up right onto the Great Slab. Climb up to the *Demon Wall* traverse, then move left to a good pinnacle belay.
3 30m 6b Climb the rib above the belay; step right to below a thin right-slanting crack in the overhanging wall. Climb the wall (cams) to a jug (peg), move right and pull into the groove above follow it and its right-hand branch to the top.
P Whillance, DW Armstrong - Aug 1984

8 Supernatural 82m E5 6a ★★★

This intricate line up the steep wall right of *Incantations* has a committing and serious middle pitch with a beckoning peg. Start at a steep shallow groove just right of a large grassy groove.

1 25m 5c Climb the groove, moving right at the top onto the wall. Move up and make a difficult pull left onto the rib which leads to a good ledge and pinnacle.

2 32m 6a Climb the steep wall to a bulge (peg out left) and move boldly onto the steep hanging slab above. Reach the base of a steep groove on the left and climb to a spike. Step right, climb a rib and groove that lead to good holds on the Great Slab. Step left and climb the slab until an easy traverse can be made leftwards to a ledge and pinnacle belay.

3 25m 5b Climb directly up the rib above the belay to a ledge on the right, then a mossy slab on the left to a sloping ledge. Traverse right along the ledge, then move up and right round the rib on good holds. Climb the wall and V-groove to the top.

P Whillance, DW Armstrong - Jul 1977

9 Breathless 26m E9 7a ★★★

A death-defying and audacious route up the smooth impending top wall of the crag. The climbing starts at **E8**, ramps up in difficulty, with the final move being the hardest. Start at the top of p2 of *Tophet Wall*.

Climb the thin crack (2 blade pegs) to a good hold (2 pegs). Climb directly to an obvious loose block (very poor thin blade peg), then climb the unrelenting hard and dynamic upper wall leftwards to gain the crux.

J Dunne, A Jack - Jun 2000

10 Tophet Wall 75m HS ★★★

Simply magnificent - it has few peers - unequivocally the greatest mountain route of its grade in the District.

1 20m Climb the wall just right of the steep crack until a step left can be made into the crack which is followed to a ledge. An ascending traverse right to a good ledge at the foot of a short dark wall

2 17m The short and bold wall to a broken ledge. Traverse left and climb a groove to a slab, spike belay on the right.

3 38m Semi hand-traverse 10m right in a sensational position to a crack and climb it to a small ledge then follow the crack up rightwards. Climb the small pinnacle on the right, step left into the crack which is followed to a thrilling pull out right onto a flake. Easier climbing up the wall leads to a belay at the start of the scramble descent to Hell's Gate Screes.

HM Kelly, REW Pritchard - Jul 1923

11 Demon Wall 76m VS 5a ★

Delicate and exposed. Start below ramp just right of *Tophet Wall*.

1 18m 5a Climb the ramp to a good spike, make a difficult and committing pull out left onto the steep wall which is followed up to a good ledge.

2 18m 4b Step right round a bulging corner into a recess. Climb its left wall on small holds to a ledge which is followed left to a large corner. (Junction with *Tophet Wall*).

3 20m 4c Follow *Tophet Wall* to a line of good flake holds on the left. Make a rising traverse across the Great Slab in a superb position to a spike belay on the edge.

4 20m Traverse left, step left round a corner and finish up the pockmarked slab.

AR Dolphin, AB Gilchrist - Apr 1945

12 Sacrificial Crack 66m E4 6a ★★★

The frighteningly overhanging intimidating off-width crack has great character.

1 18m 5a Warm up on p1 of *Demon Wall*.

2 25m 5b Poorly protected. Climb the rib just left of *Demon Wall* to a broken ledge, move right and pull over a bulge into the right-hand of two short grooves which leads to a belay just right of the crack, at a shattered pinnacle.

3 23m 6a Climb the wild crack; dynamic and strenuous.

J Lamb, P Botterill, J Taylor - Jun 1978

13 Tophet Ridge 52m VS 4c ★

The steep right arête of the crag. Start below an obvious groove to its right.

1 30m 4c Climb the left wall and a groove to gain the ridge and follow it to a good spike (ledge on the right). From the spike climb the steep wall to reach better holds leading to a grassy corner.

2 22m 4b Climb past a large block to a horizontal crack which is hand traversed into a short corner (junction with *Tophet Wall*). Pull up onto the top of a pinnacle on the right and climb more easily to the top.

S Watson, R Holmes, B Porter, C Cowen - Jun 1932

1 Lucifer Ridge VD
2 Lucifer Crack S
3 Tophet Bastion VD
4 Tophet Grooves Direct E1 5b
5 The Vikings E3 5c
6 Tophet Grooves HVS 5b
7 Incantations E6 6b
8 Supernatural E5 6a
9 Breathless E9 7a
10 Tophet Wall HS
11 Demon Wall VS 5a
12 Sacrificial Crack E4 6a
13 Tophet Ridge VS 4c
Shark's Fin
PR

10
7
12
9
8
Westmorland Crags
Hell Gate
Pillar
A
13
12
11
10
Great Hell Gate

NAPES NEEDLE

OS Grid Ref: NY 210 101
Altitude: 650m

Historical, complex, a place that'll "mak yer fash ye'r ses' seah mich aboo't"... having fun.

Approach: See page 233 and map on page 230. Follow the Climbers' Traverse below Tophet Wall passing under Napes Needle to enter Needle Gully. Up the gully to scramble left onto the Dress Circle, a ledge on the left, which gives the best viewpoint. The Traverse continues below *Eagles Nest Ridge*, a squeeze behind a flake (Fat Man's Agony) and descent into Eagles Nest Gully. Easier ground leads to *Arrowhead Ridge*, beyond which lies Sphinx Rock and Arrowhead Gully.

Caution: Take great care to avoid dislodging any loose rock as the Climbers' Traverse is a very popular path. The gullies are very unstable and should be avoided at all costs.

Descent: From *Arrowhead Ridge* and *Tormentor* scramble up then left to meet the top of the steep rocky path that leads down towards the Sphinx Rock. The descents from *Needle Ridge* and *Eagle's Nest Ridge* are quite long; scramble up until it is possible to go down the screes of Great Hell Gate - or for a mountaineering day continue up to climb Pinnacle Ridge on Westmorland's Crag before going to the summit of Great Gable.

Or use the abseil anchor above *Crocodile Crack*; another alternative is to downclimb *Eagle's Nest Ordinary Route.*

14 Arrowhead Ridge Direct 80m VD ★★★
Steep and exposed climbing to the distinctive Arrowhead. From the lowest point of the ridge on the left easy scrambling then steeper rock lead to a good ledge. The steep ridge leads to a pinnacle; step off this onto a slab then up steeply on good holds to the top of the Arrowhead. Stride across the gap, traverse a horizontal section then scramble up the ridge; belay as needed.
AG Topham, H Walker, WC Slingsby - Mar1896

15 The Tormentor 35m E4 6a ★★
Technical and intimidating climbing up the centre of the clean slab. Gain the lower left edge of the slab by climbing the short crack and stepping left along a grassy ledge. Pull onto the slab and follow a faint weakness up and right (runner), pull back to good holds at the foot of a diagonal crack. Follow this to the centre of the slab and make some scary moves straight up to the overlap (runner). Pull over and right on improving holds to another diagonal break and finish up a thin crack.
A Phizacklea, AH Greenbank - Aug 1987

16 Abbey Buttress 58m S ★★★
Classic, with a devious and exciting second pitch. Start at the foot of the buttress behind Fat Man's Agony.
1 20m Climb directly to a ledge, step right and follow a steep crack to a second ledge.
2 20m Steep moves lead to a ledge at 4m. Traverse left for 5m and then straight up for 8m followed by a traverse back right below an overhang to an arête leading to a large ledge.
3 18m Cracked blocks immediately right of the grassy gully to a ledge, then the corner on the left to a junction with *Eagle's Nest Ordinary Route.*
FW Botterill, J de V Hazard - Apr1909

17 Eagle's Nest Ordinary Route (West Chimney) 107m VD ★★
A Victorian, very traditional chimney. The wider left hand grassy chimney.
1 30m Easy rocks lead to the West Chimney.
2 12m Up and right through a crevasse then up a smooth slabby groove to a belay in the corner.
3 12m The awkward chimney above is followed by the ridge on the left.
4 18m A chimney on the left is followed by scrambling up broken rocks to the foot of a tower.
5 35m Pull up the short steep crack to an exposed rock ledge and move right into the boulder-choked chimney. Follow the scratches and scramble along the ridge.
GA Solly, M Schintz - Apr 1892

18 Long John 33m VS 4c ★★
A superb delicate pitch up the strip of rock just right of *West Chimney*. Climb straight up to the bottom of the chimney on the right, step left and climb the centre of the slab until forced left. Climb to a ledge leading back right to the centre of the slab; now trend left to a platform. Continue up or down *West Chimney*.
HG Knight, HM Kelly - Apr 1928

19 Longbow 40m E1 5b ★★
The clean wall left of *Eagle's Nest Ridge Direct*. Start below the chimney right of *Long John*. Step right onto a rib leading rightwards over a small triangular overhang to a good foot ledge. Step left and climb up the wall to join a right slanting crack leading to the Eagle's Nest. From its top, move left and climb the wall to where the angle eases. Belay in the corner at the top of *Eagle's Nest Ridge Direct.*
D Rogers, A Leece - Jun 2014

20 Eagle's Nest Ridge Direct 45m MVS 4a ★★★

The ascent of the blunt arête overlooking the Dress Circle was an amazing achievement for 1892. It shouted at them to be climbed! Two days later Solly was back, grovelling in *West Chimney*. From directly below the arête steep climbing rightwards on good holds leads to a ledge. Gain the arête up on the left using two parallel cracks, climb it past the Eagle's Nest, Crow's Nest and a bold slab to a good ledge. Belay in the corner.

GA Solly, WC Slingsby, GP Bakes, WA Brigg - Apr 1892

21 The Cayman 45m E2 5b ★★★

Excellent face climbing. Climb the overhang and crack above to meet *Crocodile Crack*. Step right and climb the thin diagonal crack to an overlap. Surmount this and continue up the wall above to the next overhang. Pull over and move up and right to a ledge on the arête. Follow the steep arête to a good ledge.

P Whillance, DW Armstrong - Aug 1977

22 Crocodile Crack 43m HVS 5a ★★★

An excellent climb up the obvious wide crack above the Dress Circle. Climb the flake crack for 8m before moving left into the main crackline leading over an overhang to a good ledge.

G Oliver, G Arkless, P Ross, N Brown - Apr1960

23 Alligator Crawl 42m HS ★

Start below a wide chimney which is bounded by an oblique overhang.

1 15m Climb the chimney to a ledge.

2 27m Step off the top of the block onto the wall to reach a good crack leading to a ledge.

G Oliver, G Arkless - May 1960

24 Amos Moses 60m E1 5b ★★

Start below the right-hand end of the Dress Circle at the bottom of a subsidiary buttress split by a wide right-slanting crack.

1 25m 5a Gain the crack from the left and climb it to a slab and pinnacle.

2 35m 5b From the pinnacle follow the prominent crack to a small ledge and move up and left to the foot of an obvious groove. Pull rightwards into the groove and climb more easily to a stony ledge.

P Long, T Parker - Jun1987

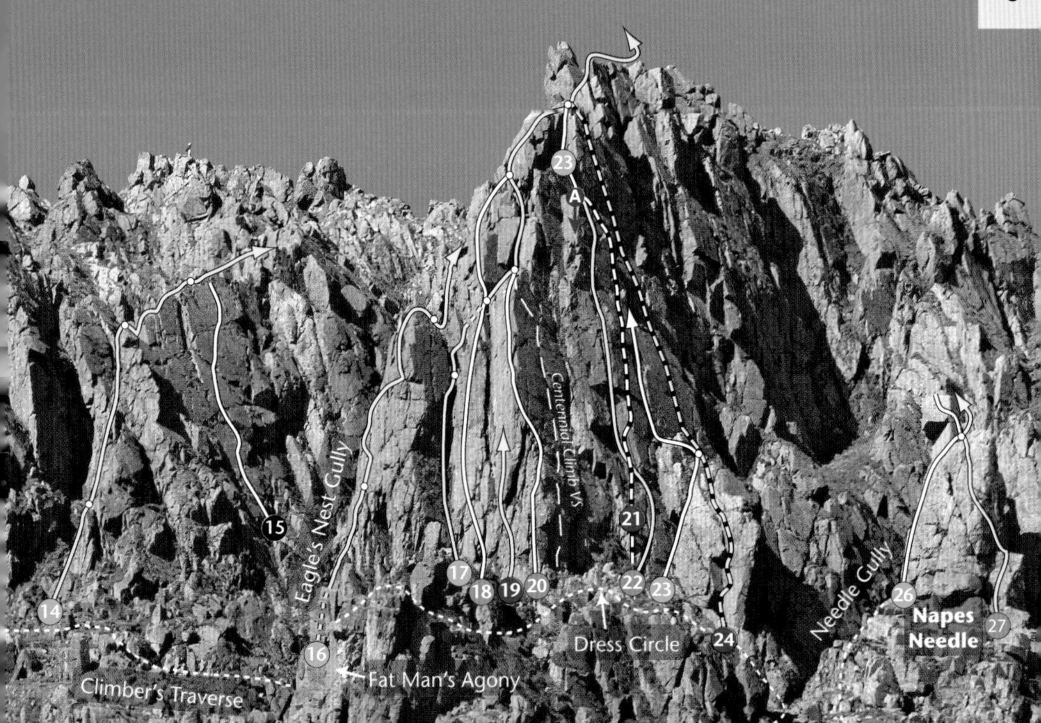

Napes Needle

A great attraction for many climbers, an ascent provides a unique and memorable experience. The first two routes share the same belay and top pitch; the final moves have acquired a particular glass-like sheen and require care.

Descent: ⚠ A good way is for the leader to lower the second to a belay on the Shoulder and then down-climb to that point protected by the second. Then, having lowered the second back to the ground, the leader down-climbs via *The Arête* safeguarded by runners placed on the ascent or by the second.

Threading the Needle (M) is a popular classic and follows the highly polished scramble through the cleft between Napes Needle and *Needle Ridge*.

25 The Wasdale Crack 17m HS ★★★
The original way. Start below the obvious wide crack.
1 13m Climb the awkward crack then an easy slab to the Shoulder.
2 4m Mantelshelf the narrow ledge, traverse left onto the face and climb delicately to the top.
WP Haskett Smith - Jun 1886

26 The Arête 20m HS ★★★
1 16m From the bottom of *The Wasdale Crack* traverse horizontally right until a pull round onto the arête can be made, climb it to the Shoulder.
2 4m Take *The Wasdale Crack*.
WH Fowler - Sep 1894

27 The Obverse Route 24m MVS 4b ★★★
A brilliant top pitch. Pass through the gap behind the Needle to reach an obvious crack on the side of the Needle facing Lingmell.
1 18m 4b Climb the steep slab right of the crack on small holds to the Platform, then a large flake, followed by a slab, to the Shoulder.
2 6m 4b Hand-traverse right, along the horizontal crack under the top block (and over the Gap) to gain its northwest arête (opposite *Needle Ridge*). Finish with steep moves up the arête on good holds.
SW Herford, W Brunskill - Aug 1912

28 Needle Ridge 114m VD ★★★
The classic mountaineering route to the summit of Great Gable. Start from the Gap behind the Needle.
1 12m Climb the very polished slab above the Gap to a short shallow chimney that trends left to a block belay on the edge of the ridge below a steep wall.
2 18m The crack in the steep wall above, followed by easier rocks to a blocky ledge. Scramble along the crest of the ridge for 7m to a stance.
3 15m Climb the chimney above for 4m, then step left onto the edge and follow this to a ledge. Climb the short corner on the right.
4 34m Climb the groove above which leads to the crest of the ridge, step around this and follow a straight crack in the wall overlooking the gully which leads back onto the crest.
5 35m Easy scrambling along the gendarmed crest to the main ridge of The Napes.

The descent down to Great Hell Gate lies 20m along the main ridge, down a red scree chute. Or continue to the summit, perhaps via *Pinnacle Ridge*.
WP Haskett Smith, JW Robinson - Sep 1884

Westmorland Crags (NY 211 102)

This quite large but broken crag offers a delightful easy ridge that is an ideal continuation to one of the Napes ridges on the way to the summit of Great Gable. Westmorland's Cairn stands on the flat ledge at the top of the buttress and offers a magnificent viewpoint.

Approach: The best approach is *Needle Ridge* or any other route to the Connecting Ridge; followed by a descent rightwards along the base of the crag.

29 Pinnacle Ridge 150m M ★★
From the lowest rocks, well to the right, scramble up well-trodden low rocks and ledges with a steeper section up a short corner, to reach the Pinnacle after 90m. Go left behind this then up a steep wall (well-marked) on the left to gain the crest. Up this then along a horizontal section with short rises for a further 60m to reach a lawn and path to the top.

27
The Wasdale Roof E3
25
26
28
AP
Langdale
Dow
Eskdale
Scafell
Gable
Buttermere
Borrowdale
Eastern
EV

GABLE CRAG

OS Grid Ref: NY 212 105
Altitude: 800m

A superb high mountain crag giving atmospheric climbing on excellent rock. The main feature is a steep crack-seamed wall with sustained well-protected routes; the walls between offer very bold and committing climbing. As it faces north, allow a good spell of dry weather to bring the climbs into condition, and pack a jumper.

Approach: From the summit of Honister Pass Youth Hostel P NY 22557 13535 the path behind the quarry car park leads onto the well-marked track that runs along the side of Grey Knotts. Break off right to a small stile and a vague path joining a better path to reach the screes below the crag. See map page 230.

Descent: Either carefully descend the precarious grassy ledges to the right (looking out); or a 50m abseil from above the left side of the face. With 60m ropes an abseil can be made from the top of *Sarcophagus*.

Alternatively follow the walkers' paths around either end of the crag, this involves a long walk.

The climbs are reached by a steep scramble or by climbing *Sledgate Ridge*.

1 Sledgate Ridge 73m MVS 4b ★★
The clean buttress starting at an obvious jamming crack in a short steep wall right next to the path.
1 20m 4b The difficult crack followed by water worn grooves on the right for 10m, then the wall on the left to a large ledge.
2 18m 4a From the left end of the ledge climb the wall, then slabs on the right to a large ledge
3 35m 4a The wall above to climb the central of three vertical cracks.
AH Greenbank, J Wilkinson, AE Wormell - Jun 1958

Scramble rightwards and descend a short gully to the base of the slabs.

2 Powder Finger 45m E3 6a ★★
Technical and absorbing. Start just right of the Chimney. Climb to a ledge and loose blocks. Pull into the slim hanging groove on the left and climb to the overhang, step right onto the arête (flake) and gain a rest. Move up to a poor flake and make committing moves rightwards over the bulge to stand on a good hold. Traverse back left and up to a crack then continue left to a shallow groove leading to the top.
C Downer, A Redfearn - May 1987

3 Dream Twister 45m E3 5c ★★
Sustained and well protected. Climb to a ledge and loose blocks. Pull into the groove on the right, exiting right at the top to a ledge on the wall. Climb the wall direct to the overhang and pull over using the crack moving left at its top into a wider crack curving to a ledge. The short crack above leads to a large belay ledge.
C Downer, A Hall - Jul 1987

4 The Troll 60m HVS 5b ★
Start directly below an obvious jammed block overhang at about 25m.
1 28m 5b Climb to the block overhang; pass it by the crack on its right to a ledge.
2 32m 5a Step right and climb steep slabs for 12m to a break, traverse right to follow a flake-line then step right into a groove that leads to the top.
AG Cram, L Rodgers - Jun 1967

5 The Angel of Mercy 60m E1 5b ★★
Quite tough and steep with a distinct crux. Take large cams.
1 25m 5a Follow *The Troll* to belay below the block overhang.
2 35m 5b Traverse rightwards across the sandwiched slab to a steep crack. Enter and follow this to where the angle eases. Climb the ramp up and right to finish up a wide overhanging crack splitting the headwall.
J Lamb, P Botterill - June 1979

6 Interceptor 65m VS 4c ★★
Complex and technical; a worthy companion to *Engineer's Slabs*.
1 30m 4c Climb to the left end of a ledge, then straight up to the right end of another ledge. An ascending traverse right leads to the twin cracks of *Engineer's Slabs* and the sentry box
2 15m 4c Climb straight up the groove above to the overhangs; traverse left to parallel cracks leading to belay by a huge flake.
3 20m 4c Layback the flake, traverse right to a groove and climb it until a prominent spike on the right can be reached. Climb the rib to the top.
P Fearnehough, NJ Soper - Jun 1967

	Route	Grade
7	**Snicker Snack**	E3 5c
8	**Engineer's Slabs**	VS 4c
9	**The Tomb**	E2 5c
10	**Sarcophagus**	E3 5c
11	**Unfinished Arête**	HVS 5a
12	**The Jabberwock**	HVS 5a

7 Snicker Snack 57m E3 5c ★★★

Superb and well protected.

1 45m 5c Climb the wall of *Engineer's Slabs* for 12m, step left and follow the straight crack through the overlap, then up the thin crack above to belay at a huge flake.

2 12m 5b Climb the flake, traverse right and cross a small overhang to gain a thin crack which has an awkward finish.

C Downer, A Hall - July 1986

8 Engineer's Slabs 60m VS 4c ★★★

Magnificent climbing up the central crack and groove line. Start just left of a groove in the middle of the face.

1 26m 4c The wall leads to the foot of a crack. Climb the crack for 5m then move across to twin cracks on the right, a chimney and the sentry box.

2 34m 4c Traverse right for 2m into a crack and climb this to a ledge, followed by a layback crack to a second ledge. The chimney above gives access to the fine groove which provides a fitting finale.

FG Balcombe, JA Shepherd, CJA Cooper - Jun 1934

9 The Tomb 68m E2 5c ★★★

Bold wall climbing with good but widely spaced protection. Start 5m right of *Engineer's Slabs*.

1 18m 4c Traverse right and up to gain and climb the obvious sentry box, leftwards up the wall above to a ledge, then step left to belay below a break.

2 20m 5c The wall on the left is climbed for 6m to a rest (runners above). Move right under the overlap to its end (runners) and pull through to a small ledge. Traverse right into a steep crack which leads to a good stance.

3 30m 5a The groove above to the overhang, step left into the open groove which leads to the top.

AG Cram, W Young - Sep 1966

10 Sarcophagus 64m E3 5c ★★★

Even bolder wall climbing, steady nerves are essential on the second pitch.

1 18m 4c As for p1 of *The Tomb* to the sentry box. Climb the wall above then step right to a large flake.

2 18m 5c Step up left to a small block at the right end of a grass ledge. Step off the block and make a series of increasingly committing moves up the wall to join *The Tomb* at the end of the traverse. Move left to a thin crack, climb up to the overlap (good runners) and pull over strenuously, stepping right onto a narrow ledge.

3 28m 5b Move up and left to climb a groove/crack-line and crack above, finish up a groove.

P Whillance, DW Armstrong - Jul 1977

11 Unfinished Arête 63m HVS 5a ★

The bold and isolated arete. Start just right of *The Tomb*, where the grass ledge begins to fall away to the right.

1 15m 4b Traverse right to below the sentry box. Climb up and right to a small groove that leads to a ledge below the arête.

2 23m 5a Climb the arête to a small overlap and traverse right, then up to a grass ledge. Continue up the arête to a sloping ledge and shattered blocks.

3 25m 4c As for p3 of *The Jabberwock*.

FG Balcombe, JA Shepherd - Jun1934

12 The Jabberwock 75m HVS 5a ★★

Beware the Jabberwock, my son! The jaws that bite, the claws that catch! It has a wild finish! Start from the lowest point of the wall, just right of the final gully on the approach scramble.

1 22m 4c Climb the cracked wall to ledges on the right of a large flake.

2 28m 5a Climb the crack, passing a large ledge at 18m, to a sloping ledge and shattered blocks

3 25m 4c The short slab on the left leads to a very exposed groove which is climbed to the top on good holds but, beware loose blocks... And, has thou slain the Jabberwock? Lewis Carroll

R Valentine, J Wilkinson - Jun 1970

The Jabberwock HVS

BOAT HOW CRAGS

OS Grid Ref: NY 199 110
Altitude: 700m

This crag has a unique feeling of remoteness and is well worth the effort needed to get there. It boasts an impressive central pillar with high quality routes on very rough rock, takes little drainage and gets the summer sun from late afternoon. The routes on the main wall were cleaned in 2013 but may benefit from a bit more cleaning before an ascent. The fine West Face receives the sun earlier.

Approach: From Honister Pass Youth Hostel P NY 22557 13535 take the route to Stone Cove below Gable Crag. Climb to Beck Head col, bear left up the east shoulder of Kirk Fell until just beyond the top of the steep section, and descend rightwards to the top of the crag. Either scramble down a short way to an idyllic gearing up and picnic spot in a grassy bowl and abseil to the routes, or follow an easy descent to the foot of the crags. Beck Head Col can also be reached from Wasdale by the relentlessly steep path up Gavel Neese on Great Gable. See map page 230.

Descent: 50m abseil from a large thread at the top of Main Wall. There is also an abseil down the West Face. Alternatively take the wide gully on the right of the main crag.

Breakwater Slabs

These lie to the left of the main wall and are composed of good quick drying rock.

1 Groyne Strain 26m E1 5b ★★

Start at the top of a large block below a grooved arête. Step delicately left to a small triangular niche, then smear leftwards to gain a higher recess in the slab. Follow the thin crack directly, moving left where it eases. Traverse right to finish up *Topsail* or abseil.

A Phizacklea, JL Holden - Jun 2006

2 Breakwater Slabs, Grooved Arête 30m VS 4c ★

Starting above a jammed block. Step onto the arête from the right and follow a stepped groove on the right edge, pulling left over a bulge to belay below broken slabs. Abseil or continue to the top.

HS Gross, G Basterfield, B Tyson - May1928.

3 Topsail 12m E2 5b ★★

This fine arête makes a good top pitch to *Groyne Strain*.

E Rogers, K Forsythe - Jun 2006

Main Wall - The Boat

The superb steep face looking directly across the head of Ennerdale receives the sun late in the afternoon.

1 Numenor Direct 50m E3 6a ★★★
One of the great E3s of the lakes. Steep and strenuous climbing up a thin ragged crack-line, well-protected throughout with good rests. Start by climbing an awkward leaning corner up to a bulge. Pull out right and move up to the foot of the sharp crack which is followed over a series of bulges to the top.
RO Graham, E Rogers - Jul 1999

2 Voyager 40m E3 5c ★★
Start from a hanging stance about 15m up Numenor. Traverse sensationally rightwards at the level of the second peg on *Flagship*; two hidden right-facing ramps provide holds and runners. From the peg, climb delicately upwards to gain the base of a groove and finish up this.
E Rogers, RO Graham - Jul 1999

3 Flagship 50m E5 5c ★★★
Superb and bold climbing taking a direct line up the wall between *Numenor* and *Fanghorn*. Micro-wires and sky hooks may prevent a possible ground fall from the crux at 12m; it is possible to place a side-runner in *Numenor* before the crux. Climb a small slab (peg). Climb straight up for about 15m past three short grooves (sustained) (peg on the right). Make delicate moves left to reach small cracks (runners). Continue straight up the small steep groove, pull out right, and follow slabs to the top.
D Birkett, S Wood, P Ross - Jun 1995

4 Voyager Direct 50m E6 6a ★★★
Fantastic climbing on very clean, rough rock. Gain the obvious ledge by a thin seam in the centre of the face. Step right and climb direct to an undercling. Reach a good foothold above and left (small wires). Layback the square flake to reach a high sidepull to the left. Further sidepulls and crimps gain the slab above and the sanctuary of the end of the *Voyager* traverse.
S Litchfield, G Read - Jul 2013

5 Fanghorn 50m E3 5c ★★★
Another classic tackling the jutting arête of Main Wall starting at the toe of the blunt arête on the right.
1 20m 5c Climb up to a small corner to the right of the rib then pull left onto the arête. Go straight up with difficulty (old peg). Continue up a shallow groove to a good stance.
2 30m 5b Traverse left across a flake and make a delicate move around a bulge into a hidden groove. Follow the groove directly to the top.
I Roper, NAJ Rogers - Jun 1969

Gable

West Face

The steep wall of excellent clean rock to the right of *Fanghorn*. Facing west it receives the sun shortly after mid-day.

6 Jolly Roger 50m E2 5c ★★
Start below the open groove, 9m right of the arête.
1 20m 5c Climb the groove to an awkward slot in the overhang. Step left and climb a groove to a grass ledge.
2 30m 5a Climb the groove then take a shallow corner on the left to finish.
E Rogers, RO Graham - Jul 1999

7 Trim and Incline 28m E3 5c ★★
Start 6m right of *Jolly Roger*. Climb to a hanging flake (poor nut) with a loose block at its top. Make a series of long reaches up a set of 'steps' (skyhook), then go right (skyhook, poor wire). Traverse left and up to reach a good hold (runners). Either move up and make a long reach left above the diagonal roof, then climb directly up a shallow scoop to a belay or step left from the runners and climb a shallow groove to the same place. Either abseil off, or finish up *Poseidon Adventure*.
A Phizacklea, K Phizacklea - Jul 1997

8 Poseidon Adventure 50m E4 6a ★★
Start 5m right of *Trim and Incline*.
1 25m 6a Climb the shallow groove/chimney and exit left at the overhang. Move left to the second skyhook placement on *Trim and Incline* (poor wire). Climb directly up the wall above with difficulty to the apex of the roof and pull over this on dramatically improving holds to a good ledge.
2 25m 5a Climb the rib defining the edge of the North and West Faces, gaining it from the right.
RO Graham, A Jones - Aug 1999

9 Scenic Cruise 45m HVS 5a ★★★
A direct line with steep sustained climbing on excellent quick drying rock. Start just left of a big chimney.
Climb a left-leaning scoop/groove for about 6m then make a couple of interesting moves right to a crack-line. Step right and climb straight up, heading for the base of the steep groove at the highest point of the buttress. Pull out left and climb a delicate slab to the top.
P Ross, P Greenwood - Aug 1996

10 The Golden Rivet 38m HVS 5a ★★
1 14m 4c Follow *Scenic Cruise* for 6m then climb the straight crack system to a ledge.
2 24m 5a Climb the flake-line up a shallow rib to where the rock bulges, then step down and traverse across the wall on the right to the edge overlooking the top of the chimney. Pull steeply up a short groove then out right onto the edge of the rib and finish directly.
A Phizacklea, JL Holden - Jun 2006

Langdale
Eskdale
Scafell
Gable
Buttermere
Borrowdale
Eastern
EV

PILLAR ROCK

OS Grid Ref: NY 172 125
Altitude: 600m

Imposing and atmospheric, offering superb climbs over a wide variety of grades on impeccable rock, and worth every bit of the long approach. Pillar Rock was a focal point for the earliest pioneers of rock climbing in the Lake District.

The Appian Way HS (page 277) Martin Attwood, Martin Armitage — Stephen Reid

This remote crag, attractive to seekers of solitude, is rightly numbered amongst the great crags of the Lake District. Ennerdale does not have a public road and crag approaches are long and arduous, though extensive forestry has resulted in a network of tracks accessible to cyclists; using a bike cuts down access times significantly. Apart from two youth hostels and a field centre, there are no facilities in the valley and the nearest campsites are at Buttermere or Wasdale.

Pillar Rock consists of two cones stuck together one behind and above the other, the summits being Low Man and High Man. High Man, the highest point of the crag, is only accessible by climbing and is awkward to descend.

From Ennerdale, the imposing North Face of Low Man is above you, horizontally split by Green Ledge, from which the climbs start. The Shamrock is to the left, the Great Heather Shelf running diagonally across its centre. Well round to the right above the scree lies the West Face.

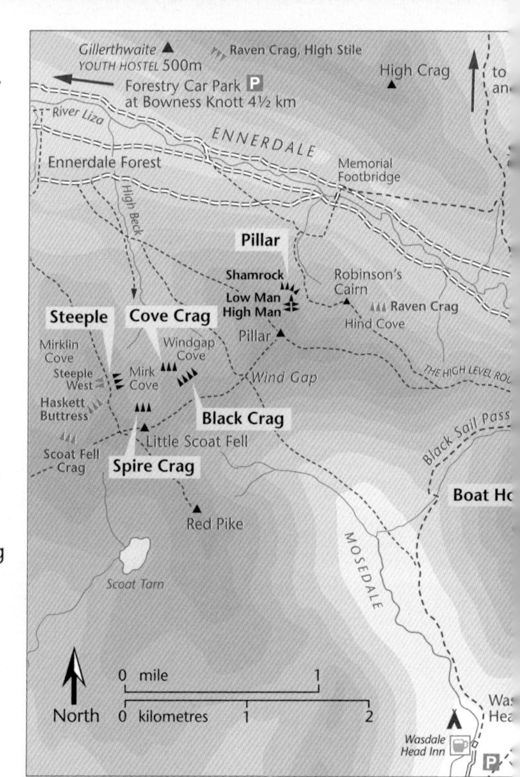

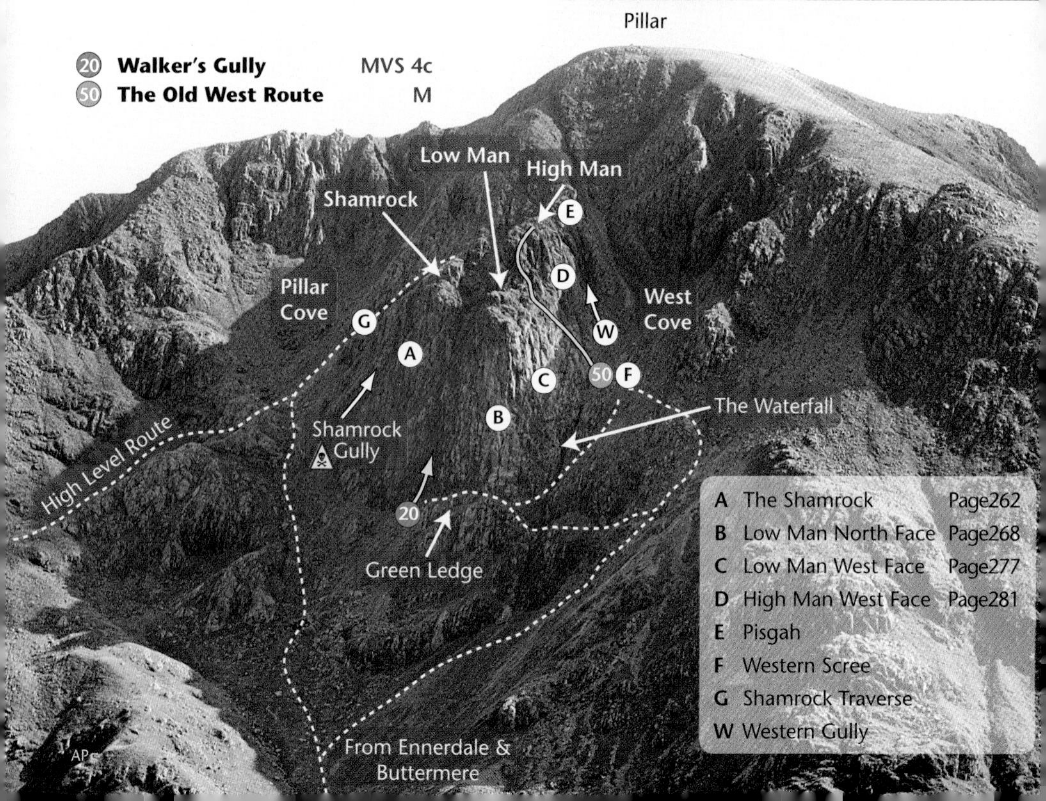

Approach, Wasdale: The traditional approach from Wasdale Head (P NY 18680 08957) takes the path towards Black Sail Pass. Just after crossing Gatherstone Beck, the path forks. Follow the upper branch to Looking Stead. Carry on a short way on the path towards Pillar where a small cairn and narrow path to the right marks the start of the High Level Route. Contour the northern slopes of Pillar. Go either way at the split, they rejoin in Hind Cove a short distance from Robinson's Cairn. In front, the magnificent eastern profile of Pillar Rock appears.

Approach, Ennerdale: No vehicles are allowed beyond the Forestry car park at Bowness Knott (P NY 10955 15433) but using bikes from here can knock an hour off the approach. Take the dirt road passing Gillerthwaite youth hostel, cross the concrete bridge and continue to a junction with the upper forest road. Turn right and after 450m hide the bikes and take the pleasant unsigned path into the cove. If walking, 50m past the concrete bridge some wooden steps mark the start of a good, wet path to the rock.

Approach, Buttermere: A long walk, but hey, the scenery is gorgeous. From Gatesgarth Farm (P NY 19527 14985), cross Scarth Gap, then diagonally down above Black Sail YH, following a path in a westerly direction to reach the valley floor at the Memorial Footbridge and a junction with the Ennerdale approach.

Camping: On the ridge to the left of the stream on the Ennerdale approach are small areas of flat ground only 15 minutes from the crag. They catch the sun early, keep it late and have a water supply.

Descent: Shamrock Gully, which is very loose and serious, should not be attempted as a descent (or an ascent for that matter). Above and left though is the start of the Shamrock Traverse, a very obvious ramp which leads diagonally rightwards to a good viewpoint above Walker's Gully. From here the short East Face of High Man is in view, home to *Slab and Notch Climb* (M), the most popular means of descent. To the left of the East Face of High Man is yet another cone, albeit a small one, Pisgah, which is separated from High Man by a deep cleft, the Jordan Gap. Leading up to the Jordan Gap from near the start of *Slab and Notch Climb* is East Jordan Gully, an easy scramble. Do not try to descend West Jordan Gully. Western Gully lies between Pisgah and Pillar and can be descended with care into West Cove.

South-West Climb MVS (page 284) Chris Cox, Harry Ellis — Stephen Reid

East Face of High Man

Sunny short climbs reached by following the Shamrock Traverse.

Climbs from Jordan Gap

Approach: From the east via the scramble of East Jordan Gully.

Descent: Reverse *Slab and Notch Climb* or abseil from a block near the summit cairn.

Slab and Notch (in descent): From the summit move 10m north to find an obvious cleft and chimney splitting the East Face. Descend the chimney easily for a few metres, move left (facing in) onto a stepped slab. Downclimb to a good ledge leading left (facing in) to a short steep broken arête. Descend the arête for 5m to another ledge. From the ledge move left (facing in) to the Notch and descend either of the steep grooves beyond to gain the Slab. Traverse the Slab leftwards (facing in) and climb up its left edge slightly, then descend to the foot of East Jordan Gully.

1 Jordan Bastion 20m VS 4c ★
The steep thin crack is awkward, sustained and strenuous - a bit of a test. From the middle of the Gap, stride across a cleft and approach the crack from the left.
CG Crawford, CF Holland - Aug 1919

2 Central Jordan Climb 20m VD ★
Immediately right of the highest part of the Gap a block corner with a crack leads to a big sloping ledge. The steep wide crack in the corner, a huge flake, and a short wall lead to High Man.
WP Haskett Smith - Aug 1882

3 East Jordan Climb 30m VS 4c ★
Above two large jammed chockstones near the bottom of East Jordan Gully is an open-angled corner. Get established and climb to a ledge on the left. A tiny spike on the right unlocks the way on.
WP Haskett Smith - Aug 1884

(4) East Jordan Wall 30m VS 4b ★★

A superb, bold route unmarred by suspect rock towards the top. From East Jordan Gully climb a short corner, wiggle left and right into an open groove to reach a niche at 10m. Leave this up and rightwards to a vague slim groove, climb this to the wall below the top.

CG Crawford, CF Holland - Aug 1919

(5) Slab and Notch Climb 60m M ★★★

Wanders around finding the easiest way up and down. Start at the foot of East Jordan Gully well below Jordan Gap. Climb onto the large easy-angled Slab on the right at its top left-hand corner and descend slightly. Traverse easily across its base and climb either of two steep grooves to the Notch (20m). Move right along a narrow ledge for 4m and then climb the wall/arête direct to another ledge. Move right and climb slabs before stepping right into the upper section of a large gully on the left - The Great Chimney.

JWE Conybeare, AJ Butler, E Leeke, JC Leeke, TRC Campbell, JD Poyer, JW Pratt - Aug 1863

(6) Pendlebury Traverse 20m M ★

From the Notch follow a ledge on the left to a short chimney. Climb over or round a block at the top onto a moderate upward traverse to a chimney in the corner.

F Gardiner, WM Pendlebury, R Pendlebury, J Hasking, HJ Priest - Sep 1872

(7) The Curtain and The Arête 78m HS ★★

This climb runs up the curtain of rock forming the left side of Great Chimney. Start on a flat grassy ledge (cairn), just above the lowest short wall of the arête.

1 26m *The Curtain*. The wall with good if dodgy holds is followed by an awkward wide crack which starts from a precariously poised block on the right. Continue up rightwards on good holds and following the narrowing ridge to a good spike belay just before a large flat ledge.

2 7m Traverse the ledge leftwards and climb up to the Notch.

3 45m *The Arête*. Just right of the Notch, climb a slightly overhanging right-hand corner on good holds to a slight headwall overcome via a thin left-slanting crack. The arête leads to the top.

WP Haskett Smith (The Arete) - Prior to 1884

(8) The Great Chimney 110m S ★

This prominent cleft splits the East Face and runs from near the top of *Walker's Gully* to the summit of High Man. It makes a good continuation to *Walker's Gully*.

WP Haskett Smith - Mar 1887

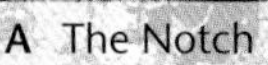

The Shamrock

A large rambling crag with several long and interesting routes, in the main on excellent rock though it can be lichenous and mossy in places. Grassy ledges abound and dry conditions are desirable. *Photon, Eros* and *Thanatos*, do dry quickly, as this section of the crag catches the morning sun.

Descent: From the Tea Table scramble down to the head of Shamrock Gully, above the scree funnel of Walker's Gully, then scramble up rightwards and back leftwards to emerge at the top of the Shamrock Traverse descent (see photo page 256).

The Upper Tier

Approach: By a steep vegetated scramble from its left-hand end or a route on the Lower Tier.

9 Graviton 145m HVS 5a ★★

Of similar character to *Eros*.

1 20m 4c Climb to the left arête. Go boldly up this to a slight break and continue until it eases. Downclimb the grassy chimney on the left to a stance at the foot of another arête.

2 30m 4b Climb the crack just right of the arête to a small ledge. Gain the arête and follow it (hidden wires on right) to a groove which leads to a stance.

3 40m 4a Climb the broken grassy wall to an easy arête overlooking Shamrock Gully. Follow this and climb a cracked slab round to the left of the smooth diamond-shaped wall to regain the arête; go up to a stance.

4 25m 5a Climb up a couple of metres to the left of the steep wall of the final tower, then traverse one metre left along a grass ledge (above Shamrock Gully) and climb boldly up the first shallow groove to the crest of the ridge.

5 30m Easier climbing along the ridge to the Tea Table.

SJH Reid, C King - May 2005

10 Photon 147m VS 4c ★★

A long and varied climb of a mountaineering character.

1 25m 4c Climb the steepening groove to below a sharp arête (*Eros*).

2 30m 4c Move right and go up a slabby corner to the foot of a groove. Ascend the steep corner to a bulge, climb the steep crack on the right to reach a good ledge on the left.

3 37m Climb the corner above and continue past a huge chockstone to a good ledge. Climb the mossy slab on the left to finish on a ledge overlooking Shamrock Gully.

4 25m 4b Climb up a couple of metres to the left of the steep wall of the final tower, then traverse 3m left along a grass ledge under a shallow groove and up into a broken groove leading to the crest of the ridge.

5 30m Follow the ridge to the Tea Table.

WA Barnes, A Jackman, JC Eilbeck, DA Elliott - Sep 1967

11 Eros 152m E2 5b ★★★

The bold ribs produce an extremely good climb.

1 25m 5a Bold. The rib direct and a mossy slab lead to a good ledge at the foot of a sharp arête.

2 30m 5b Even bolder. More of the same, the steep rib on its right side for 18m; up the slab above to a ledge then traverse left to a grassy corner.

3 22m 5b Tricky. Climb the corner-groove in the right edge of the diamond-shaped wall.

4 20m 4a Continue to a ledge on the right. Step left across the groove and climb the left edge of a slab then a ridge to beneath the final tower.

5 & 6 55m 4b Join *Photon*.

WS Lounds, JC Eilbeck - 18 May 1968

The Shamrock Chimneys VD. It's routes like this that give climbing on Pillar a bad name! "Those who visit will find much chimney-sweeping awaiting them." G Abraham FRCCJ 1908

12 Photogenic 124m E1 5b ★★

The highlight of this climb is a fine arete.

1 26m 5a Start up a short scoop right of the deep chimney, and follow the slab above, slightly rightwards at first, then back leftwards, until a traverse can be made left under a square-cut overhang to reach a belay in *The Shamrock Chimneys* at the foot of the arête.

2 28m 5b Gain the arête and climb it on excellent rock. Diligent searching will reveal runners.

3 35m 5b Climb the short rib just right of the grassy gully to a step right onto the other rib. Move up and right, to a grassy recess, a few metres below the big grassy ledge; a bold traverse leads across to the left arête and belay above.

4 35m Traverse along the ridge to the Tea Table.

P2 C King, SJH Reid - Jul 2005, p1 & 3 A Phizacklea, JL Holden - Jul 2005

13 Pauli Exclusion Principle 85m E3 5b ★★

A very serious undertaking.

1 25m 5b Virtually protectionless where it matters. Climb the arête on its right-hand side to a good hold at 10m; moves up and right lead to a small spike (side runners on right). Move up the thin crack above and then trend back left to the arête and follow it to a grass ledge.

2 20m 4c Climb the large flake crack above and an easier wall to a grass ramp which leads to a belay under a short diagonal chimney.

3 25m 5b Another very serious pitch. Climb out rightwards, onto the slabby base of the buttress and move up leftwards to reach the edge of a grassy gully above the chimney. Pull straight up the blunt leftmost arête above and climb it on a series of flat holds.

4 15m The slab on the left and the corner beyond to the top of the Shamrock.

RE Wightman, A Phizacklea - May 1988

The Lower Tier

Below the Great Heather Shelf the best reference point is the large left-facing corner with the left-facing overhang at the top - this is the line of *Thanatos*.

14 Thanatos/Electron 182m HVS 5b ★★★

This combination is one of the best and longest routes on the Shamrock. The layback crack, not technically difficult, is bold and intimidating and the first pitch is hard, especially if wet, which it usually is. Start from the lowest part of the crag, directly beneath the large roofed corner.

1 27m 4b Work up slabs, corners, grass, heather and bilberry to the base of the main corner.

2 30m 5b An excellent, well-protected pitch. Climb to the first overhang. Traverse left onto a rib and enter a groove below the second overhang. Make difficult moves on the left to reach a good ledge.

3 25m An easy groove then the grass and heather of the Shelf leads to a belay.

Electron lies round the corner to the left, reached down, then up, at the foot of a vast vertical right-angled left-facing corner with a short hour-glass shaped chimney on its right.

4 26m 5a Climb the corner past an awkward bulge to a large grass ledge.

5 24m 4b Climb up the broken groove for 12m to a grass ledge and surmount the wall beyond to a large block. Belay at the foot of the imposing, not to mention intimidating, off-width crack.

6 20m 4c The crux! Climb the crack with bravado. A fine character-building pitch.

7 30m 4b Move right and go up the grey arête to a slim ledge 2m below the top of a pinnacle. Traverse 6m right to the foot of a continuation arête and reach the Tea Table.

WS Lounds, JC Eilbeck - May 1968
AG Cram, JC Eilbeck - Sep 1966

15 Thin It Is 177m E1 5b ★★

1 27m 4b *Thanatos* p1 to the second bilberry ledge.

2 20m 5a Starting on the right, follow cracks in the right wall to the left end of a small grass ledge. Climb the groove and arête on the left for 4m before traversing rightwards to a somewhat convoluted belay on a higher ledge.

3 35m 5b Climb the thin crack in the left wall, passing a slot with difficulty, to gain a good hold over the bulge. Pull immediately left using a hidden sidepull into the base of a hanging groove. Follow the groove to the Shelf and scramble up this to belay.

4 20m Scramble rightwards up the Shelf to a massive upstanding flake overlooking *Walker's Gully*.

5 40m 5b Go straight up for 5m and traverse to the right along a flake into a short corner. Climb this and the left-trending groove for about 10m until just below a kink rightwards at the start of a long crack. Finger traverse left to the arête, step round it onto a good foothold and make another move to a crack. Follow this with decreasing difficulty up the fine wall to a big grass ledge. Belay in the corner on the left.

6 35m 5a Climb the corner, moving right to avoid the bulge. Continue up a second corner, at its top step right to a slab. Follow cracks up the slab to a short juggy headwall.

Lower Tier, SJH Reid, C King - Jun 2004; Upper Tier, C King, SJH Reid, R Kenyon - Jul 2005

16 Shamrock Eliminate 183m HVS 5a ★★

Varied climbing the full height of the Shamrock.

1 23m Follow p1 of *Thanatos* as far as the first bilberry ledge and belay in a small corner on the edge of the right arête.

2 35m 5a Climb the stepped corner on the left of the arête for 4m. Move up and right, round the arête, and up into the bottom of the V-groove. At its top follow the obvious corner above to a grass ledge. Take the left-hand of short twin grooves to a stance in another short groove.

3 45m 4a Traverse horizontally left for 3m round the arête and gain easier rock which leads to the Shelf. Scramble diagonally right up this to a massive upstanding flake overlooking *Walker's Gully*.

4 20m 4b It is awkward to enter the obvious left-slanting hanging groove. Climb to a block belay just over the top on the right under a V-groove.

5 25m 4b Avoid the V-groove by stepping out right from the base of the block onto the steep buttress. Move up, right, then up on excellent rock to a good belay in a left-facing corner crack.

6 20m 5a Above on the left, is an obvious V-groove just right of the prominent buttress. Climb the steep wall on small holds to gain a grass ledge at the foot of the groove. The smooth groove is difficult. After about 6m escape right and climb the rib. All quite "top-end".

7 15m 4c The V-groove above to the top.

P Ross, CJS Bonington - Oct 1965

17 Shamrock Tower 176m VS 4b ★★

Enjoyable climbing.

1 23m 4b As for p1 of *Shamrock Eliminate*.

2 18m 4b Step onto the arête on the right, climb up a little, and then rightwards into a corner. Ascend the corner to a small ledge and very large block belay.

3 25m 4b Traverse left for 3m and step round the arête into a V-shaped groove; climb this and the wide groove above (mainly on the right) to a pair of small grass ledges at its top. Move up the

right-hand of two short corners to another grass ledge and belay in a short V-corner by a large block to the right.
4 45m 4a Move up right onto the block, step right and climb a cracked slab to a grass terrace. Climb a rock barrier diagonally right and up to reach the Shelf. Cross this diagonally up and rightwards to a massive upstanding flake overlooking *Walker's Gully*.
5 40m 4b Go straight up for 5m and traverse to the right along a flake. Turn the arête and climb straight up and then slightly rightwards to gain the huge left-facing corner. This is followed to a ledge on the right.
6 25m Continue up an easy rock ridge to the top of the buttress.
SH Cross, AT Hargreaves, AB Hargreaves, RE Hargreaves, AM Cross - May 1940

(18) Odin 178m HVS 5b ★★

An excellent route. 30m of grassy scrambling leads to the left side of a bay and a spike belay a few metres up and left of a short corner.
1 18m 4c Step off the spike and go directly up the steep wall and a short groove to a slim ledge on the right and large block belay.
2 25m 5b Stand in the niche above with difficulty, step right to avoid the roof and climb directly up steep rock to reach a long slim groove on the right. Climb this for 2m, then move back left across the wall to a grass ledge. Mantelshelf another grass ledge; block belay.
3 45m 4b Climb over the bulge on the left and cross the Shelf diagonally up and rightwards to a massive upstanding flake overlooking *Walker's Gully*.
4 50m 4c Go straight up for 5m and traverse to the right along a flake into a short corner. Climb this and the left-trending groove and continue up a long crack to a ledge. All very satisfying.
5 40m Continue up the easy ridge and scramble to the Tea Table.
P1-3 B Ingle, P Crew - Apr 1960; P4-5 AG Cram, K Robson - Apr 1967

(19) The Magic Rainbow/ Necromancer 175m E1 5b ★★

A worthwhile route, slightly harder than *Thanatos*. Scramble 15m up rushes to a short left-facing corner 10m right of *Thanatos*.
1 20m 5b Climb the corner for 2m until it is possible to move across the steep left wall to gain a slim left-facing groove. Climb the groove to a grass ledge on the right.
2 30m 5a Climb a short groove just up and right of the belay, or its left wall moving back right at the top to a ledge. Climb up the steep wall above to gain the left end of a narrow ramp. Follow the prominent crack above, pulling out left at the top, and scramble up 8m.
3 20m Climb the short wall to the Shelf. From the right-hand end of the Shelf scramble down into *Walker's Gully* to a block belay. Or skip p4 and climb by traversing rightwards 10m from the huge flake at the upper right end on the Great Heather Shelf (4b) to belay below p5.
4 35m 5a Climb a grassy groove on the left into a wet cave. Exit right from the cave onto a steep slab keeping to the centre for the best climbing. Move up and right to a small stance and large block belay in a fine position overlooking the gully.
5 30m 5a Climb the slab below the impressive final wall. Move to the left edge and climb the flake crack until it is possible to traverse right to the centre of the wall. Climb boldly up to a small flake, then move right and continue up the slab to a ledge and block belay.
6 40m Continue up the easy ridge and scramble to the Tea Table.
DW Hodgson, J Workman - Oct 1972, p1 W Young, I Singleton, 1966
AG Cram, W Young - Apr 1968

(20) Walker's Gully 182m MVS 4c ⚠ ★★★

A very imposing and atmospheric route calling for techniques seldom seen at climbing walls! Helmets are strongly advised as there is much loose scree in and above the gully.
1 32m 4a An easy chimney then scramble to the foot of a high green chimney. The right wall and a step right onto sloping grass. Descend slightly and belay from a crack in the smooth right wall.
2 45m 4a Return to the edge of the chimney; an exposed groove with poor holds to a step left on to the first chockstone. Up to another chockstone - problematic. Scramble up the gully bed overcoming a large chockstone en route, and belay at the foot of a steep chimney.
3 30m 4b Climb on the left of the chimney to a cave in the gully; usually wet. Climb up behind, then over, a chockstone; then bridge the gully to reach a sloping chockstone. Another chockstone just above gives access to scree.
4 25m 4b Above, a cave is formed by a large chockstone. The through route is strenuous but short. Or climb the left wall outside the cave, missing out the fun.
5 15m 4a A further through route followed by an awkward chockstone.
6 35m 4c Overcome yet another chockstone to gain the final cave. Take the right wall until forced out right to avoid the capstone. Strenuous moves gain the top, though it is rumoured that the tall can back and foot this last bit. Scramble up scree to find a belay. A good continuation in the same vein is to follow The Great Chimney to the summit of High Man.
OG Jones, GD Abraham, AE Field - Jan 1899

High Man
Low Man
Stony Gully
The Hand Traverse
The Nose
Savage Gully MVS
Proton E1
5
7
8
50
29
23
26
21
27
28
24
22
21
22
26
21
23
24
20
SR

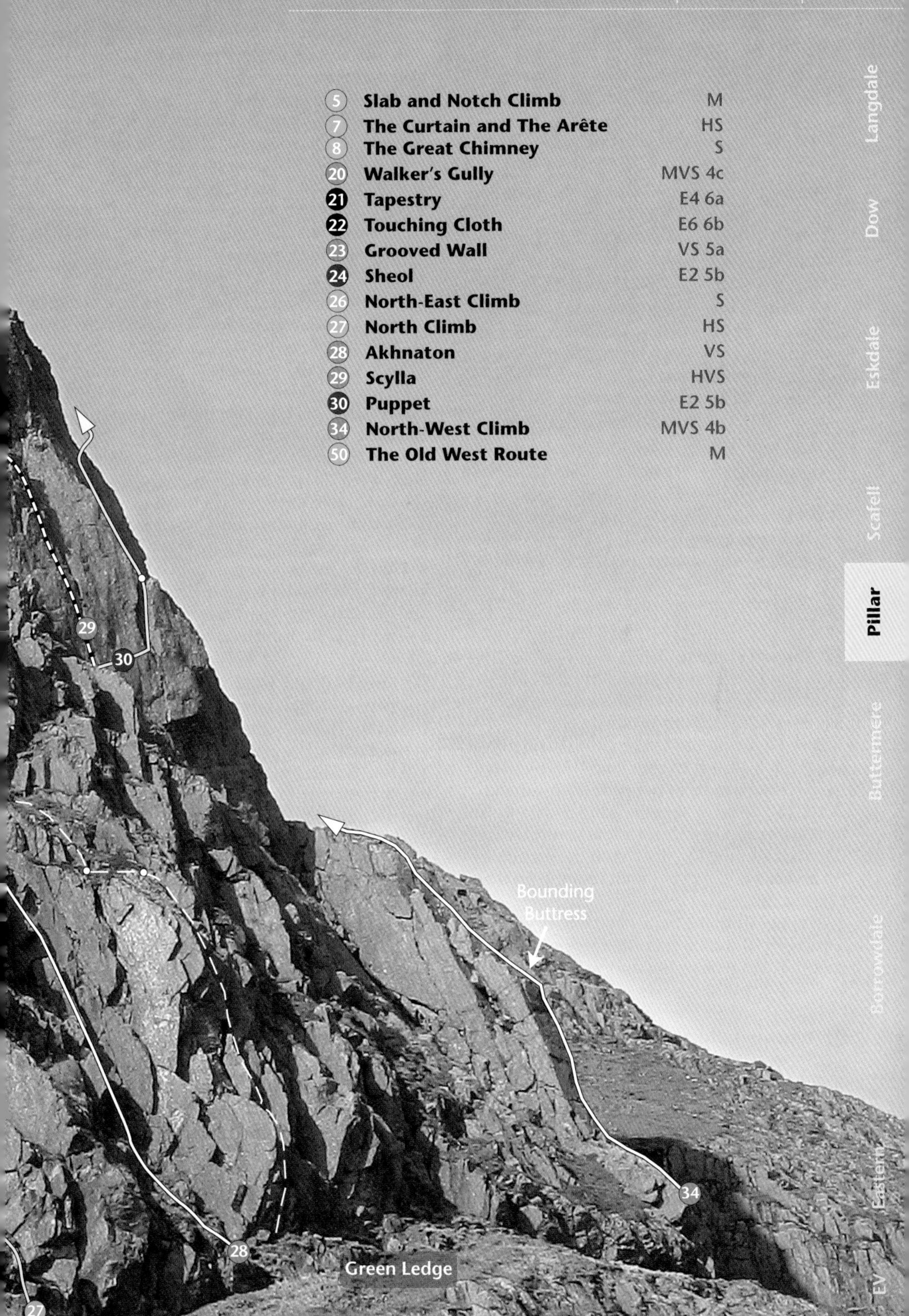
5 Slab and Notch Climb M
7 The Curtain and The Arête HS
8 The Great Chimney S
20 Walker's Gully MVS 4c
21 Tapestry E4 6a
22 Touching Cloth E6 6b
23 Grooved Wall VS 5a
24 Sheol E2 5b
26 North-East Climb S
27 North Climb HS
28 Akhnaton VS
29 Scylla HVS
30 Puppet E2 5b
34 North-West Climb MVS 4b
50 The Old West Route M
29
30
Bounding Buttress
34
28
Green Ledge
27

North Face of Low Man

Diffs and **Extremes** side by side, many of which are among the best in the district. Grassy ledges in abundance mean virtually all the routes become very unpleasant in wet conditions.

Most of the climbs start from Green Ledge which crosses the cliff rightwards from the bottom of *Walker's Gully*. From the right-hand end it is possible to scramble round to the West Face via the Waterfall (see page 256 & 277).

Descent: Stony Gully (the grassy gully on the east side of Low Man) to just above a rock step then climb a short wall on the left (looking in) and traverse leftwards over grass and bilberry ledges to the scree above *Walker's Gully* from where the Shamrock Traverse is easily reached.

Or descend *The Old West Route* (M), then scramble down and cross the Waterfall with care to gain Green Ledge; if this does not appeal, after descending The Old West Route, a path on the opposite side of the scree leads to open hillside that can be descended more easily. Or follow *The Old West Route* to the summit of High Man (see page 256 & 281).

21 Tapestry 70m E4 6a ★★★

Fit to hang on any wall - excellent climbing in good situations and reasonably clean to boot! Scramble 12m up from *Walker's Gully*.
1 25m 5b Climb the centre of the huge pinnacle and finish by its left edge. Climb the chimney fault leftwards to belay beneath the overhang.
2 20m 6a Serious. Surmount the overhang, immediately step right to a shallow corner. Follow this almost to the top, then gain the wall on its left and climb it, moving right to finish on the belay ledge.
3 25m 5b From the right-hand end of the ledge, a groove in the arête leads to a soaring leftward hand-traverse. Follow this and then climb a crack back right to finish.
A Stephenson, C Sice, W Young, RG Willison - Apr 1980

22 Touching Cloth 70m E6 6b ☆☆☆

A collectable piece of modern art worthy of its position; a phenomenal middle pitch - solid rock, fabulous moves.
1 25m 5b As for *Tapestry*.
2 22m 6b Follow *Grooved Wall* for 3m to a grassy ledge. Step right and gain a left-trending groove system which is followed on good holds. At the final jug arrange gear; a traverse right on underclings gains a crimp. Head straight up (gear) and commit to the long crux (pocket on right) passing a good slot/undercling. A jug brings welcome respite. Step up to a couple of slots and either finish direct or traverse right to avoid the grass cornice.
3 23m 6a The Bayeux Tapestry pitch. From above the *in-situ* belay at the foot of the blank wall left of the final pitch of *Tapestry*, a rising line of good holds lead up the left-hand side of a black streak to a tough cruxy move off a poor crimp (poor RP). Rejoining *Tapestry* at its finishing crack brings relief and gear.
S Litchfield, G Read - 26 May 2012

23 Grooved Wall 124m VS 5a ★★★

A good well-protected climb up difficult grooves in the wall right of *Walker's Gully*.
1 50m 4a Grassy ledges lead to a wide broken chimney composed of a vast flake for its left-hand side; climb to its top. Take the left-hand groove above to a ledge; belay.
2 30m 5a Above is an overhanging crack, the crux of the climb. Gain the groove above and continue up to a good spike belay.
3 20m 4b Continue up the sustained groove to belay by a corner on the side of the groove.
4 24m 4c The final groove above is not without interest, but ends after 12m. Continue up ledges and grass to a rock gateway which opens onto the scree just above *Walker's Gully*.
HM Kelly, HG Knight, WG Standring - Apr 1928

24 Sheol 86m E2 5b ★★

The jagged soaring crack gives an excellent pitch. Low in the grade. Scramble up grass to the foot of the crack.
1 22m 5b The sustained and awkward crack is nearly vertical and tilts slightly to one side, at its top is a good stance and chockstone belay.
2 22m 5a Follow a slabby groove up, first rightwards then back leftwards. Now traverse right to gain the very steep, and cleaner looking, right-hand groove. Sustained bridging gains a ledge and belay.
3 15m 4c Climb the groove on the left exiting right a few metres below the top to a ledge.
4 27m 4a Climb straight up to finish up the wide square chimney.
AG Cram, T Martin - Apr 1965

25 Sheol/Tapestry Connection 62m E2 5c ★★★

An impressive and very rewarding way up the crag. Scramble up grass to the foot of the crack.
1 22m 5b *Sheol* p1.
2 15m 5c Left across the overhanging wall to a flake-crack on the arete. Levitate strenuously to a ledge, up twin jam cracks to belay. Or avoid the 5c section by following *North-East Climb*.
3 25m 5b *Tapestry* p3.

Tapestry E4 Paul Platt — John Kettle

19 Necromancer E1 5b
20 Walker's Gully MVS 4c
21 Tapestry E4 6a
23 Grooved Wall VS 5a
24 Sheol E2 5b
26 North-East Climb S
27 North Climb HS
28 Akhnaton VS
50 The Old West Route M
Stony Gully
High Man
Shamrock
Savage Grooves HVS
Savage Gully MVS
SR

29 Scylla HVS
30 Puppet E2 5b
31 Megaton E1 or HVS
32 Goodbye to All That E1 5b
33 Ximenes HVS 5b
34 North-West Climb MVS 4b
Bounding Buttress
Green Ledge
Pillar

The next climbs start above the step up at the start of Green Ledge.

26 North-East Climb 116m S ★★

A classic route with atmosphere and good situations in the upper half, despite an abundance of grass. Start from the very left end of Green Ledge at a patch of gravel where a short wall leads to a square platform.

1 10m An easy mantelshelf and short slab lead to a large ledge at the foot of a broken groove.
2 26m Climb the gully for 10m to the second ledge at about half height. Move up a metre, then traverse 3m across the rib on the left. A 3m chimney leads to a small stance. Move round the rib on the left on to a slab. Traverse the slab to grassy ledges.
3 23m A short chimney leads to a longer one with an awkward finish. Climb the short slab on the left, then walk left to a long V-groove on the wall of *Walker's Gully*.
4 24m Climb the groove to a corner with a belay.
5 18m A mossy wall on the right leads to a good ledge behind a big block. A steep chimney is followed by easier climbing to a grassy corner.
6 15m Another steep chimney is followed by grassy ledges. From here a traverse can be made right to Low Man or left to the scree above *Walker's Gully*.

GD Abraham, AP Abraham - Apr 1912

27 North Climb 104m HS ★★★

A superb classic **D** with a **S** finish. It has been the scene of many epics and should not be underrated. Take lots of slings and start from the very left end of Green Ledge, at a patch of gravel, where a short wall leads to a square platform.

1 10m An easy mantelshelf and short slab lead to a large ledge at the foot of a broken groove.
2 25m Follow the gully/groove until it steepens at a small grassy bay. On the left, the smooth double groove of **Savage Gully** (MVS 4b 1901) continues in a soaring line. On the right is the deep Twisting Chimney.
3 34m Climb Twisting Chimney and then trend leftwards up an open groove. Scramble up to a belay on a small ledge at the meeting of two narrow chimneys.
4 9m The Stomach Traverse. Squeeze up and along the right-hand chimney which curves to the right in its upper half.
5 18m The be-chockstoned corner is climbed via a capstone, followed by a walk of 6m to the Split Blocks. Climb into the Split, turn left and wriggle up the chimney to the top of the Blocks. Traverse to the left, making an exposed stride across the fearful void of the Strid, to a big ledge below and right of the Nose.
6 8m The Nose. Go left along the ledge to a corner (high runner). Work out leftwards to stand on the tip of a projecting flake. Will it-won't it moves up and left gain better holds and a ledge just above; belay. Or take The Hand Traverse. An excellent finish, particularly in the case of a runny Nose! From the right end of the ledge below the Nose, climb the steep wall for about 3m on tremendous holds until the sharp edge of a flake is reached. Traverse boldly left to the top of the Nose.

The easy grassy Stony Gully leads to the summit of Low Man from where *The Old West Route* can be joined. Alternatively a rising traverse across bilberry and heather to the left of Stony Gully crosses a rock ridge after 50m and lands you at the foot of Great Chimney from where a further traverse left and up gains the descent of the Shamrock Traverse.

WP Haskett Smith, G Hastings, WC Slingsby - Jul 1891

28 Akhnaton 88m VS ★

A fine direct line up the massive corner, the first major feature encountered after *North Climb*. Rather dirty and escapable but still well worth doing. Scramble a few metres up a grassy bay to the base of the corner.

1 47m 4c Climb the groove, surmounting two bulges, to a grass ledge; continue up grass a couple of metres to join the polished corner-crack on *North Climb* p3.
2 33m 4c Traverse left into the bottom of the continuation groove which is marked at half-height by a large pinnacle on the right. Carry on up the groove with increasing difficulty and belay just right of the Nose on *North Climb*.
3 8m 4b From the belay, step right and go up the steep wall to hand-traverse left and finish on the top of *North Climb*.

W Young, R Schipper - Apr 1967

29 Scylla 133m HVS ★★

A mountaineering route, which climbs the crack in the centre of the huge wall on the North Face of Low Man. Start at the last major groove on the left side of the grassy bay, just right of a short impending band of rock. When looking up, high on the crag will be seen a blank wall with a crack in it. Below the wall is a square chimney which forms p2 of *Scylla*. If you can see this chimney then you are in the right area. Start up left a few metres at a grassy groove.

1 35m 4a Climb up to the central groove and follow this exiting right. Making the most of the rock above, trend right to a short wide gully and climb it to a stance at a huge chockstone below the very large square chimney.
2 25m 4b Climb the chimney to belay below a

A The Terrace
B Split Blocks
C Le Coin
D Dowlen's Chimney
E Block Ledge
H The Hand Traverse
L Lamb's Chimney
N The Nose
O Oppenheimer's Chimney
T Taylor's Chimney
High Man
Low Man
Proton E1
West Wall Traverse
Green Ledge
Pillar
27 North Climb HS
29 Scylla HVS
30 Puppet E2 5b
31 Megaton E1 or HVS
32 Goodbye to All That E1 5b
33 Ximenes HVS 5b
34 North-West Climb MVS 4b
35 Charybdis HVS 5a
36 Goth E2 5b
37 Gaul HVS 5a
38 The Appian Way HS
50 The Old West Route M
AP

crack in the wall.
3 30m 4c Climb the crack in the centre of the wall: it becomes a chimney-groove at 12m. Avoid a large wedged block by a crack on the left and continue up this crack, and ledges above, to belay on the highest ledge at a hollow block.
4 25m 5a From the top of the ledge, pull up an overhanging wall. Traverse down and left to the foot of a groove and jamming crack, which is climbed to the top of a pinnacle, from where a swing right leads to easier ground. Take a stance immediately on the grass ledge.
5 18m 4a Traverse rightwards to the arête on the right and follow it to the summit of Low Man.
AG Cram, W Young - 9 Jun 1963

30 Puppet 130m E2 5b ★★
A varied climb with difficult and exciting upper pitches.
1 26m P1 of *Scylla.*
2 24m 4c Move to the right and climb a short corner for 6m, then step back left above the overhang and go up a pleasant crack. Continue over ledges and an overhanging chockstone to below the crack of *Scylla* in the centre of the large wall.
3 18m 5b Ascend *Scylla* for 6m (thread). Traverse across the wall on the right, ascending slightly to gain the deep lichenous pod-like groove. Climb this, or the arête on the right, to a small stance.
4 18m 4b Continue up the corner and vague arête above until a few moves to the right lead to a small stance at a rather worrying detached spike.
5 20m 5b Climb the steep shallow groove above and left; continue up the steep wall on improving holds to a good ledge: a bold pitch.
6 24m 4a Move left and follow an easier ridge to the top of Low Man.
AG Cram, B Whybrow - Apr 1966; p5 D Yates and party - Jul 1963

31 Megaton 120m E1 or HVS ★★★
Mega! Varied, interesting and sustained at a good level. Start 7m left of the Bounding Buttress, below the steep grassy bay.
1 18m 4b Make the best of the rock rib to the lower end of a rightward-rising grass ramp under a steep slab and take a thread chockstone belay about halfway along the grass ramp under the slabs.
2 26m 5a From the lower end of the grass ramp, starting 5m from the Bounding Buttress wall on the right, climb very boldly up the slab for 9m before moving left to gain a vague rightward-curving fault. Follow this to easier ground. Climb diagonally leftwards to a stance well up on the left by a pile of blocks on a ledge under the impressive overhung deep V-groove.
Alternatively climb the better protected **HVS** variation:
2 4c Start 2m to the left of the belay and follow a thin crack directly up the slab until about half-height branch up leftwards to easier ground. Climb diagonally leftwards to a stance well up on the left by a pile of blocks on a ledge under the impressive overhung deep V-groove.
3 36m 5a Traverse right along two rock ledges to a groove. Climb this for 2m then leave it to move leftwards up a gangway to a thin corner-crack which soon widens and is followed until the angle eases. Climb up rightwards for 12m or so to a recess with a dubious spike and a loose pebble thread in a corner.
4 20m 4c Pull directly over the bulge above into a groove and follow it to a mossy shallow niche. Stepping left avoids the moss and leads up to easier ground under a steep crack. Don't get confused as there is a similar crack 7m right - Oppenheimer's Chimney on *North-West Climb.*
5 20m 4c Dowlen's Chimney. Climb the crack (not as bad as it looks!) to the top of Low Man.
W Young, WA Barnes - May 1972. P4 WF Dowlen, R Greenwood - Mar 1954

32 Goodbye to All That 124m E1 5b ★★★
A direct line on excellent rock culminating in a sensational top pitch. Start 7m left of the Bounding Buttress.
1 18m 4a As for Megaton to below the slabs.
2 26m 4c Two metres left of the Bounding Buttress wall is a thin crack in the slab. Climb this direct to a narrow bilberry ledge and huge block belay.
3 36m 5b Climb up into an overhung scoop just left of the belay and pull out awkwardly onto a small ledge on the left. Climb directly up to and climb a crack, pull out rightwards to easier ground. Climb directly up over bulges and slabby rock to belay in a recess with a dubious spike and a loose pebble thread in a corner.
4 20m 5a Stride out rightwards onto a ledge on the right with a spiky block on it. Climb the arête above on its left side to emerge into a rock bay. Climb the wall on the right to a square pocket and traverse right to a flake on the arête. Go straight up to easy ground below a deep chimney/crack (Oppenheimer's Chimney). The best belay is well below the chimney on a small quartz ledge on a superbly exposed rib out on the extreme right.
5 24m 5b A bold pitch. Climb up to the base of Oppenheimer's Chimney and fix some good runners! Traverse horizontally leftwards on blocks to some tiny footholds on a rib and make a long reach up left for a jug - much easier if you are tall. Climb directly up the wall above in an exposed

Megaton E1/HVS Harry Ellis, Chris Cox — 📷 Stephen Reid

position on good holds but with no further protection until a placement under a chockstone on the left in a crack. Move back right and follow more jugs up a rib to easy ground and the top.
SJH Reid, SR Stout - Sep 1996

33 Ximenes 51m HVS 5b ★★
A good approach to several routes on the West Face (such as *Goth*), which takes the front of the buttress leaning against Low Man. Start 2m right of the left edge of the Bounding Buttress at an overhung recess below the left-hand of two cracks.
1 18m 5a Gain the crack from the recess and follow it strenuously to an easing. Move left and climb the slab to the foot of the crack in the prow of the buttress, just left of the wide chimney on *North-West Climb*.
2 33m 5b Climb the crack, which is awkward and strenuous but well-protected, to a ledge and continue up easy slabs to the Terrace at the left-hand end of the West Wall Traverse.
AG Cram, W Young - Apr 1968

34 North-West Climb 130m MVS 4b ★★★
A fine route, varied climbing and good situations seeking to avoid obvious difficulty. Start at the right-hand end of Green Ledge, at an obvious rightwards-slanting short gangway.
1 20m Climb the gangway to a ledge and follow a chimney for 10m to a slab. Avoid the continuation by a traverse left across the slab to belay at the foot of a much wider chimney.
2 36m 4a The wide chimney is taken direct to finish on a grassy slab in a corner. Up a short crack onto the crest of the buttress on the left and follow another crack up this until the angle eases at the Terrace. Cross rightwards for 9m to belay at the base of a smooth slab.
3 25m 4b The slab and a short grassy corner lead to a grassy ledge under a prominent steep V-groove. Traverse leftwards around a rib and climb up into the first of a series of three recesses (Le Coin). Carry on up into a second recess with a dubious pointed spike, a solid blunt spike, and a loose but threadable pebble in a short corner.
4 25m 4a Lamb's Chimney, quite bold. To the left of the undercut groove above are three vague grooves. To gain the first, traverse left to a nose and ascend it to Block Ledge. Climb the groove above and pull out left at its top. Stride immediately back right and go up to a belay below an impending crack.
5 24m 4b Oppenheimer's Chimney - Traverse rightwards under bulges and go up to the foot of another impending crack. After an awkward start it becomes more reasonable and easy scrambling then leads to the top of Low Man. Oppenheimer's Chimney can be avoided by traversing rightwards lower down and then ascending a crack and going to the right round the corner.
FW Botterill, LJ Oppenheimer, A Botterill, JH Taylor - Jun 1906

35 Charybdis 129m HVS 5a ★★
1 15m Follow p1 of *North-West Climb* to a stance and belay at the top of the 10m chimney.
2 30m 4c Continue up the chimney then ascend a wall split by cracks to the Terrace.
3 20m 4c Move to the right to a slab. Ascend this and go up the corner. Belay below the obvious deep overhanging groove.
4 15m 5a Climb into the groove, descend a little and climb the left wall using a big flake. Return along an awkward gangway to the top of the groove and go over a loose block to a sloping stance and thread belay on the right.
5 12m 5a Climb the left-hand green groove above moving left at the top to a ledge.
6 15m 4b Climb the fine bold arête on the right of the groove to a large block belay.
7 22m 4c Climb the shallow groove above, just to the right of Oppenheimer's Chimney. Move to the right over the bulge, then follow a slanting crack back left up the wall to the top.
AG Cram, W Young - Sep 1964

West Face of Low Man

Excellent rock, dries quickly after rain and catches the afternoon sun.

Approach: Follow Green Ledge rightwards to where it drops away into a wide wet gully which cuts deeply into the hillside below the West Face of Low Man. An awkward horizontal scramble leads, starting with a 1m rock step, crosses the gully and goes up a short slimy wall onto the scree on the other side of the Waterfall and leads up to the West Face of Pillar. This is all very nasty if wet and has serious prang potential if you muff it. Another option is to leave Green Ledge before the 1m rock step and scramble down a steep grass trench to cross the gully at a lower point by a dripping black wall. Go under this wall via a fault-line and continue in this line, well beyond the steeper rocks, until you gain open hillside to the west of the Rock. A scrambly ascent can be made to join the normal path to the West Face. Alternatively avoid crossing the waterfall by climbing **Waterfall Climb** (50m D) up a groove system in the rocks which bound it on the left side to the same point.

When approaching this face from Buttermere or Ennerdale, the Waterfall crossing is avoided by ascending the unremitting scree well to the right of the waterfall until a horizontal path is gained which leads round to the West Face.

From the Western Scree, under the West Face, the climbs are reached by following the West Wall Traverse, a slightly worn scramble that starts some 10m up the scree from the head of the waterfall. Traverse slightly downwards, passing under a long low smooth wall, then rising a little to a huge block on a grass ledge at the foot of *The Appian Way*. A slight descent from here leads round the edge of the crag to the Terrace, half way up the North Face at the top of the Bounding Buttress and at the start of *Goth*.

Descent: From just below the summit of Low Man, scramble rightwards down a well marked way to an exit onto scree; the lower section of the *Old West Route*. Alternatively follow the upper section of *The Old West Route* to the summit of High Man and descend from there (see page 256).

36 Goth 75m E2 5b ★★★

A well positioned yet intimidating crux requires very small wires for protection. Follow the West Wall Traverse leftwards to a huge block on a grass ledge. Scramble down and left, passing a smaller block, to another grass ledge at the foot of an open-book corner with an undercut arête on its left. A good alternative is to climb *Ximenes* from Green Ledge to the Terrace.

1 20m 4c Climb the vague open groove to a hanging stance in the grassy V-groove, 4m below the huge overhang.

2 35m 5b Traverse left for 2m to the foot of a mossy groove. Climb the groove until a dubious block in the roof of a small overhang is reached; then break out left across a small slab to an arête and runners. Climb the overhanging wall (crux) to a narrow sloping ledge and either hand-traverse strenuously to the corner on the right, or move up and foot-traverse instead. Continue up this corner until a small overhang bars the way. Traverse left across the wall to a stance on a quartz ledge.

3 20m 4a Climb up to a short curving crack on the right. Ascend this and finish up rough slabs taking a line almost on the left arête.

M de St Jorre, N Hannaby - Jun 1959

37 Gaul 73m HVS 5a ★★

An excellent main pitch at the upper limit of the grade makes this a route not to be missed. Start as for *Goth* at the blunt spike belay.

1 20m 4b Cross grass rightwards to a short greasy chimney-groove. Climb this and the left slanting slab above to a grass ledge in a V-groove below the big roof on *Goth*.

2 35m 5a Climb onto the slab on the right and cross it to a groove. Follow this and the wall above with sustained difficulty to an easier groove (*The Appian Way*) which leads to a grass terrace and block belay. A good pitch.

3 18m 4a *The Appian Way*.

JD Wilson, T Martin - Jun 1974

38 The Appian Way 65m HS ★★★

A very pleasant and exposed route with delicate wall climbing and good situations. Follow the West Wall Traverse leftwards for some 70 metres, to a huge block on a grass ledge.

1 20m Avoid the mossy groove by climbing up grassy rock on the left for 3m and then traversing to the right across the top of the groove to gain a grassy corner-ramp which is followed to its top.

2 15m Climb the thin corner-crack and, from its top, traverse delicately left across the imposing wall to a worrying spike on the skyline. (Wires left of the base of the spike backed up using a crack on the left.)

35 Charybdis HVS 5a
36 Goth E2 5b
37 Gaul HVS 5a
38 The Appian Way HS
39 Appian Wall VS 4c
40 Triton Direct VS 4c
41 Mirror, Mirror... E2 5b
42 Nook and Wall Climb S
43 The Devil's Eliminate HVS 5a
44 The Devil's Entrance VS 4c
45 Thor VS 4c
46 Err VS 4c
47 Ledge and Groove Climb S
48 West Wall Climb VD
49 Mallory's Route VS 4c
50 The Old West Route M
West Wall Traverse
A The Terrace
FN First Nook
SN Second Nook
P The Pedestal
SR

3 12m Move left and ascend a series of steep ledges straight ahead (bold) to a grassy terrace and a large block leaning against the wall (thread).
4 18m Left of the block climb the slightly overhanging right-hand branch of an 8m crack followed by slabs.
REW Pritchard, HM Kelly - Jul 1923

39 Appian Wall 77m VS 4c ★★

A direct line through *The Appian Way* - superb but scary! Start as for *The Appian Way* at a large block.
1 25m 4c Bridge the mossy groove direct and continue up the clean rock groove above until just below the right end of an overlap. Step right onto the arête and follow cracks up the wall to join the traverse on *The Appian Way*, take this leftwards to a dodgy spike.
2 25m 4b A serious pitch. Move carefully up off the spike and traverse boldly rightwards towards the middle of the wall before climbing straight up to grass ledges. Go right up these to a crevasse stance.
3 27m Climb the blunt arête above the stance. Scrambling up 20m to a belay.
C King, SJH Reid - Sep 2004

The next routes all start from the lowest rock on the face above the waterfall.

40 Triton Direct 95m VS 4c ★★

An enjoyable eliminate. Start 3m left of the chimney of *Nook and Wall Climb* at an easy-angled groove.
1 38m 4c 1m up before the groove gets dirty, pull blindly out rightwards into a good crack. Climb this and the rough slab above to a terrace. Follow the rightward-slanting grassy ramp above to its top, then pull awkwardly leftwards into a broken groove on the left wall and go up this to easy slabs. Climb up to a shallow open groove on the right-hand side of a sharp arête. Climb this on the right, almost moving into the grassy First Nook, before pulling back left. From the top of the groove, move up, then stride out left to a stance on top of the sharp arête, under a flake hand-jam crack.
2 28m 4c Climb the hand-jam crack and take a shallow groove above to easier ground. Overhead is the Bad Corner - a steep grass-filled corner-crack: climb up to get established in the base of this, then make an exposed traverse leftwards to the arête which is climbed to a huge block belay.
3 29m 4c Stand on the block and make a long reach up the smooth wall to a high jug. Heave up and climb a slab; spike belay 20m higher.
A Stephenson, RG Willison - May 1974

41 Mirror, Mirror... 90m E2 5b ★★

An out there "on the wall" experience, with pesky distractions such as runners kept well below the minimum on p2. Take several thin slings and a cool head and start as for *Nook and Wall Climb*.
1 33m 5b Step left onto the wall and move left into the chimney which is climbed to a terrace. A narrow rightward-slanting grassy ramp is followed until moves can be made straight up the wall to gain a standing position on a blocky projection. Sidle round the arête and up to easy slabs, then trend left to belay in a leftward-facing corner.
2 30m 5b Step one metre left from the corner and climb straight up the wall on incuts to the traverse-break (spike on left). Step right to the left-hand end of a slim overhang and move up through the bulge (wire beside hollow hold). Climb boldly up the wall above, firstly rightwards, then leftwards, on good holds until finally a barely adequate spike allows breathing to resume just below the steeper headwall. Climb directly through the headwall to a crevasse stance.
3 27m Climb the blunt arête above the stance and scramble 20m to a spike belay.
C King, SJH Reid, J Preston, K Wigglesworth - Jun 2005; p1 C King, SJH Reid, May 2006

42 Nook and Wall Climb 101m S ★★

A meandering, interesting and historic route featuring some very exposed climbing. Start from a flat rock platform on the West Wall Traverse, just right of the bottomless chimney towards the left-hand end of the smooth vertical wall. The best belay will be found in a crack 3m right.
1 33m Step left onto the wall and move left into the chimney which is climbed to a terrace. A narrow rightward-slanting grassy ramp is followed until it steepens. Climb up for a couple of metres then traverse right to a grassy corner. Follow the rib ahead on the right to a flake belay.
2 15m Traverse the flake leftwards into the First Nook. Climb the corner to a rock ledge about halfway up then traverse left along a huge flake and left around the arête into the Second Nook. There is a very mossy wall on the left.
3 24m Easy rock on the right leads to below the Bad Corner. Avoid this by moving one step down to the right and boldly cross the wall using a flake to regain the main corner. Climb the corner moving out left below a bulge at its top to gain a large sloping ledge and huge block belay.
4 29m A short chimney, just right of the belay, leads to a grassy terrace; spike belay 20m higher.
HM Kelly, CF Holland, REW Pritchard - Sep 1920

43 The Devil's Eliminate 66m HVS 5a ★★

An exciting final pitch is the making of this climb. Start as for *Nook and Wall Climb*.
1 26m 4b Pull out left towards the chimney but immediately step back right and climb a thin crack up the wall to a terrace. Step off a perched block and climb directly up the wall to a grassy niche. Climb rock to the left of a grassy crack to gain the left edge of a large flake. Belay on the

right of the flake under an impressive slab.
2 40m 5a Step off the flake and climb boldly up the left edge of the slab to a small quartz ledge at its apex. Above is the corner of *The Devil's Entrance.* Make an exposed stride of 1.5m horizontally rightwards to a steep crack and climb this to a small ledge. A short groove leads to a bigger ledge. Climb the short mossy wall above, moving out left to semi-mantelshelf up a clean rib to another ledge. The groove above the pinnacle on the right is part of *West Wall Climb* and the groove around the arête to the left is *The Devil's Entrance.* Climb boldly up the shallow groove between and take the rough slabby rib above. Belay slightly higher on a chockstone.
BJ Clarke, SJH Reid - Sep 2004

The next three routes start at the steep dark right-hand crack in the smooth vertical 5m wall which slants down slightly leftwards just above the West Wall Traverse.

44 The Devil's Entrance 65m VS 4c ★★

1 25m 4c Climb the jamming crack of *Thor* and move up right onto the slab then back left immediately onto a rib. Climb the rib to grass and step right into a slim rightward-facing groove/crack; follow this to a flake belay.
2 40m 4b Step off the flake and climb the left edge of the slab for 1m, before traversing left into the left-facing corner of *Nook and Wall Climb,* just above the First Nook. Climb the corner to a small quartz ledge at the apex of the slab on its right. Continue up the steeper corner above, moving right at a bulge near its top to belay on a chockstone.
R Bennett, R Lavender - Aug 1972

45 Thor 65m VS 4c ★★

An enjoyable climb with good situations and excellent rock.
1 30m 4c Climb the jamming crack and move up and right to ascend an easy-angled rightward-slanting slab using a flake-crack. Climb directly up a steeper slab above, just right of a corner-groove, to just below a slim open groove on its right-hand side. Traverse right 2m, past a large flake, and climb up to a small rock ledge and flake belay.
2 35m 4c Climb a steep crack/groove above to a small overhang. Turn this on the left and continue up to the top of a pinnacle. Move up and then make an airy rising traverse across the wall on the right to a grass ledge; scramble up to a belay.
R Schipper, CJS Bonington - Jun 1967

46 Err 75m VS 4c ★★

Initially indecisive, linking together bits of several other climbs, this culminates in a fine top pitch.
1 35m 4c Follow *Thor* to the slab. Traverse to the right across the broken slabs to a perched block (*Ledge and Groove Climb*) and then follow *West Wall Climb* rightwards to a slab.
2 40m 4c Climb the corner-crack behind the belay then step left onto easy-angled rock; ahead is a lichenous groove. Make a bold move onto the clean rib to the right of this and pull rightwards into the base of a hanging capped groove. Climb the groove to the overhang which is avoided by some timely holds appearing on the slab on the right. Continue up grassy ledges to a belay on *The Old West Route.*
WL Robinson, KS Perry - Aug 1970

47 Ledge and Groove Climb 80m S ★★

Meandering and enjoyable climbing on excellent rock - an exposed downward traverse on p2 makes this route unsuitable for nervous seconds. Start at a one metre high groove, below a smooth wall, at the top of clean slabby steps on the West Wall Traverse, and more or less directly above the Waterfall.
1 22m Climb the groove then diagonally rightwards up a narrow ramp to below a V-groove. Traverse delicately left along the exposed ledge to its end and ascend slabby rocks rightwards to a grass ledge 5m below a large flake.
2 34m Climb up to just below the flake and then step down and cross a little wall on the left. Climb up to a detached flake crack system and follow this until it is possible to move out right. Climb the slab to a tiny ledge at its top. There is a short groove leading up to a scoop with cracked blocks up on the left and a steep mossy groove up high on the right. Keep traversing awkwardly rightwards, well below the mossy groove, to make an exposed downward step across the top of a groove to a good stance on the Pedestal on the right.
3 24m The left-hand steep shallow groove directly above is hard to attain, but once entered the holds improve, though still quite bold. Exit on the right, cross grass to the right, and go up a short easy crack behind a block, beyond which easy steps lead to *The Old West Route.*
AT Hargreaves, G Barker, RE Heap - Oct 1933

48 West Wall Climb 65m VD ★★★

An excellent route of continuous interest. Follow the West Wall Traverse a few metres to a platform below a 3m wall.
1 15m A short crack leads to a grass rake. Cross this and make a hard start up a V-groove until it is possible to pull out left to a sloping ledge and flake belay.
2 15m Step right; steep rocks then lead to a slab. A superb crack in the wall on the right, to the right of the corner-crack, leads to a small sloping ledge 3m below the end of the crack. Belay on the Pedestal.
3 15m Descend leftwards slightly from the Ped-

estal and make an awkward traverse leftwards, well under a mossy groove, to a short groove on the left. Climb this to a large scoop and belay on blocks at the base of a cracked pinnacle.
4 20m Climb the pinnacle via its left arête and from its top climb a short awkward groove, or the wall on its left. Easier rock leads to the top of Low Man.
HM Kelly, CF Holland, CG Crawford - Jul 1919

49 Mallory's Route 65m VS 4c ★★ (North-West-by-West)
Long overlooked - an outstanding lead for its day. The first 15m are in common with *West Wall Climb*. Follow the West Wall Traverse for a few metres to a platform below a 3m wall.
1 40m 4b A short crack leads to a grass rake. Cross this and make a hard start up a V-groove until it is possible to pull out right onto a sloping ledge. Traverse right and climb up behind a large block. Gain a V-groove above and then follow the prominent crack in the right wall to a fine belay on the Pedestal.
2 25m 4c Quite bold and hard. Step right off the Pedestal and climb awkwardly up into the right-hand shallow groove. Climb this, still awkward, to grass, then a corner on the right and so to the top.
GHL Mallory, A Goodfellow - Sep 1913

50 The Old West Route 150m M ★★★
Pillar's Low and High Men are separated by this obvious and well marked scramble: the original route of ascent. From the Western Scree, follow the left-slanting rake-line that divides the West Faces of Low and High Men to the summit of Low Man. From there, move towards High Man and up to slightly higher grassy ledges until a more rocky right-to-left stepped diagonal line leads to a short steep corner and small pinnacle. A determined heave-ho will gain you easier terrain that leads to the summit of High Man.
J Atkinson - Jul 1826

West Face of High Man

The most impressive face of Pillar Rock and also the quickest to dry.

Approach: from the Western Scree or by scrambling a short way up *The Old West Route*.

Descent: Reverse *Slab and Notch Climb* (see page 261), reverse *The Old West Route* (see page 281), or by abseil from near the summit cairn into the Jordan Gap, followed by descending East Jordan Gully and then Western Gully. Care is needed in Western Gully which starts where the separate pinnacle of Pisgah merges in with the mountainside. Don't try to descend West Jordan Gully from the Jordan Gap.

51 Gondor 70m E2 5c ★★★
Impressive and exposed, strenuous and delicate. Start at the base of the ridge left of the prominent groove of *Gomorrah*.
1 25m 4a P1 of *Gomorrah*.
2 18m 5b Climb the groove in the arête to the bulge. Above on the left is a large triangular hold. Pull up and move boldly up right until the angle eases. Belay in a small corner below a grass ledge.
3 27m 5c Climb down from the stance for 2m and traverse delicately right round the nose onto the wall. Climb up and left to easier climbing, following a groove to a large ledge and block belay.
AG Cram, K Robson - Apr 1967 PA; FFA G Tinnings, 1978

52 Gomorrah 80m VS 4b ★★★
A superb climb. Start on a small grass ledge, well below and left of the huge triangular roof, reached by scrambling up *The Old West Route* 40m to a belay on a spike just left of a rough rib.
1 25m 4a Follow the rib to a green ledge on the left. A wall and slab lead to huge block belays.
2 20m 4b Step up right and traverse round the rib and across the corner to ledges. Step down and climb an awkward right-slanting crack/groove on the right to gain a ledge below the big groove. Climb the groove, taking care with poised blocks, to a stance under a roof.
3 35m 4b Either overcome the bulge and finish up the groove or take the wild Ridge Variation (4c); traverse left with difficulty to gain the foot of a steep crack. Climb this over a slight overlap and pull onto a slab that forms the left side of a slight groove. Exit left into another groove which leads to a ledge and blocks from where easy climbing attains the top of High Man.
HM Kelly, CF Holland - Aug 1919; P3 M Linnell, AS Piggott - May 1932

53 Vandal 80m HVS 5a ★★★
A fine route, steep and well-protected in its lower half but becoming rather worrying with height. Start directly below the large triangular overhang of the West Face.
1 25m 4c Climb the grassy corner to about 5m below the triangular roof where a line up the wall on the right leads with a difficult move to a small ledge. The short curving crack on the right is followed to a good stance.
2 55m 5a Climb the main crack passing another large overhang on its right to a small overhang at 12m. Move left round this and either traverse left to the left arête or move up and traverse left a few metres higher. Climb boldly up the slab above until it is possible to traverse right into an easier slabby amphitheatre and eventually find a runner. Climb up leftwards to a poor flake belay on a ledge at the foot of a flaky rib. Climb the hollow rib to the top.
G Oliver, JM Cheesmond, L Willis - Jun 1959

	Route	Grade
50	**The Old West Route**	M
51	**Gondor**	E2 5c
52	**Gomorrah**	VS 4b
53	**Vandal**	HVS 5a
54	**Pillar of Salt**	E1 5c
55	**Hawkeye**	HVS 5a
56	**Sodom**	VS 4b
57	**Cheekwoolly**	S
58	**Rib and Slab Climb**	HS
59	**Rib and Rib Climb**	E1 5a
60	**New West Climb**	VD
61	**The South-West-by-West Climb**	VS 4c
62	**Sundance**	MVS 4c
63	**South-West Climb**	MVS
64	**West Jordan Gully**	S

54 Pillar of Salt 85m E1 5c ★★
An eliminate with clean and very rough rock, particularly on the final pitch. Start as for *Vandal*.
1 25m 5a Follow *Vandal* as far as the small ledge. Climb the thin crack on the left to a stance.
2 30m 5a Move up one metre and then make a rising traverse rightwards along an obvious series of holds across the wall on the right to the arête. Climb the arête direct until it eases under a bulge and traverse right along a slim ramp to belay on the chockstone at the foot of the chimney on the *New West Climb*.
3 30m 5c Pull up the short wall on the left to a ledge. Make a hard series of moves up the wall above (microwire) to get established on a sloping ledge on the arête. Follow the arête more easily to a slab on the left of the continuation arête. Reach and mantel a huge jug on the edge of the arête. Continue above on fine holds to another break. Finish directly up the jagged edge above.
SJH Reid, J Preston - Sep 1997

55 Hawkeye 84m HVS 5a ★★
1 17m 5a Climb the crack 3m right of *Vandal* onto a pedestal below a blunt arête. Climb the arête directly (quite bold) moving right at the top to a flake belay and stance on the right.
2 30m 5a Climb the prominent groove directly above the stance and, when it eases, step left onto a rock ledge on the front of the rib beneath a shallow groove. Go up this to a large flake (runner). Continue a short distance until a short ramp leads rightwards to the foot of the chimney on *New West Climb*.
3 12m 5a Immediately on the right of the chimney is an overhung V-groove. Climb this over a bulge and step right to a grass stance in a prominent groove.
4 25m 4b Climb to the overhang. Go up the groove on the left a short distance and pull out right to finish up another groove and short wall.
P3 A Phizacklea, RE Wightman -May 1988; C Read, GL Swainbank - Aug 1995

56 Sodom 88m VS 4b ★
Enjoyable but scary friction climbing. Be warned it is a bold climb. Start 12m up *The Old West Route*, on a ledge 3m above.
1 20m An easy slab is climbed for 12m then a groove followed by steep rock which leads to a grassy niche.
2 20m 4a Move 3m to the right to a clean corner. Climb the corner to a resting place below a steep slab then traverse horizontally left on sloping rock steps to the left-hand side of a grassy corner (spike belay high up on the rib on the left).
3 28m 4b A serious lead. Ascend the rib on good holds stepping left into an exposed groove. Follow this and where it eases move up the left-hand side of the rib, overcoming a bulge and thin slab to gain a shallow corner. Step up left to blocks and climb the wall just left of these to gain a slab. Traverse rightwards and down slightly, passing through a gap in the rib, to gain the chimney on *New West Climb* at the point that that route quits it to traverse right - chockstone belay.
4 20m 4b The chimney.
HM Kelly, CF Holland - Aug 1919

57 Cheekwoolly 85m S ★★
An excellent line on superb rock. Protection is spaced but adequate. Start in the back of a huge groove, reached by scrambling 5m leftwards up grass from the pale dike at the start of *Rib and Slab Climb*.
1 45m Climb the open groove-line which trends slightly to the right, to belay under the right-hand of two grooves to the right of a chimney.
2 40m Climb the right-hand groove to where it opens out. Traverse left into the left-hand groove and climb its left rib to the top.
P1 R Bennett, R Lavender - Jul 1974; P2 A Phizacklea, RE Wightman - May 1988

58 Rib and Slab Climb 90m HS ★★★
One of the best climbs of its grade in the Lakes and an extremely enjoyable way to the summit of Pillar Rock. Start just above the start of a right-slanting intrusion of pale rock, 2m below the large embedded block at the foot of *New West Climb*.
1 26m Traverse left along a footledge and continue leftwards to a steep rib with a groove. Climb this to break out left at a small ledge. Climb the slab right of the groove, or the rib on its right, to a ledge. A bold pitch.
2 20m The groove above is hard to start (crux) but the difficulties soon ease. Climb the steep rib on the left of the groove of *New West Climb* to a stance at the top.
3 20m Traverse right and upwards, crossing a groove, onto a superb rough slab; climb it, rising rightwards to a rib which is followed to the "pile of blocks" belay on *New West Climb*.
4 24m Follow the crack of *New West Climb* for about 3m then traverse leftwards via a block. Climb the blistered slab and rib above directly.
CF Holland, HM Kelly, CG Crawford - Jul 1919

59 Rib and Rib Climb 90m E1 5a ★★
An eliminate style series of variations on *Rib and Slab Climb* giving great climbing on fantastic rock. Start at the foot of a great right-slanting pale rock intrusion, just a couple of metres below the start of *Rib and Slab Climb*.
1 30m 5a Follow the intrusion for 5m to a short shallow wide chimney. Step leftwards onto a rib and climb to a jagged overhang. Step left onto *Rib and Slab Climb* and go up a few moves to

place an inadequate selection of paltry protection. Traverse horizontally rightwards onto the overhang, pull over it, and follow the rib to below a short V-groove. Climb the wall to the right of the groove and go up a few metres to a stance just below a small square roof. A bold pitch but never desperate.
2 36m 5a Climb a slim groove to the left of the roof until good jugs on the right wall allow a traverse rightwards above the roof to the arête. Follow the arête to gain the traverse on *Rib and Slab Climb*, then climb diagonally leftwards up the fine slab to its left edge before bold moves up rightwards allow the arête to be regained. Follow it to the "pile of blocks belay" on *New West Climb*.
3 24m 5a Step out leftwards off the top block and make a fingery hand-traverse onto a nose on the left. Continue the traverse leftwards round into a slim groove and climb this to join the last moves of *Rib and Slab Climb*.
C King, SJH Reid - Jul 2005

60 New West Climb 87m VD ★★★
A very fine climb which finds its way through areas of rock usually reserved for harder things. The situations are superb making it one of the best routes of this standard in the Lake District. Start just above a big embedded block in the scree, 25m or so down from West Jordan Gully.
1 20m Follow easy rock in a shallow chimney trending slightly to the left to a rib which leads to a small corner. Follow a steep staircase on the right to belay on a good ledge.
2 10m Climb a wide shallow chimney which leads to a small platform and traverse horizontally left for 4m to step down to a good belay.
3 17m The obvious groove to ledges and make an awkward traverse left to the foot of a chimney.
4 20m The imposing chimney above is climbed or thrutched, depending on ability and girth, to a chockstone at 9m. Avoid the chimney above by traversing horizontally right and around a rib with difficulty. Continue rightwards, then up, to surmount a pile of blocks which form a magnificent belay.
5 20m Climb the crack up the slab above to a small ledge and finish via the slab on the left.
GD Abraham, AP Abraham, CW Barton, JH Wigner - May 1901

61 The South-West-by-West Climb 80m VS 4c ★★
A contrived but worthwhile and increasingly good climb. Start a few metres to the right of *New West Climb*, by the big boulder under West Jordan Gully.
1 18m Traverse left on loose rock to the rib which bounds *New West Climb* on the right and follow it to belay on that climb.
2 25m 4c The left edge of a smooth rectangular slab on the right leads to a horizontal ledge below another larger slab. Climb this until the rock steepens, then move left across a crack to a good foothold before making a few hard moves up to a stance.
3 15m Traverse left into an easy groove and climb this to the traverse of *New West Climb*.
4 22m 4c Traverse left and climb the groove above to the overhang; turn this on the right (crux, and quite bold) and pull out right onto the arête.
A Birtwistle, WK Pearson - Jun 1938

62 Sundance 75m MVS 4c ★★
An unbalanced but pleasant climb directly up the face. Start 6m below and left of *South-West Climb*.
1 16m 4b Climb the wall and corner above to a grass ledge and traverse 3m right to a flake belay.
2 35m 4c Move one metre left and ascend a thin crack up the slab to a bulge. Pull over this via a crack and ascend the slab on the left to a rock ledge. Go directly up via a second ledge to a corner. Climb the corner or the wall on its left to a ledge. Continue up the slab to a stance beneath the prominent arête.
3 24m 4b Bridge up into the corner above and pull out right onto the arête as soon as possible. Follow the left-hand side of the rib above to join *South-West Climb* for the last few moves.
GL Swainbank, C Read - Aug 1995

63 South-West Climb 75m MVS ★★★
Delectable climbing on small but positive holds. The start is one metre left of the entrance to West Jordan Gully.
1 35m 4b A short groove leads to a small ledge under a slab containing a deep-cut hold. Gain the hold from the left, move awkwardly right and continue up the slab to where it steepens. Pull up boldly on good holds which lead to a small ledge. Continue up the rib on the edge of the gully for another 10m to a good square ledge.
2 22m 4b Traverse diagonally left for 3m, then step up, move back right onto the slab and climb it, keeping to the right until a slight steepening is reached. Climb boldly up the slab above until a short traverse right under a large block can be made, towards Jordan Gap, to a small stance. Quite a serious pitch.
3 18m 4b Return under the block and climb a rib and short crack to the summit of High Man.
P1 HR Pope, WB Brunskill - Sep 1911; P2 CF Holland RF Stobart, DE Pilley - Jul 1919; P3 HM Kelly, CF Holland, CG Crawford, NE Odell - Jul 1919

64 West Jordan Gully 30m S ★
This is the prominent cleft separating Pisgah from High Man. An interesting and atmospheric climb deep inside the mountain.
WP McCullock, WR Reade - Jul 1898

MIRK COVE

OS Grid Ref: NY 160 123

Mirk Cove is one of the most beautiful and remote coves in the Lake District.

Two small coves, Wind Gap Cove and Mirk Cove, are divided by vague ridge with Black Crag near the top. See map page 258.

Approach, Ennerdale: Park Ennerdale Bowness Knott P NY 10955 15433 Alongside High Beck (a tributary of the Liza). The upper woodland part of this path is not marked on the OS map but is actually easy to follow; and boggy. With a bike follow the Pillar Rock approach; keep cycling westwards along the upper forest track until, just after crossing High Beck, a path will be seen leading up through the trees - or take an open path up a firebreak a few metres further on.

Approach, Wasdale: Park at Wasdale Head P NY 18680 08957 More interesting and involving less scree crawling, follow Mosedale Beck to source, then reach the col between Red Pike and Scoat Fell; a path traverses rightwards to join the ridge and passes near Black Crag. Or Wind Gap via Mosedale then westwards along the ridge to a cairn (828m); the summit is now only 50m away. To the base strike leftwards, at the same level as Wind Gap, across the rather steep and rough fellside.

Camping: Any approach is very long for a single day's climbing. Conveniently, good flat ground in the bottom of the cove makes an excellent campsite less than half an hour from the crags.

BLACK CRAG

OS Grid Ref: NY 164 117
Altitude: 750m

The rock in the main is superb, though it can be very blank in places - begin well within your grade and carry a good range of gear including micro-cams and micro-nuts and thin slings.

Descent: Via the gully to the right of the crags or the wide scree-filled Descent Gully, easy but unpleasant.

Lower Slabs

A superb face of rock about 35m high recognised by a mossy recessed step towards the right and a leftward-trending grassy area on the left.

1 Lower Slabs Ordinary Route 42m VD ★★

A good little route. Start 4m left of the mossy recess. Follow grassy rocks up left for 6m to an obvious foot-ledge which leads rightwards to a grassy ledge and block. Step back left and climb a shallow groove with a crack to a rock ledge on the right. Now left to follow the left side of the arete pleasantly to a rock platform.

E Wood-Johnson, EW Milne - Jun 1929

2 Lower Slabs Climb Direct 38m HVS 4c ★★

A very pleasant though quite serious climb. Start 2m left of the large mossy recess. Climb a rightward-trending (near horizontal) dog-leg crack to reach a shallow left-slanting groove, immediately above the top of the mossy recess. Follow this to a grass ledge (Friends 2 & 3.5). From the right side of the ledge, easy but unprotected climbing up a slightly left-slanting ramp leads to a rock ledge. Traverse right past a reasonably solid flake, then a worryingly poised one, to a long stride right. Now go up and rightwards through a small triangular niche to a ledge.

E Wood-Johnson, CJ Astley Cooper, A Wood-Johnson, WG Hennessy - Jun 1929

3 Debutante's Slab 30m VS 4b ★★

A good slab climb on fantastic rock with a wild finish. Very bold in the lower two-thirds. Start beneath a very thin left-facing corner at some wonderfully bubbly rock. Climb to easy ledges (side runners in the *Direct* - cams). Continue up and leftwards until a large blunt spike on the right can be gained. The intimidating headwall above the spike through a small triangular niche leads to a good ledge.

J Loxham, A Loxham - Jul 1990

4 Ellison's Eliminate 30m HVS 5a ★

Pleasant climbing on fine rock up the edge of the slab. Start at the right-hand side of the buttress at some mossy streaks. Big holds lead to a ledge. Move right and follow, a leftward-slanting diagonal crack to a step right and up with an awkward mantelshelf onto a tiny ledge under the headwall. Stride left and move up to the base of the triangular niche, then traverse right a metre or so and climb diagonally rightwards up the steep headwall on excellent holds.

SJH Reid, S Baxendale - Sep 2006

AP

Middle Buttress

A Terrace can be reached a few metres round from the large mossy recess, or from the top of the Lower Slabs by a short descent.

5 Poet Laureate 46m E1 5b ★

A direct route up the highest section of Middle Buttress with a distinct crux mid-way. Take small wires. Start 6m left of the toe of the buttress at a clean arête which bounds a right-facing corner.

1 24m 4b Climb the arête direct to a block belay on a grass ledge.

2 22m 5b Boulder off the block leftwards and climb the groove for a few moves before difficult moves lead right to a small crack in the rib. Delicate then pleasant slabs, via a left-facing corner, lead upwards.

J Loxham - Apr 1987

6 Perfect Day 25m E1 5b ★★

An excellent pitch on superb rock with a well protected crux followed by a long bold section to reach the top. It makes a good start to *Limerick*. A clean rib at the lowest point of the wall has a hard first move, then climb up to a small roof above a grass ledge. Traverse left down a ramp to a short corner, up this, pulling out left at its top. Climb the shallow blocky left-facing groove above until it peters out then traverse rightwards and gain a slim groove in the arête (hidden wires). Climb the groove to gain a good ledge above. Exit the ledge on the left, move up 2m and traverse horizontally right to another slim groove in the arête. A couple more moves up this will allow your heart rate to return to normal.

SJH Reid, S Baxendale - Sep 2006

Upper Buttress

From the right-hand end of the Second Terrace, a rock and grass rake slants up rightwards to a terrace and a short upward scramble leads to the foot of the impressive Upper Buttress.

Descent: Walk left to a slanting grassy gully.

7 Tower Buttress 57m VD ★★★

A superb climb on excellent clean rock and with considerable exposure. Start at the lowest point of the buttress.

1 18m The pleasant slab to a large grass terrace.

2 27m Climb the right edge; traverse left to the base of a wide crack by the overhang. Step left then go straight up to ledges below the final slabs; or climb the wide crack.

3 12m Several options - the slab to the left; the thin crack in a shallow groove above or use the crack to reach a ledge, then just below the top make a hand-traverse right - this last is most spectacular.

E Wood-Johnson, CJ Astley Cooper, A Wood-Johnson, WG Hennessy - Jun 1929

COVE CRAG

OS Grid Ref: NY 162 118
Altitude: 675m

Not named on the maps. In the centre of Windgap Cove, 250m west of and slightly lower than Black Crag, lies a low rocky spur which curves up to join the main Scoat Fell ridge. The base of the spur terminates at a set of water-streaked slabs of immaculate rock. Most of the rock is quick-drying and compact, but a few wet streaks on the right can linger for several days. Take a good selection of microcams and microwires.

See map page 258.

1 No September Blewes 40m E1 5b ★★
Just left of the main part of the crag are two sharply defined ribs: this route climbs the right-hand one. A good pitch and quite low in the grade. Climb the rib with interest to a brief interlude below the final crack which requires a determined approach.
R Jervis, SJH Reid, T Daley - Sep 2014

2 Ewes Ahead 40m HVS 4c ★★
A direct line with spaced protection.
1 15m 4c Climb the slab to a ledge. Belay just up on the right at a short wall under an open corner.
2 25m 4c Either climb the corner direct or step right to a flake and climb over a short bulge to a huge sloping ledge. From its top left corner step across left onto a rib containing two slim grooves and climb to easier slabs. The delicate rib above has a great finishing hold. Scramble off left.
N Kekus - Jun 2010

3 Pushmepullewe 40m HVS 5a ★★
An excellent and quick drying eliminate. Start at a block just left of the left-hand left-leaning ramp.
1 25m 5a Step off the block to gain the top of the ramp. A short corner leads with difficulty to a rising traverse line leftwards. From its high point climb the short wall to a large ledge. From its right edge climb straight up a short wall to an even larger ledge.
2 15m 5a Climb diagonally up leftwards to a rib and up to under a horizontal crack. Reach a small foothold on a rib on the right and climb up the right side of a large flake. Belay a little higher. Scramble off left or climb the easy groove.
SJH Reid, T Daley, R Jervis - Sep 2014

4 Deja Ewe 65m VS 5a ★★
Superb rock and the quickest drying line on the crag. Start at the left leaning ramp.
1 25m 5a Climb the left-hand ramp then traverse left to a short corner (microwire). Make a hard move up this and right onto the slab. Immediately move up left and easily up to a large platform. Follow a grassy right-slanting groove on the left to a large mossy ledge.
2 20m 4b From the right-hand side of the ledge climb the wall diagonally leftwards to a pull right across an open left-slanting groove to reach a crack in the far wall. Climb to a ledge and zigzag up to a huge block belay on the right.
3 20m Climb between a large block and a smaller poised block to a grass ledge, then climb the groove on the right behind the tower.
C King, SJH Reid, S Baxendale - Jul 2006

5 Prophylactics 65m E1 5a ★★
With an exciting finale this route hardly lives up to its name being very poorly protected at the start.
1 25m 5a The short impending crack and scoop directly above the ramp is difficult. Climb it with trepidation then move slightly right and follow a rib to a large mossy ledge.
2 20m 4c From the left-hand side climb up to the edge of a slab and cross it leftwards until overlooking a black groove. The delicate rib above ends with a superb flake; finish at a higher ledge.
3 20m The easy groove.
A Phizacklea - Apr 1988

6 Bitter Pill 45m E2 5a ★★
Excellent face climbing with poor protection.
1 25m 5a Follow the short ramp to the impending crack of *Prophylactics*. Walk 2m right and climb the wall on small holds trending leftwards towards the top. Move up into a left-leaning scoop leading to a small roof and bulge. Climb directly over the bulge to belay on a large mossy ledge.
2 20m 4c Climb the wall just right of the right-hand mossy streak and step right round the edge to to climb the scoop and arête on the left of a groove to a ledge and belay. Scramble off left.
N Kekus - Jun 2010

⑦ No Ewe Turns 67m MVS 4b ★★

A great climb - don't be put off by the mossy start.

1 25m 4a The central right-leaning ramp leads to a ledge, follow the crack on the right of a smooth wall until it trends left, then climb straight up to a ledge, 2m down and right of the large mossy ledge.

2 20m 4b Move up rightwards until 2m right of a blocky lump in the left-leaning central corner. Climb the slabby wall above to follow a diagonal crack leftwards to its high point, then continue up the wall above, via a short groove, to a huge block belay.

3 14m 4a Stand on the block then trend left and then right up the rib. Belay beneath a cracked tower.

4 8m 4b The left-hand crack provides a strenuous finish.

A Phizacklea - Apr 1988

⑧ Baxi's Bomber Beetles 67m HVS 5a★★

An interesting route on good rock with a great second pitch. The wet streaks can be avoided. Start at the rightmost left-leaning ramp.

1 25m 5a Climb the ramp to a junction with *No Ewe Turns* and follow it to the foot of the crack on the right of the smooth wall. Swing out left and hand-traverse up a slim ramp to a short groove. Climb this to a ledge, then a smooth corner on the left to a stance.

2 20m 4c Climb up rightwards and up block holds just left of the right arête until just below a grass ledge on the right. Climb the clean left-leaning groove on the left and continue in the same line up a short corner to a big ledge and huge block belay.

3 14m 5a Stand on the block then step out onto a tiny foothold on the arête and sidle round rightwards into a corner. Climb this to a grass ledge then go up a short corner to a cracked tower.

4 8m 4b Climb diagonally rightwards to the right arête of the tower and then follow this to the top.

SJH Reid, Sally Baxendale - Jul 2006

Langdale
Dow
Eskdale
Scafell
Pillar
Buttermere
Borrowdale
Eastern
EV

SPIRE CRAG

OS Grid Ref: NY 160 114
Altitude: 770m

Truly remote, this small slab of immaculate clean rock dries very quickly, provides phenomenal friction and solitude. Not named on maps it lies on the steep headwall of Mirk Cove. Using the 1:25000 OS map, it is just above the '8' of spot height 841 of Little Scoat Fell. See map page 258.

1 Spire Route 23m HS 4a ★
Corners lead to a traverse right to reach a crack. Despatch this and finish up the groove.
A Phizacklea, JL Holden - Jun 2005

2 Where the Ouzel Wasn't 23m HS ★
Pleasant wall climbing with a bold finish.
SJH Reid, C King - Jul 2006

3 Inspired Slab 24m E2 5b ★★
Immaculate rock and a direct line.
A Phizacklea, JL Holden - Jun 2005

4 Fred Dibnah, Steeplejack 24m E2 5c ★
More good rock on the slabs left of the big corner of Impatience Slab. For comfort fix side runners.
A Phizacklea, JL Holden - Jun 2005

5 Impatience Slab 22m S ★
The pleasant corner starting at the foot of a large block.
M Cocker, Pippa Cocker, C Wells - Jun 2003

6 Perspire Crack 15m E3 6a ★
The slanting crack is thin and sustained. Use a sky-hook to protect the start, then the gear is good.
A Phizacklea, JL Holden - Jun 2005

STEEPLE - EAST FACE

3 hr 

OS Grid Ref: NY 158 116
Altitude: 700m

① **Steeple Buttress** 160m VD ★★
A satisfying long mountaineering route with many variations, ending on the summit.
1 35m Scramble easily leftwards up broken rocks to a slightly undercut rib. Follow the rib on superb rough rock to a square ledge where the rib widens to a flat wall with a crack in it.
2 25m Climb the left edge of the wall (or the crack) and follow the rib to a horizontal intrusion of banded rock.
3 20m Directly up the ridge above on good holds to a grassy area.
4 25m Easy scrambling up the edge of the buttress leads to more grass. On the left is a hanging rib leading to the summit. Belay to the left of this.
5 25m Climb the steep rib, on its left side at first, then up the crest and bypass a large block on its left, or climb straight over it, and scramble up to belay at the foot of a wide groove with a slim groove splitting a hanging rib to its left.
6 30m Tricky moves up the slim V-groove followed by easier rock lead to a fine finish at the summit.
DA Elliott - Apr 1957

Steeple Buttress, Steeple East Face VD (page 291) Emily Brooks, Fiona McCarthy — 📷 Stephen Reid

BUTTERMERE & ST BEES

Buttermere & St Bees

FRCC GUIDE

Buttermere & St Bees
Definitive Guidebook

☐ *Oxford and Cambridge Direct* MS (page 321) Martin Armitage — Al Phizacklea

BUTTERMERE & HONISTER PASS

'I have no sympathy with the ever-increasing number who look on the tramp to the foot of the crags as a "beastly grind". It will be disastrous to the sport of climbing if its devotees cease to love the mountains as a whole, as the older men did, and wish only for the crags.' Lehmann J Oppenheimer 1908

A beautiful valley with a rich variety of crags and rock type in some of the loveliest settings. Easily accessible yet offering solitude and remoteness.

Peascod's Ladies' Day Out

A challenging long day out climbing all of Peascod's ladies named routes...

1. Delilah, High Crag	VS 4c
2. Salome, Great Round Howe	E1 5a
3. Cleopatra, Buckstone How	HVS 5a
4. Jezebel, Miners Crag	VS 4c
5. Eve, Shepherds Crag	VS 4c

YEW CRAG KNOTTS

15 mn

OS Grid Ref: NY 219 145
Altitude: 350m

Good climbing on clean and quick drying rock. The first steep clean buttress on the left when ascending Honister Pass from Buttermere.

Approach: Directly from the road, P NY 21517 14565, to its foot. See map page 294.

Descent: To the right.

The following routes tackle the highest most continuous area of rock.

1 Face the Music 35m E1 5b ★
Good climbing. Start below the main corner of *Substitute*. Climb left then up the left-hand of the twin grooves to a good ledge. Finish up a groove above.
C Downer, E Rogers, RE Wightman - Apr 1987

2 Backlash 35m E1 5b ★
Easier than it looks.
C Downer, RE Wightman, E Rogers - Apr 1987

3 Substitute 40m E1 5b ★★★
Steep and sustained yet well protected; the main corner on the left-hand side of the buttress. Gain the corner from the right and climb it until a glacis on the right can be gained with difficulty. Continue up the steep corner above.
A Grieg, J Moore - Aug 1977

4 Eternal Spring 40m E1 5b ★
The groove to the right of a small square overhang and the overhanging chimney above.
1 22m 5b Up to a thorn bush. Move up and gain the groove via a large detached flake; up the groove and exit right to a tree belay.
2 18m 5a Step left then climb straight up the wall to gain the chimney; up this to the top.
TW Birkett, K Forsythe, W Peascod - Mar 1981

5 The Garden Wall 40m S
Interesting climbing. Start left of the main arête at an upstanding flake.
1 15m Climb the wall up and to the left to a thorn bush. Climb the narrow chimney behind to a recess.
2 12m Traverse horizontally right, nearly to the arête, then work up left over vegetation to a stance with thread belays below a steep little groove.
3 13m Climb the groove then ascend the steep wall on the left to a flake belay at the top of the crag.
W Peascod and Party - Nov 1941

Below the main arête are two well defined corners.

6 Poker 30m E2 5c ★
The left hand corner, finishing up the arête. Climb the thin crack in the right wall to a traverse. The hanging ramp above (crux) is climbed by its right edge onto the wall above. Finish up the arête on good holds
RO Graham, W Williamson - Mar 1987

7 Hearth 40m E1 5b ★
A devious route avoiding the bulge on Hearth Direct. Climb the right-hand corner for 7m then traverse left and back right to regain the true line above the overhang. A wall and short groove above on the right lead to the top.
JA Austin, E Grindley, C Heap - Aug 1974

8 Hearth Direct 30m E2 5c ★★★
A sustained exhilarating pitch tackling the overhang avoided by *Hearth* on big flat holds.
RO Graham, TW Birkett - Mar 1981

9 Chimney Buttress 27m HVS 5a
The buttress immediately left of the chimney. Climb a smooth wall for 4m to a ledge, traverse left 3m and climb an open groove until forced back right. Finish up the rib. Or climb directly (**E1**) from the ledge to the rib
R Valentine, J Wilkinson -Sep 1969 : Direct - W Williamson - Mar 1989

10 The Chimney 20m VD
An enjoyable wriggle up the chimney.
W Peascod & Party - 31 Dec 1941

11 Sweep 20m MVS 4b ★
A series of entertaining variations. Climb the corner right of *The Chimney*, exit right to the gap behind *Yew Crag Needle*. Move left by a large flake and cross *The Chimney* to finish directly up the buttress on the left.
J Grinbergs, SJH Reid - Oct 1990

12 Yew Crag Needle 20m VS 4c ★
Fun. Climbs the miniature Napes Needle to the right of *The Chimney*, then continues up the crag behind.
1 10m 4c Climb the left-hand arête to a small roof and hand-traverse right along the break to the right edge. Pull directly over the bulge to the top; pinnacle belay.
2 10m 4b Descend into the gap and traverse right to a corner follow this past a loose block to the top.
SJH Reid, J Grinbergs - Oct 1990

Substitute E1 (page 297) Eric Parker — Ron Kenyon

ZORRO BUTTRESS

OS Grid Ref: NY 220 145
Altitude: 430m

Great routes, an open sunny aspect and absorbing climbing – well worth the walk.

Belay at an embedded block up the heather about 15m from the top of the climbs.

Approach: Walk right from Yew Crag Knotts. See map page 294.

Descent: Go left (west) above a wing of the crag. Down a grassy gutter then turn back towards the crag.

In the centre of the buttress are two distinctive left-facing corners. A striking crack lies on the left and a deep cleft on the right.

1 Mark of Zorro 30m E1 5b ★★
A fine climb taking the obvious crack. Start below a tree on a ledge. Pull up onto the ledge and climb the crack to the overhang. Follow it awkwardly onto the left-hand face. The impending crack above is strenuous.
C Downer, D Nicol - 1977

2 Zeta 27m E2 5c ★★
Good steep and strenuous: the left-hand corner, directly above the tree. Pull onto the ledge and ascend right into the corner. Pass the first overhang via a hollow flake. Move up to the lip of the second overhang (hard), pull up and round the right arête to a resting place. Step up the edge and move back into the corner. Climb the third overhang and immediately traverse left to climb the arête.
C Read, GL Swainbank - Oct 2006

3 Banderas 25m E1 5b ★★
Interesting throughout. Climb the short steep wall to a ledge in an overhung recess, right of the tree. Move up and right onto the arête. Move back left and up onto a sloping ledge in the corner. Climb the corner (crux) to sharp flake holds and swing right at the top to a resting place. Move up and step across to the left edge of the wall. Climb the wall above directly, on sometimes alarming but apparently secure holds
C Read, GL Swainbank - Oct 2006

4 Sabre Cut 23m HVS 5a ★
This is the prominent chimney/crack at the right-hand side of the face. Follow the crack, which develops into a chimney. Squeeze up as far as possible to the overhang and step left out onto the wall moving up to a small ledge. Pull up into the line of the continuation crack and, using sharp stacked flakes that form the right arête, follow it to the top.
C Read, GL Swainbank - Oct 2006

CR

MAIDENSTONE BUTTRESS

OS Grid Ref: NY 220 144
Altitude: 380m

A compact, quick-drying, sunny buttress with a lovely outlook. The short stiff walk is rewarded with a vigorous workout for an afternoon or evening.

All the routes are good, *Maiden's Cheek* being the boldest and best of the bunch.

Approach: A mere 150m above and opposite the first lay-by - P NY 21787 14310 - after crossing the bridge on the descent from Honister. Or walk right from Yew Crag Knotts.

See map page 294.

1. **Maiden's Nose** HVS 5a
2. **Maiden's Groove** HVS 5b
3. **Maiden's Cave** E1 5b ★
4. **Maiden's Twins** HVS 5a ★
5. **Maiden's Cheek** E2 5b ★
6. **Maiden's Gangway** VS 4c ★
7. **Right Arête** VS 5a ★
8. **Maiden's Chimney** D

BUCKSTONE HOW

OS Grid Ref: NY 223 143
Altitude: 400m

Very accessible, steep and exposed. Despite its reputation, the routes are comfortably sound and will reward with memorable experiences. Dries quickly.

Approach: From Honister Pass YH - P NY 22557 13535 - take the old quarry track, cross unstable slate spoil and follow a descending traverse to the right-hand end of the crag.

See map page 294.

Descent: To the right on loose slabs.

1 Groove Two 48m HVS 5a ★★
A classic pitch made difficult by the stone-ground smoothness of its walls. Start 20m left of the right extremity of the crag.
1 20m Scramble up to and climb a worn chimney-groove to a birch.
2 28m 5a Climb the main groove. The steep entrance can be avoided by the polished black groove on the left.
W Peascod, SB Beck, G Rushworth - Jul 1947

2 The Asp 48m E2 5c ★★
Start right of a small pillar, beneath the brown stain.
1 16m 5c Climb the thin V-groove 2m right of *Cleopatra* to the right end of the gangway then go up a smooth groove (crux) to a roomy ledge.
2 32m 5b Climb the open groove to an overhang then gain a crack on the right wall and climb it to a grassy ledge. Finish up the rib on the right.
J Lamb, P Whillance - Jun 1976

3 Cleopatra 71m HVS 5a ★★★
The classic of the crag; an ingenious and airy way through the layers of overhangs. Start below the smooth brown-stained wall.
1 25m 4c Climb onto a pillar then move right over a bulge to a gangway. Follow this up left to a crack and climb it for 3m. Traverse the wall on the right to gain a large ledge.
2 20m 5a Move delicately up the rib on the left then traverse left to the left-hand of two grooves. Climb this and step left to good belays.
3 26m 4b Move right to gain a bottomless groove then climb its left wall and the continuation, to the top.
W Peascod, B Blake - May 1951

4 Encroacher 60m E1 5b ★
1 35m 5b Climb steeply between jutting flakes to gain the end of a gangway. Continue thinly up the groove above to the overhang, over this on good holds and up to gain a leftward-facing corner. Climb this and pull right onto the rib. Climb over an overlap to a ledge.
2 25m 4c Step left and climb over broken rocks to a spike. Swing left onto the face and climb up left to a groove that leads to the top.
D Knighton, M Brown - Jul 1978

5 Alexas 64m HVS 5a ★★
Interesting throughout with a fine second pitch. Start at the foot of a lower buttress.
1 12m 4c Climb a shallow groove and move up to a shattered ledge.
2 26m 5a Traverse right below the overhangs to a perch at the foot of an undercut groove. Climb the groove steeply to a ledge on the right below the overhangs, then climb diagonally left until it is possible to move up right to a ledge.
3 26m 4b Move right to gain a bottomless groove then climb its left wall and the continuation to the top.
B Ingle, P Crew - Sep 1962

6 Caesar 72m HVS 5a ★
Enjoyably steep on good holds. Start at a green groove on the left of the lower buttress.
1 9m Climb the groove past a large jammed flake to a shattered ledge below the overhangs.
2 26m 5a Pull up into a niche then step up right and climb a fine groove to a niche with spikes.
3 13m 4c Move left to a ledge, up to a little overhang, turn it on the left and climb to a ledge.
4 24m 4b Climb a curved groove over thin flakes to the top of the crag.
L Brown, AP Turnbull - Sep 1959

7 Honister Wall 95m HS ★★
A fine series of typical Buckstone How pitches! Start just right of a large block.
1 20m Climb the wall to a stance below the overhangs.
2 13m Traverse left and climb a steep arête to a niche behind a small oak.
3 14m From the bollard on the right, climb a short wall and groove to a large grassy corner.
4 13m The Black Wall. Traverse diagonally right then climb the rib.
5 20m Traverse diagonally left across a slab and under a small overhang before moving up to a ledge.
6 15m Climb the short wall on the right and scramble to the top of the crag.
W Peascod, SB Beck - May 1946

8 Cumbrians' Climb 82m HVS 5a ★
Varied climbing. Start 3m left of the large block.
1 25m 5a Climb a crack that splits the small overhangs and continue to a ledge below a wall. Either make a very long stride left to gain a bottomless niche or climb straight up on good holds to gain the stance below the V-groove of *Sinister Grooves.*
2 13m 4b Climb diagonally right across one groove into another and follow this to a large grass ledge below a black wall.
3 26m 4b Traverse left into a groove with an overhang. Turn it on the right and climb to a stance below a corner stacked with blocks.
4 18m Climb the corner to easy ground.
W Peascod, R Wilkinson - Jul 1949

9 Octavia 80m HVS 5a ★
A climb of continuous interest. Start beneath an obvious curving crack-line, 7m left of the large block.
1 25m 5a Climb the crack, passing an overhang at 6m. Continue up and climb into a groove on the right-hand side of a large block. Pull right onto the arête then go up to the block belay below a V-groove.
2 35m 5a Climb the wall above and surmount a block on the right. Ascend just left of a groove until a pull right can be made. Move up left to the bottom of a steep wall and step left next to a horizontal slot. Pull up onto the steep slab above and climb it directly towards the foot of a steep groove until a move left gains a rock ledge. Climb directly between the prows up the wall above to a rock ledge. Climb the narrow arête on the left to a stance level with its top; anchors 3m higher.
3 20m 4b Move right from the rib to ledges. Above is a steep left-slanting groove; gain and climb it to the top.
GL Swainbank, C Read - May 1997

10 Sinister Grooves 80m VS 4c ★★★
A climb of unforgettable character; a benchmark at the top of the grade. Start beneath an open groove 10m left of the large block.
1 25m 4a Climb the groove beside a heathery central crack-line and move up through a more defined groove to step right to a stance below a deep V-groove.
2 25m 4c Climb the groove to its top. Step right and go up round the arête. Climb a tapering slab until it is possible to traverse 4m left round a rib and go up into the bay below a long crack.
3 30m 4c Climb the crack and then the chimney to the top.
W Peascod, SB Beck - Mar 1946

11 Catalyst 80m E2 5b ★
Start up a shallow groove just right of an arête and 12m left of the large block.
1 20m 5a Climb straight up a vague corner to a ledge at 8m, move right onto the wall and climb to an overhang. Cross the slab on the left and pull up over blocks to a ledge.
2 25m 5b Climb the recessed wall to a detached flake. Step up left into an easier groove and climb it to a spiky arête. Traverse left on bilberry ledges and move up to a tree.
3 35m 5b Go left round the corner to an embedded flake and step off it onto the wall. Move right over a bulge to gain an overhanging groove and climb it (peg) to exit onto the left arête. Climb the steep grooves above trending right to the top.
C Read, J Adams - May 1972: FFA J Lamb - Mar 1975

11
10
8
9
7
6
5
3
4
2
11
10
9
8
7
6
5
4
3
2

1	**Groove Two**	HVS 5a
2	**The Asp**	E2 5c
3	**Cleopatra**	HVS 5a
4	**Encroacher**	E1 5b
5	**Alexas**	HVS
6	**Caesar**	HVS 5a
7	**Honister Wall**	HS
8	**Cumbrians' Climb**	HVS 5a
9	**Octavia**	HVS 5a
10	**Sinister Grooves**	VS 4c
11	**Catalyst**	E2 5b

From Honister Pass

GREAT ROUND HOW

OS Grid Ref: NY 207 128
Altitude: 520m

Set among the hummocks and little tarns of the secluded upland between Haystacks and Gillercombe the crag has a superb outlook, dries very quickly, catches the early evening sun and offers clean rough rock.

Approach: P NY 22557 13535 From the quarry at Honister Pass Youth Hostel follow the footpath past the upper quarries. At the stone building, strike downhill across Warnscale Beck and beneath the outcrop of Little Round How. Branch left then skirt the western end of the crag.

See map page 294.

Descent: To the south.

Four long routes in the centre of the crag have indistinct lines, yet they are all worthwhile. Sharing a common start (1) **Farandolle** MS ★ and the slightly easier (2) **Starchaser** MS ★ take the centre of the buttress. (3) **Route 2** D ★ and (4) **Stargazer** D ★ climbs from the grassy bay, sandwiching the harder routes. One 50m rope is plenty.

(5) **Tambourine** 35m VS 4b ★
Make a steep start 3m to the left of a corner with a juniper at its foot. Saw-edged flakes trend left to a clean groove trending back right.
D Craig, W Peascod - May 1982

6 Salami 25m E1 5b ★★

The steep fingery unprotected wall to a widening in the slanting crack. Follow the crack right to a small block. Move up (crux) and trend left to finish.

N McAllister, G Higginson, J Lawrenson - May 1997

7 Salome 25m E1 5a ★★

A fine steep pitch; hard to protect. Small holds on the bulging wall and a delicate traverse right and up gains the foot of a downward pointing fang. Climb the right side (crux) and from its top climb the rough wall.

D Craig, W Peascod, N Craig - Jun 1983

8 Pepperami 25m VS 4b

The scruffy left side of the blunt arete for starters.

N McAllister - 25 May 1997

9 Bratwurst 25m VS 4c ★

The open groove on the right side completes lunch. Poorly protected.

J Lawrenson - May 1997

HIGH CRAG

OS Grid Ref: NY 182 145
Altitude: 450m

45 mn

With some of the most enjoyable routes in the valley it is well worth an early start to make the most of the morning sun.

Samson HVS (page 310) Fiona Sanders — PETER STERLING

Approach: Paid P at Gatesgarth Farm NY 19527 14985. Follow the scarth gap path to a gate, then take the left side of a fence on the right directly up to the crag. See map page 294 and photo page 314.

Descent: Well to the left (east) along a well-defined path to a short steep corner to a long clean groove. Or with care abseil by *Dry Trim.*

1 The Three Kings 42m VS 4c ★
Interesting climbing up the first steep wall at the left. Start from a small rock ledge beneath three distinctive small triangular niches, 15m left of the rock table.
1 20m 4a Climb the wall crossing a diagonal crack, to reach easy slabs, up then left to the foot of a steep clean wall.
2 22m 4c Trend right to blocks (care). Move up and traverse diagonally left to reach and follow a slightly cracked groove to the ledge above. Move up and pass the first of two overlaps on its right. Pull up, step left, then up the steep wall.
C Read, BR Shackleton - May 2000

2 Ludo 55m HS ★★
A direct line giving some good climbing. Start 4m left of the rock table.
1 30m Take a left-rising line up the wall, crossing a heather-filled fault-line, to some whitish layers and a scoop. Step left; move right over a bulge and then climb directly up to ledges.
2 15m Take the slim groove up the right edge of the slab to the right of a corner (bold). Move up to gain and climb a scoop, belay on a sloping rock ledge beside a huge block.
3 10m Move up the ledge leftwards for 2m and pull into a shallow bottomless groove in the final tier. Head up rightwards.
B Masson, P Gomersall - Jun 1984

3 Nameless Route 58m HS ★
A pleasant climb on good rock. Start at the foot of the crag, immediately left of a short chimney.
1 30m Climb a short wall to a ledge below a small overhang. Step left then climb the steep slabby rock above the overhang, trending right-wards at first, then more easily straight up to a sloping rock ledge. Move up and belay on a gen-tle slab below an obvious crack in the wall above.
2 18m Climb the steep crack to a small veg-etated ledge. Step immediately up left around the exposed arête and move up steeply to gain and climb the scoop above (crux) to a ledge and large block belay.
3 10m Gain the top of the block from the right and pull onto the slab above. Another short wall leads to block belays.
W Peascod, E Banner-Mendus - Sep 1941

4 Artefact 67m MVS 4b ★★
Popular. Scramble up from the left to start on the rock table below a corner.
1 24m 4a Climb the corner, exit right by a grass mantelshelf. Continue to the large glacis below a crack.
2 16m Scramble left to a ledge below an over-hung corner.
3 27m 4b Move directly up the corner to an overhang. Turn this on the right and climb an easier groove to a sloping rock ledge below an undercut crack. Climb the crack to easier rocks.
NJ Soper, JA Austin, S MacLean, BL Griffiths - Jun 1965

5 Resurrection Route 75m VS 4b ★
A satisfying route. Start below and right of the rock table.
1 25m Ascend a short corner to the table. Step onto the rib on the right and follow it to a large glacis below an imposing corner-crack.
2 15m 4b The crack.
3 20m 4b Step down onto the right wall along a short ledge, move into a mossy crack and climb this to a block belay.
4 15m The pleasant slab is climbed to the top.
W Peascod, E Banner-Mendes, A Barton - Sep 1941

6 Dry Trim 33m E1 5b ★★
Good edges lead directly up the wall right of the crack of *Resurrection Route.*
S Howe, R Cassidy - 21 Jul 1984

7 Samson 33m HVS 5b ★★
A fine pitch up the centre of the smooth central wall. Make an ascending traverse right, just above the overhang to gain the crack in the centre of the wall, climb it; it eases just before it turns into an **E1**!
L Kendall, A Clarkson - May 1963 FFA P Botterill - May 1978

8 Close Shave 33m E1 5b ★★
A good steep climb though close to its neigh-bours. Start under the overhang beneath the crack of *Samson.*
Make a difficult pull left through the overhang. Step right to a thin crack. Climb this for 2m and move right onto *The Philistine.* Move back left and climb the wall to step right onto a small ledge. Climb the thin crack on the left, which slants left and follow cracks though the bulges above.
SJH Reid, SR Stout - Jun 1999

9 The Philistine 35m E1 5b ★★★
A great climb up the clean blunt arête. Protection is only good when it is most needed. From the left climb to the overhang and traverse right to a good foothold on the arête (or direct at **5c**). The crack yields stubbornly with a poor resting place above. The move down to the left side of the arête is precarious; once completed relish the superb situation and climbing above.
E Cleasby, TW Birkett - Jun 1975

10 Lost Colonies Direct 46m E3 6a ★★
Excellent climbing starting 4m right of *The Philistine*. Move delicately right to a good runner in a shallow corner. Traverse left and up (thread on *Psycho*), move right and climb the superb crack and the capped groove to finish up the fine wall above.
P Livesey, J Sheard - Jul 1976 ; Direct start - J Lamb, J Taylor, P Botterill - May 1978

11 Psycho 50m E1 5b ★★
Technical climbing. Start beneath the left hand cave.
1 15m 4c Gain the top of the detached flake and climb the cracks above to the cave.
2 35m 5b Move left and climb a difficult shallow groove to a thread. Move up and left with difficulty to gain a V-groove. Climb this and easier rock to the top.
L Brown, JS Bradshaw - Sep 1964

12 High Crag Buttress 55m HVS 5a ★★★
Very fine climbing directly up the main face passing between two caves. An especially route when climbed as a single pitch with 60m ropes. Start beneath the right hand cave.
1 30m 4c A short corner-crack on the right leads to a grass ledge, an awkward wall crack gives access to the belay in the left-hand cave. Make an intimidating move onto the rib between the caves; continue up the chimney-crack above to a small square cave.
3 25m 5a Climb the rib on the right (thread); a delicate traverse leads up to a slab further right; easy grooves lead off.
JJS Allison, L Kendall - Sep 1962 FFA P Nunn, PL Fearnehough

13 Fellwanderer 53m HVS 5a ★
A good way up the crag at this grade. Start beneath the right-hand cave.
1 18m 5a Climb up to the right-hand cave and exit right onto ledges. Belay down and right.
2 25m 5a Climb up left onto a rib and follow it into a small cave. Hand-traverse left along the fine flake to its end, make a difficult mantelshelf then step left to better holds. Step down and traverse left on jugs to easier ground and reach a huge block belay.
3 10m 4a The slab on the right.
A Cammack, SJH Reid - Jun 1996

14 Nebuchanezzar's Dream 54m E1 5b ★★
Quality climbing up the thin crack right of *High Crag Buttress*. Start beneath the right-hand cave.
1 18m 5a Climb up to the cave and exit right onto ledges. Belay down and right.
2 36m 5b Climb the thin crack to where the angle eases. Step right to a groove and climb it over an overhang to easy ground.
J Lamb, M Hetherington, A Dunhill - Jun 1979

15 Gethsemane 47m E1 5b ★★★
The prominent crack-line in the centre of the right-hand wall gives an excellent climb.
JA Gosling, JA Brooder - May 1970; FFA C Read, J Adams -1972

16 Delilah 50m VS 4c ★★★
Sustained and delectable climbing, the upper section takes a fine groove. Start just left of the deep chimney defining the end of the main buttress.
1 18m 4a Move left onto a grass ledge then gain a narrow ledge just above. Traverse this back right and follow a crack to a stance.
2 32m 4c Ascend left into the groove and climb it exiting right just below the top.
W Peascod, SB Beck - Aug 1951

1	**The Three Kings**	VS 4c
2	**Ludo**	HS
3	**Nameless Route**	HS
4	**Artefact**	MVS 4b
5	**Resurrection Route**	VS 4b
6	**Dry Trim**	E1 5b
7	**Samson**	HVS 5b
8	**Close Shave**	E1 5b

9	**The Philistine**	E1 5b	13	**Fellwanderer**	HVS 5a
10	**Lost Colonies Direct**	E3 6a	14	**Nebuchanezzar's Dream**	E1 5b
11	**Psycho**	E1 5b	15	**Gethsemane**	E1 5b
12	**High Crag Buttress**	HVS 5a	16	**Delilah**	VS 4c

BIRKNESS COMBE

Overlooking the south shore of the lake this combe is the traditional heart of Buttermere climbing.

Approach: From Gatesgarth Farm, paid P NY 19527 14985, follow the track south-west towards the far fellside. At an intersection take a less distinct path that rises below a dank outcrop (plaque) before crossing some boggy ground to enter the combe.

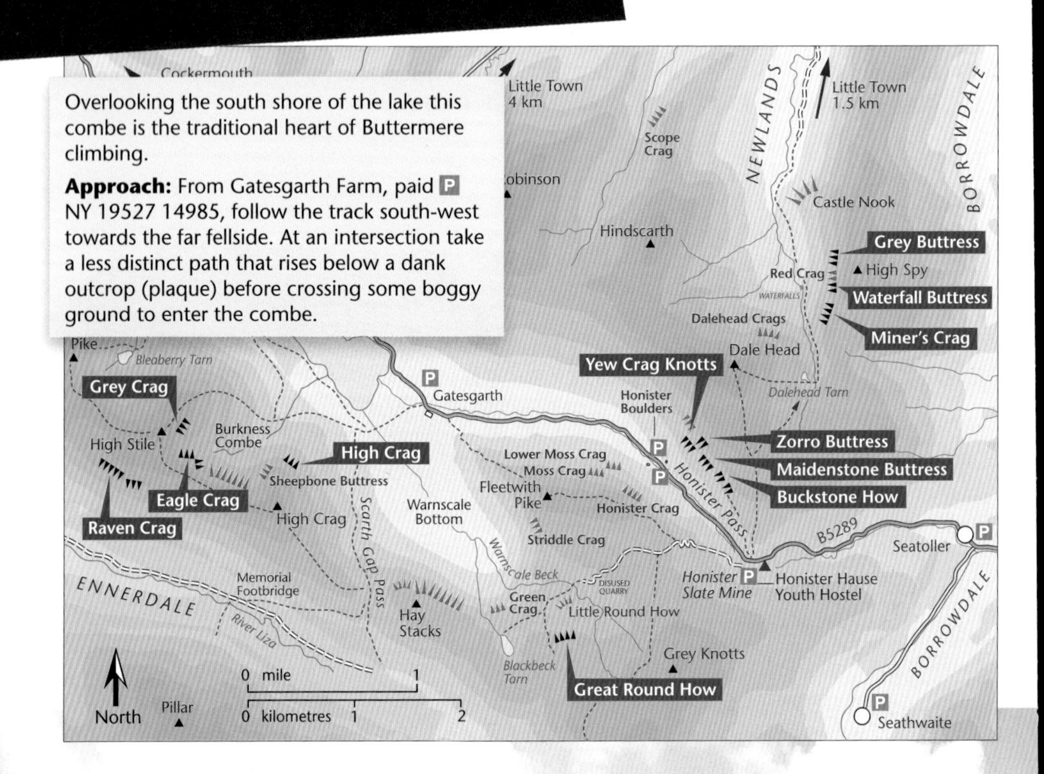

EAGLE CRAG

OS Grid Ref: NY 172 145
Altitude: 600m

This impressive buttress dominates the upper combe and offers great climbing. The routes become much harder in anything other than perfect conditions. Luckily Grey Crag is conveniently close.

Descent: The broad scree gully on the right.

1 Easter Buttress 74m VS 4c ★★
A classic: a typical Lakeland adventure. Start from the vegetated terrace at the lowest point of the rock ribs.
1 30m 4b Easy rocks lead to a steep groove, at the top pull out right to a ledge. Climb left to a flake and then right to an overhung platform.
2 14m 4c Step right into an undercut crack and jam past a suspect flake, continue up a short corner, pull out left onto a ledge.
3 30m 4a Climb the steep crack and continue to the top.
F Graham, M Wood, J Hirst, JF Burton - Apr 1925

2 The Hanging Chimneys Direct 45m HVS 5a
A pitch of character, unfortunately dirty. Start in the highest grassy bay, reached by traversing very steep, vegetated and exposed terrain right from *Easter Buttress*. Climb the groove, moving right to a resting place. Move left and climb up to a flat ledge immediately below the overhangs. Move up to the right to gain good holds and easier rock which leads to the Chimneys which are followed to a resting place; finish up the V-groove above.
J Earl, RG Hutchinson - Jul 1974

3 Fifth Avenue/ Central Chimney 150m VS 4c ★★
This combination has a long delicate and sustained pitch which links with the upper pitches of *Central Chimney*. If the chimney finish doesn't appeal, equally good alternatives are *Carnival* (**HVS 5a**), *Eagle Front* (**VS 4c**) or *Easter Buttress* (**VS 4c**).
1 30m Climb to the right hand side of the alcove via steep grassy cracks and corners.
2 42m 4c From the alcove, move left and make a difficult move up the wall. Trend right to an open groove which leads to the Terrace - junction with *Eagle Front/Carnival*.
3 16m 4b Traverse left into *Central Chimney*. Easter Buttress can be reached from here by scrambling up left.
4,5 & 6 62m 4c The intimidating cleft. Another steep chimney. More easily to the top
P1-2 W Peascod, SB Beck, F Monkhouse - Jul 1940 ; P3-6 W Peascod, SB Beck, G Rushforth - May 1948

4 Carnival 139m E1 5b ★★
Enjoyable and at the lower limit of its grade; one of the quickest drying routes on the crag.
1 30m As for *Fifth Avenue/Central Chimney*.
2 35m 5b Climb the steep crack at the back of the alcove, cross a slab on the right and continue by a crack and V-groove to the Terrace.
3 12m 4b Traverse left to a stance in a grassy bay.
4 27m 5a A spooky pitch. Climb the shallow grooves on the left and then move right to a small ledge. Move up and traverse right to a groove and belay on a ledge above.
5 35m 4b Follow the cracked rib and move left to follow the arête left of the grassy trench to the top.
I Roper, JA Austin, NJ Soper - Jul 1965

5 Deimos 134m E3 5c ★★★
A sustained expedition; solid climbing all the way.
1 30m As for *Fifth Avenue/Central Chimney*.
2 10m 4c Go round to the right and up a shallow groove to a small ledge.
3 36m 5c From the corner a few delicate moves up the slab gain a line of undercuts and layaways. Follow these below the overhangs slanting away to the right to below a bulging groove with an excellent jug on its smooth left wall. Climb the groove with a hard exit (crux) to the Terrace.
4 25m 5b Up on the right is a rightward-slanting groove. Enter this from the left and climb it to a ledge on the right. Climb the steep wall above on good holds to a good ledge.
5 33m 5b The bulging crack and groove above lead, without loss of interest, to the top.
C Read, J Adams - Oct 1972; FFA P Whillance - May 1975

1	**Easter Buttress**	VS 4c
2	**The Hanging Chimneys Direct**	HVS 5a
3	**Fifth Avenue/Central Chimney**	VS 4c
4	**Carnival**	E1 5b
5	**Deimos**	E3 5c
6	**Shape of Things to Come**	E3 5c
7	**Eagle Front**	VS 5a
8	**Mardi Gras**	E1 5b

6 Shape of Things to Come 97m E3 5c ★★★

An excellent way up the crag, finishing on a superb arête. As for p1 of *Eagle Front* then traverse 6m left to a blunt spike below mossy slabs.
1 12m 5a A knobbly ramp leads left. Climb a groove above and step left to belay.
2 30m 5c Climb the overhanging groove above to a resting place. Move left to a sloping ledge and climb the bold wall above to the Terrace.
3 25m 5a Climb onto a large detached flake and up the bubbly groove above to a scoop. Continue delicately then follow the traverse on *Eagle Front* rightwards to the foot of the final crack.
4 30m 5b A niche in the arête to the right is the next objective. From here move back onto the wall and delicately out to a small ledge above the overhang. Climb the arête; awkward at first.
SJH Reid, TW Birkett - Sep 1986

7 Eagle Front 150m VS 5a ★★★

An exhilarating route which strings together a succession of excellent pitches on good rock. Start up an obvious rib which protrudes from the foot of the crag about 20m left of the right-hand edge of this face
1 18m Climb the rib and traverse right to a nook.
2 28m 4c Climb into the steep groove above, move right to gain a ramp sloping back left, follow this to the 'Difficult Bit' up a steep shallow corner. Move up to reach a small ledge, swing up right to a higher ledge, traverse left across some slabs. Flake handholds lead to a ledge up on the right.
3 20m 5a The shallow groove above is hard to enter, step right around a rib to a grass ledge then easily to the Terrace and a block thread belay.
4 22m The 'Long Green Traverse' (aka The Terrace). Go horizontally left, crossing a slab to reach a prominent grass ledge on the skyline. Move up left to a small ledge.
5 14m 4c Climb the steep wall, trending slightly left, before stepping back right across a delicate slab into a groove. Climb this to 'Nail Ledge'.
6 20m 4b Traverse right, crossing exposed ribs to a water-worn slab. Ascend the corner to a large stance.
7 28m 4b The fine corner crack, step right at its top to an easy finish.
W Peascod, SB Beck - Jun 1940

8 Mardi Gras 137m E1 5b ★★

Interesting and varied climbing; mostly **VS** with a short, well-protected crux. Start below a groove 2m left of the blunt arête bounding the face on the right.
1 22m 4c Climb the groove, trending left at its top, move up and follow a slabby ramp left until moves down gain a ledge and spike belay.
2 25m 5b Move back onto the ramp and follow it to merge with *Eagle Front* just before the Difficult Bit. Step right and climb an awkward crack and groove (crux) to a sloping ledge beneath some slabs. Traverse right and pull up round the skyline onto a good ledge, move right and up to a large ledge, then traverse left to a block belay.
3 22m 5a Right 2m and make a difficult pull up onto a large foothold on the wall above. Step left and climb direct to a grass ledge. Continue up to the Terrace and block belay (thread).
4 18m Move right and climb easily to gain a large grass ledge. Climb onto a short slab and belay in the crack above on its left.
5 50m 4b From the top of the slab, pull up left onto the wall and climb direct until the angle eases. At about 30m trend right on good rock passing a small spike/block runner. Move up right onto the rib and climb it until a move left leads to the final slab. Stretch the rope out to a block belay.
C Read, GL Swainbank - Jul 2006

GREY CRAG

OS Grid Ref: NY 171 148
Altitude: 700m

A series of short buttresses superbly positioned in three tiers high above the Combe with a great collection of easy to mid-grade routes that takes no drainage, the clean rough rock dries quickly.

"Too much of Grey Crags after an army diet is like champagne on indigestion", CWF Noyce, Buttermere & Boat Howe FRCC Journal 1942.

See map page 314.

Harrow Buttress

Descent: Descend to the left (for *Mitre Buttress*) or right. To reach Chockstone Buttress and *Sol* scramble up rocks above to a saddle.

1 Harrow Buttress 45m D ★★
Starts at the usual point of arrival. Enjoyable with a steep start.
1 10m Climb the corner or the arête on its right, to a ledge.
2 15m Climb the chimney above, traverse 3m left and move up to a ledge.
3 20m Climb the groove and scramble up to an overhung corner. Pull up left and climb to the top of the buttress.
W Bishop, WA Woodsend - 1912

Mitre Buttress

The left-hand buttress of the lower crag. The routes are described from right to left

Descent: Down the worn scree-chute to the left, or continue up to below the upper tier of Oxford and Cambridge Buttress.

2 Mitre Arête 35m VS 4b ★
The steep left arête of the buttress is good but serious for its grade.
1 20m 4a The arête over several bulges.
2 15m 4b Follow the ladder of ledges leading left across the steep exposed wall to the apex of the buttress.
J Greaves, F Poulter - Apr 1946

3 Mitre Mouse 37m HS
A good second pitch. Start above the scree slope where a pinnacle rests against the face.
1 25m Step left and climb up to a triangular roof on the pinnacle. Move left, enjoyable climbing up the front leads to the top of the pinnacle. A short wall on the left then easy ground leads to a belay at the foot a corner-chimney.
2 12m Climb the crack just right of the corner-chimney. Continue up a slight groove and pull up into a crack; go up this to easier ground.
BJ Clarke - Jun 2005

4 Mitre Buttress Ordinary 64m M ★
The easiest way up the buttress. Start where a pinnacle rests against the face.
1 20m Climb easily to a cave with a pointed roof.
2 8m Traverse left and slightly down, before stepping left along a ledge to its end. Pull up on good holds and climb up to block belays.
3 14m Climb a wall to a grass ledge, step left along the ledge and climb the steep corner-chimney.
4 22m The enjoyable ridge to the top.
CA Elliott and Party - 1912

Grey Crag Link-ups

Grey Crag offers brilliant opportunities to link climbs. Some of the best are:

1.	**5 Mitre Buttress Direct : 16 Oxford and Cambridge Direct**	MS
2.	**15 Fortiter : 17 Dexter Wall**	VS
3.	**1 Harrow Buttress : 12 Chockstone Ridge : 16 Oxford and Cambridge Direct**	MS

1 Harrow Buttress D
2 Mitre Arête VS 4b
3 Mitre Mouse HS
4 Mitre Buttress Ordinary M
5 Mitre Buttress Direct MS
6 Ribbon Wall MVS 4b
7 Rib and Wall D
8 Sol VS 4c
Oxford and Cambridge Buttress
The Slabs
Grey Wall
Chockstone Buttress
Chockstone Ridge
Link path
Mitre Buttress
Harrow Buttress
9 Slabs West Route HS
10 Slabs Ordinary Route VD
11 Return with a Vengeance MVS 4b
12 Chockstone Ridge M
16 Oxford and Cambridge Direct MS
17 Dexter Wall VS 5a
CR

5 Mitre Buttress Direct 80m MS ★★

A varied route up the front of the buttress from its lowest point.

1 13m Climb the wall leftwards to a ledge.

2 15m Climb a short wall and walk right to the steep right (east) face of the buttress.

3 15m The left side of the wall has a mantelshelf onto a narrow ledge on the right. This ledge leads left to the edge of the buttress.

4 22m Climb directly up the steep exposed wall above to a ledge.

5 15m The natural line above is easy; alternatively climb a steep chimney/crack to the left.

AC Pigou and Party - Jul 1915

6 Ribbon Wall 46m MVS 4b ★★

Pleasant wall climbing. Start by scrambling to the base of the wall.

1 25m 4b Climb blocky flakes on the left to a thin horizontal flake, pull up right, then work up and left to a small protruding flake. Move up to a shallow corner which leads to a belay on the arête.

2 21m Step right and climb the cracked face to the crest of the rib. Continue up easy ground.

P1 A Phizacklea, JL Holden - May 2006 ; P2 C Read, GL Swainbank - Jun 2006

7 Rib and Wall 96m D ★

A logical continuation to *Harrow Buttress*. Start in the bay between *Harrow* and *Mitre Buttresses*.

1 25m Climb the right face of the steep rib to a grass nook, continue up to a belay below a large block.

2 7m Climb the block on its right and cross its top to the main wall.

3 15m Climb some shattered rock, trending right to beneath an obvious V-groove.

4 12m Move up the groove a few metres, pull right round the corner to a narrow ledge and follow it across the wall to a block/cave.

5 12m Climb the wall right of the block, move right and climb a short steep crack to a ledge.

6 25m Climb easy-angled slabs to the top.

W Peascod, GG MacPhee - Aug 1945

8 Sol 36m VS 4c ★

Combines delicate and fingery climbing with vigorous jamming. Start beneath the blunt rib of a huge boulder near the saddle.

1 25m 4a Step off a block under the right side of the left face and climb the right edge on superb crinkly rock to the top of the boulder. Continue easily to a ledge beneath the prominent left-facing corner.

2 11m 4c The excellent corner.

C Read, SW Pollington - Jun 2006

Chockstone Buttress

The middle tier comprises The Slabs, rising from the gully on the left and Grey Wall, the fine wall to the right.

Descent: An easy open scree gully well to the right or the badly eroded scree gully to the left.

9 Slabs West Route 55m HS ★★★

Interesting throughout. Start up the gully on the left of the slabs at a stepped rightwards rising traverse.

1 32m Follow a thin crack in the slab to where it steepens then climb the wall to the left and move up right to a ledge. Move leftwards, then straight up the slab to a ledge below a pile of blocks beneath an overhang.

2 23m Climb left of the overhang into a shallow niche. Step right, make a few moves up, step left and finish straight up the slabby wall.

W Peascod. A Barton - Sep 1942

10 Slabs Ordinary Route 61m VD ★★★

Varied climbing up the right side of the slabs. Start up the gully at a rightwards rising traverse.

1 18m Follow the traverse to blocks, climb over them and up to a large sloping ledge; belay at its right end.

2 23m From the left end of the sloping ledge go up easy-angled rock which leads to a crack and clean slab above, to the foot of a wide right facing corner/groove.

3 20m Climb the corner on good holds to the top.

H Bishop, WA Woodsend - Aug 1913

11 Return with a Vengeance 69m MVS 4b ★

A memorable top pitch.

1 25m 4a From the lowest point of the slab climb easily to a sloping grass ledge at 3m. Pass the bulge by a thin crack on its right, follow this to a step left onto the crest and up to a belay on the right side of a large sloping ledge.

2 20m From the ramp on the right step into a left trending crack leading to a ledge. Trend right up slabs to a stance at the foot of the right-facing corner/groove.

3 24m 4b Traverse 4m right to the edge of the buttress and climb up keeping as close to the arête as possible; protection is only available where most needed.

WF Hurford, CB Fitzhugh - 21 Aug 2000

12 Chockstone Ridge 67m M ★

Takes a stepped ridge beyond the gully right of the slabs from a ledge a few metres up on the left side. Follow the crest past a gendarme at 30m climbing a steep chimney endowed with good holds below the final easy section.

JH Clapham and Party - Apr 1914

Grey Wall

The next routes are on Grey Wall, the fine wall 30m horizontally to the right.

13 **Suaviter** 48m S ★★

A delightfully exposed second pitch. Start beneath the left end of a long ledge.

1 10m Climb the corner, move right then up to the long ledge.

2 16m Step down from the left end of the ledge, traverse delicately left to a crack with a protruding block and climb it past a ledge with doubtful blocks to a roomy ledge on the left.

3 22m Climb the ridge above to an area of ledges and blocks, then a groove with a wide crack at its back to the top.

W Peascod, SB Beck - Jul 1941

14 **Grey Wall** 45m VS ★★

Steep and direct.

1 9m 4a Climb a crack to the long ledge.

2 28m 4c From the left end climb the shallow corner, step left onto the wall and follow cracks. Step right and up into a niche, pull out right, then ascend twin cracks to a small ledge. The corner-crack on the left leads to a large ledge.

3 8m Move right and follow an easy rib to the top.

J Adams, C Read - Feb 1972

15 **Fortiter** 42m MVS ★★★

The prominent excellent crack-line right of centre is clean and direct.

W Peascod, SB Beck - Jul 1941.

Oxford and Cambridge Buttress

The final tier is a compact buttress of rock.

Descent: The gully to the left of the buttress. Alternatively, traverse right to where easy ground leads down and back in.

16 **Oxford and Cambridge Direct Route** 42m MS ★★★

An outstanding route for its grade taking the main arête of the buttress.

1 15m Start under the arete and wend your way up.

2 27m Move up left, climb a short bulging crack, move back right to a ledge. Follow the right edge over a bulge to the top.

HW Reade - Sep 1914

17 **Dexter Wall** 42m VS 5a ★★★

A classic test piece; at the top of its grade. The highlight is the technical crack splitting the just off-vertical wall. Start 5m right of the arête.

1 24m 4a Climb a crack to a V-niche beneath an overhang, step right and climb a crack to a narrow ledge. Traverse right, climb a slim corner, move right to a small ledge and belay.

2 18m 5a Climb the thin vertical crack.

W Peascod, SB Beck - Mar 1941

RAVEN CRAG HIGH STILE

OS Grid Ref: NY 164 144
Altitude: 610m

Stunningly situated on the Ennerdale face of High Stile, these buttresses are composed of rough, firm and quick drying rock. Choose a fine calm day to make the most of your visit.

Approach: From Buttermere, off-road P NY 17736 17060, cross Red Pike then descend in the direction of Pillar Rock.

See map page 314.

Western Buttress

The first buttress at the left-hand end.

Descent: To the left or go right over the top of Spearhead Buttress and down scree beside it.

The right end of the buttress has an attractive arête above a subsidiary buttress.

1 Chrysalis Arête 48m VD ★
Varied climbing: start just above and right of the toe of the subsidiary buttress.
1 25m Climb the steep curving crack above the grassy bay to an overhung ledge. From a slab on the right, pull round a bulging block and scramble up to a ledge.
2 23m Climb easy slabs, trending left up to the left side of the arête and step delicately round to the right. Pull up and follow it to a large block.
J Carswell, A Barton - Sep 1935

Spearhead Buttress

The steepest of these buttresses.

2 Butterfly Crack 33m S ★★
Direct and steep. Gain the crack by awkward moves slightly right. Climb it on good holds, carefully pass a poised block and jam up the narrowest part until it eases as it deepens into a chimney.
J Carswell, A Barton - Sep 1935

3 Painted Lady 33m E3 5c ★★★
Exposed and exhilarating climbing taking an intricate line of least resistance up the wall between *Butterfly Crack* and the right-hand edge of the front face. Start in a recess beneath a bulge, 3m left of the right-hand edge and above an embedded flake. Pull over the bulge to holds on the right, move left then up passing a perched flake on the left. Step onto the flake and ascend the left side of the wall, continuing up steepening rock, to outflank the first band of overhangs (dubious hold). Pull up to beneath the second band of overhangs and traverse right beneath them (peg). Climb the wall direct and move straight up the corner (peg). Continue to the third overhang, pull directly over to gain a hanging groove and ascend this to the top.
B McGowan, G Wilks - Sep 2003

4 Alpine Ringlet 30m E4 5c ★★★
Excellent steep climbing based on the right edge of the main face and incorporating the impressive crack in the left wall of *The Emperor*. Start just above the right edge of the front face. Climb the shallow groove until it steepens. Having placed a skyhook on the obvious hold up on the right make a long reach for big flat holds on the left and pull up again (peg). Step left around the arête (peg), step up and make a difficult step right for a small flat spike. Gain a jug on the arête, pull up and make a long reach for a block hold and climb the crack until a ledge is reached on the left. Balance to the arête and a make a finely positioned move to the top.
E Rogers, K Forsythe - Jul 2006

5 The Emperor 33m E1 5b ★★★
Sustained climbing up the fine bulging ramp/groove-line on the right flank of the main buttress, low in the grade. Start above the right edge of the front face, beneath a prominent wide crack. From below the crack step left off blocks onto the wall and move up a steep narrow ramp over two bulges to gain a long wedged block in the groove above. Continue to the final overlap, climb the crack and groove above through the notch at the top.
C Read, SW Pollington - Jun 2005

⑥ **Family Plot** 35m HS ★

A difficult first pitch leads to easier climbing. Takes the prominent wide crack right of the front face,

1 10m 4a Climb the crack, make a short traverse right to a corner; small stance.

2 25m Climb the wall above and pull into the looming groove which widens into a chimney. Pull over blocks (care) and up the wall on the left to the top.

DN Greenop, CJ Crowther - May 1965

Eastern Buttress

Beyond a gully is the final buttress.

Descent: Left down scree beside Spearhead Buttress, or right past the end of the crag.

⑫ **Boulder and Crack** 36m VD ★

Worthwhile for the top crack. Start at the boulder below the eastern end of the buttress.

1 16m Reach the top of the boulder from the left; pass a chockstone up a chimney-crack to a ledge.

2 20m Move up, then step right to the crack.

DN Greenop, G Benn - May 1958

3 Painted Lady E3 5c
4 Alpine Ringlet E4 5c
5 The Emperor E1 5b
6 Family Plot HS

Eighty Foot Slab Buttress

A sweep of fine slabs situated below and left of Spearhead Buttress.

Descent: To the left, down scree beside Spearhead Buttress.

7 Outside Edge 25m VD ★
Start immediately right of an overhang at the left side of the face. Climb steeply and awkwardly over a bulge to a slab, pull out left, traverse up left to the edge of the buttress and follow this to a small ledge. Climb a short scoop and continue right to the top.
IM Banner-Mendus, J Carswell, A Barton - Sep 1935

8 Zig Zag 30m S
Use the *Outside Edge* entry to reach the foot of a right-facing corner. Climb the corner to a short traverse left to ledges and the top.
J Carswell, A Barton - Sep 1935

9 Crazy Diamond 25m E1 5a ★★
Excellent climbing up the centre of the face. Step off some blocks and climb directly for about 12m to a large hold on the left. Move up and diagonally to the right, continue up the steepening wall, moving slightly left. Easier rock to the top.
C Read, P Fleming - Sep 2003

10 Shine On 25m E2 5b ★
Thin, bold, flawed only by its contrived escapability.
A Phizacklea - Sep 2005

11 Kona Nu Nu 27m VS 4c ★
Good climbing up the conspicuous crack on the right side of the main slab. Climb the crack which runs up the left side of a subsidiary slab to reach a glacis beneath an impending groove. Pull up and follow the crack above until it ends, continue more easily to the top.
C Read, NF Tonkin, GL Swainbank - Oct 2003

NEWLANDS

The Newlands is a quiet backwater, yet this delightful secluded valley offers varied climbing on contrasting crags which enjoy the afternoon sun and are rarely busy.

Approach: From the track which leaves the road at Little Town P NY 2325 1950 follow the east side of the valley (bike useful). Just beyond the spur of Castle Nook, take the left branch which narrows to a path (leave bikes here). The crags now come into view on your left.

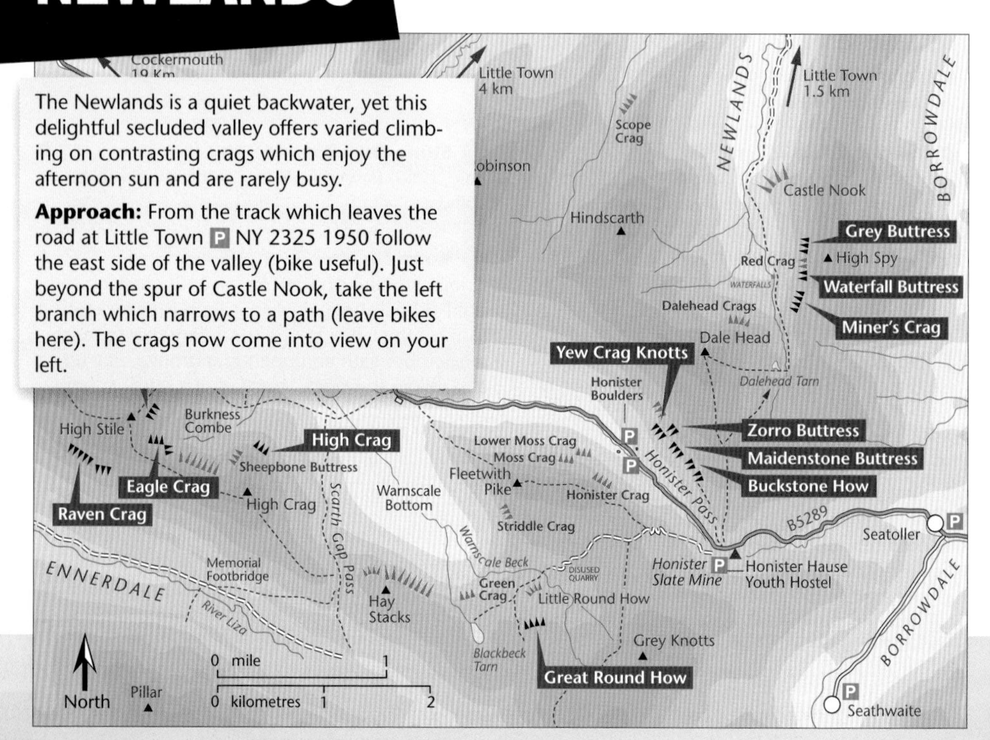

GREY BUTTRESS

1 ¾ hr

OS Grid Ref: NY 232 163
Altitude: 450m

Approach: Directly from the main path up the valley. The crag appears insignificant from below but has some very good routes on steep solid rock.

Descent: Abseil down right from a block immediately above *Grey Slab*, or thread a sling and abseil directly down the front face. Alternatively, traverse well above the gullies to the left (north) of the buttress (care), before moving down through steep heather.

1 Buckfast 45m E1 5b ★
A direct route with interesting climbing. Start beneath the groove on the left side of a detached pinnacle.
1 28m 5b Climb the groove and pull right onto the top of the pinnacle. Step up right into a shallow groove which leads to a ledge on the left. Move directly up, then up right, then left (delicate and quite bold, crux), to a triangular foothold. Climb straight up and pull left into a recess. The short groove leads to a ledge and block belay
2 17m 4b Directly up the front of the arête above to the top.
C Read, GL Swainbank - May 1996

2 Pinnacle Wall 46m S ★
Interesting.
1 13m Climb the pinnacle using the crack on its right, swing round to the left and follow a crack up a short left-slanting groove to a stance beside a holly.
2 20m Climb right of a steep grassy fault to a large holly.
3 13m Climb into the corner, traverse right and pull over the large block.
G Rushworth, SE Dirkin - Jul 1948

3 Brandywine 67m VS 4c ★★★
Intricate, enjoyable and technically high in its grade. Take care to protect the second. Start behind a perched block sitting atop a broken rib.
1 23m 4c Step off the block into a steep corner, pull left over a large block onto a gangway which leads to a step left into a niche. Move up and traverse left to a ledge.
2 20m 4c From the left end, climb cracks until it is possible to traverse the wall on the right to a triangular foothold; boldly up to a slab on the right. Traverse right, up to the edge of the slab, step right and move down to belay in a scoop.
3 24m 4b Move up right on slabby rock into a groove; follow this by its right edge. Continue in the same line then work back left over steep rock (minimal protection). Just before reaching a heather-choked groove, pull up steeply right to finish.
JA Austin, DE Roberts - Jul 1964

4 Direct Route 44m HVS 5a ★★
An extremely fine first pitch.
1 22m 5a Climb the corner above the block to a niche under bulges. Bridge out right, pull up steeply onto a flake and from its crest climb the wall. When it eases, move left round a rib, then up left to belay in a scoop.
2 22m 4a Move up left and climb the steep right-hand groove on the left side of the final tower.
JA Austin, AH Greenbank, NJ Soper, DW English - Jun 1965

5 Grey Slab 50m VS 4b ★★
Fine gymnastic moves on good clean rock.
1 20m 4b From the block, step into the corner then right onto an undercut shelf. Mantel up then traverse right to a steep crack leading to slabby rock. Traverse right across a heather ledge to a stance.
2 30m 4b From above the belay, move left and climb the impending wall to a small quartz ledge up on the right. Follow the steep slab on the left and the arête above to a large block. Climb round it to the top.
G Rushworth, SE Dirkin - Jul 1948

6 El Scorchio 47m E1 5b ★★
Nice climbing with a short crux. Start at the foot of a groove with a large flake belay on its left.
1 19m 4b Up the groove then up right to a block, pull right and continue up the slabby wall, then trend right to belay beneath the obvious crack.
2 28m 5b Move up and traverse left onto a ledge, a difficult pull up the wall (crux) gains an alcove. Move up a few metres, step left onto the fine wall and continue, passing right of a flake, to gain slabby rock. Finish up a short rib on the left.
C Read, C Jones - Jul 2006

To the right of the main buttress there are two chimneys at the back of a hidden alcove.

7 Alcove Ridge 60m S
An interesting climb across unlikely terrain.
1 15m Climb the left-hand chimney to a vegetated slope with a dead tree at its apex.
2 30m Traverse right to an arête. Climb a narrow gangway on the left, step left to a broken groove, climb this, then the arête on the right to a ledge with a big block at its left end.
3 15m The cracked wall leads to the top.
W Peascod, G Rushworth - Aug 1948

The Alcove
A
1 Buckfast E1 5b
2 Pinnacle Wall S
3 Brandywine VS 4c
4 Direct Route HVS 5a
5 Grey Slab VS 4b
6 El Scorchio E1 5b
7 Alcove Ridge S

WATERFALL BUTTRESS

1 ¼ hr

OS Grid Ref: NY 232 161
Altitude: 400m

1 Direct Route and The Bolt Finish 117m S ★★

Interesting and varied climbing. Start 5m left of the broken pinnacle at the foot of the buttress.

1 33m Climb direct to a wall which leads past a flake and small tree on a ledge. Gain the slab above, trend left to a nook below the main rib of the crag.

2 12m Traverse left under the rib; follow a crack, past a dubious block, to a large block belay.

3 30m Climb onto the block, step right and move up to a large ledge. From the back of this a gangway leads to the arête on the right, step right onto a small ledge, up the cracked wall to a large ledge.

4 26m Move to the right and climb clean rock left to the foot of a stepped corner, climb it and traverse right along a narrow ledge to a stance below a black corner.

5 16m Climb left into the corner and up this to a storming finish.

W Peascod, GG Macphee, G Rushworth - Jul 1948
P4 & 5 N Allinson, PT Kay - May 1969

This buttress is situated directly above the cascade in the upper dale and offers a long and quick drying route on good rock with a mountain atmosphere.

Approach: Directly from the main path up the valley. See map page 326.

Descent: A steep but easy path in the gully to the right (south) of the buttress.

MINERS' CRAG

OS Grid Ref: NY 231 157
Altitude: 480m

A large and complicated mass of slatey rock some of which needs careful handling; the routes are atmospheric, they feel exacting for their grade and big for their length. The climbs are on the right (southwest) face of the crag.

Approach: From Honister Pass, P NY 22557 13535. Follow the fence heading for Dale Head, until the angle eases at 570m; a vague path forks right (don't go too soon). Cross the shoulder and pass Dale Head Tarn to reach Miners' Crag. For routes on Terrace Wall, head to the top of the crag and go down the descent gully.

See map page 326.

Descent: Make for the highest point above the crag, and then walk down to the right (south) into the first gully and the scree below. Alternatively, scramble awkwardly rightwards down the Quartz Rake which passes below Terrace Wall.

1 **Miners' Grooves** 80m VS 4b ★★
Good steep problems, best combined with *Talulah.* Start at a slab below a steep V-groove 10m right of the gully at the left edge of the southwest face.
1 13m Climb to the foot of the groove.
2 30m 4b Climb the groove for 15m to a perch. Swing out onto the left arête and follow it and a shallow gully to a stance below a grooved wall.
3 37m 4a Climb the deepest groove, trending right, and then easy ribs to the top just left of the Quartz Rake.
G Rushworth, W Peascod, GG Macphee - Jul 1948

2 **Corkscrew** 63m HS ★★
Memorable climbing in exposed positions. Start at a rib below and left of a large slab.
1 13m Climb the rib to a niche left of the slab.
2 23m Traverse left and climb the steep slab and the groove above. Move right to a groove, climb it stepping left across its top, then go up to a ledge below a sweep of slabs.
3 27m Traverse the slabs to the right arête, climb it, then more easily to the Quartz Rake.
G Rushworth, W Dennison - May 1948

3 **Counterbalance** 65m VS 4c
These variations on *Corkscrew* offer steep open climbing.
1 30m 4c Climb the rib to below a much steeper rib. Ascend the slab on its immediate right for 4m then climb a short steep groove (crux). Trend left up an open groove then follow easier rocks left to belay on a ledge below a sweep of slabs.
2 35m Climb the rib above on the left; first on its left, then the crest to the top.
C Read, FM Cox – Jul 2006

4 **Double Slab** 63m VD ★
Good climbing on the double-tiered slabs.
1 23m Climb the initial rib of *Corkscrew* and then move right to follow the slab to a stance right of an open groove.
2 10m Step left and up the open groove to a corner.
3 30m Climb the right wall of the corner, then the centre of the upper slab. Trend right to a left-sloping ridge leading to the Quartz Rake.
W Peascod, SB Beck - Apr 1948

Terrace Wall

The remaining climbs start from the terrace of Quartz Rake.

5 **Talulah** 28m VS 4c ★
A good continuation to routes below Quartz Rake. Start near the top of the Rake. Climb the obvious rightward-facing groove/crack then easier rock, trending left to the top.
J Robinson, A McWatt – Aug 1996

6 **Jezebel** 42m VS 4c ★★
A fine second pitch. Start from above a rock step in the Quartz Rake, beneath the lower part of the offset corner-line.
1 17m Climb the blocky corner to a juniper ledge, move to the right to belay beneath the upper corner.
2 25m 4c Climb the corner past a holly to stand on cracked blocks below the steepening upper section. Traverse airily left; pull onto the arete and follow it to the top.
W Peascod, SE Dirkin - Jul 1950

7 Bathsheba 39m E1 5c ★★★
Excellent climbing, steep and with continuous interest, taking a direct line up the obvious big corner. Start directly below the upper corner.
1 17m 5b Pull up directly onto a triangular slab below a short impending groove, up this and pull out left to reach good holds on the steep wall. Climb this until it eases at the base of a short open groove. Traverse to its right edge then up and back left to a ledge beneath the upper corner.
2 22m 5c Climb the corner past a holly.
C Read, P Fleming - Nov 2006

8 Harlot 37m HVS 5a ★★★
Good steep climbing finishing directly through the central headwall. Start 8m right of the big right-angled corner where an obvious quartz fault on the face runs down to meet the fellside.
1 20m 4a Step up and work steeply left on good holds to gain the slabby groove; follow this to a good ledge.
2 17m 5a Climb up and enter a sentry box, pull out left and continue up the fault-line.
GL Swainbank, C Read - May 2004

ST BEES

OS Grid Ref: NX 939 145

Accessible with calm waters

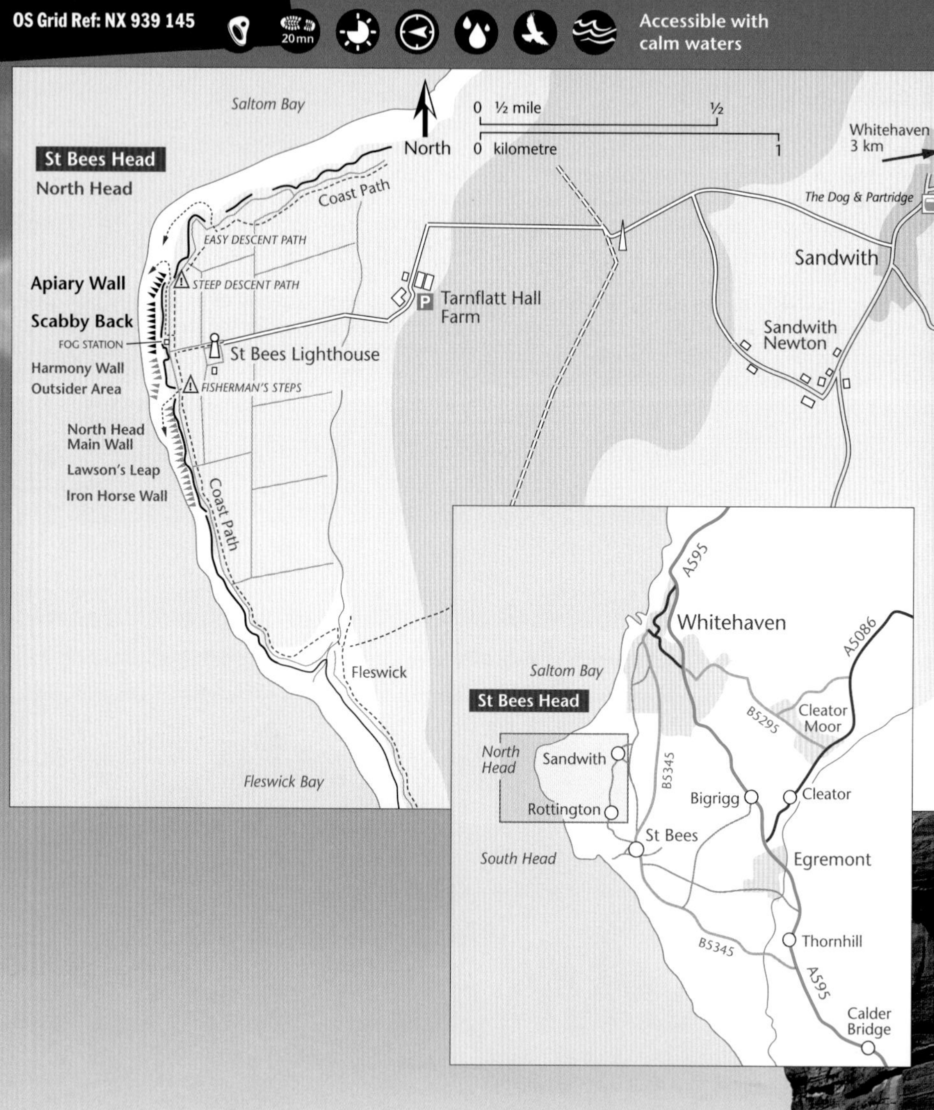

Fisherman's Friend F5 (page 337) Stephen Coughlan — DAVID SIMMONITE

St Bees is situated 5km south of Whitehaven. The weathered sandstone cliffs face west and catch a great deal of sun. They offer great friction and are very quick to dry. They also present endless bouldering opportunities, for more see: www.LakesBloc.com
Approach: P Tarnflatt Hall Farm NX 94813 14615 From the lighthouse and foghorn station go north for 50m and cross the fence. The path dives down a a short gully then steeply towards the sea. Some fixed rope.
From Foghorn Station
1
2
3
4
5
6
7
8
Slippery descent
Apiary Wall Boulders

	Route	Grade
1	Absolutely Fabulous	F6b
2	Kleenze	F6c
3	Blooming Marvellous	F6c ★★
4	Just Nice	F6a
5	Ancient Mariner	F5+ ★
6	Nectarine	F6c+ ★★★
7	Drone	F7a+ ★
8	Virgin Queen	F7a ★★
9	Royal Jelly	F6b
10	Honey Pot	F6b+ ★
11	Beeswax	F6b
12	Swarm	F7a ★★
13	Bee Line	F6b+ ★
14	Bee Hive	F6c
15	The Apiarist	F6b+ ★★
16	Bee Sting	F7a ★★
17	Foul Brood	F7a+ ★
18	Promenade Crack	F7b ★★
19	Aurora	F6a+ ★

Access Groove from Apiary Wall
18 Promenade Crack F7b ★★
19 Aurora F6a+ ★
20 Toxic Rock F7a ★★★
21 Nuclear Seepage F7b ★
22 Scurvy F6a
23 West Coast Crack VS
24 Andy's Route F6b ★★★
25 Andy's Route variation F6a+
26 Quantum Leap F6b+
27 Route One F4 ★
28 Recharge F6a+
29 Feeling Groovy F6c ★★★
30 Stage Fright F6b
31 Route Two F4
32 Megadrive F6b+ ★
33 Dreaming of Red Rocks F7a+ ★★★
34 Run Wild, Run Free E5 ★★
35 China Syndrome F6a+
36 Driller Killer F6a ★
37 The Wasp HVS ★★
18
19
20
21
22
23
24
25
41
42
43
44
45
46
47

28
29
30
31
32
33
34
35
36
37
38
39
40
41
38 Molly Malone F6c
39 Westworld F7a+ ★
40 Whisky Galore F7a ★★
41 Dave's Route F7a+
42 Pieces of Eight F6a ★★
43 Rainbow Warrior F6b+ ★★
44 Scorpion F6a ★
45 Screamadelica F7a+ ★
46 Twilight Zone F3
47 Northern Lights F6b+ ★
48 The Adventures of Pinocchio F7a ★
49 Nasal Passage F6a ★
50 Legend's Friend F7a ★
51 The Steal F7a
52 Natural Habitat F6c ★
53 I Wish I Was F8a
54 Friggin' in the Riggin' F6b
55 Frigging Friends F6c
56 Fisherman's Friend F5 ★★★
57 Elysium F7b ★★★
PJ
55
49
50
51
52
53
54
56
57
PJ

BORROWDALE

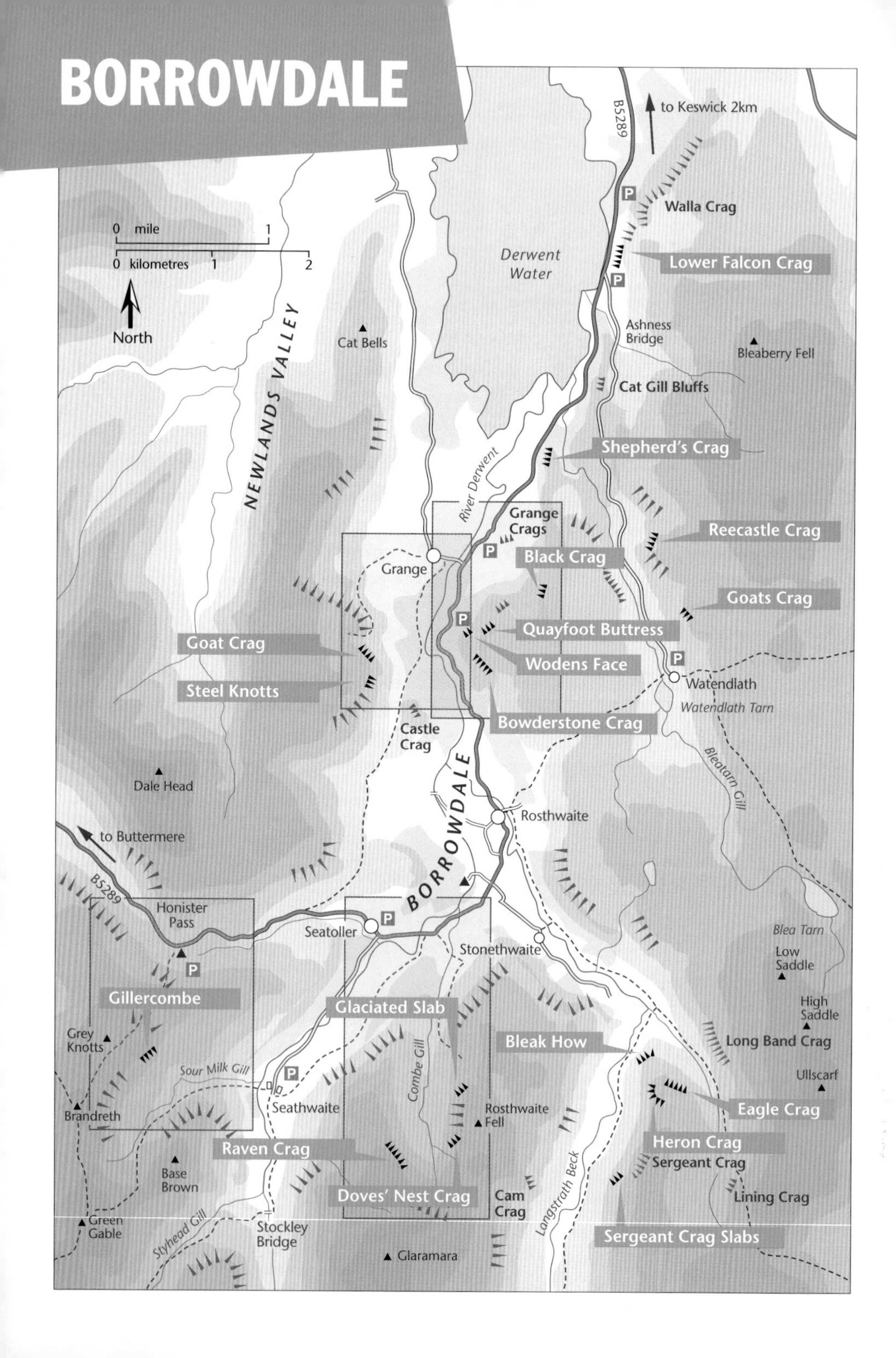

0 mile 1
0 kilometres 1 2
North
NEWLANDS VALLEY
Cat Bells
Derwent Water
B5289
to Keswick 2km
Walla Crag
Lower Falcon Crag
Ashness Bridge
Bleaberry Fell
Cat Gill Bluffs
Shepherd's Crag
River Derwent
Grange Crags
Reecastle Crag
Black Crag
Grange
Goats Crag
Quayfoot Buttress
Goat Crag
Wodens Face
Watendlath
Steel Knotts
Watendlath Tarn
Bowderstone Crag
Castle Crag
BORROWDALE
Bleatarn Gill
Dale Head
Rosthwaite
to Buttermere
B5289
Honister Pass
Seatoller
Stonethwaite
Blea Tarn
Low Saddle
Gillercombe
Glaciated Slab
High Saddle
Grey Knotts
Bleak How
Long Band Crag
Combe Gill
Sour Milk Gill
Ullscarf
Seathwaite
Rosthwaite Fell
Eagle Crag
Brandreth
Heron Crag
Raven Crag
Sergeant Crag
Base Brown
Doves' Nest Crag
Cam Crag
Lining Crag
Langstrath Beck
Green Gable
Styhead Gill
Stockley Bridge
Sergeant Crag Slabs
Glaramara

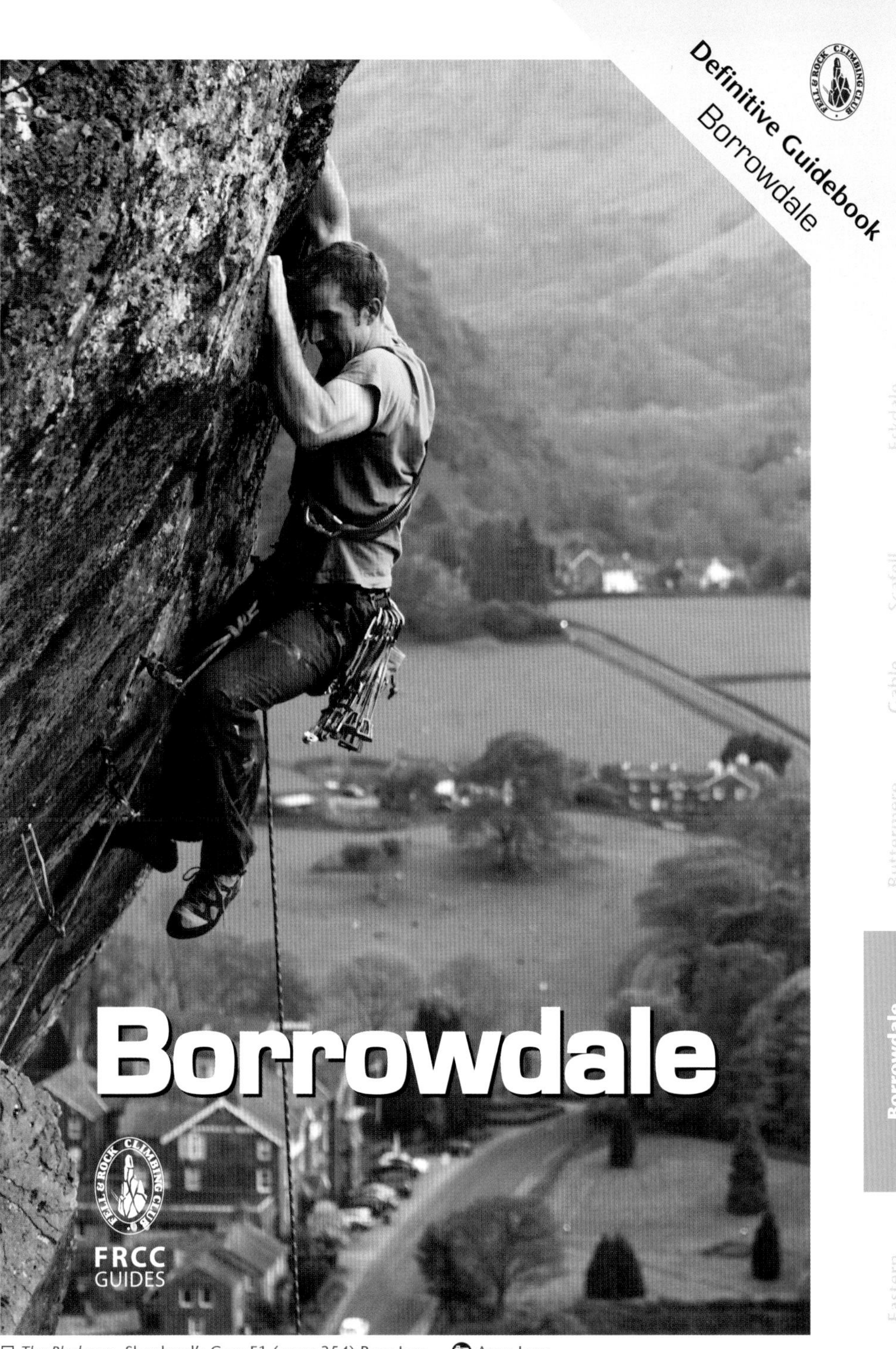

☐ *The Bludgeon*, Shepherd's Crag E1 (page 354) Rory Juss — ADAM LEWIS

LOWER FALCON CRAG

OS Grid Ref: NY 270 204
Altitude: 180m

Long, exciting and memorable routes with a reputation for loose rock and tricky protection.

Kidnation E1 (page 343) Wes Hunter — DAVID SIMMONITE

Old unreliable fixed gear on most routes. Long extenders ease drag.

Approach: Lay-by below the crag, P NY 27007 20850. Or P on the left at the start of the Watendlath road NY 26937 20335.

1 Spinup 50m VS 4c ★★

Popular amenable climbing in exciting situations.
1 20m 4c Leftwards up a slab and around a rib to a ledge. Keep left and climb to a gangway; left again for 3m; now right to belay just left of a black groove. A bit bold.
2 30m 4c Follow the black groove for 5m; gain an exposed traverse right above the overhangs. Follow this to its end and continue diagonally right.
P Ross, D Sewel - 1957

2 The Dangler 42m E2 5c ★★

Steep and strenuous – very good.
1 12m 5a Gain the block belay.
2 30m 5c Power up the steep groove to a ledge on the left and rest. A traverse right on large flat holds leads into a grooveline and the top.
S Clark, T Martin - May 1963; FFA R Fawcett, C Gibb - 1976

3 Hedera Grooves 40m VS 4c ★★

A good introduction to the crag.
1 24m 4b Wander up to the holly.
2 16m 4c The groove and ramp above.
P Ross, P Lockey - Aug1956

4 The Niche 60m E2 5c ★★★

A tough classic, sustained with excellent positions.
1 26m 5c Climb the bulging wall and rib on the left to a position where you can make the crux traverse right into the niche..
2 34m 5b Exit top right; move right, up through the overhang to reach the groove leading to a slabby wall on the right.
A Liddell, R McHaffie - Aug 1962

5 Interloper 50m E1 5c ★★

An enjoyable top-end **E1**.
1 29m 5c Right then left, cross a sloping ledge to the ledge above with a steep groove on it's left. Climb this to a small stance on the left.
2 21m 4c Over the bulge to a gangway; follow this leftwards.
A Liddel, R McHaffie - Jul 1962; FFA C Read, J Adams - Jun 1971

6 Kidnation 50m E1 5b ★★★
A great route; the best way up this part of the crag. 60m ropes. Climb the groove and continue to the overhung niche. Move left and pull into an open groove. Solve the short crux moves across to the fine slanting corner and a finish left.
P Ross, E Metcalfe - May 1957

7 Kidnapped 42m E2 5c ★★★
Tremendous, sustained climbing at the top of the grade. Climb the groove and continue to enter an overhung niche. Move up to the roof, left to the arête, then follow the groove above.
P Botterill, J Lamb - Apr 1978

8 Plagiarism 48m E2 5c ★★
A justifiably popular route and for once, at the lower end of the grade. The rust coloured groove leads leftwards steeply across to join *Kidnapped*. Above the niche take the roof on its the right, move left and climb the groove..
P Nunn, O Woolcock - Aug 1962

9 Usurper 50m E1 5a ★★
Enjoyable steep climbing with fine, open and improbable positions. 60m ropes. Where *Illusion* moves right; move left on a steep gangway to a ledge. Weave through roofs right and left. Wow!
P Gomersall, N Bulmer - Jun1975

10 Illusion 44m HVS 5a ★★★
Pleasant climbing across the wall below the large overhang but with a big feel. Remember to extend your runners.
P Lockey, P Ross - Jun 1956

11 Lamplighter 40m HVS 4c ★★
An interesting route up the big slanting groove with some hard moves in a couple of places.
L Hewitt, S Glass – May 1964

12 Extrapolation 42m E2 5c ★★
A good route with a tricky crux bulge. Gain the steep slabs by a thin step right. The red groove above leads to an overhang and a steep wall.
D Nicol, I Conway, R Wilson - Jul 1975; FFA J Lamb, P Botterill - Jul 1975

REECASTLE CRAG

OS Grid Ref: NY 273 176
Altitude: 300m

Good rock, clean and steep, strong fingers are an asset. Off-road P NY 27122 17810

1 Ador 25m VS 4c ★
Steep juggy climbing.
R McHaffie, M Wingrove - Apr 1979

2 Bold Warrior 24m E1 5b ★
A good, steep route with an awkward start.
R McHaffie, M Wingrove - Apr 1979

3 The Executioner 26m E4 6a ★
Technical climbing up the left hand side of the bulging wall. Bold to reach the scoop.
P Whillance, D Armstrong - Apr 1979

4 The Torture Board 26m E7 6c (F7c+) ★★
Desperate – the conspicuous twin cracks.
P Cornforth - May 1987

5 Grievous Bodily Arm 26m E7 6c (F7c+) ★★
Tough climbing up the right hand of the two crack systems.
P Ingham - Jun 1987

6 Daylight Robbery 26m E6 6c (F7b+) ★★★
Steep and crimpy; hard above the peg.
C Sowden, M Berzins - May 1984

7 Burn at the Stake 26m E7 7a ★★★
Bold, powerful and technical The central crackline right of *Daylight Robbery*. Climb a pale green streak to reach the crack and climb it!
P Cornforth - summer 1992

8 The Whipping Post 26m E7 7a ★★
Hard moves to pass the break.
D Birkett - Apr 1992

9 Penal Servitude 30m E5 6b ★★★
Brilliant. Climb the bulging wall to three horizontal quartz breaks (peg and microwire). Move up (crux) and left to the groove, follow this to the top.
D Armstrong, P Whillance - May 1981

10 White Noise 30m E3 5c ★★★
Pumpy and well protected. Climb up to a small overhang; pull up left to gain and follow the crack.
J Lamb, R McHaffie - Aug 1978

11 Rack Direct 30m E2 5b ★★★
A good warm-up - a bit of a soft touch; the central faultline.
S Miller, R Parker - Sep 1977

12 Squashed Racquet 30m E5 6a ★★
A serious eliminate with some great climbing. Top end 6a, top end E5!
C Sowden, M Berzins - Jun 1984

⑬ The Rack 40m HVS 5a ★★
A good route with great situations which weaves its way up the crag at an amenable grade.
R McHaffie, B Mallaghan - Oct 1973

⑭ The Rack Finger Flake Finish 30m E2 5c ★★★
Fine, steep, well protected climbing with a short, sharp, steep section.
P Whillance, D Armstrong - Jul 1981

⑮ Guillotine 30m E3 5c ★★★
A superb route giving sustained varied climbing - well protected.
J Lamb - Sep 1978

⑯ Inquisition 30m E4 6a ★★★
An excellent bold eliminate.
C Downer, R McHaffie - Aug 1984

⑰ Thumbscrew 30m E3 5c ★★★
Steep, fingery and sustained, up the bubbly wall.
J Lamb, D Cherry - Aug 1978

⑱ The Gibbet Direct 30m E2 5c ★★
Tough for the grade. Sustained and with a hard move to gain the gangway.
C Downer, R McHaffie - Jul 1984

⑲ The Gauntlet 30m E1 5b ★
An eliminate. The move left is made at a block 3m up in the corner crack.
C Downer, R McHaffie - Aug 1984

⑳ The Noose 30m HVS 4c ★★
Well protected up a fine natural line.
R McHaffie and party - Apr 1972

㉑ Breach of the Peace E7 6b (F7b+) ★

㉒ Short Sharp Shock E6 6c (F7b+) ★
The crux is passing the peg.

GOATS CRAG

OS Grid Ref: NY 277 170
Altitude: 400m

20 mn

An idyllic setting, splendid views, quick drying, plenty of sun and only 20 minutes from the road. P NY 27232 17270

Descent: To the left (facing out).

1 Mort 15m E1 5b ★
Open climbing past the small triangular overhang.
R Davies - Sep 1989

2 Balancing Act 14m E15b
Another fine climb up the lower wall.
M Turner, A Blyth - May 1996

3 Light Fantastic 14m E2 6a
Pulling above the horizontal break provides the interest.
R Davies, K Telfer - Sep 1989

4 Pussy Galore 13m E2 5c ★★
The obvious left-slanting crack that maintains interest.
K Wilkinson, P Hirst - May 1989

5 Lucky Luke 14m E4 6a
The leaning wall provides a serious undertaking.
T Ralph, M Charlton - summer 1993

6 Munich Agreement 15m E1 5b ★
A good route with a sting in its tail.
N Brunger, J Gilhespy - Sep 1989

7 Optional Omission 14m E1 5a ★
Nice wall climbing.
J Gilhespy, N Brunger - Sep 1989

8 Inner Limits 14m HVS 5a ★
Right side of the wall to finish in a fine position.
R Kenyon, C Kenyon - Sep 1989

9 The Green 18m S 4b ★
Crosses some steep ground for the grade.
RA Smithson, D Heard - May 2004

10 The Slab 13m D
The obvious slab just right of the blunt arête.
R Davies - Sep 1989

11 Nightmare Zone 14m HVS 5b ★
A direct route finishing up the arête.
R McHaffie, J Bosher - Oct 1989

12 Poland 15m MVS 4b ★
A cunning climb.
N Brunger, K Telfer - Sep 1989

13 Everybody's Dream 15m S 4a
The centre of the slab right of *Poland*.
J Bosher - Oct 1989

14 Berlin Wall 15m E2 5b ★
A good steep wall.
1989

15 Emma Line 16m HVS 5a ★★
The sharp arête in a fine position.
J Gilhespy, N Brunger, R Davies, K Telfer - Sep 1989

16 Low end in sight 15m HVS 5b
Try not to touch the climbs on either side.
M Dunne, J Timney, A Desmond - Sep 2012

17 Son of Oz 15m HS 4c ★
The corner-crack, the line is obvious.
S Telfer, R Sharpe - Sep 1989

18 Rogue Herries 15m E4 6a ★
A poorly protected route which thankfully relents towards the top.
K Telfer, R Davies, N Brunger, J Gilhespy - Sep 1989

19 The Colour of Magic 15m E4 6a ★
A bold, strenuous and committing route.
R Davies, K Telfer, N Brunger, J Gilhespy - Sep 1989

20 Stranger to the Ground 12m E2 5c ★
An enjoyable technical climb.
K Telfer, R Davies, N Brunger - Sep 1989

21 Mull Wait 12m HS 4c ★
Another wide crack.
G Baum, J Meeks - Jul 1999

Derwent Water and Falcon Crags — Jon Allison

SHEPHERD'S CRAG

OS Grid Ref: NY 263 185
Altitude: 140m

5 mn

Described by Paul Ross as the 'super-boulder', Shepherd's is with good reason the most popular crag in the valley. A wide selection of enjoyable routes across all the grades, quick and easy access, generally good, varied, quick-drying rock and a café at the bottom - what more could you want?

Little Chamonix VD (page 354) Chris Bonington — Jamie Paluch

EV
Eastern
Borrowdale
Buttermere
Gable
Scafell
Eskdale
Dow
Langdale

SHEPHERD'S CRAG

Climbers have traditionally used the customers' parking at Shepherd's Café, High Lodore Farm, P NY 26207 18320. If you park here, then please spend freely at the café so that we can continue to enjoy the friendly relationship that has developed. Besides that, it is the best café in the world!

Approach: Via the gate behind the café.

Jackdaw Ridge Area

Crossing the stile leads to the Jackdaw Ridge Area offering a number of long and relatively easy routes.

Descent: Walk south from The Belvedere, the flat area at the top of the crag, down to the top of a gully and up the other side to a good path that leads back to the stile. Alternatively, descend the gully itself or head right (west) just before the gully and scramble down over blocks to Jackdaw Terrace.

1 Jackdaw Ridge 66m D ★

A route which clearly gives much pleasure.

1 26m 7m left of the stile is a rib; climb this for 8m. Continue directly above to a ledge and oak. Easier blocky rock leads to a good ledge and large oak. Or climb the less pronounced rib 3m left of the ordinary start at **VD**.

2 23m The right-slanting V-groove above the oak leads to the easier-angled ridge: tree belay.

3 17m Follow the ridge to reach The Belvedere; first by an awkward V-groove and then a rib.

B Beetham - Aug 1946

2 Donkey's Ears 67m HS ★★

A classic climb with a decisive final pitch. Start 5m left of the deep chimney where an ash tree is guarded by a slim flake.

1 26m An easy wall leads to a conspicuous scratched line and a wide, grassy trough. Scramble up to belay by a small cave below the huge projecting block.

2 20m Stand on an outward-pointing spike using the outside or inside route from the cave. A hand-traverse left and up, or a struggle between the two 'ears' gains a ledge. Over the pile of blocks above, trending right, to belay at a tree on *Jackdaw Ridge*.

3 21m Traverse left to a corner, teeter delicately along an obvious traverse line to V-cracks. Climb these precariously and continue to The Belvedere.

B Beetham - Apr 1947

Monolith Crack Area

Three mid-grade routes offer a good introduction to this varied area.

Approach: Follow the base of the crag up and left to a large yew. Now scramble up and right to a broken terrace beneath a vertical, smooth, orange/brown wall. Continue up right over large blocks to Jackdaw Terrace. At the upper right-hand end of the terrace is an open corner and steepening.

3 Monolith Crack 32m HVS 4c ★★

Varied and popular tackling the centre of the wall and sporting a classic off-width finish.
1 12m 4c The slanting break leads past the stunted oak to a short chimney and trees.
2 20m 4c The Monolith is on the left. The idea is to get up the off-width crack to its right; a short corner and wall follows.
B Beetham - Jul 1947

4 Porcupine 28m E3 6a ★★

Above the jumble of jagged blocks a pleasant first pitch leads to a short technical corner.
1 18m 5a Carefully pull directly up the overhanging rib on the right, and follow the groove and wide crack above to the large ledge and tree belay of *Monolith Crack*.
2 10m 6a The intense, well protected prominent short corner finishing rightwards.
P Ross, E Ray - July 1955; FFA P Whillance - Feb 1977

5 The Black Icicle 30m E1 5b ★★★

Take care to protect the start; on p2 the protection is good but spaced. Start left of *Porcupine*.
1 14m 5b The thin, black quartz crack running up the steep wall. Tree belay.
2 16m 5a The blunt arête yields arborially to an airy finish.
D Fielding - 1958

Wild Sheep Area

An area of ramps, grooves, steep walls and arêtes. Reference points are the hanging arête of *Wild Sheep* and, 8m to the left, a large oak tree at the base of the crag. This area of Shepherd's is sheltered and stays dry.

Approach: Follow the base of the crag up left to a large yew tree and scramble to broken ledges.

6 Shepherd's Chimney 32m VS 5a ★★

This direct version of the original gives a good line, finishing in a fine position.
1 17m 5a Climb the short corner at the left end of the steep orange brown wall to a grassy ledge. Go up the groove/corner above to an awkward exit (crux).
2 15m 4a Climb the slanting chimney/corner; steep initially, followed by easier climbing on the left wall.
Original, B Beetham - Jul 1946

7 Wild Sheep 33m E2 5b ★★★

Absolutely brilliant! The striking arête to the left of the final section of *Shepherd's Chimney*. Start directly below a large bush at the bottom right-hand side of the arête. and climb directly up easy ramps and corners to a ledge. Move left past the bush onto the overhanging side of the arête and climb it on superb incut holds.
K Wilkinson, D Booth, A Morris - Mar 1989

8 Derision Groove 34m MVS 4b ★★

A popular and absorbing route with good holds taking the steep, stepped groove and gangway - take care at the top.
P Ross, JA Wood - Feb 1955

9 Battering Ram 33m E3 6a ★★

A great route tackling the right side of the arching overhang then the fine, steep finger crack on the right. Left of the large oak is a prominent flake; start here and weave your way to the right-hand end of the overhang. A diagonal groove above leads to a ledge and traverse right to an oak. The thin right-hand crack directly behind the oak leads to the finishing groove.
R Smith, J Earl - May 1984

Chamonix Area
10 Little Chamonix VD
11 The Bludgeon E1 5b
12 Crescendo MVS
Fisher's Folly Buttress
13 Chamonix HS
14 True Cross VS 4c
15 The Grasp E2 5b
16 Creeping Jesus HVS 5a
17 Kransic Crack VS 4c
18 Kransic Crack Direct HVS 5a
19 Fisher's Folly VS 4c
20 M.G.C. E2 5c
21 C.D.M. VS 4b
The Belvedere
Wild Side E3
Thin Air Variation VS
Double Cream HVS
Chamonix Area
Fisher's Folly Buttress

Inclination E5
Bob's Exasperation E3
Jackdaw Terrace
Ant Highway VS
Jackdaw Ridge Area
1 Jackdaw Ridge D
2 Donkey's Ears HS
Monolith Crack Area
3 Monolith Crack HVS 4c
4 Porcupine E3 6a
5 The Black Icicle E1 5b
Wild Sheep Area
6 Shepherd's Chimney VS 5a
7 Wild Sheep E2 5b
8 Derision Groove MVS 4b
9 Battering Ram E3 6a
Jackdaw Ridge Area
RT

Chamonix Area

Very popular sporting classic multi-pitch routes including what is probably the most photogenic climb in The Lake District.

Descent: Go right, cross The Belvedere and take any of the descents.

10 Little Chamonix 71m VD ★★★

Varied climbing, good positions and a spectacular final pitch have rendered this to a fine sheen – deservedly so...

1 30m Vague grooves lead to a flake crack on the left; tree belay.

2 12m Scramble up right through trees to below two V-corners.

3 16m The left-hand corner leads to an overhang. An enigma - gain and cross the slab on the right to reach its right arête to the Saddle.

4 13m Step right and reach the top of the pinnacle. A couple of steep moves gain The Belvedere.

B Beetham - May 1946

11 The Bludgeon 54m E1 5b ★★★

Magnificent; well named for a strenuous and spectacular finale.

1 30m 4c Climb the black slab and wall above; belay at a 3 stemmed oak on the right-hand side of a large arboretum.

2 24m 5b Whiz up the easy angled rib and groove to to reach the base of a pinnacle. Using the crack on its right manoeuvre onto its top. Finish directly.

P Ross, P Lockey - Apr 1957

12 Crescendo 68m MVS 4b ★

Challenging.

1 35m 4b The chimney right of the 'aiguille' leads past the chockstone to a platform. Climb boldly up the polished wall, trending first left, then right, to reach an easier line of grooves and a ledge. Move left over blocks, then scramble through trees to belay on a large oak tree below a triangular block under a steep wall.

2 33m 4a Move up past the block to reach a steepening in the wall. Left for 3m on good holds to reach another tree covered ledge. The ridge on the right leads to The Belvedere.

B Beetham - Aug 1948

Fisher's Folly Buttress

Left of Chamonix Area is a compact buttress with the prominent *Kransic Crack* at its centre.

Descent: Carefully follow a clear path leftwards. Please do not abseil off, or top rope, from the trees as they won't last!

13 Chamonix 25m HS ★★

Rather devious. From the right-hand end of the huge flake climb rightwards to gain the arête, then continue to a pinnacle. Step right onto the wall and climb up and left into the wide crack, or climb the crack direct (harder) to a tree belay.

B Beetham - Apr 1946

14 True Cross 30m VS 4c ★★

Steep, sustained; a well protected natural line. The blunt arête leads to a juggy break. Follow this leftwards, above the overlap, to join *Fisher's Folly*. Step down left onto the wall below the roof and traverse left to finish.

SJH Reid, W Phipps - Apr 1996

15 The Grasp 24m E2 5b ★★

Bold with ground-fall potential. Climb the left-hand side of the flake and up to the scoop, right of the black overhang. From a good hold on the left make a committing move over the overhang onto the wall. Continue carefully up, cross *Kransic Crack*, to finish up a leftwards-slanting gangway.

D McDonald, R McHaffie, N Robinson - Oct 1978

16 Creeping Jesus 24m HVS 5a ★★★

A positive approach with your wall-honed fingers leads to the top of the flake; move up the scoop then go right to finish up the wall.

J Healy, A Mitchell - Jul 1978

17 Kransic Crack 22m VS 4c ★★

Grit men will find the big left-hand crack easy. Traverse to the right along the flake and make an awkward move onto the wall. Rightwards again to the wide crack of *Chamonix* and finish up this.

GB Fisher, D Oliver, F Bantock - Jul 1952

18 Kransic Crack Direct 20m HVS 5a ★★★

Excellent, well protected and varied. From the right-hand end of the flake haul over the bulge to reach the crack on the left and huge holds.

D Peel - 1956

19 Fisher's Folly 25m VS 4c ★★★

The exposed wall above the corner is delicate, passing the overhang on the right to gain the cracks in the top wall can prove tricky.

M Thompson, P Nicol - Easter 1955

20 M.G.C. 20m E2 5c ★★

A well-chalked test piece. Three well protected phases up the steep wall using a peg-scarred crack.

B Roberts, G West - 1958

21 C.D.M. 20m VS 4b ★

The juggy crack. Step right; left of bushes at the top.

Illusion, Lower Falcon Crag HVS (page 343) Adam Hocking — DAVID SIMMONITE

North Buttress

This soaring tower offers fine long pitches; some of the best at Shepherd's.

Descent: Walk up the hill behind the crag a few metres to a path that leads north to the top of Brown Slabs and an easy descent to the left.

22 P.S. 38m E1 5b ★★
An exhilarating climb, starting at the obvious broken groove 8m up and right from the foot of the buttress. Climb the groove to a ledge. Continue up the fault above to a wedged block, then swing right using good technique or a long reach to side pulls and follow the easy arête to the top.
P Ross, B Aughton - Apr 1959

23 North Buttress 45m E1 5b ★★
A long and exciting pitch starting on the left side of the large flake a few metres up and right from the foot of the buttress. Climb the flake and the bulge above. Continue up until a short traverse left gives access to a gangway trending back right. Immediately step left and tackle the tricky obvious overhanging groove.
PJ Greenwood, D Whillans, P Whitwell - 1954

24 True North 40m E2 5b ★★★
An excellent direct pitch, with thin fingery climbing up the hanging slab and a magnificent finish, just warranting the grade. Climb the blunt arête just left of the flake crack of *North Buttress.* and groove above to a broken ledge. Continue straight up the ragged crack in the black wall above to a ledge, just right of a hanging slab. The slab leads to a ledge. Swing up and right to finish up the steep rib in a fantastic position.
J Lamb, R Allen - summer 1981

25 Crunchy Frog 40m E1 5b ★★
An exciting and bold climb taking a direct line up the buttress. The blunt arête and a groove lead to the broken ledge. Now move slightly left and tackle the tricky groove. At its top move steeply up and right on magnificent holds to reach a ledge and continue direct to the top.
TW Birkett, R McHaffie - Aug 1975

Troutdale Pinnacle, Black Crag S (page 364) Paul Ross — Al Hinkes

22 P.S. E1 5b
23 North Buttress E1 5b
26 Adam VS 5a
27 Eve VS 4c
29 Ardus MVS 4b
30 Aaros E1 5b
31 Jaws E1 5b
32 Finale HVS 5a
AP

26 Adam 40m HVS 5a ★★★
A superb, well protected companion to *Eve*. From the toe of the crag take the corner to the belay on *Eve*. Climb up right then back left and up a short crack to a holly. Climb straight up and then slightly leftwards up the wall above. Move up to a corner and swing left on to the nose. Straight up to finish
P Ross, B Wilkinson - Aug 1955

27 Eve 50m VS 4c ★★★
A popular and memorable route weaving up the buttress. P2 is quite serious and demands competence from both leader and second. Start 8m left of the lowest point of the crag behind a large oak and beside a split block.
1 13m 4b The short slab and steep crack lead to a ledge.
2 22m 4c Ascend the groove for 2m and step left to gain a slab. Arrange the best runners you can and climb the slab diagonally leftwards to reach a stance at the top left corner overlooking *Ardus*.
3 15m 4b Climb the short rib above to the overhang. Move right onto the face and continue to the top using a good crack.
W Peascod, B Blake - Aug 1951

28 Delight Maker 40m HVS 5a ★★
An excellent direct line up the buttress with a bold middle section, starting just left of *Eve*. Climb the shallow groove then move left onto the arête and follow this in an improbable position to meet Eve at the start of the traverse. Climb the overlap at a thin crack then the slab to an obvious depression above grassy cracks. Climb its right-hand side and continue up and left, cross *Eve* and finish up the groove.
R McHaffie, B Johnson - May 1982

29 Ardus 42m MVS 4b ★★★
A wonderful and very popular climb using the dominating large corner. Start at a well marked ramp leading up right to the base of the steep corner.
1 18m 4a From its foot climb the ramp line to a block belay at the foot of the corner.
2 24m 4b Ascend the block and the corner above to a ledge. The crack 5m to the left across the exposed slab is reached with difficulty and followed to the top.
V Veever, H Westmorland - May 1946

30 Aaros 40m E1 5b ★★★
An outstanding pitch of fine, fingery climbing up the steep wall with the crux saved until the end. Move up the ramp for 4m then follow the narrow right-slanting gangway, just left of *Ardus*, for another 4m. Gain a shallow V-shaped sentry box in the wall on the left and follow the groove above for 3m. Move right and climb straight up the steep wall. Continue in the same line to the traverse of *Ardus*. Follow this right a short distance and finish up a thin slanting crack in the headwall, 2m left of the corner.
R Graham, R McHaffie, TW Birkett, K Forsythe - Oct 1978

31 Jaws 39m E1 5b ★★
A good first pitch with some strenuous climbing.
1 24m 5b Climb the blunt arête above the start of *Ardus* on its right side to join *Finale*. Go up this for a metre or so and follow a line of stepped grooves on the left to a small overhang. Climb this, using a thin crack on its right, and continue up the wall to a tree belay.
2 15m Climb the wall behind the tree and go directly up the arête above.
M Lynch, E Cleasby - Sep 1975

32 Finale 34m HVS 5a ★★★
This great test piece spits out a lot of contenders. Strenuous and sustained climbing. Protection is excellent, assuming you can hang around to place it.
1 21m 5a The short, steep corner just left of the blunt arête. After 6m, step right and climb the bulge and crack to a tree.
2 13m 4a Move right and finish up the open groove and crack in the slab on the right.
T Savage, P Ross - Jul 1965

Brown Crag

Brown Crag is the home of a number of excellent single pitches where many a climber has been introduced to the sport.

Approach: This crag can be easily reached through the trees from the road 200m north of Shepherds Café, High Lodore Farm. Alternatively from the stile walk along the base of all the other areas described.

Descent: Scramble down the right hand side (as you look down) of the easy sloping ground behind the slabs. Cross a stile over the northern bounding wall and walk back round under *Brown Crag Wall*. Please do not abseil off the trees unless you leave a sling.

33 Brown Slabs Crack 30 m VS 4c ★★

The occasionally slippery arborial corner at the right-hand end of the Brown Slabs Area.

B Beetham - Apr1947

34 Brown Slabs Scoop 35m HS ★★

A great direct through the right-hand side of the sccop starting immediately left of *Brown Slabs Crack*.

R Tolley, P Latimer - Apr 2007

35 Brown Slabs 36 m D ★★

The well-worn line behind a tree, 5m left of *Brown Slabs Crack* passing just right of a battered oak.

B Beetham - April 1946

36 Brown Slabs Direct 38m VD ★★★

A popular and polished route. Halfway between two obvious trees at the base of the slabs a line leads diagonally left. Straight up at first, then rightwards through a scoop to a large block on the left, level with a battered oak. Step off the block and climb the wall slightly leftwards on good flake holds.

B Beetham - April 1948

37 Brown Slabs Arête 44m D ★★★

Very popular. Start as for *Brown Slabs Direct*.

1 16m The scratched line leads leftwards to a conspicuous notch in the arête.

2 28m Enjoy the pleasantly exposed crest.

CD Frankland, B Beetham - 1922

38 Brown Slabs Face 42m HVD ★★★

Fine and open - Just right of the oak at the left-hand edge of the slab a scratched line up the shallow rib crosses *Brown Slabs Arête* to finish up a shallow, broken groove and rounded rib.

B Beetham - Sep 1947

Down and left of Brown Slabs Area lies the impressive right-facing corner of *Conclusion*. Left of this, the beetling lower wall is severely undercut.

39 Conclusion 42m E1 5b ★★

The striking, steep, strenuous prominent right-facing corner leads to a junction with *Brown Slabs Arête* and an amble to the top. Keep cool and it's OK.

P Ross, P Whitwell - Oct 1955

40 Brown Crag Wall 45m VS 4b ★★

A classic - varied and interesting; inevitably polished. A weakness in the wall at a twin stemmed oak is the key to the start.

1 30m 4b Gain and climb the scoop for 3m and step right onto an arête. Move up boldly into a corner, onto a ledge then traverse left for 2m onto the slab. Pass a sloping ledge, continue up the slab and scoop then traverse right to a tree.

2 15m 4a A shallow corner then trend left to the top.

R Wilkinson, KC Ogilvie, JDJ Wildridge - Apr 1950

41 Brown Crag Grooves 40m E1 5b ★★

An unyielding but fine climb taking the groove line just right of the undercut wall with two crux sections on P1. Start at a smooth shallow corner 4m left of the twin stemmed oak.

1 24m 5b Climb the steep wall for 3m, move right and ascend a steep corner leftwards to the wall above. Move left to the base of a prominent groove and climb this with interest to a ledge.

2 16m 4b Climb delicately onto the block above and move left to climb a groove for 10m. Finish to the right.

F Crosby, P Muscroft - Sep 1959

Borrowdale

BLACK CRAG

OS Grid Ref: NY 263 172
Altitude: 260m

North Buttress

A superb crag in a wonderful location, undoubtedly one of Borrowdale's best with something for everyone.

The crag dominates the small valley of Troutdale and is clearly visible from the road after passing the Borrowdale Hotel.

Approach: Park in a lay-by where the road enters a series of bends, P NY 25682 17675. Walk up the track adjacent to the hotel into Troutdale, cross the stream and take a steep path.

Descent: Follow tracks up and right across the top of the crag then below the right-hand side of the crag.

1 The Coffin 70m VS 4c ★★

Adventurous climbing through grooves, overhangs and walls at the left end of the buttress. Start just left of the open corner of *The Shroud*.

1 15m Climb a slab leftwards, then a corner past a tree to a ledge. Belay on the right.

2 33m 4c The steep wall behind, passing a bulge. Avoid the roof by moving left and climb the groove above to a niche. Make a steep step left to a short groove which splits the overhang and leads to a ledge.

3 22m 4a Move rightward for 3m then go left past ledges to below a steep wall. Avoid this by a groove round the left arête and go easily to tree belays.

R McHaffie, D Brownlee - Feb 1967

2 Jubilee Grooves 104m El 5b ★★

Fine climbing through some impressive ground with a serious first pitch.

1 44m 5a Climb easily up a scoop in the wall just left of the corner to a ledge. Step right and climb the wall to a ledge with no belay. (Poss. belay 5m right on *The Shroud*). A short wall and the groove above on the left lead to a traverse right down the slab to belay below the overhang.

2 33m 4c Left for 5m a wall and groove on the left, back right at the top, down to a peg belay.

3 36m 5b Climb leftwards for 3m to a groove at the end of the overhang. Surmount this, pull out right and continue up the slabby groove to a heather ledge. Walk right - large block belay.

4 24m 4a Retrace to the top of the groove, directly up a rib and continue to a tree.

W Freelands, R McHaffie - Jun 1977

3 The Shroud 72m VS 4c ★★★

An imposing route of great interest.

1 12m 4b The corner, belay on the right.

2 15m 4c Climb the groove to the overhang (peg). Difficut moves right lead to magnificent jug pulling and easier ground. Belay below the large overhang.

3 21m 4c Traverse left for about 7m; then leftwards and up a short groove left of a nose. Continue up to the right to pass another small overhang on its left. Up the short groove above and step left to a ledge.

4 24m 4b Move onto a rib on the right and climb a series of mossy slabs and grooves to pass a bulging wall on the right. Easy to the top.

P Ross, P Lockey - Jun 1958

4 Grand Alliance 57m E4 6a 

Memorable, delicate, intricate climbing requiring commitment and competence.

1 10m 4c Climb the arête on the right of the corner of The Shroud to a ledge.

2 15m 5b Traverse right to twin blocks on the ledge. Climb into the overhung corner, pull out right and then the wall to a block belay on the slab.

3 32m 6a Go right across the slab to the left end of a long overhang. Mantelshelf onto a ledge on the wall above, traverse delicately right between the overhangs. Climb with less difficulty to foot ledges then trend left to small undercuts. Step right, the difficult moves up the wall soon relent. Scramble to the top or abseil.

R Matheson, E Cleasby - Jul1976

5 Vertigo 80m E2 5c ★★

Interesting, exposed and strenuous.

1 12m Walk up the right trending gangway (above a large holly), climb a short corner and step right to a yew.

2 14m 4c Gain a corner on the left which leads to a large slab. Move left for 5m - block belay.

3 24m 5c Cross the slab rightwards to the left end of a long overhang, mantelshelf onto a ledge on the left wall. Climb a series of short left trending corners, pull over the final roof and move right to a small ledge. Traverse 2m left then up the wall above to a small ledge on the left.

4 30m Climb the rib on the right and the groove above, crossing a hanging block. Easy slabs above.

P Ross, W Aughton - Oct 1958
FFA P Whillance, D Armstrong -Jun 1977

1
2
3
4
5
6
A
TL
Langdale
Dow
Eskdale
Scafell
Gable
Buttermere
Borrowdale
Eastern
EV

6 Prana 54m E3 5c ★★★

Brilliant climbing on the gully wall with reasonable protection.

1 12m 4b A neat fault in the black slab leads leftwards to a tree belay below the wall.

2 42m 5c Take the wall, 3m left of the gully, pulling up left onto the slab below the overhangs of the half-way break. Pull over on small holds. Move up until a step left can be made to a ledge. Now tackle the bulging wall above. Abseil or scramble to the top.

P Gomersall - Sep 1977

South Buttress

The arrival and gearing-up point is at the toe of this buttress, beside an obvious fallen tree.

Expect some congestion as the next few routes share the slab start left of the fallen tree.

7 Troutdale Pinnacle Direct 99m VS 4c ★★★

Delightful delicate climbing.

1 25m 4b Climb the steep slab then up the corner crack beyond the ledge. Over an overlap to a second ledge, traverse right and then up to a block belay.

2 25m 4c Step left and climb the wall direct for 10m. Step left and continue more easily to a small ledge.

3 & 4 49m 4a Join *Troutdale Pinnacle* to your right.

JD Oliver, M Nixon, K Pepper - 1952

8 Troutdale Pinnacle Superdirect 96m HVS 5a ★★★

A great route featuring both delicate and strenuous climbing and a memorable finger traverse.

1 & 2 50m 4c *Troutdale Pinnacle Direct*.

3 21m 5a The imposing steep crack is climbed to its top and a move left.

4 12m 5a A broken groove and an awkward move gains the sensational finger traverse leading right (**5b** for fat fingers). Continue up an easier groove to the top of the pinnacle.

5 13m Finish up *Troutdale Pinnacle*.

P Ross, D Oliver - Aug 1954

9 Obituary Grooves 100m VS 4c ★★

Sustained technical climbing, high in the grade.

1 30m 4b Above the slab step left and climb the wall and crack just right of the dirty corner to a ledge. Move left, climb a short corner and then left again to a birch tree.

2 34m 4c Climb a groove to a yew below an overhang. Move to the right and up to the top of the groove where a memorable move leads left. Climb the groove above, moving left, then up and out to the right to belay.

3 36m 4c Easier rock to a large flake. Climb leftwards into a leftward-slanting corner (awkward) from which an exit is eventually made on the right. Gain the groove above, move left to a holly and back right via twin cracks to the top.

PJ Greenwood, P Ross - Jul 1955

10 The Mortician 93m HVS 5a ★★★

Absorbing groove and crack climbing; sustained and high in the grade.

1 30m 4b *Obituary Grooves* to belay at the birch.

2 40m 5a Starting the undercut clean groove proves stubborn. Above, climb the wide crack.

3 10m 4c Move into a broken groove and continue directly to the top of the pinnacle, or take the finger traverse.

4 13m *Troutdale Pinnacle*.

B Thompson, WA Barnes - Aug 1969

11 Troutdale Pinnacle 105m S ★★★

One of Britain's best Severes finding the easiest way up an impressive buttress with positions normally only found on much harder routes.

1 21m Behind the fallen tree the short wide crack leads to a ledge. From an oak on the right, climb the wall for 6m and then a broken groove to a large block belay.

2 28m Follow the groove on the right to slabs which lead rightwards to a ledge and belay below a shattered corner.

3 10m The steep corner on good holds followed by an awkward pull up and left to a small stance on the right extremity of a sweep of slabs.

4 21m Traverse left and down the slabs to a corner. Swing across the steep left wall and pull up to ledges.

5 12m Steep but easy climbing to the top of the pinnacle; very exposed belay.

6 13m A sensational climax. The groove, then spectacularly left across the overhang to an easy finish.

F Mallinson, R Mayson - May 1914

12 Raindrop 90m El 5b ★★★

A classic taking a direct line up the pinnacle.

1 15m 5b Climb the very obvious thin, left-slanting crack to a ledge then up the slab behind, trending left a second ledge.

2 27m 5a Climb straight up to the left end of a small overhang, then move left along a diagonal crack to below a shallow scoop which is followed to a stance.

3 33m 5b Climb the wall to a good foothold on the right. Move left for 2m, then straight up to gain and climb a rightward-slanting groove and arête to reach the top of the pinnacle.

4 15m 4c Climb a little way up the groove, swing round the arête to the left and so to the top.

P Livesey J Sheard - Jun 1973

11
9
8
A
6
8
12
7
10
9
7
6
11
12
RT

QUAYFOOT BUTTRESS

OS Grid Ref: NY 254 167
Altitude: 135m

2 mn

Very accessible high quality climbing on superb compact rock.

Approach: P NY 25452 16860 Go over a stile and strike directly up to the crag.

Descent: To the right (south) side of the crag.

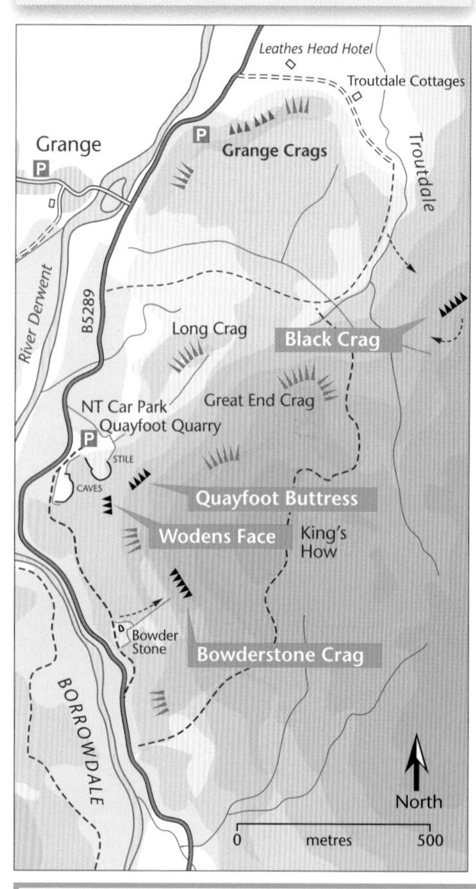

1 Quayfoot Buttress 60m VD ★★
Enjoyable and varied – much better than it looks! Start 3m right of the fence.
1 30m At the foot of the left side of the crag, 3m right of the fence a groove trends right to a block overhang. Avoid this by an awkward move on the left and climb to a ledge. Move left above a small birch, now follow a groove and arête to a ledge below a large scoop on the left.
3 30m Climb the scoop, move left at its top, and follow slabs.
B Beetham - Apr 1946

2 The Crypt 40m HVS 5a ★★
Fine and exposed climbing taking the shallow groove on the left side of the main wall. Start from a grass ledge.
1 22m 4a Up and left to a ledge over an awkward bulge and up to a tree.
2 18m 5a Move right onto the ledge, up slightly left and climb a scoop to a small overlap. Take the rib on the left..
R McHaffie, J G Alderson - May 1969

3 The Crypt Direct 40m E1 5b ★★
A more difficult finish tackling the overhang *The Crypt* side-steps.
K Rudd - Apr 1971

4 The Go Between 36m E2 5c ★★★
Delicate climbing up the wall to the right of *The Crypt Direct.*
J Lamb, P Botterill - Jun 1981

5 Aberration 38m VS 4c ★★
Pleasant with good positions.
1 20m 4c The corner and short chimney above to a ledge on the right.
2 18 m 4c A difficult step left gains a steep slab. Up this to a chimney/groove and follow this
O Woolcock P Nunn - May 1965

Ray McHaffie's (Mac's) Borrowdale Enchainement

1. The Niche, Falcon Crag	E2
2. White Noise or The Rack, Reecastle Crag	E3 or HVS
3. Crunchy Frog or Aaros, Shepherd's Crag	HVS or E1
4. Jubilee Grooves, Black Crag	E1
5. The Crypt, Quayfoot Buttress	HVS
6. Icarus Direct, Eagle Crag	E2
7. Lakeland Cragsman, Sergeant Crag Slabs	HVS
8. Easy Street, Raven Crag	MVS

⑥ **Mandrake** 44m HVS 5a ★★★

A superb and popular climb with an exposed and committing finale.

1 20m 4c From *Aberration's* corner hand traverse left for 3m then climb up to a ledge

2 24m 5a A crack leads to the bottom of the chimney/groove. 6m across right another crack leads to an overhang; cross this and continue to the top.

A Liddle M Burbage - Jul 1964

⑦ **Irony** 40m HVS 5a ★★

Good, with sustained interest.

1 18m 5a Grooves cross grass ledges to a slab on the left. Then head rightwards to a crack leading to a ledge.

2 12m 4c Cross the broken overhang and continue to the top of a thin crack. A swing right leads to a ledge (peg).

3 10m 5a Move up left under the overhang (peg) then pull over with great difficulty and continue to the top.

R Belden; FFA A Liddel, R McHaffie - 1961

WODEN'S FACE

OS Grid Ref: NY 253 167
Altitude: 90m

This delightful and sunny little wall of superb compact rock has a short approach and a nice collection of routes in the **S – VS** grades; a great venue for a short day. P NY 25452 16860.

Descent: The routes finish on a terrace, either scramble off down left (care!) or climb a short wall to the top.

① **Wimpey Way** 24m S ★★
An obvious stepped flake and groove line.
W Robinson, K Perry - 1970

② **Woden's Face** 25m MVS 4b ★★
Avoiding the overhang makes this the harder option.
B Beetham, C D Frankland - 1921

③ **Woden's Face Direct** 24m S 4a ★★
Another favourite up the middle of the wall.
B Beetham, C D Frankland - 1921

④ **Woden's Cheek** 22m MVS 4b ★★
The shallow groove in the right arête to the front face has a committing start.
B Beetham - 1935

⑤ **Tantalus** 20m VS 4c ★
An enjoyable route that's high in the grade.
K Jones, W Baddet - May1969

Conclusion, Shepherd's Crag E1 (page 361) Iain Robinson — LUKE ARMITAGE

BOWDERSTONE CRAG

OS Grid Ref: NY 256 165
Altitude: 220m

Above the incomparable Bowderstone, hidden on the wooded hillside, are the pleasant *Bowderstone Pinnacle* and the modern testpieces around Hell's Wall.

Approach: From the Bowderstone Quarry car park P NY 25452 16860 take the Bowderstone track. Just before the Bowderstone a track, on the left, leads directly up the hillside to below Bowderstone Pinnacle.

Bowderstone Pinnacle

Descent: Well to the right of the crag.

1 Bowderstone Pinnacle 36 m VD ★★
The classic easy route of the crag. Start 10m up the gully to the right.
1 12m Polished ledges and a broken crack lead to a stance on the arête. **2 The Arête Start** is VS 4c.
2 18m Continue into the cleft between the buttress and the Pinnacle on the right.
3 6m Either climb onto the Pinnacle direct, or climb the buttress on the left, then leap across the gap onto the top of the Pinnacle. Continue up the ridge and a short step.
F Mallinson, R Mayson May 1914

Woden's Needle

A small buttress fronted by a prominent pinnacle about 50m down and left of Hell's Wall – well worth the detour.
Descent: To the left.

3 Woden's Needle 30 m S ★★
An interesting climb starting on the left. Flakey cracks lead to the top of the pinnacle, moving left to a ledge at half height. The stepped wall above.
B Beetham 1936

4 Creeping Bentley 30m VS 4c ★
From the very foot of the pinnacle a crack up right leads past a wobbling flake, and a pocket, to the top of the pinnacle. Step up then move left towards an oak and follow the left edge of the wall.
R Smithson, D Heard - Aug 2004

1
2
1 Bowderstone Pinnacle VD
2 The Arête Start VS 4c
RK
Langdale
Dow
Eskdale
Scafell
Gable
Buttermere
Borrowdale
Eastern
EV

HELL'S WALL

20 mn

Hell's Wall

An impressive area for the talented and strong; the nearest thing to a hard sport crag the Lakes has to offer.

Descent: use a broken ramp on the left of Hell's Wall.

Inferno E7 (page 373) Mary Birkett — Steve Crowe

	Route	Grade	Stars
1	**Lucifer**	E5 6a	★★
2	**Bleed in Hell**	E8 6c (F8a)	★★★
3	**Inferno**	E7 6c (F7c+)	★★
4	**Hell's Wall**	E6 6c (F7c+)	★★★
5	**Mesrine**	E6 6b (F7c+)	★★
6	**De Quincy**	E7 6b (F7a)	★★
7	**Hellish**	E8 6c (F7c)	
8	**Wheels of Fire**	E4 6a	★★★
9	**Valhalla**	E1 5c	★★
10	**The Bulger**	E5 6b	★★★

EAGLE CRAG

OS Grid Ref: NY 277 122
Altitude: 500m

This crag has real character, yet is no longer fashionable. Dominating the view from Stonethwaite the imposing rectangular wall screams – climb me! Closer acquaintance reveals a complex crag of good, sometimes green, steep, lichenous rock; difficult to approach and slow to dry.

Approach: From Stonethwaite, P NY 26147 13830, head up Greenup Gill. A short rake left to right gives access to ledges below the climbs.

1 Where Eagles Dare 51m E2 5c ★★★
A soaring classic. Start at the large flake.
1 15m 5c Jam the crack into the absorbing groove; belay in the corner.
2 36m 5b Climb the obvious scoop, then go left to a thin crack. Pull up and swing left round a rib on good holds to gain a ledge. Follow the steep rib for 5m (peg), step right, up across a ledge to a rib and the top.
P Whillance, S Clegg - Aug 1975

2 Verdict 49m E4 6a ★★★
Real quality - technical climbing with a serious finish.
1 15m 5b Climb the groove to a jammed block overhang. Pull up and hand-traverse right to a ledge. Climb the crack on the left and continue over blocks to a belay in a corner.
2 24m 5c Pockets lead right across the wall. Move into a groove, pass an overhang to a small cave. Mantelshelf left to a grass ledge below the final corner.
3 10m 6a Entered from the left the technical groove has a superb jug just below the top.
S Clegg, P Botterill - Aug 1975; FFA M Berzins, R Berzins - Aug 1976

3 Falconer's Crack 58m VS 5a ★★
Alternating strenuous cracks and bold faces. Start mid-way between *Verdict* and *The Cleft Direct* at a crack.
1 18m 5a The crack and groove above to belay in a corner.
2 18m 4c Move 5m left to a rib, teeter up the wall beyond and then easier climbing left to a belay below a prominent chimney.
3 22m 4b The rib right of the chimney leads pleasantly to the top.
W Peascod, S B Beck - Jun 1946

4 Daedalus 48m E3 5c ★★★
The awesome undercut chimney makes a fine, powerful climb.
1 30m 5c Gain and climb the chimney and gangway above. A bulge bars access to a steep groove (peg). Climb this and the wall above to finish diagonally rightwards on good holds.
2 18m 5b Leftwards across the steep wall to a small ledge below a faint groove; follow this.
P Nunn, B Griffiths, P Ross - May 1965

5 The Cleft Direct 45 m E3 5c ★★★

A good strenuous route.

1 27m 5c The corner crack crossing a large ledge until moves can be made left to a sloping ledge and large flake. Continue up the groove above, then move rightwards to a ledge.

2 18m 5b Follow Daedalus leftwards.

P Botterill, S Clegg - Jun 1975

6 The Restraint of Beasts 52 m E5 6b ★★★

An outstanding route tackling the prominent arête; protection is good where it matters.

1 16m 6b Precarious moves up the shallow groove (small blue Alien, Rock 2) lead to the obvious fin. Layback boldly to a protruding block (peg). Continue to a ledge.

2 36m 5c A diagonal break runs rightwards to the arête - pull steeply up this on good holds. Continue more easily to finish up the fine grooved arête of Icarus Direct.

W Hunter, C Downer - Jun 2000

7 Icarus Direct 50m E2 5c ★★

A good steep crack gives access to a rounded smooth buttress.

1 30m 5b Climb the steep crack to a ledge. From its right extremity mantelshelf onto a ledge on the face. Continue direct to climb a short steep crack to large holds. Go easily up to a grass ledge and spike belay.

2 20m 5c Climb the grooved arête above directly to good holds. Swing rightwards onto a ledge, then up and left onto another ledge. Go easily to the top.

C Downer, R McHaffie - Jun 1984

8 Post Mortem 42m E3 5c ★★★

A crack of unusual character provides the final decisive pitch. A classic of its type! Start on grass ledges.

1 24m 5a Follow a flake crack diagonally rightwards to a dirty vegetated crack leading directly to the ledge below the wide crack.

2 18m 5c Climb the crack and continue to the top.

P Ross, P Lockey - May 1956

Ambling Ant, Steel Knotts MVS (page 392) Cath Sullivan — RON KENYON

BLEAK HOW

OS Grid Ref: NY 273 125
Altitude: 270m

Good rock and a lovely outlook make this a wonderful venue. P NY 26147 13830

Descend: To the left or by abseil.

1 Rub Off 40 m HVS 5a ★
The thin crack above the vegetated ledge goes through a small niche then direct to the top.
M Armitage, D Falcon - Jul 1984

2 Brush Off 35m HVS 4c ★★★
A featureless but extremely good and bold route.
C Downer, C Bacon, S Kysow - May 1984

3 Fancy Free 30m E1 5a ★
A striking route up the curving arête right of the slabs.
C Downer, C Bacon, S Kysow - May 1984

4 Breathless 30m E3 6a
The technical groove.
C Downer, S Kysow - May 1984

The central buttress has three excellent climbs

5 The Boj Eliminate 36 m HVS 5a ★★
A short corner leads to a spike at the top of the oval slab. Climb the groove moving right to pull onto a large slab, follow this to a short crack leading to an exposed traverse horizontally right, on superb quartz holds the *The Reiver*. Step left and follow flakes to finish along the final break.
SJH Reid, L Steer - Jun 1985

6 Bleak How Buttress 36m E2 5c ★★★
A first class route just making the grade for a precarious couple of moves across the slab.
D Hellier - Nov 1983

7 The Reiver 36m HVS 5a ★★★
Compelling – must be climbed.
C Downer - Jun 1984

8 Front Runner 30m E1 5b ★★

Monolith Crack, Shepherd's Crag HVS (page 351) Michael Kenyon — Ron Kenyon

UPPER HERON CRAG

OS Grid Ref: NY 275 122
Altitude: 440m

1 hr

❶ **Traverse of the Frogs** 30m E2 5b ★★★
A strenuous pitch with excellent protection. Climb a short crack to gain the obvious rightward-slanting hand-traverse, follow this to join and finish up *Heaven Knows I'm Miserable Now!* Take care to avoid rope drag.
J Hughes, SJH Reid - Jun 1996

❷ **Heaven Knows I'm Miserable Now!** 22m E15b ★★
The jagged rock on this route makes it easier than it looks. Climb the left-hand groove and crack to a ledge. Exit just left of a nose of rock the right.
C Dale, R Curley - Jun 1984

❸ **Flamingo Fandango** 22m E1 5b ★★★
Climb a layback crack to a small ledge. Move up and left onto another ledge. Follow the flutings over a slight bulge to a ledge and finish left of the nose.
R Kenyon, C King - Jun 1984

❹ **Big Foot** 24m E2 5c ★★★
Climb the crack to a ledge, up to a jug, then up and left to a sinuous crack which leads to a ledge. Finish up the nose on the left.
C Dale, R Curley - Jun 1984

❺ **The One that Got Away** 28m E2 5c ★
Climb *Little Nose* to the flake overlap. Pull up left to climb the flake crack and short walls to the top.
J Arnold, K Arnold - Jun 2001

❻ **Little Nose** 30m E2 5b ★★★
The shallow corner and wall to a hollow flake overlap. Stand on this, move right to a jug and make a long reach to gain and climb the groove above.
C Dale, R Curley - Jun 1984

❼ **Shooting Fish in a Barrel** 28m E4 6a ★
Pull left on to the ramp, step right and climb the wall past two horizontal breaks, make difficult moves left to gain the obvious crack. Step back right and climb the wall and slab with difficulty to easier ground. Or finish up *Little Nose* at **E3 5c.**
J Arnold, K Arnold, S Prior - Jun 2001

❽ **The Question** 28m E2 5c ★★★
The obvious grooved arête. A short corner leads to the groove and wall above.
R Kenyon, C King - Jun 1984

❾ **Bilberry Topping** 28m E2 5c ★★
Climb the short wall and slanting crack then move right to an open groove below a crack in the upper wall. On the right is a ledge with a vital block. Use a good handhold to get established on the wall, overcome a small overlap and gain the large ledge above. Move slightly left and climb the obvious corner in the short wall.
R Kenyon, M Armitage - Jul 1999

SERGEANT CRAG SLABS

1 hr

OS Grid Ref: NY 271 113
Altitude: 400m

Superb climbing on immaculate rock; justifiably one of Borrowdale's most popular crags. Magnificent surroundings, basking in late-afternoon sun.

Approach: Follow Stonethwaite Beck, P NY 26147 13830, cross the bridge and turn right up Langstrath until directly below the slab.

Descend: By abseil.

1 Revelation 45m VS 4c ★★
The left hand crackline through a block-step in the overhang
R McHaffie, J Bosher - Jul 1991

2 Endurance 45m HVS 5a ★★★
The thin crack through an overlap can be slow to dry in the upper section.
R McHaffie, J Bosher - Jul 1991

3 Between the Lines 45m E1 5b ★★
The narrow slab between the cracks finishing up a pebbly pillar with a rounded top.
J Campbell, SJH Reid - May 1995

4 Lakeland Cragsman 45m HVS 5a ★★★
The wider crackline splitting the slab is superb.
R McHaffie, J Bosher - Jul 1991

5 Terminator 2 45m HVS 5a ★★★
More great climbing. Climb through the left-hand break in the overlap into the right slanting ramp/groove.
R McHaffie, J Bosher - Sep 1991

6 Aphasia 45m E2 5b ★★★
The centre of the main slab is intricate, technical and a bit bold, simply brilliant!
C Downer, C Bacon, R HcHaffie - Jun1992

COMBE GHYLL

Exploration reveals outcrops of beautiful, clean, rough rock in abundance in this peaceful, heavily glaciated valley.

Approach: P NY 25022 13560, a path leads up into the bottom of the Combe.

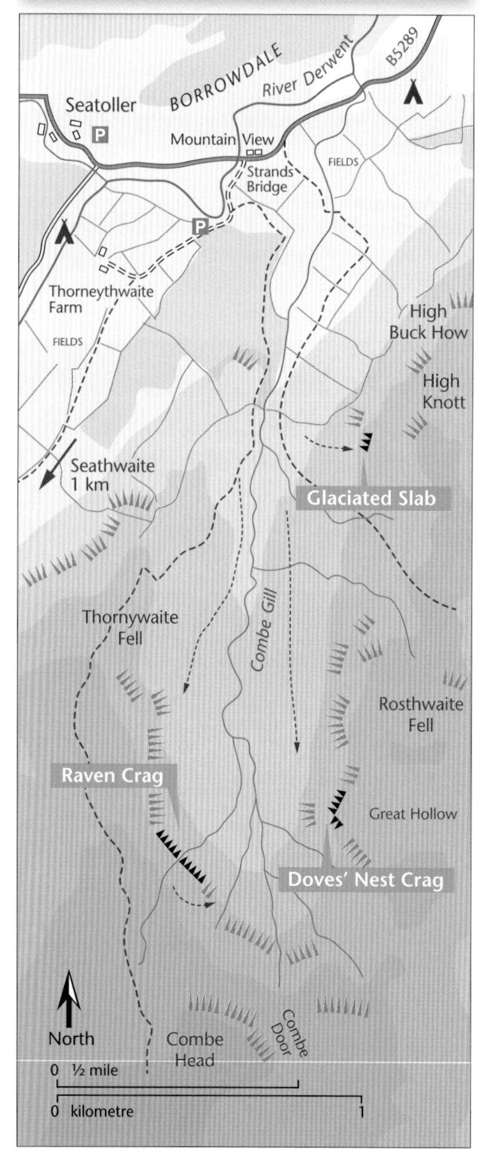

Deep passages create unusual and enjoyable climbs on excellent rock in a very fine setting. It could all move again – take care!

Descent: Either side of the crag, both are steep with left perhaps being easier on the left.

1 Adam's Slab 38m MVS 4b ★★
An excllent pitch; poorly protected at the start.
R Kenyon - Jun 1985

2 Meet Your Maker 38m HVS 4c ★
Climb directly left of moss passing right of a block.
D Johnson, E Ostell - May 1997

3 Horizontal Pleasure 80m HVS 4c ★★
Varied; the spectacular finale is virtually unprotected and not for the faint hearted!
1 30m A mossy scoop trends rightwards; cross a ledge, the short crack leads to the left edge of the buttress. Belay under the left branch of a chimney.
2 8m 4b Squirm up left to stand on the jug, cross to the right and up to a pinnacle.
3 12m 4c Stride across and climb the long narrow slab to the large chockstone on the right. Go up to a stance.
4 30m 4c Traverse along the lip to a small ledge; trend leftwards to reach the top.
SJH Reid, JE Reid - Sep 1995

4 Face Route 82m VD ★★
Traditional techniques yield dividends.
1 30m A crack trends left. From the ledge the right arête leads to walk 8m right below the South Chimney.
2 8m Left along the detached block to an interesting belay.
3 16m Drop down, disappear up the chimney (Central Chimney) to emerge in the Attic Cave.
4 28m Step down and stride right across the top of Central Chimney to reach a fine crack; the wider crack above leads to a pinnacle on the right. Move left and up to the top.
RST Chorley, B Beetham, RW Somervell - 1944

5 Clubfoot 70m VS 5a ★★
A sharp crux reserved for the final moves. P2 is bold; with poor protection and an awful landing.
1 26m 4m Easy slabs and corners to belay below the South Chimney.
2 22m 4a Cross the slab up left. Climb, right of Central Chimney.
3 16m The rib on the right and rocks above to a stance.
4 6m 5a The stiff corner groove has good protection.
B Evans, S Burns, B Hunt - 1954

DOVE'S NEST
50 mn
OS Grid Ref: NY 253 117
Altitude: 475m
Attic Cave
1
2
3
4
5
RT
Dow
Eskdale
Scafell
Gable
Buttermere
Borrowdale
Eastern

GLACIATED SLAB

OS Grid Ref: NY 254 128
Altitude: 300m

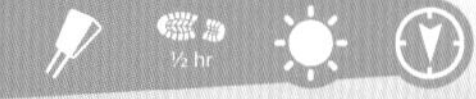

A clean, quick-drying, slabby outcrop giving relaxed climbing on superb, ice-planed rock.

Descent: Up and to the right.

RT

1 **Trod Pip** 32m MVS 4b ★
D Byrne-Pearce, P Ross - Oct 1988

2 **Trod Dovera** 32m VD
B Beetham - Oct 1944

3 **Trod Lethera** 30m D ★
B Beetham - Oct 1944

4 **Trod Too Far** 28m S ★★
P Latimer R Tolley - Sep 2008

5 **Trod Pimp** 28m S ★★
B Beetham - Oct 1944

6 **Trod Methera** 24m S ★★
B Beetham - Oct 1944

7 **Trod Tethera** 22m VD ★★
B Beetham - Oct 1944

8 **Trod 'A' Tween** 18m MVS 4a ★
Be careful - this one has ground-fall potential.
R Kenyon - Oct 1988

9 **Trod Tan** 16m D ★
B Beetham - Oct 1944

RAVEN CRAG

OS Grid Ref: NY 248 114
Altitude: 360m

Dominating the head of Combe Ghyll this crag offers long mountaineering routes together with a pleasant short wall. *Raven Crag Gully* and *Corvus* also provide classic entertaining climbs for wet days.

Corvus D (page 387) Dee Gaffney — Cath Sullivan

EV Eastern **Borrowdale** Buttermere Gable Scafell Eskdale Dow Langdale

The Pedestal Wall

1 Pedestal Wall S ★★
B Beetham - Aug 1940

2 Cock It HVS 5a ★
T Langhorne - Jun 1987

3 For the Record VS 4c ★
T Langhorne - Jun 1987

4 Just a Quickie VS 4c ★
R Kenyon - May 1984

5 Crystal Slab 94m MVS 4b ★★
This excellent route starts at a groove below the big slab up and to the right.
1 45m 4b Climb a spiky groove and a shallow scoop onto a slab below a wall. Step up and traverse left across the wall to a jug, move up and continue to the right end of the overhung ledges at the top of the slab.
2 16m From the left of the ledges climb an overhung slab on the right to below a crack in a groove.
3 33m The crack and groove above.
P Hirst E Hirst - Jun 1985

Raven Crag Buttress

6 Midge Ridge 121m VS 4b ★★
1 18m 4a From a pinnacle, the right arête leads to a narrow ledge. A short wall, follow a scoop and short groove to a large ledge.
2 30m 4a Move left and climb to a large ledge. Take a slab leftwards and step round the arête to a narrowing ramp, up (bold) to some dubious spikes on the left. Climb a short chimney and wide ramp, move right up a short slab to a stance.
3 50m 4b Make a delicate traverse left (spike) and pull into the scoop; climb to a large ledge. The left slanting crack system leads to a slim hanging groove followed by a short chimney. Pass left of the large flake then up the wall above, stepping out left to a block. Moves left avoid the short arête, gain the protruding block and finish up the crack in the wall.
4 23m Easy ground.
SJH Reid, CAJ Reid, SA Baxendale - Jul 2006

7 Raven Crag Buttress 112m VD ★★★
Continuously interesting and great value.
1 33m Climb the open chimney/groove and

ledges above to a good ledge.
2 26m Bear slightly left and climb up to a ledge overlooking the gully. Continue past a projecting flake to a ledge.
3 30m Climb grooves to a large ledge.
4 23m Scrambling remains.
B Beetham & members of the Goldsborough Club - Sep 1939

8 Corax 145m HS 4a ★★
An enjoyable climb.
1 30m 4a Gain and follow twin cracks in the slab leading directly to a ledge and block belay.
2 30m 4a Pass the block and follow a crackline up the exposed buttress above; slabby rock leads to a belay.
3-5 85m Move easily left to join *Corvus*.
B Beetham - Jul 1950; P1- 1951

9 Corvus 147m D ★★★
A route for all seasons, traditionally in the rain.
1 26m Start up slabs then move right to a ledge in the gully. Climb the first V-cleft in the left wall to a ledge and block belay
2 36m Traverse left along ledges to a corner. Climb the corner, which deepens into a chimney, and a slabby scoop to a good stance.
3 35m A rib 5m right is climbed to gain a steep slabby wall. Belay on the right.
4 10m The Hand-Traverse - a line of flake handholds leads left across the wall to a recess.
5 40m Pass a large ledge, up a rib then a scoop and so to the top.
B Beetham - Jun 1950

10 Raven Crag Gully 178m VD ★★★
A classic and thoroughly entertaining. Keep right passing the first chockstone, then easily left past a cave. Pass another cave on the right, continue up, then right past another chockstone. Traverse below and pass left of the capstone.
WA Wilson, JW Robinson, CN Williamson - Sep 1893

11 Easy Street 60m MVS 4c ★★
1 30m 4b Trend left from blocks crossing a ledge onto a gangway. Move right across a small overlap to belay below a slab.
2 30m 4c Climb the slab passing an overhang on its left and continue by a precarious flake to a groove. Finish up the rib.

Atmospheric mountaineering climbs plus a selection of shorter routes.

Descent: By the obvious ramp to the left; take care on the steep path, or follow the ridge to the valley.

GILLERCOMBE

OS Grid Ref: NY 223 124
Altitude: 480m

Gabbro VD (page 390) Trevor Langhorne — Richard Tolley

This large mountain crag basks in day-long sunshine and offers some great climbing on superb rock.

Approach: From Honister Pass Youth Hostel P NY 22557 13535 or Seathwaite P NY 23547 12290.

Descent: Use the gully on the right (north).

Gabbro Buttress

This buttress lies high of the left hand side of the crag and is most easily reached from the top.

1 Gabbro 47m VD ★★

A bit broken but really enjoyable. Start just above a large embedded boulder in the scree gully.

1 27m Go right from the top of the pinnacle into a small V-corner. Exit the corner above on the right and belay under a large flake.

2 20m Swing round to the right and continue up the delightful slab above.

B Beetham - Apr 1941

The next three routes start from grassy ledges reached by scrambling 8m up the grassy ramp that starts at the big embedded boulder in the scree gully. Alternatively descend a grassy gully on the right of the buttress.

2 Rough Magic 38m HS 4a ★★

Bold, enjoyable and exposed.

1 18m From some large blocks climb the steep wall and exposed rib to join *Gabbro*.

2 20m 4a Up the corner to a swing right onto the front of the buttress. Enjoy the bold edge on wonderful rock to where the angle eases, then the centre to the top.

B Clarke - Jun 2005

3 Rough Stuff 32m MVS 4b ★★

More lovely climbing on incredible rock. From a juniper, below a short, clean slab, climb to a small cave. Reach the slab above, either from the block on the left side of the cave (better), or by the right rib (4c). Continue up the fine slab, move a few metres left and follow clean rock to the top.

W Hurford, S Reid - May 2005

4 Just Say Non 35m MVS 4b ★

Climb right into a groove and gain the slab from the right. Pad up to a ledge. Climb the wall right of a thin crack and continue up the slab and rib above.

S Reid, W Hurford - May 2005

Gillercombe Buttress

5 Gillercombe Buttress 195m S ★★★

A quick-drying pre-war classic. Start at the lowest point of the buttress left of a ramp right of a gully.

1 15m From the lowest point slabby rock leads to a stance.

2 15m Head right past a flake to the upper ramp.

3 40m The traverse left is awkward at first to a platform below a corner crack.

4 20m The crack.

5 40m Climb a short steep scoop/corner on the right to a large ledge. Scramble up an open corner to a large ledge and flake belay.

6 40m Step left and climb a groove to a ledge. Continue up slabs to easier ground.

7 25m Scrambling.

H B Lyon, W Woodsend - May 1912;
P6 & 7 J Ray, H Harland, GA Solly, C Wilson - May 1921

6 Grey Knotts Face 131m VD ★★

A good and character building mountaineering route, with a traditional squeeeeze...

1 13m From the fence climb to a large grass ledge.

2 25m Diagonally right into a corner, pass a square ledge to slip through the letter box and wriggle up the cleft to the top of the block; move left and up to a large ledge. To avoid the slot either climb the short corner above or move right then up a wall using a wedged flake (S).

3 33m Climb the chimney crack passing a chockstone to a grass ledge.

4 60m Finish up the right rib of the shallow gully.

B Beetham -Jun1939

STEEL KNOTTS

OS Grid Ref: NY 246 164
Altitude: 240m

Excellent rock with pleasant climbing.

Approach: From Grange P NY 25262 17505 or south of Grange P NY 25226 173360.

Descent: To the left.

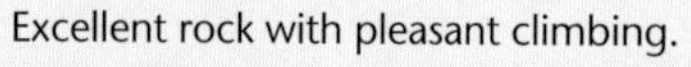

South Face

1 Stinger 21m E2 5c ★
A good finish up the narrow pillar.
J Williams, P Rigby - Aug 2003

2 The Sting 23m E2 5c ★★★
A fine jamming exercise. A must at the grade.
RT Marsden, TE Dunsby - 1973

3 Smoker's Delight 21m E2 6a ★
A hard start makes this a challenge for the grade.
M de Vaal, C Reid,T Suddaby - Jul 2004

4 Meandering Maggot 26m E1 5b ★★
The wall to the right of *Smoker's Delight*.
R Kenyon, T Price - 1984

5 Lurching Leech 30m HVS 5a
Deceptively awkward.
K Leech, T Taylor - Aug 1965

6 Samurai Jack 30m E4 6a ★
Very bold climbing up the centre of the steep clean wall.
T Suddaby, C Reid - Jul 2004

7 Rashomon 30m E3 5c
The left side of the fractured arête.
J Timney, M Dunne - Oct 2012

8 Ambling Ant 30m MVS 4b ★★
A pleasant open climb.
R Kenyon, T Price, L Jordan - Oct 1985

9 Route 2 30m VS 4c ★
The obvious crack forming the left side of the pinnacle.

10 Tottering Tortoise 40m HVS 5a ★★
An entertaining off-width.
T Taylor, K Leech - Aug 1965

East Face

11 Loss Adjustor 30m E2 5c ★★
The wall right of the arête with a difficult finish.
R Graham, P Graham - May 2013

12 Lost in Space 50m HVS 5a ★★
A good trip across the crag starting up *The Lost Boys*.
R Kenyon, M Kenyon - Jun 2014

13 The Lost Boys 30m HVS 5a ★★★
The prominent arête after an interesting start.
P Whillance, D Armstrong - Apr 1984

14 Paint it Black 30m E3 5c ★★
The obvious black crack with a step out left.
B Davison, D Smart - Jul 1982

15 Free Falling 28m E4 6a ★★
Quite sustained, but just makes the grade.
D Messenger, J Sharpe - Sep 1995

16 Terminal Velocity 28m E3 5c ★★
The fingery wall direct - a challenge for the grade.
P Graham, R Graham - May 2013

17 B.M.C. 1 30m VS 4c
The easiest way up this part of the crag involving a long traverse to finish.
M Armitage, J Unsworth - Sep 1986

GOAT CRAG

OS Grid Ref: NY 245 165
Altitude: 350m

1 hr

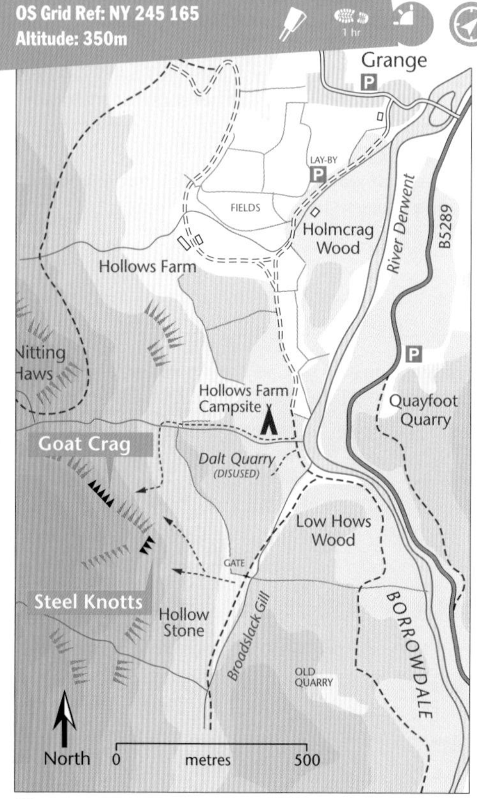

1 D.D.T. 40m HVS 5a ★★★

An impressive, technical corner of considerable character. It's easiest to use the big holds to your right.

J Lee, A Tackman, P Ross - Oct 1965

2 The Voyage 83m E3 5c ★★★

A magnificent trip; sustained, absorbing.

1 30m 5c Climb *D.D.T.* for 10m then step right below a bulge. Straight up (peg), traverse right to a groove in the arête and follow this to a tree.

2 30m 5c Traverse right; first below an overlap, always finding the easiest line. Join *Footless Horse* and use a ramp (bolt and pegs) then continue to follow *Bitter Oasis* finally gaining an easy slab and ledge.

3 23m 5c The steep wall, left then right to gain a flake crack. Over a bulge to a corner and wall.

S Clegg, P Botterill - Jul 1976

3 Tumbleweed Connection 56m E2 5c ★★★

Tremendous; you may be blown away. Start below the wide crack of *Praying Mantis*.

1 26m 5c Hand traverse round the arête to the foot of twin cracks. 3m left, climb up crossing a bulge (peg). Traverse delicately right 3m to take a groove in the arête to the tree.

2 30m 5b Left and up to make a spectacular move left across the undercut arête onto the slab. Can be done in one amazing 50m pitch using the *By-Pass* (1979); from the peg continue straight up to the exposed move left onto the arête.

P Botterill, D Rawcliffe - Jul 1976

4 Praying Mantis 85m E1 5b ★★★

The impressive original route, now a classic, weaves up the frowning buttress right of *D.D.T.*

1 25m 5b The insecure wide crack leads to a slab and tree.

2 16m 4c A ramp and traverse left across a smooth wall leads into a V-groove. A step right leads to a small stance; belay below block overhangs.

3 44m 4c Technically right to a wall and a vague depression in the buttress above; a step left gains a final slab. (Extend the left rope runners and run 2 and 3 together if using 60m ropes.)

L Brown, S Bradshaw - May 1965

5 Athanor 73m E3 6a ★★★

Excellent, strenuous and delicate.

1 28m 6a The rib on the left of a vegetated groove, the blank-looking groove then a short steep crack lead to a traverse left under a small overlap.

2 45m 5c A prominent V-groove on the right with overhangs at its top (peg). More grooves and overhangs, until a pull right gains the slabs.

J Adams, C Read - Sep 1968

6 Footless Horse 57 m E6 6b (F7b+) ★★★

This powerful combination gives arguably the best **E6** in the valley. Climb *Athanor* into the niche and climb out right to gain the rightward-trending ramp. Pass the belay (bolt and pegs) below the roof. Climb directly up the undercuts (peg) and continue (peg) to the undercut fang. Continue directly to the top.

Chris Hope - Jul 2003

7 Mirage 60m E5 6b ★★★

A magnificent challenge - first delicate and bold, then steep and strenuous. The groove 3m right of *Athanor* to beckoning undercuts. Haul leftwards, then climb a thin crack to an awkward pull up right. Above is a large flat hold, stand on it, step right, round a rib then up rightwards to a pocket. Left from the pocket to a slight rib, then straight up (bolt and pegs). Climb rightwards (old bolt) then straight up to beneath a bulge (old bolt). Step left, and climb the weakness through the bulges (thread) to pull into the scoop to join *Bitter Oasis* at the hanging spike. Follow this to the top.

RO Graham, D Lyle - Apr 1981

8 Bitter Oasis 54 m E4 5c ★★★

Another magnificent route. Scramble to a birch.

1 28m 5c Gain the groove on the left which leads to a slab, the 'bitter oasis' and, higher, a commodious stance.

2 26m 5c A rising traverse left across to a pedestal and out of sight of your second, then leads to a small foothold below a hanging spike. Climb the left side of the spike, then move left up a wall on finger pockets to a ledge; easily up leftwards to finish.

P Livesey, J Sheard - May 1974

Excellent steep rock topped by 'beetling yellow overhangs' make an impressive crag by any standard, giving consistently challenging routes. Take 60m ropes. Climb in the morning after giving it a day or two to dry. Shady and cool on warm afternoons.

Approach: From Grange P NY 25262 17505 or south of Grange P NY 25226 173360. Use the slabby wet diagonal rake arriving at a belvedere by a large boulder.

Descent: Abseil.

EASTERN CRAGS

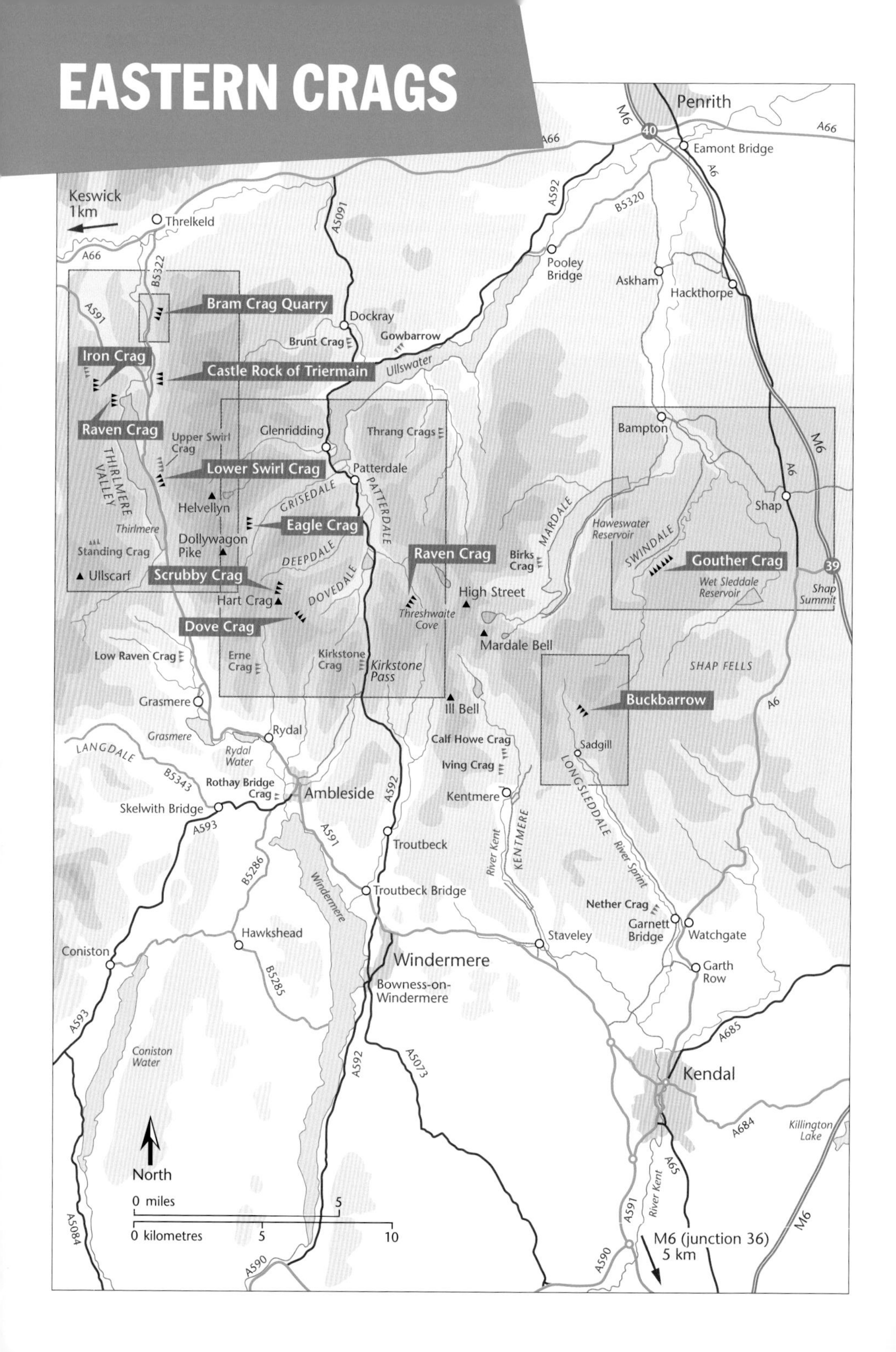

Up Hellya E8 Dave Birkett — Alastair Lee

BRAMCRAG QUARRY

OS Grid Ref: NY 320 220

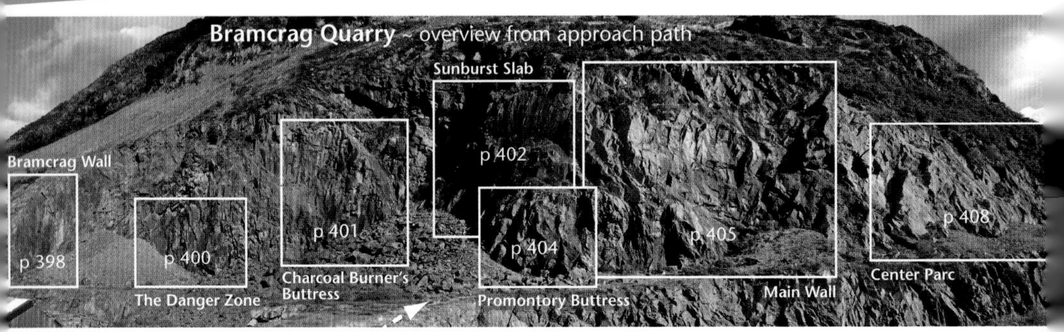

A high-quality sport venue with fun climbing, clean sticky rock and a superb outlook; the quarry attracts many climbers.

Danger: Rockfall frequently occurs almost anywhere, even below the 'safer' right hand Center Parc sector.

Access: The quarry is privately owned. Climbers are on good terms with the landowner and the user of the quarry. In the past selfish parking has created issues. Park sensibly where shown: in the lay-bys on the road and follow the approach indicated.

Do not block the access track.

If you do not observe these simple courtesies you risk losing this super venue.

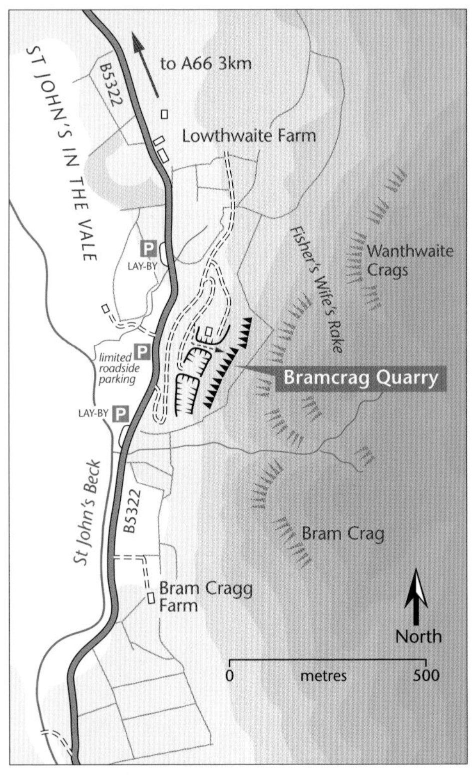

P NY 31792 21755

P NY 31867 22380

P NY 31867 22015

Bramcrag Wall

1 Michelangelo 16m F6c ★★

A stubborn bulge, a technical sustained traverse and difficult crack lead to the niche.

M Norbury - Jun 2010

2 Middle Earth 16m F7b ★

The shield has a stopper move.

M Norbury - Jun 2010

3 Bramcrag Wall 19m F7a ★★

Great moves lead to the niche. The crux is where it should be.

M De Vaal - Jun 2010

4 Wai Lord 19m F7b+ ★

The obvious curving line has desperate moves to gain the lower off.

M Greenbank - Aug 2010

1

2

3

4

BY

The Danger Zone ⚠

Beware. Very high incidence of rockfall makes this area dangerous. In 2013 rock peppered the aptly named *Dancing in the Danger Zone!* - nobody has been injured, yet!

5 Vanished Times 25m F6b ★
The corner - awkward moves to the lower off.
C Fowler, C Downer, L Jones - May 2012

6 Cool Hand Luke 25m E2 5c ★★★
The obvious well-protected diagonal crack.
L Jones, C Downer, D Sperry - May 2012

7 Dancing in the Danger Zone! 35m F6b
A stunning route but sadly, the main slab is in the firing line - note the rock scars!
C Downer, L Jones, D Sperry - May 2012

Charcoal Burner's Buttress

8 Best Western 25m F6a+ ★★
Superb juggy climbing up the overhanging crack and arête. Best seconded to retrieve the gear.
C Downer - Aug 2014

9 The Deviant 25m F6c+ ★★
A devious line - beware of rope drag.
C Downer, W Young, C Wornham - Sep 2014

10 Keep the Car Running 27m F6a+ ★
A fine route up the large flake; traverse left with tricky moves to a large block and the slab above.
C Downer, P Ross - July 2013

11 Arcade Fire 25m F6a+ ★★★
An expedition! It is easier for a second to retrieve the gear rather than the leader.
C Downer, T Daley, S Murphy - Aug 2014

12 Silicone Crack 15m F6c ★
Short and sharp.
C Fowler, C Downer, C Wornham - Sep 2014

13 The Culling 20m F6c ★★★
An excellent groove line.
C Downer, C Fowler - September 2013

14 Slaying the Badger 25m F6a+ ★★★
An intricate line with a long tricky traverse left.
C Downer, C Fowler - Aug 2013

15 Ripping Yarns 25m F6a ★
The step left may be harder than the pull over the overlap.
C Downer, D Sperry - May 2014

16 The Charcoal Burner 25m F6b ★★★
Superb, continuously absorbing climbing up the groove and arête above.
C Downer, D Sperry - Jun 2013

17 Sunbeam Talbot 20m F6b ★
An easy crack leads to a difficult finish.
D Sperry, C Downer - Jun 2013

Sunburst Slab

From *Grand Union* to *Stoker* take care when lowering off if you only have a 60m rope.

18 Tin Can Alley 20m F6a+ ★
Worth waiting for a dry spell.
C Downer, M Armitage - Jul 2014

19 Coup-de-Grace 20m F6b ★★★
So enjoyable! Be decisive.
C Downer, M Armitage, D Sperry - Jul 2014

20 Grand Union 30m F6c ★★★
L Jones, C Downer, D Sperry - May 2012

21 The Sunshine Gang 30m F6a ★★★
Fun climbing up the cracks and grooves.
C Downer, L Jones, C Fowler, D Sperry - May 2012

22 The Shooting Gallery 30m F6a ★★★
A brilliant pitch across impressive ground. It's best for a second to retrieve the gear. Head left from the tree stump along the juggy traverse.
C Downer, M Armitage, C Wornham

23 Sunburst Slab 30m F6a ★
Grooves lead to a rising ramp and an awkward move into the wide crack.
C Downer, L Jones, D Sperry - Jun 2012

24 The Woodcutter's Lullaby 30m F6c+
A contrived variation from the ramp.
C Downer, C Fowler - May 2014

25 Stoker F6c+ 30m
Difficult climbing up the right side of the slab.
L Jones, C Downer, C Fowler - Jun 2012

26 Bring Me Sunshine F5 20m
The pleasant slab and groove.
C Downer, W Young - Dec 2014

Coup-de-Grace F6b Pete Winterbottom — BILL YOUNG

Promontory Buttress

27 Yopo 15m F5+
The arête has an awkward move.
C Downer, L Jones - Apr 2013

28 Benghazi Burner 15m F6a+ ★
The obvious overhanging crack heading for the open groove.
C Fowler, C Downer - Dec 2013

29 Morley Street Mission 15m F6b ★★
Burly moves to a ledge then aim for the slim groove on the left. Variant left is **6a**.
C Downer, L Jones, D Sperry - Apr 2013

30 Last Dash 15m F6b ★★
An excellent route up the obvious crack and groove.
C Bainbridge, PJ Kane - May 1997

31 Con Artist 15m F6b+ ★
A contrived line but excellent climbing.
C Fowler, C Downer - Mar 2014

32 Twilight 15m F5
PJ Kane, C Bainbridge - May 1997

33 Hound-dog 15m F6a
Not bolted; but you can clip those next door.
PJ Kane, C Bainbridge - May 1997

34 The Quarryman 15m F6a
The black-streaked bulge to gain the corner..
PJ Kane, C Bainbridge - May 1997

35 The Wetherby Whaler 15m F6a
The crack in the wall above Promontory Buttress.
C Downer, C Fowler - Jun 2014

Main Wall

36 The Tipton Slasher 30m F6c ★★★
Superb technical climbing. The lower step right needs working out and for the full Slasher experience the top arête is climbed direct; holds barred on the right wall!
C Downer, L Jones, C Fowler - Jun 2012

37 Yorkshire Ripper 30m F6b+ ★★★
Absorbing sustained climbing following the central line on this buttress.
C Downer, M Armitage - May 2014

38 Usain Bolt 30m F6b+ ★★★
Another superb route up the impressive cleaned corner.
C Fowler, C Downer - Aug 2012

39 Middle East Crisis 30m F6b ★
An eliminate line.
C Downer, J Spencer, J Rigg - Jun 2014

40 Eastern Promise 35m E2 5c ★★
Bring your rack for this superb trad climb. Climb the little groove to its top, swing right, up, cross a small ledge. Continue up (small wires - crux), grassy ledge. Continue up trending left.
A Phizacklea, J Holden - Apr 1991

41 Coup d'État 36m E2 5c ★★
Climb to a doubtful block and pull over to a shot-hole. From the shallow groove embark on a rising traverse to the right aiming for 2 bolts close together and a difficult pull over the overhang.
A Phizacklea, J Holden - April 1991

42 The History Boys 30m E2 5c ★★★
Continually interesting climbing.
Climb to ledges and a flake then pull directly over the roof. Climb the groove and slab to a projecting block. Move right and over to a ledge. Climb the groove (cams) to the lower off.
C Downer, G Lee, G Proctor - May 2010

43 Desperate Dan 30m F6b+ ★★★
Use a massive span, confident smearing or a belayer with broad shoulders. There is a difficult overhang higher up.
C Downer, M Armitage, C Wornham - May 2014

44 Arc-de-Triomphe 25m F6a+ ★★★
Excellent. Amenable and with fine positions.
C Downer, C Fowler, M Armitage - May 2014

45 Bobby Dazzler 30m F6b ★★★
An excellent and very enjoyable cruxy route.
C Downer, C Higgins, D Ferguson, C Fowler - Jul 2009

46 Hell Bender 30m F6c ★★★
Intricate climbing in a fine position up the arete. Please leave the maillon in place.
C Downer, T Daly - May 2014

47 Bon Courage 30m F6a ★
The slabby groove and slab leftwards to the obvious bay. Traverse left and up the slab.
C Downer, M Nicholson - Sep 2009

48 Mr Angry 18m F6b ★
Delicate balancy fun.
C Downer, M Nicholson - Sep 2009

49 Bonne Chance 18m F6c ★
The highlight is the desperate move to gain the groove.
C Downer, M Nicholson - Sep 2009

50 Take It or Leave It 20m F6a
The rib and crack.
RJ Kenyon, C King - Jun 1991

51 Welcome to Rio 25m F6a ★
Climb the corner and follow the flake handrail.
C Downer, D Sperry - May 2014

36	**The Tipton Slasher**	F6b+
37	**Yorkshire Ripper**	F6b
38	**Usain Bolt**	F6b+
39	**Middle East Crisis**	F6b
40	**Eastern Promise**	E2 5c
41	**Coup d'État**	E2 5c
42	**The History Boys**	E2 5c
43	**Desperate Dan**	F6b+
44	**Arc-de-Triomphe**	F6a+

45 Bobby Dazzler F6a+
46 Hell Bender F6c«
47 Bon Courage F6a
48 Mr Angry F6b
49 Bonne Chance F6c
50 Take It or Leave It F6a
51 Welcome to Rio F6a
Borrowdale
Eastern
BY
EV

Center Parc

52 Bambino Bolero 25m MVS
The ramp system beneath the large overhangs (which fell down) is in the firing line and should be avoided.
RJ Kenyon, G Baum, G Irvine - May 1991

53 On the Edge 23m F5
The pleasant arête.
RJ Kenyon - Dec 1991

54 Tyke's Teeter 23m F6b
A serious route with difficult bold moves above the grass ledge.
RJ Kenyon, A Davis - Dec 1991

55 Tyke's Teeter Direct 20m F6c
Tenuous on the initial slabs.
C Bainbridge, PJ Kane - May 1993

56 Gorilla Monsoon 20m F6a+ ★
The tricky groove through the obvious notch. The rib then make exciting moves left.
C Downer, M Nicholson - Apr 2014

57 Good Luck Mr. Blair! 20m E3 5c
Total belief is required to pull this off.
P King, RJ Kenyon - 1997

58 Farewell to Adventure? 20m F6a ★
Enjoyable climbing with tricky moves through the overlap.
RJ Kenyon, J Bardgett - Feb 1992

59 Sorry, No Bolts 25m E2 5a
Unprotected originally - the nearby bolts haven't made it any safer.
S Miller - Jul 1991

60 A Miller's Tale 25m F6a ★
An enjoyable pitch.
C Downer, C Fowler - Apr 2014

61 Fargo F5 ★
Pleasant slabby fun.
C Downer - Apr 2014

62 Whicker's World 25m F5+ ★
Another enjoyable line up the left side of the pleasant water-worn slabs.
C Fowler, C Downer, L Jones - Jun 2013

63 The Rookie 25m F5 ★
More pleasant climbing up the slabs though the bolts are sportingly spaced.
C Downer - Jun 2014

64 The Comfort Zone 25m F5 ★
And another similar pleasant amble up the slabs.
C Downer - Jun 2014

65 Blencathra Badger 27m F5+ ★★★
Would win best in class, if not in show!
A Phizacklea, J Holden - 1991

66 The Long Good Friday 27m F5+ ★★
From *Blencathra Badger*'s second bolt, a fine arete leads to the large hanging groove.
C Downer, M Armitage - Apr 2014

67 The Good Friday Agreement 30m F6b
A short but neat eliminate.
C Downer, C Wornham - Apr 2014

68 Brothers in Arms 30m F6a+ ★
The black-streaked wall and head for the obvious overhang which is climbed with surprising ease unlike the slab above.
C Bainbridge, S Bainbridge - Jun 1992

69 Ship of Fools 27m F6a ★★
A fine line heading for the black-streaked wall and the grooved arête above.
C Downer, K Forsythe, A Tilney - Apr 2014

70 Vale of Secrecy 30m F6a+ ★
Climb to the second bolt and pull into an open groove then a slim groove and the final rib.
A Phizacklea, J Holden - Apr 1991

71 Barrow Boys' Day Out 30m F6a ★★
Good open climbing following a natural line rightwards across the buttress.
A Phizacklea, J Holden - Mar 1991

72 Ripper Street 30m F6b
Climb up to and cross *Barrow Boys' Day Out*. Climb the slim groove directly above with difficulty.
C Downer, D Sperry - Nov 2013

73 Goodbye Mr Major! 31m F6a ★★
Follows the dark rock leading to a pleasant slab.
P King, RJ Kenyon - 1997

74 Goodfella's 27m F5+ ★★
Direct and satisfying.
P Botterill, A Davis, C Downer, C Fowler - Jun 2013

75 St. John's Ambulance 30m F4+ ★
Trust they aren't needed!
A Phizacklea, J Holden - April 1991

76 Endgame 20m F5+
The slabby rib.
M Armitage, W Young - Apr 2015

The North Crag

A magnificent crag towering above St John's in the Vale. It catches the afternoon sun, has enjoyable quality routes of all grades and is deservedly popular.

Steep and juggy in character, confidence in what lies above pays dividends, but treat the flaky holds with caution. Protection is sparse outside the comfort of the crack and groove lines.

Approach: From Legburthwaite car park P NY 31802 19580follow the track across the field, cross the culvert and through the wood.

Descent: Walk right and use the path below the South Crag or abseil from the routes on the right of North Crag.

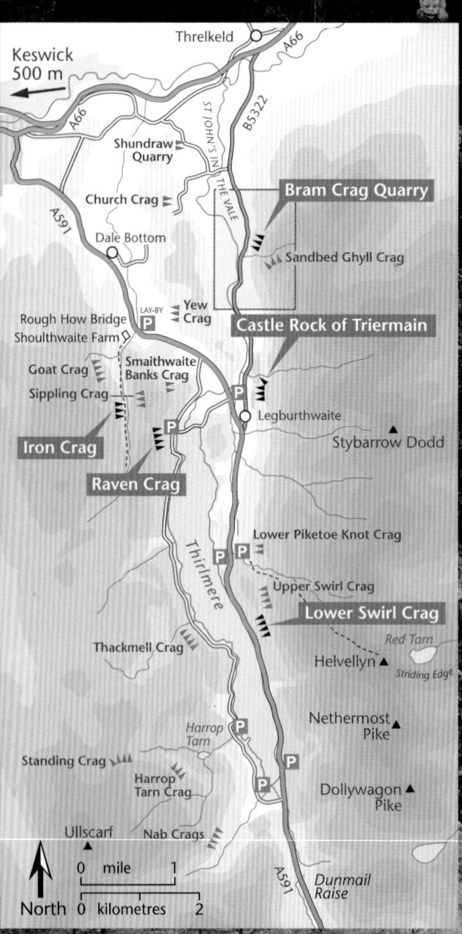

Danger: A geological fault is actively opening at the left side of the crag, releasing a block of megalithic proportions, rendering a number of classic routes unsafe. This is moving and is being monitored. Sadly, several classic excursions are threatened, including two mega classics - **North Crag Eliminate** (NCE) and **Overhanging Bastion** (OB). All of the routes left of *Thirlmere Eliminate* are threatened. On NCE the crucial traverse uses the very fault that's opening!

CASTLE ROCK OF TRIERMAIN

OS Grid Ref: NY 322 197
Altitude: 275m

10 mn

1	**May Day Cracks**	HVS 5a	6	**Harlot Face**	E1 5b
2	**Thirlmere Eliminate**	E1 5b	7	**Triermain Eliminate**	E2 5b
3	**Rigor Mortis**	E2 5c	8	**Angel's Highway**	E1 5a
4	**White Dwarf**	E4 6a	9	**Ted Cheasby**	E2 5c
5	**The Ghost**	E3 5c	10	**The Final Giggle**	E1 5b

1 May Day Cracks 70m HVS 5a ★★★
A series of sustained, well-protected cracks is the clear divide between the potential danger zone and the remainder of the crag. You need to decide if you are far enough away! A ledge collapsed here in 2011.
1 46m 5a Climb a shallow groove, cross a ledge, through a tree, to continue up the chimney and V-groove above. Belay at the base of a large slab.
2 24m Take the big slab on the left.
RJ Birkett, L Muscroft - May 1947
If you get nervous you can step boldly from the chimney onto the arete of *Thirlmere Eliminate.*

2 Thirlmere Eliminate 55m E1 5b ★★★
Superb - starts below a 2m high perched flake.
1 37m 4c The flake and corner lead to a ledge. Traverse diagonally left into a corner and take the arête above.
2 18m 5b Work to get gear in the very steep corner moving onto the right wall.
P Ross, PJ Greenwood - Jun 1955

3 Rigor Mortis 57m E2 5c ★★★
Brilliant - technical and exposed.
1 15m 4c Climb the wall and follow a steep crack to the long narrow ledge.
2 20m 5c Climb the corner on the left and crack to the top of the 'white cone'. Traverse up leftwards and up a shallow scoop.
3 22m 5a Right round the corner to a sensational line of interrupted gangways leading to a chimney.
P Ross, B Aughton -Apr 1959

4 White Dwarf 30m E4 6a ★★
An eliminate climbing the face of the 'white cone' and into the steep corner above. Reaching the gangway can be trying.
TW Birkett, KW Forsythe - May 1978

5 The Ghost 30m E3 5c ★★
Steep strenuous and committing. Climb into the bottom of the groove to the right of the 'white cone' (cam). Hard moves right gain a large flake, step up left and climb a V-groove and the steep wall above. **The Loop** (E2 5b) avoids the committing moves by continuing into the groove from the top of the 'white cone'.
AG Cram, WA Barnes, W Young - Jul 1964; *The Loop* R Matheson, G Fleming - Sep 1969

The following routes lead to a tree-covered ledge which gives a convenient abseil descent. The ledge above the first pitch of the next four routes may be more pleasantly (and safely) reached by climbing p1 of *Rigor Mortis.*

6 Harlot Face 50m E1 5b ★★★
Probably the first extreme in the Lakes; with a short sharp crux.
1 15m 4c Climb the line of corners rising leftwards.
2 15m 5b Climb a short way up the overhanging corner to a move right round the rib then steeply up the corner.
3 20m 4c The groove above.
RJ Birkett, L Muscroft - Jun 1949

7 Triermain Eliminate 49m E2 5b ★★★
Superb and very strenuous.
1 16m 5a Climb to a small ledge and a corner above.
2 33m 5b Don't underestimate the thuggy overhanging corner. Recover, then follow the chimney and shallow groove above.
DD Whillans, J Brown, D Cowan - Mar 1953

8 Angel's Highway 52m E1 5a ★★
An exposed climb.
1 36m 5a Climb to a small ledge then right to a corner. Move right round the arête and back left up to a shallow groove to a small tree then left to a ledge.
2 16m Climb the wall.
PJ Greenwood, P Whitwell - Sep 1955

9 Ted Cheasby 45m E2 5c ★★★
A strenuous and sustained crack.
1 30m 5c Climb directly up the thin crack and the groove above, step right above the bulge and back left up a shallow groove.
2 15m The wall above.
P Gomersall - Easter 1977

10 The Final Giggle 45m E1 5b ★
1 30m 5b From the left end of a ledge (cam under the overhang) climb the shallow groove and step right (pegs). Climb the groove, step right, climb the wall to a small tree, now left to the ledge.
2 15m Steep but easier rocks lead to the top.
MA Toole, P Ross - Jul 1965

SOUTH CRAG

OS Grid Ref: NY 321 195
Altitude: 300m

An open sunny aspect, good clean rock and easy access - perfect for an afternoon or evening

Approach: From Legburthwaite car park follow the track across the field and break off right up to the top right corner, cross the culvert and follow a rising path through the wood to cross a ladder stile.

1 Via Media 38m S ★★
Steep with a hard crux. From the foot of the big groove climb the rib on the right to slabs. The obvious crack on the left side of the steep wall leads to the top.
GF Parkinson, W Rae - May 1945

2 Gazebo Direct 38m HVS 5a ★★★
Superb climbing; the positive holds provide an enjoyable route directly up the centre of the wall.
G Lee, C Downer - 1971

3 Romantically Challenged 36m E1 5a ★★
Climb past the yew then straight up the wall to a rightward-rising crack-line. Cross this and continue directly up.
SJH Reid, T Lywood - 2002

4 Direct Route 36m VS 4b ★★
Take the intimidating wall, moving leftwards after 6m (ledges). Climb up to a sentry box and take the crack over a bulge onto the slab above.
AT Hargreaves, GG McPhee - May 930

5 Failed Romantic 36m E1 5b ★★
Very good climbing. A steep rib leads to a small ledge. Climb to the leftward-slanting seam then to the top.
S Hubbard - Aug 1984

6 Kleine Rinne 36m VS 4b ★★
Excellent. Climb the groove; the slab to its left edge, place gear, then haul up into the groove and easier slab.
JJS Allison - Apr 1963

7 Yew Tree Climb 38m VD ★★
Ubiquitous!
1 9m The slab on the left leads to an overhung corner.
2 17m The broken rib on the right; ledge (yew tree- surprised?) then left and follow the slab to a wall.
3 12m Climb the wall to the right of the crack and the slabs above.
GG McPhee, MM Barker - Mar 1928

8 Gangway Climb 34m VD ★★
Superb but serious - not for your first lead! Near the right hand corner a rib leads to a gangway on the left; continue up the slab above.
GG McPhee, JW Baxter - May 1928

9 Wall Climb 25m S ★
At the right-hand corner. From a ledge on top of the blocks step right up the short steep corner groove. Up the slab to a slim groove with a slightly bulging entry; climb this direct.
D Armstrong - 1978

10 Slab Climb 25m S ★★
More of a reachy groove! 5m from the right-hand corner climb the slab to a short steep corner which is climbed direct.
MM Barker, GG McPhee - Jul 1928

Gangway Climb VD Jackson Nixon — Ron Kenyon

1 Via Media S
2 Gazebo Direct HVS 5a
3 Romantically Challenged E1 5a
4 Direct Route VS 4b
5 Failed Romantic E1 5b
6 Kleine Rinne VS 4b
7 Yew Tree Climb VD
8 Gangway Climb VD
9 Wall Climb S
10 Slab Climb S
4
2
3
2
1
4
AP

7
6
9
10
8
7
5
6

LOWER SWIRL CRAG

OS Grid Ref: NY 321 159
Altitude: 330m

15 mn

A lovely place to climb on summer evenings - a steep wall of excellent rock which offers high quality climbing with a superb outlook

Approach: From the Swirls car park P NY 31712 16845 cross a footbridge through a gate onto the open hillside. Follow the wall south just above the forest. Lower Swirl Crag is 1½ kilometres from the gate, where the wall drops down the hillside.

1 Hot Dog 24m E2 5c ★
The left-hand groove in the twin-grooved corner.
D Armstrong - May 1984

2 Burger 24m E1 5a ★
The right-hand side of the obvious corner. The long reach to enter the corner is hard for short climbers.
D Armstrong - May 1984

3 Swirled not Shaken 24m E3 6a ★
Up right to stand on a flat-topped spike (pegs). Straight up (jug) to rock up on an incut foothold to reach dinks. Step right and continue up right to an easy groove.
P Carling - Nov 1989

4 American Pie 24m E2 5c ★★
It's serious starting the thin crack in the wall.
D Armstrong, P Whillance - Apr 1984

5 Supertramp 21m E3 5c ★
The thin crack up the blunt arête.
JW Earl, R Smith - Jun 1985

6 Frank 21m HVS 5a ★
Climb the groove past the holly and continue over a small overlap. Move up and left with difficulty and direct to the top.
D Bowen, R J Kenyon, C King - Jun 1983

7 The American Cowboy 18m E4 6a ★
Climbs the rib with a hard bold start.
A Hocking, J McHaffie - Jul 1997

8 Breakfast in America 18m E4 6a ★
An eliminate up the wall using blinkers, but holds are required and they are on the other routes.
P Whillance, D Armstrong - Apr 1984

9 Californian Weirdo 15m E2 5c ★★
The prominent right-slanting crack.
R J Kenyon, C King, D Bowen - Jun 1983

20 mn

OS Grid Ref: NY 304 188
Altitude: 350m

A steep and impressive place, its main attraction is the high density of quality hard routes. Due to the impending rock, routes in the cave area stay surprisingly dry in wet spells. The pegs and slings on a number of routes were replaced in 2009. Check the BMC RAD as the best time is late-spring.

Approach: Park P NY 30622 18925 at the road junction or in a lay-by 100m north. A path heads up through the trees to join a forestry road. Go left to a right-angled bend; after 20m a vague path climbs to the crag.

Descent: Steeply on the right or abseil.

1 Peels of Laughter 36m E5 6b ★★★
A superb route combining thin wall climbing with a brutal roof. To the left is a steep wall capped by a large overhang. Start directly below the middle of this wall, 3m left of a sycamore. Climb a very shallow loose groove to a large break. Pull leftwards off a block onto the steep wall using small holds. Step back right to the shallow scoop which is climbed to beneath the roof. Traverse left and surmount the roof with difficulty at the obvious weakness to a good hold. Continue more easily up the groove above to a block belay and abseil.
P Livesey, P Gomersall - Jun1977

2 Medlayer 27m E3 5c ★★★
Left of the medlar tree move up left of the arete then round right to a ledge. Traverse left up the rib to a junction with *The Medlar* which is followed left to its abseil point.
Relayer - J Lamb, B Berzins, M Berzins, P Botterill - Jun 1979

3 The Medlar 27m E4 6a ★★★
An excellent route with a very technical section up the open-book corner rising from the left side of the Cave. Start at the medlar tree.
Climb the curving grey-green wall left of the tree to the overhang. Move left round the nose and pull up to a ledge at the foot of the corner. Bridge up the corner with increasing difficulty to a hard move left to a jug. Continue traversing and then climb up to a good ledge.
M Boysen, CJS Bonington pa - Aug1964; FFA C Jones - 1976

4 Close to the Edge 37m E4 5c ★★★
An excellent pumpy eliminate picking the easiest way up this section of the crag. Follow *The Medlar* to the foot of the corner. Traverse right with difficulty across the overhung slab and pull round and up to a foothold stance and peg belays. Step up and swing left to the left arête of the groove. Continue up the fine groove system to a large ledge.
S Clegg, P Botterill - May1977

5 The Second Coming 30m E6 6b/c ★★★
Pumpy to start and technical to finish - awesome. Climb direct to the taverse on *Gates of Delirium*. Move out left and climb the groove to reach a good slot. Make a move up and then climb diagonally rightwards to beneath the bulge (old peg). Pull straight through, using a good undercut, to a thin crack in a groove and climb this to its top (good gear and a good rest). Move a little left, then up and back rightwards aiming for a stainless steel peg. Make technical moves past this and up awkwardly into the hard part on *Das Kapital*, follow this (peg) to a small sapling. Continue left to Ab off or if your arms can take it...
D Booth, M Weeks - Aug 2003

6 Infestation Finish 20m E7 6c ★★★
Follow *Das Kapital* up a short groove above the belay and step right onto a gangway. Move rightwards along this to two good incut jugs by a spike. From these, make some hard technical moves in a fantastic position up the steep headwall to a big flat hold. Move slightly right and up to a small triangular niche. Climb up a few moves before going left and up the centre of the slab to reach the top.
D Booth, J Robertson, J Beveridge - Aug 2003

7 The Gates of Delirium 57m E4 6a ★★★
This brilliant classic starts as for *Blitzkrieg*.
1 18m 6a Climb the groove to the hole. Traverse left (two old pegs) then up leftwards to a foothold stance in a groove (pegs).
2 21m 6a Step up and right to attain a standing position in the groove. Climb the groove pulling out left with difficulty passing a sloping ledge to gain another ledge. Step right above the groove and climb the wall moving right to a grass stance. Abseil point.
3 18m 6b *Relayer* finish - From the abseil point, step left and scramble up to the foot of the headwall. Climb up 5m until it is possible to swing right across the overhanging wall to a good hold on the lip. Pull over and follow the slab to the top. A fantastic finish.
P Botterill, S Clegg - Aug1976

1 Peels of Laughter E5 6b
2 Medlayer E3 5c
3 The Medlar E4 6a
4 Close to the Edge E4 5c
5 The Second Coming E6 6b/c
6 Infestation Finish E7 6c
7 The Gates of Delirium E4 6a
8 Das Kapital E6 6b
9 Blitzkrieg E4 6a
Medlar Tree
10 Communist Convert VS 4b
11 Totalitarian E1 5c
12 Empire E3 6a
13 Creation E5 6a
PR

8 Das Kapital 46m E6 6b ★★★
A tremendous route with steep sustained climbing requiring total commitment.
1 28m 6b Climb the groove to the hole as *Blitzkrieg* and follow the crack (threads) straight over the large roof (peg). Follow the intermittent crack until it is possible to swing right to the top of the flake of *Blitzkrieg*. Go back left and up *Blitzkrieg* for one metre and then traverse left for 3m (pegs) to a shallow groove which is hard to enter and initially equally hard to climb (peg) to the ledge. Move 2m left to a block belay.
2 18m 6b Climb the crack above the belay to an overhang. Move right onto an undercut slab and follow this rightwards to a niche. Move up a couple of metres and then step left to gain a thin crack. Climb the wall on the left of the crack to gain the final crack leading to the top.
P Livesey, P Gomersall - Summer1978

9 Blitzkrieg 58m E4 6a ★★★
A fine strenuous assault on the cave headwall. The climbing is well-protected with a short technical crux section. Start in the back of the cave.
1 19m 5b Climb the groove to a hole below the roof, swing right and traverse rightwards (peg) to a recess.
2 39m 6a Traverse back left to a niche and climb the flake to the overhang. Move left and break through the overhang with difficulty to belay below the chimney. Climb the chimney and exit left. Move up and follow a line of flakes out left onto the wall. Follow this to the top.
P Gomersall, P Livesey - Jul1977

10 Communist Convert 42m VS 4b ★★
Exposed and delicate on sound rock arcing from left to right across the *Totalitarian* buttress. A popular climb; a sheep among wolves. The crux is slow to dry. Start at the right-hand side of the short wall below the cave.
1 15m 4a Climb slabs and move right onto the nose.
2 27m 4b Move diagonally right to an open groove, mantelshelf onto a small ledge and continue rightwards to a small rock ledge. Traverse right and upwards, step down into a crack and move up to a large ledge and spike belay on the right and a walk off rightwards.
AR Dolphin, D Hopkin, M Dwyer, J Ramsden - May1953

11 Totalitarian 78m E1 5c ★★★
An outstanding climb, testing from the off although there is only one really hard move, by the peg near the top. Ape up to the top of the vegetated bowl to belay by a large block directly below the right-hand corner of the cave.
1 18m 5a Move left round a rib and climb a shallow corner on the right. Step down to the left across a steep wall and climb up to a niche. Move up and right on good holds and continue to a good ledge and belay below an open groove to the right of the rib flanking the cave.
2 20m 5b Climb the groove. At the top, step up right and continue slightly rightwards to belay.
3 22m 4b Move diagonally right to an open groove, mantelshelf onto a small ledge and continue rightwards to a small rock ledge. Traverse right and upwards, step down into a crack and move up to a large ledge and spike belay on the right.
4 18m 5c Step back left and climb the corner (peg) leading up to the roof and pull out right to the edge. Climb the crack above to the top.
CJS Bonington, M Thompson (pa) Sep1964; FFA E Grindley

12 Empire 63m E3 6a ★★★
An excellent wall climb. The usual arrival point is below a shallow vegetated bowl; belay at the top of this, just right of a large block; in situ sling.
1 18m 5a Move right and climb directly into a shallow groove. Continue straight up to ledges.
2 33m 5c Go left into the niche and out of its right-hand side. A ramp leads rightwards and up to a small ledge. Continue up the slab above to the obvious steep groove. Climb this and move left to easier rock. Continue rightwards to a good stance below the roof.
3 12m 6a Climb up to the overlap and pull awkwardly onto the wall above (peg) and up to the top.
K Myhill, K Jones - Sep1973; FFA J Lamb - 1974

13 Creation 33m E5 6a ★★
A fine, hard and serious undertaking. Start at an oak tree reached by abseil.
1 24m 6a Climb the left side of the arête to a groove (peg) and climb to the small overhang. Hard moves lead right and over the small overhang then up the wall.
2 9m 6a An awkward move up the wall above leads to the crack of *Totalitarian*.
P Botterill, S Clegg - Sep 1976

IRON CRAG

OS Grid Ref: NY 297 193
Altitude: 350m

Left-Hand Buttress

A steep wall high on the left has plenty of routes at the bottom of the extreme range plus a few harder ones. The rock is generally solid and clean, the lines pleasing and the climbing very worthwhile. Right-Hand Buttress, a steep subsidiary buttress lower down on the right with the clear horizontal break taken by *The Committal Chamber*, is home to one of the toughest collections of hard extremes in the region, all incredibly steep.

Approach: Park in the lay-by P NY 30022 20640, cross the main road and through the farm caravan site. Between the farm buildings go through a gate and immediately turn right uphill on a small path through the wood. Head right at the forest road and down to a bridge. Follow the beck up the valley until beneath the crag and make a short slog up the hill.

Descent: The only safe descent on foot is down the left-hand side. Or abseil.

1 Martial Law 42m E1 5b
Takes the higher of the two obvious diagonal breaks in its entirety, or finish up *The Steel Band* instead.
RO Graham, C Downer - Mar 1982

2 The Steel Band 45m E2 5b ★★
Pleasant climbing using the lower of the two diagonal breaks. Low in the grade, though the top wall requires a bold approach. Start at the foot of a small greenish ramp just right of *Martial Law*.
P Whillance, D Armstrong - Jul 1981

3 Granolithic Groove 35m E1 5b ★★
A groove running almost the full height of the crag provides excellent climbing. The hardest section is above the start, but can be protected; a cleaned rib higher up provides great climbing on positive holds.
P Whillance, J Loxham - Jun1981

4 Solidarity 35m E1 5b ★★
A thin steep crack guards the next groove to the right. The strenuous little bulge can be sidestepped right and back left using *Kryptonite*.
P Whillance, J Loxham - Jun1981

5 Kryptonite 32m E5 6b ★

The meat of this difficult route is on the otherwise blank wall in the middle of the crag. Quite tough? It's nails! Start up *Solidarity* moving steeply rightwards to a small overlap, continue right to a steep crack and climb to a break. Step up into the flake-crack, go high on the flake then smear to the break; pull through the roof. Most folk sidle off rightwards, apeing to a sloper, joining *Marble Staircase* at its crux: **E4 6a**.

RO Graham, C Downer - Apr 1982

6 Marble Staircase 32m E4 6a ★★★

A fine climb that takes in the leftward-slanting flake-crack at half-height. The steep groove slanting rightwards steeply eases at a kick back left. Climb straight up to regain the groove following it to a prominent horizontal break. Traverse right to the left-facing flake-crack, up this, then make delicate crux moves leftwards to reach the upper break below an overhang and haul over into a short groove.

P Whillance, D Armstrong - Jul 1981

7 Amabilite 32m E4 6a ★★

Good climbing, run-out between reasonable gear. Climb the slanting groove to its end. Move up and right making a mantelshelf onto a ledge. From the left side of the ledge, climb the wall above arriving at a niche on the horizontal break. Stand in the break; climb the wall above and left, reach the next break and continue directly up the wall.

N Wharton, C Gore, T Whiteley - Jun 2009

8 Hiddenite 32m E2 5c ★★★

A fantastic route with an easy start and a tricky but well-protected crux. Take a belay at a big flake. The traverse left along sloping ledges can be protected with a small cam. Go up the groove to an overhang and then move right climbing the right wall to a thin horizontal break; lace this with gear. Now you need to figure out how you will reach the next holds at and above the small overhang. Once done finish up and left.

D Armstrong, P Whillance - Jul 1981

Right-Hand Buttress

Home to some mega-hard test pieces.

Descent: To the left.

9 The Committal Chamber 57m E5 6a ★★★

Exposed and strenuous; a tremendous outing across very steep ground giving an excellent insight into the nature of the other routes. Start at the left-hand end of the buttress at a short crack in a corner below and left of the yew tree.

1 12m 4c Climb to the yew.

2 24m 6a Follow the crack to a good rest in a niche; step down right (chockstone). Set solid jams and reach a good jug before embarking on a series of committing and strenuous moves on jams and undercuts to reach the obvious sloping ledge. Well-protected; if you are strong enough to hang around.

3 21m 4c Traverse right to the end of the ledge. Move up and keep moving right round the corner to a steep grassy finish. A better alternative is to finish up the *Phoenix in Obsidian* groove.

RO Graham, C Downer - Jul 1983

10 Western Union 39m E6 6b (F7b+) ★★★

An amazing direct line up steep and difficult ground starts below a grassy ledge at 5m. Pass the grassy ledge, then climb a difficult wall (peg) and move left into a sentry box. Climb this, then the crack above and wall on the right to the bottom of a groove. Get as much of a rest as possible in the niche, then launch up the groove to the top (5 pegs - replaced 2008).

D Hall, top hat and tails... - Sep 1986

11 The Iron Man 36m E7 6c (F7c) ★★★

An awesome route incorporating the top section of *Pumping Iron*, up the wall to the left of *Western Union*. Climb *Western Union* to the break. At the base of the thin groove is a flake which sports a peg. Climb boldly up the thin groove onto the head wall, one metre left of *Western Union*, before "out-there" moves left gain undercuts and on up to a small niche. The reward for tough moves left is improving holds.

G Sutcliffe, J Fletcher - Aug 1993
A Wilson, M Johnston - Jun 2008

⓬ If 6 was 9 40m E9 7a (F8a+) ★★

This impressive route tackles the all-too-obvious blank wall in the centre of the crag with an "evilly placed ledge - finely placed to kill you if you fall from the redpoint crux! ...The gear is ...; crap." D MacLeod prior to the second ascent in 2007. Climb the initial wall (peg) to a large ledge. Move left to below the left end of a small overlap. Climb directly (3 pegs) to the break. Finish up the steep V-groove above.

D Birkett - Aug 1992

⓭ Phoenix in Obsidian 40m E7 6b (F7b) ★★★

A fairly direct line up the right-hand side of the buttress below the obvious overhang at two-thirds height. Extend your runners to avoid drag. Climb the initial wall (peg) to a large ledge. Climb up (two poor pegs) then make some hard committing moves to gain a good hold (peg; wires). Move up into the niche. Swing right and make difficult moves to gain a good hold below the roof (Rock 5). Make a difficult traverse left and pull through the overhang at its narrowest point to gain the ledge below the groove. Climb the steep V-groove above.

M Radtke - Jul 1989

9	**The Committal Chamber**	E5 6a
10	**Western Union**	E6 6b (F7b+)
11	**The Iron Man**	E7 6c (F7c)
12	**If 6 was 9**	E9 7a (F8a+)
13	**Phoenix in Obsidian**	E7 6b (F7b)

PATTERDALE

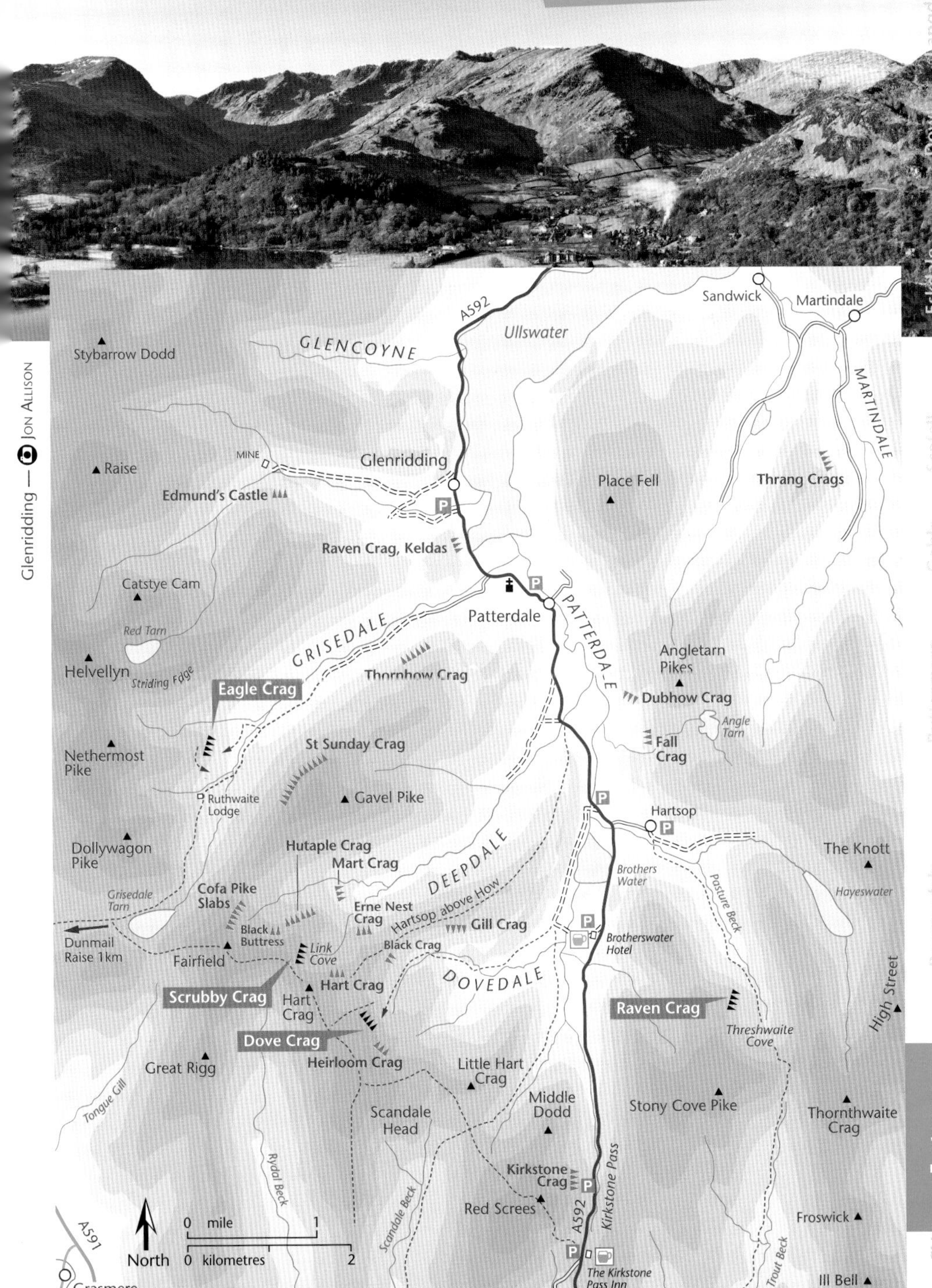

Glenridding — Jon Allison

EAGLE CRAG

OS Grid Ref: NY 357 143
Altitude: 395m

Sunny, open climbing in a delightful situation.

Approach: A road turns into a good track running all the way up the valley from Patterdale. No parking is available once you leave the A592; there's a large pay car park in Glenridding P NY 395 170 or Patterdale P NY 39592 15985.

A mountain bike knocks an hour off the long approach.

① **Hawkeye** 25m VS 4b ★★
Excellent with good positions. Climb up to a shallow groove then rightwards onto the rib. Climb straight up to The Pasture keeping left of the large perched block.
T Marr, M Tooke - Jul 2008

② **Kestrel Wall** 45 m S ★★
A simply superb climb.
1 27m Follow the crack directly to The Pasture.
2 18m The steep slab, 8m right of the stone wall then the scoop moving right to the rib.
RJ Birkett, AH Griffin - Jul 1954

3 Pericles 45m HVS 5a ★
A good route with an intimidating crux.
1 27m 4c Climb the groove to step right and up to a big spike and The Pasture.
2 18m 5a The overhanging V-chimney with a quartz jug. Climb the chimney and slab above.
O Woolcock, MS Wild - Sep 1960

4 Warbird 27m VS 4c ★★
Good enjoyable well-protected climbing. The corner/groove then step left onto the wall. Trend left to a corner/crack and the wall above to The Pasture.
T Marr, M Tooke - Aug 2008

5 Horse Power 65m E2 5c ★★
Sustained.
1 35m 5c Up the slab to just right of the V-groove and continue to better holds and crack-line up leftwards to a big spike. Back right to the steep delicate slab and reach The Pasture.
2 30m 5c The black-streaked slab to a short hanging groove. Steeply out right and up with difficulty to the steep corner above, finishing out left.
D Musgrove, G Arthur, D Musgrove - May 1989

6 Grand Day Out 37m HVS 5a ★★
Superb with good positions. Easily right to a grass ledge. Step right and climb a steep rib/groove then leftwards onto the slab. Trend slightly left to gain a small shelf. A steep shallow groove leads to The Pasture.
T Marr, M Tooke, F Fitzgerald - Jun 1999

7 Sobrenada 59m VS 4c ★★
An excellent climb with a fun crux chimney.
1 36m 4b The slab to a cave and the corner to the left. Right to the nose then direct to The Pasture.
2 23m 4c Traverse 5m right and up to a spike and back left to gain the large shallow chimney. Ascend the chimney with interest; left to a slab and ribs.
MA James, GA Leaver, KA Brookes - Jun 1957

8 Soliloquy 76m E2 5a ★★
Superb and scary.
1 36m 4b Climb to the cave and out onto the right-hand rib. Pull out of the groove and follow the edge of the rib to The Pasture.
2 40m 5a Traverse right to the prominent rib. Climb up to an obvious flat hold; the groove on the left leads to a ledge leading back to the rib and slabs.
N Allison, C Greenhow - Jun 1975

Pericles HVS Eric Parker — Ron Kenyon

SCRUBBY CRAG

OS Grid Ref: NY 367 115
Altitude: 710m

Superb climbing on steep rock with good holds in an atmospheric mountain setting.

Approach: From the car park P NY 40257 13415 at the north end of Brotherswater via the Hartsop above How ridge or slightly shorter from the top of Dunmail Raise via Grisedale Tarn and the summit of Fairfield.

① Juniper Crack 51m HS ★
A mossy start but things quickly improve.
1 23m Climb the mossy corner to the slabs.
2 11m Move up the corner until difficulties force you to step onto the left wall.
3 17m Climb the crack, move round the rib and up by the corner crack.
JC Duckworth, G Batty - May 1952

② Beowulf 54m VS 4c ★★★
Excellent spooky climbing.
1 27m 4c Up to a grassy ledge. Climb the wall above first trending right over a slight bulge then an ascending traverse to the left.
2 27m 4b Climb up to then over the left end of the prominent overhang and up the curved crack to a flake. Traverse right 5m and then up.
NJ Soper, PE Brown - Sep 1959

③ Heorot/ Darth Vader 50m HVS 5a ★★
Excellent hybrid.
1 36m 4c Climb up into the groove and follow it to a step left onto the rib then continue more easily.
2 26m 5a Climb the left edge of the wall to a wide crack leading to the top.
JW Earl, RG Hutchinson -May 1974; C Read, BWilson -Jun 1978

④ Grendel 67m MVS 4b ★★★
Superb classic.
1 39m 4b Climb up right to the groove, follow this with a move on to the right wall at the top.
2 28m 4a Climb the right hand corner of the big recess passing a pedestal and straight up past poised blocks to the top.
H Drasdo, G Batty - Jun 1956

⑤ Hrothgar 84m HVS 5a ★★
A fine route.
1 17m A grass ramp to a rock corner leading to the groove.
2 37m 5a Move right then back left up a gangway then up the groove. As it steepens, move onto the left wall and up to the ledge. Belay 11m right.
3 30m 4c Climb to a ledge then right and over a bulge then more easily.
NJ Soper, DMcE Dixon, CD Curtis - Apr 1960

DOVE CRAG

OS Grid Ref: NY 376 109
Altitude: 580m

One of the most impressive pieces of rock in the district, being sheer or overhanging for most of its height. A day here will give a memorable adventure whatever grade you choose to climb at. The concentration of sheer quality on the North Buttress makes this a 'must visit' venue for those operating competently at **F7**.

Approach: From the car park at the north end of Brotherswater P NY 40257 13415.

Descent: To the right; abseil/lower off points on North Buttress.

Main Crag

1 Westmorland's Route 110m MS ★★
An interesting mountaineering route which takes the ridge that abuts the left end of the main face. Much harder in anything less than perfect conditions, it should not be underestimated.
1 21m Easy rock leads rightwards to the grassy ridge which is followed easily to a large ledge.
2 36m Ascend the ridge on its slabby right side. Continue directly to a grassy ledge below a wall.
3 20m Traverse right on spiky brackets above a gully for 5m and ascend the mossy leftward-slanting slab to a grassy ledge on the ridge.
4 21m Climb the little wall and traverse up to the left to the end of a gangway. Move up to a large bilberry ledge; traverse right to a belay.
5 12m Climb the final wall.
H Westmorland, J Mounsey, WA North - Oct 1910

2 Dovedale Groove 54m E1 5b ★★
A classic product of the 'Rock and Ice' which takes the impending crack-line. Start at the foot of the crack behind a large boulder.
1 15m 5b From the top of the slab make an awkward move into the groove and continue, bridging and jamming, to a stance below a conspicuous overhanging crack.
2 18m 5b Climb the crack to a chockstone then pull awkwardly left onto a slab. Continue more easily up a groove and slab to a large grass ledge.
3 8m Move up to a grass ledge below some overhangs.
4 13m 5a Climb through a gap in the overhangs and step left into the left-hand groove.
DD Whillans, J Brown, D Cowan - May 1953; p4 JA Austin, NJ Soper - Jun 1963

3 Phobos 69m E2 5c ★★
A steep wall climb accepting the challenges that Hiraeth avoids. Take at least 6 long slings. Start where the path at the foot of the crag steepens to a scramble leading up to the crack of *Dovedale Groove.*
1 30m 5c Climb vegetated rock to reach a clean crack on the left of an overhang. Follow this to the middle of the traverse of *Hiraeth* and move up right to the highest of the flat rock ledges. Climb leftwards up the steep wall for 6m then move right to a shallow niche. Step back left and climb the groove, stepping left below the bulge, turning the overhang on the right to reach a stance at the foot of a terrace.
2 15m 4b Step right and climb leftwards to a gangway parallel to the terrace. Follow the gangway and the chimney above rightwards to a stance on *Hiraeth.*
3 24m 5a Climb the short corner (Hiraeth) and move right, past a large spike, to below a large corner. Ascend the corner and hand-traverse right along a thin crack below a roof, then move up to gain easier ground.
C Read, J Adams - Aug 1972 PA. FFA P Long, R Valentine - Spring 1974

4 Extol 92m E2 5b ★★
"*Extol* is rather like Whillans; direct, uncompromising and hard." Chris Bonington: Hard Rock. This route forces its way up the centre of the crag and, like its neighbour, suffers from lack of use. The start to *Hangover*, at the right side of the triangle of slabs just left of a big boulder.
1 47m 5a Climb the grassy groove and then traverse right to a belay below the corner. Climb the corner for 12m then traverse left with difficulty for 3m. Step up and re-enter the corner over a bulge. Move up and climb a small chimney then step round the rib to a good stance.
2 45m 5b The grassy leftward-slanting ramp 6m left of the stance is the initial objective. Cross on a series of good jugs to reach the ramp. Climb this to reach the short steep wall and the big overhang. Step right and pull into a bottomless groove which splits the overhang. Follow this until forced to move right to finish up the rib.
DD Whillans, C Mortlock - Apr 1960 PA.

North Buttress

All the climbs on this tremendous leaning wall offer spectacular and strenuous climbing on accommodating rock covered with generally good flat or incut holds. Protection is adequate, with

1
2
3
4
4
Hiraeth E2
Hangover HVS
AP

1 Westmorland's Route MS
2 Dovedale Groove E1 5b
3 Phobos E2 5c
4 Extol E2 5b
5 Dusk till Dawn E7 6b (F7c)
6 Bucket Dynasty E7 6b (F7c)
7 Vlad the Impailer E7 6b (F7c)
8 Fear and Fascination E5 6a (F7a+)
9 Bucket City E6 6b (F7b)
10 Fast City E5 6a (F7a)
11 Fast and Furious E5 6a (F7a)
12 Flying Fissure Finish E5 6b (F7a+)
Pail Face E6
A
9
8
11
12
5
7
6
9
11
8

a selection of small cams up to size 2 useful. The routes on the North Buttress are generally clean and equipped with *in-situ* gear. French grades are not intended to suggest a clip-up! They merely give some idea of the technical climbing you can expect to find – but without the security of bolts.

5 Dusk till Dawn 30m E7 6b (F7c) ★★★
An awesome route, one of the steepest lines in the Lakes. A double set of small cams is recommended. Start at the obvious layback crack below the right end of the grassy terrace. Follow *Bucket Dynasty* through its crux and move right for a couple of metres to good holds (Friend 0.5 or Wallnut 6). Make moves up and rightwards to gain the right side of the pillar. A series of big moves on good holds following a leftwards-leaning ramp leads to a huge shake out below a ramp (cam 1). Make hard moves up (peg) and leftwards to superb jugs on the left side of the pillar. More huge moves lead to a small ledge. The tricky groove above is climbed to another ledge.
C Hope, A Wilson - Jul 2003

6 Bucket Dynasty 25m E7 6b (F7c) ★★★
Another steep exciting climb on good rock. Climb the flake crack to its top and follow the wall above until a move left leads to huge holds (2.5 Friend). Climb the intimidating wall above to a good layaway (1 and 00 Friends). Pull up again to gain *Vlad the Impailer* at the Friend 3. Finish up this.
M Berzins, N Foster - May 1991

7 Vlad the Impailer 35m E7 6b (F7c) ★★★
Stupendous, bold and very strenuous climbing make this an unforgettable route. This is the obvious fault-line leading out leftwards from *Fear and Fascination* to the bay above. The pegs and *in-situ* tat were replaced in 2011. Long slings essential. Start at the foot of the rock step. Follow *Fear and Fascination* to the good flake. Swing left to a jug and then another (0 Friend), then traverse left (in situ Rock 1 and vital Friend 2.5). Undercut left to a downward pointing spike and good footholds, then pull up left (Rock 1 and crucial Friend 0.5 or Wallnut 6). Swing down across left (Friend 3) then climb up (peg) to a jug (Friend 1 or 1.5 on right). Gain the block and niche up and left (crux) (peg) and continue up the fault-line (peg and thread) (krabs). The second climbs to the rock shelf to lower.
M Berzins, N Foster - Aug 1990

8 Fear and Fascination 48m E5 6a (F7a+) ★★★
A classic climb; bold, strenuous, intimidating and maintaining interest right to the top. Brilliant. Climb the flake crack to the rock shelf and pull up the wall at the right end (old peg). Continue up the wall to a good flake and then less easily to a short crozzly crack. Hand-traverse right and pull into the niche on *Bucket City* (old pegs). Step right and up, passing an obvious spike, to gain the right end of the ledge system and a good rest. Climb the fine groove-line above, making a sneaky step out right when all the holds seem to run out, finishing via the obvious deep groove.
RO Graham, TW Birkett - Jun 1980

9 Bucket City 45m E6 6b (F7b) ★★★
Another tremendous pitch, this time taking the obvious diagonal crack to the left of *Fast and Furious* and an intricate line up the superb headwall. Layback the starting flake and step left into a shallow cave. Pull over the bulge and climb up to the break. Step left round the rib to the base of a thin diagonal crack sporting several old pegs. Fight the stubborn crack to a rest in the niche (*Fear and Fascination* gains this point from the left) then climb up and rightwards as for *Fear and Fascination*, passing a conspicuous spike to gain the right end of the obvious ledge system and a good rest. Make a couple of moves up the groove above before breaking out left via a line of holds on the lip of an overlap. These lead to an obvious slot from which a line of reasonable holds, breaks and ledges lead directly up the wall (peg).
M Berzins, N Foster - May 1988

10 Fast City 37m E5 6a (F7a) ★★★
Follow *Fast and Furious* to the top of the groove. Move left to the prominent spike, follow *Bucket City*.

11 Fast and Furious 45m E5 6a (F7a) ★★★
Bold, sustained and memorable. The name suggests the required approach! Several long narrow tapes are useful for the small spikes. Layback to the top of the flake then climb the short bold rib to the base of a smooth wall guarding entry to the groove. Neatly avoid this obstacle with a step up to the right before hand-traversing back left to the base of the groove (peg). Layback boldly up the groove to better holds and runners then trend rightwards passing a tiny spike. Extend to gain a superb hidden jug on top of a short rib (crux). Climb the wall (bold) right, left, then straight up, aiming for the obvious finishing chimney. Belay above this or continue up to a better anchor on the left.
RO Graham, D Lyle, TW Birkett - May 1982

12 Flying Fissure Finish E5 6b (F7a+) ★★★
A superbly steep and deservedly more popular right-hand finish to *Fast and Furious* following the hanging groove right of the chimney of *Fast and Furious*. From the superb jug after the crux move right (peg) then race up the tough wall (thread) to gain a line of buckets which lead up the sensational groove to the top.
N Foster, M Berzins - Aug 1990

Fast and Furious E5 Craig Smith — Steve Crowe

RAVEN CRAG THRESHTHWAITE

OS Grid Ref: NY 419 112
Altitude: 450m

¾ hr

For those operating at **E3** and above this is one of the best crags in the Lakes. The rock is solid, compact and steep, providing tremendous, athletic climbing. A great days climbing is assured.

Redex E2 (page 434) Keith Phizacklea — Rob Matheson

1 Grand Prix 40m E3 5c ★★★
Strenuous, well-protected and justifiably popular. Climb the corner to below the overhang at the break. Move right slightly and pull into the steep crack. Gain the leftward-slanting ramp above with difficulty and follow the line more or less directly into the final groove/crack system.
P Whillance, R Berzins, P Botterill - Sep 1980

2 Internal Combustion 40m E6 6b ★★★
High octane fuel recommended. A superb wall climb; bold, then technically demanding. Climb the groove a few metres right of *Grand Prix* to the break. Committing moves over the first overlap (peg) reach better holds leading diagonally right. Climb up to a small overhang (pegs), then firing on all cylinders, unravel the difficult sequence directly up wall.
R Smith, JW Earl - Jun 1986

3 Top Gear 40m E4 6a ★★★
Top Route! Climb the wall, crack and groove to reach ledges below the right edge of the Shield. Move right and climb a short flake-crack until a pull up left can be made into a steep groove. Swing left to gain a large sloping foothold on the bottom right-hand edge of the Shield. Reach the obvious line of holds which trend leftwards across the Shield until a vague groove is reached. Follow this then step right and mantelshelf onto the large sloping ramp. Step right and climb the short corner to the top.
P Whillance, D Armstrong - May 1981

4 Redex 30m E2 5b ★★
This classic diagonal line gives fine sustained climbing. Climb the diagonal crack to the horizontal fault. Hang in there to get good protection! Follow the crack to the small tree. Step right into the steep, awkward groove and follow this with a move right at the top.
CW Brown, TW Birkett - Jul 1976

5 G.T.X. 40m E3 5c ★★★
An impressive and sustained route taking a direct line through *Redex*. Start 5m right of *Redex* at a shallow groove. Climb the groove rightwards to the scoop, step left and climb steeply to the horizontal fault. Follow the crack to the small tree and then climb left and up to the overhang. Pull over this into the groove and up to a second overhang. Climb this on the right to finish.
P Whillance, R Parker - May 1980

6 Running on Empty 35m E4 6a ★★★
You may well be by the time you reach the top! Excellent climbing. Take small wires. Climb the groove (bold) heading for the right end of the large overhang where a large spike will be found. Use this to swing right with a committing move onto the wall above, which is climbed delicately to a large groove right of *Redex*. Follow the groove to the top with an awkward finish.
J Lamb, P Botterill - Jul 1981

7 Boy Racer 37m E4 6a ★★★
A great climb! Climb the right-hand side of the arch with a tough move into a slim groove on the right. Follow this boldly to a good ledge and up the ramp to the break near the ravens' nest. (possible belay but better to continue). Climb the short left-slanting ramp/groove past a quartz crack then make a thin move up and left to reach the next crack and so into the groove. Climb the groove and rib on the left up to the break. Excellent climbing into and up the groove above leads to the top.
P Botterill, J Lamb - Jun 1981

8 Liquid Engineering 38m E6 6b ★★★
Sustained, steep and sparsely protected with a most deceptive and serious top pitch. Start at a vague white scoop.
1 24m 6b Climb into the scoop; either head up and leftwards until above a peg (wires) then step down left to clip, or move across left and up on layaways to the peg. Above the peg tentatively move left across the blank slab to a good side-hold. Climb the wall above to a diagonal crack then more easily to a ledge. Step right to a scoop and follow the slab to a large block.
2 25m 6b Move up the ramp for 2m and pull into a large bottomless groove (tape) reaching good footholds. Climb the groove making some very technical moves and then continue more easily. Spike belays well back.
P Rigby, A Murray - Sep 1984

9 High Performance 40m E5 6b ★★★
A wide repertoire is needed for this tremendous climb; aptly named. Start below the vague white scoop in the lower wall.
1 25m 6b The thin diagonal crack; the meaty bit above the slot is hard.
2 15m 6a Climb into the large groove above. Move across right to a good jug on the arête and then step back left into the groove which is followed to the ledge above the capping roof. Finish up the wall above. Belay well back to the left on spikes.
P Botterill, J Lamb - May 1981

Approach: From a small car park in Hartsop P NY 41032 13020 follow the path until the crag can be clearly seen on the right, slanting diagonally up the hillside. Best to take the line of the old dry stone wall to the crag. Steep!

Descent: Abseil.

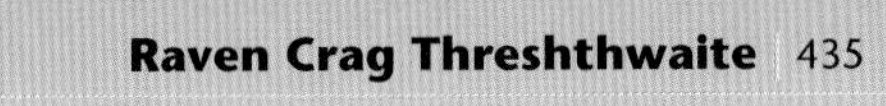

1 The Blunder 25m HVS 5a ★
The steep chimney/crack.
S Hubbard - Mar 1982

2 Express Crack 33m E1 5b ★★★
The burly corner is well-protected by large cams.
JA Austin, DG Roberts, JJS Allison - Oct 1969

3 The Clangers 33m E1 5b ★★
Climb to the obvious line of flakes and follow them to the ledge and the slab above.
JW Earl, R Smith - Jul 1986

4 The Hog's Back 34m HVS 5a ★★
A fine route with a hard move to enter the the groove.
JD Llewellyn, A Sutton - Sep 1956

5 Slab and Rib 32m VD ★
Enjoyable and worthwhile. Climb the slab then work left to the rib.
D Atherton, JD Llewellyn - Sep 1956

BUCKBARROW CRAG

30 mn

OS Grid Ref: NY 483 073
Altitude: 335m

6 Dandle Buttress 46m S ★

A good climb up a fine feature.

1 14m Easy rocks to a corner and then twin cracks.

2 15m The broad ridge to a ledge then a chimney on the left to Spike Minor.

3 17m Continue to the top.

JD Best, M Linnell, H Johnson - Jun 1926

7 Sadgill Wall 100m S ★★

A very good climb.

1 20m Climb the slab until it steepens. Step right and ascend to a grassy ledge.

2 20m Climb the rightward slanting flake/crack then the slab on the left.

3 30m Traverse sensationally right across the steep slab to its right edge and ascend directly up into the grassy bay above.

4 30m Cross the right wall of the bay, up the broken ridge and easy rocks above.

AH Griffin, CE Arnison, T Philipson - 1949

Approach: From Sadgill, P NY 48326 05743, follow the main track up the valley for two kilometres until below the crag. A stile gives access to the steep final approach. A mountain bike speeds up access along the good track.

GOUTHER CRAG

OS Grid Ref: NY 515 127
Altitude: 330m

Excellent climbing across the grades in an unspoilt secluded valley – often dry when the central Lakes areas are wet.

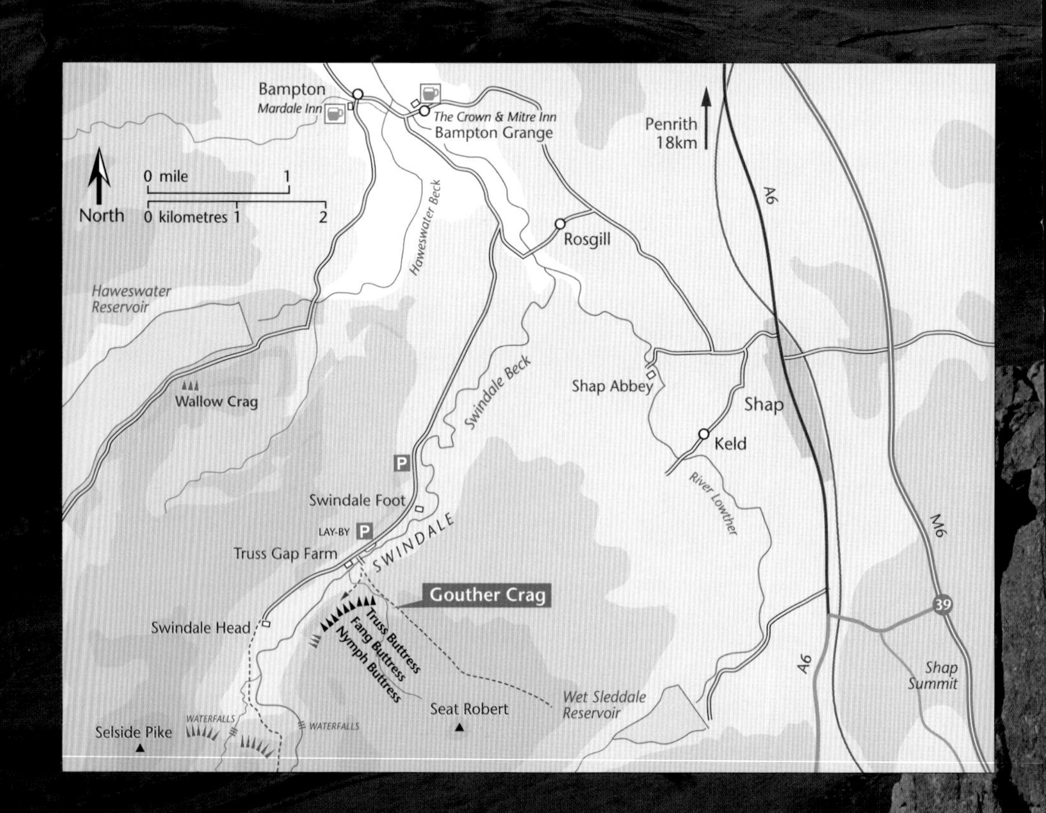

The Dalesman E5 (page 443) Nick Wharton — Tim Whiteley

Fang Buttress catches the afternoon sun.

Approach: There is no parking at Truss Gap Farm. A few hundred metres east is a large open parking area, P NY 52139 14219. From the farm cross the river and follow tracks to the crags.

Truss Buttress

1 Castration Crack 27m E3 6a ★★
Great climbing with a high crux up the thin crack-line.
P Whillance, P Botterill - Jul 1980

2 The Bone 22m S
Climb up leftwards and follow the right side of the slab and the groove above.
RJ Kenyon - Jun 1974

3 Slab Start 20m S ★
Climb the slab and right facing groove above.
S Miller - Aug 1974

4 Truss Buttress 38m VD ★★
Delightful climbing up the arête onto a little slab to the left and the rib above.
RH Fidler, CE Arnison - Aug 1933

5 Sam 20m S ★
An enjoyable pitch up the slab and V-corner.
S Miller, A Miller - 1976

6 Times of Stress 30m E3 6a ★★
Well-protected crack climbing. Take a short steep crack onto a slab. Pull up past a break to reach a thin crack which leads, with a brief deviation right at a spike, to a good ledge and the scoop above.
P Whillance, P Botterill - Jul 1980

7 Hernia 22m E1 5b ★★
Entertaining, well-protected moves offer a devious start to *Scabby Horse*. Leftwards to gain the top of the flake, then steeply rightwards round a bulge to go directly up the groove.
B Rogers, W Day - 1976

8 Scabby Horse 20m VS 5a
A pleasant ramp and groove. Or at **E3 5c** go directly up the steep wall.
RJ Kenyon, A Greenhow - Aug 1973

Borrowdale Buttermere Gable Scafell Eskdale Dow Langdale
Eastern

The Fang MVS Rob Thomas — Ron Kenyon

Fang Buttress

1 Sostenuto 36m HVS 5a ★★
A splendid route.
1 28m 5a Climb the flake crack and then the steep wall to ledges. Move left along a crack and up an easy rib.
2 28m The easy crack on the right.
H Drasdo, RB Evans, NJ Soper, RP Harris - Aug 1958

2 Fang Direct 30m HVS 5a ★★
A very enjoyable route. Climb the crack past the overlap and continue up to gain the shallow scoop; exit rightwards. Finish easily up the blunt rib.
RM Flood, JR Sutcliffe - Jul1974

3 The Fang 40m MVS 4a ★★★
Superb with great positions.
1 20m 4a Climb to the holly, traverse diagonally left to ledges and climb a steep thin crack.
2 20m Ascend the steep arête at the right end of the ledge to a platform and the rib above.
JS Williams, CR Wilson, T Nicholson, RA Ewin - Oct 1946

4 Left Edge 39m S ★
A steep but well-protected route.
1 24m Climb the groove and move out left. Surmount the small overhang and climb a crack and wall to finish in the V-corner.
2 The wall and groove above.
C Griffiths, G Oliver - Mar 1966

5 The Doghouse 39m MVS 4b ★★
Climb the groove and walk left to a niche. Climb the steep crack and the wall to the foot of the right-facing V-groove. Finish up the groove.
R Wilkinson, B Peace - Aug 2003

6 Kennel Wall 37m S ★★
A delightful route.
1 26m Ascend the crack and groove above.
2 11m The crack to the right.
JS Williams, CR Wilson, T Nicholson, RA Ewin, GH Tyson - Oct 1946

7 Bloodhound 37m E2 5b ★★★
Brilliant, absorbing, sustained slab climbing. Easily up right (side runners). Cross the slab to gain an obvious flake to the left. Directly up then right to the base of an obvious groove. Climb the groove.
RG Hutchinson, JW Earl - Jul 1978

8 Hindleg Crack 22m S ★★
A classic struggle up the obvious chimney.
JS Williams CR Wilson T Nicholson RA Ewin GH Tyson - Oct 1946

9 The Dalesman 24m E5 6b ★★
From *Dogleg Crack* go left, directly through the roof (peg) and finish up the slab.
R Patterson, A Scott – Jun 1998

10 One Step Beyond 24m E4 6a ★★★
Superb climbing in a great position. Follow the crack then traverse down above the lip to reach a resting foothold. Bold climbing just right of the arête leads to the top.
I Williamson, J White - May 1980

11 Dogleg Crack 13m HVS 5a ★
Battle your way up.
RJ Kenyon, S Howe - Aug 1977

EDEN VALLEY & SOUTH LAKES LIMESTONE

Armathwaite

An excellent quality sandstone outcrop in a beautiful woodland setting. A reliable wet weather alternative to the Lakes; best in the winter and spring.

Chapel Head Scar

With perfect, smooth, compact limestone and rough tufa formations Chapel Head Scar is a brilliant all-year sport climbing destination. Impressively steep, the crag overlooks the idyllic Witherslack valley on the sunny west side of Whitbarrow only a short walk from the car. Routes have been re-equipped over recent years.

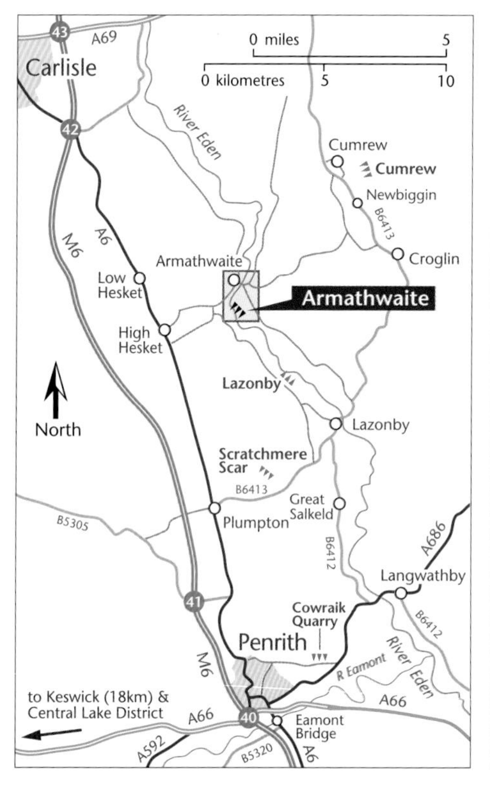

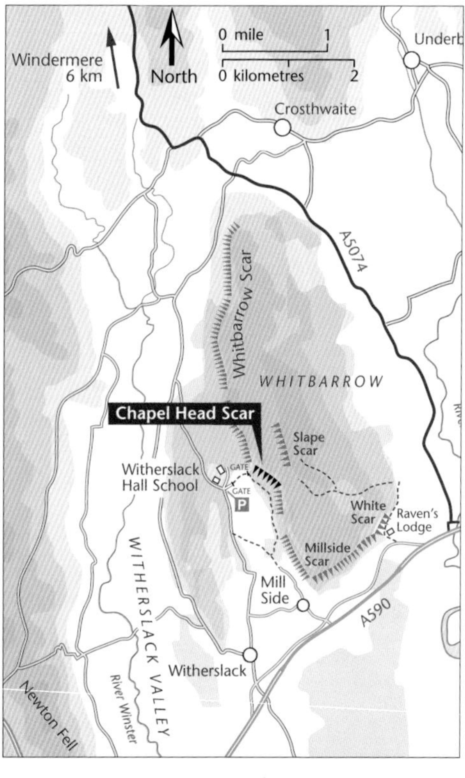

Definitive Guidebook
Eden Valley &
South Lakes Limestone

Eden Valley & South Lakes Limestone

☐ *Up Town* F6c (page 464) Yan Preston — Nick Wharton

ARMATHWAITE

OS Grid Ref: NY 505 452
Altitude: 50m

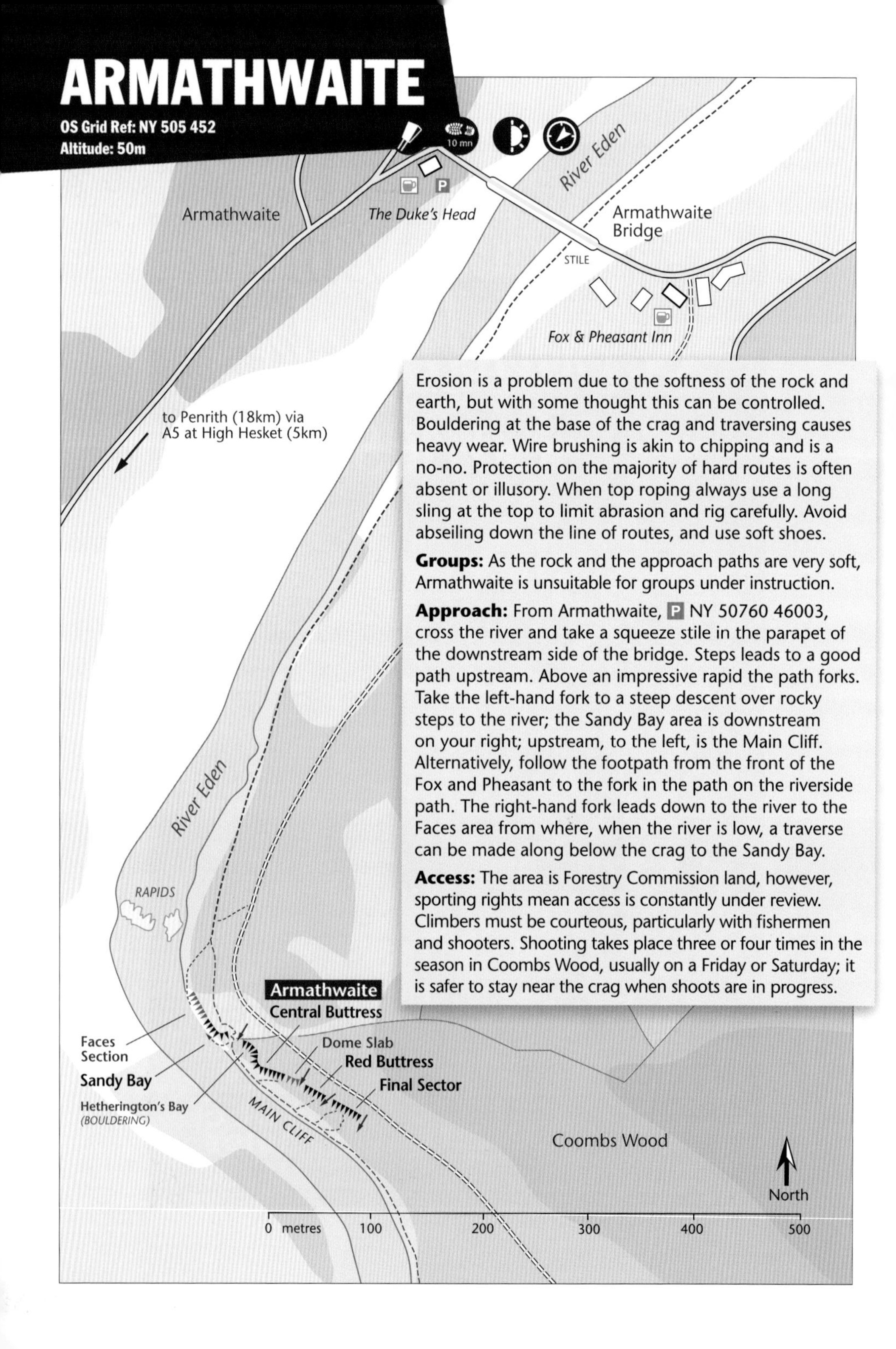

Erosion is a problem due to the softness of the rock and earth, but with some thought this can be controlled. Bouldering at the base of the crag and traversing causes heavy wear. Wire brushing is akin to chipping and is a no-no. Protection on the majority of hard routes is often absent or illusory. When top roping always use a long sling at the top to limit abrasion and rig carefully. Avoid abseiling down the line of routes, and use soft shoes.

Groups: As the rock and the approach paths are very soft, Armathwaite is unsuitable for groups under instruction.

Approach: From Armathwaite, P NY 50760 46003, cross the river and take a squeeze stile in the parapet of the downstream side of the bridge. Steps leads to a good path upstream. Above an impressive rapid the path forks. Take the left-hand fork to a steep descent over rocky steps to the river; the Sandy Bay area is downstream on your right; upstream, to the left, is the Main Cliff. Alternatively, follow the footpath from the front of the Fox and Pheasant to the fork in the path on the riverside path. The right-hand fork leads down to the river to the Faces area from where, when the river is low, a traverse can be made along below the crag to the Sandy Bay.

Access: The area is Forestry Commission land, however, sporting rights mean access is constantly under review. Climbers must be courteous, particularly with fishermen and shooters. Shooting takes place three or four times in the season in Coombs Wood, usually on a Friday or Saturday; it is safer to stay near the crag when shoots are in progress.

Sandy Bay

This popular area has many good boulder problems in the "Bay", notably traverses.

1 Kingfisher 16m S ★★
Steep and satisfying, with big holds and Deep Water Soloing potential. Traverse left just above the river and with inital difficulty up an open groove. An easy corner is followed to an awkward move over an overlap and up to the top, or move left and finish up an awkward slab.
S Wilson, A Yarrow - May 1973

The following three routes are extended boulder problems that gain a big ledge half-way up the crag: either finish up *Time and Motion Man* or jump into the river!

2 Kaleidoscope Eyes 15m E2 5b (V2) ★
Start from the top of the sawn stump; move up and leftwards to tackle the arête direct.
M Tomlinson - Aug 1986

3 Grey Duster 15m E3 6a (V4) ★★
An entertaining climb with a steep start. 2m right of the stump climb the centre of the bulging wall into a very shallow groove. A good hold on the left enables the final crack to be viewed; climb to the ledge.
J Lamb -1975

4 The Arête 15m E3 6b (V7) ★★
A slap happy problem which should quarantee hours of fun! Levitate up the slopers to the conspicuous little blackened pocket at 3m, rejoice, and continue on better holds.

5 Time and Motion Man 16m E1 5c ★★
A popular challenge starting in the alcove. Move up and leftwards with great difficulty and some contortions onto a very narrow wall under some small square-cut overhangs. Better holds lead to jugs below a little bulge guarding a fine groove. Enter the groove with some relief and exit almost immediately on its left wall to gain a good ledge. Either move left and climb a slight groove to an awkward finish or go straight up at a slim corner.
R Kenyon, T Dale, S Wilson - May 1973

6 The Exorcist 18m E4 5c ★★★
This route put the "arm" in Armathwaite. An excellent, steep and compelling line on good clean rock. From the base of *Glenwillie Grooves Direct* a hard pull onto a ledge leads up to a peg at 5m. Move out with trepidation to a pocket on the right. A sequence of strenuous and technical moves lead back left then straight up. Rising doubts as to the peg's solidity urge one upwards to a good ledge. From the sanctuary of the ledge a bulge is climbed into the top groove. It is best to exit on the left.
J Lamb - 1974

7 Glenwillie Grooves Direct 16m MVS 4b ★
S Wilson, A Yarrow - May 1973

8 Glenwillie Grooves 18m HS 4b ★★
A popular climb with a short, sharp and very safe crux in a fine position right at the top. Start from a tar-spattered ledge just right of the corner. Climb the wall and slab to a sheaf of saplings. Climb to the left of the saplings and finish with a steep pull to a ledge below the final corner,
S Wilson, A Yarrow - May 1973

9 Harry's Arete 16m E1 5b
Climb the narrow groove just right of *Glenwillie Grooves* and, from large footholds, swing awkwardly left onto the arête and around to an easier angled slab. Climb the slab and finish as for *Harry's Groove.*
R Kenyon, S Thompson - 1978

10 Harry's Groove 16m HS 4b
Climb the main right-sloping groove towards a loose break in a bulge. Move over this into a heathery recess then left along a ledge and layback the stepped corner.
R Kenyon, J Morton - Jan 1975

11 Smiling Faces 16m VS 4b ★
Climb the blunt arête on the right of the wall on small but good holds until a hard move enables one to step up onto a slab. Gain a ledge and follow the short slab rightwards, as for *The Thirty-Nine Steps*, until steep moves lead up to finish at a solid tree.
M Holden, D Holden, M Tomlinson - Aug 1986

12 The Thirty-Nine Steps 13m VD ★
Climb the slab using small ledges to a triangular ledge. Gain a higher bigger ledge, then ascend the short slab rightwards until steep moves up the wall above lead to a satisfying pull out at a solid tree.
S Wilson - 1980

	Route	Grade
1	**Kingfisher**	S
2	**Kaleidoscope Eyes**	E2 5b (V2)
3	**Grey Duster**	E3 6a (V4)
4	**The Arête**	E3 6b (V7)
5	**Time and Motion Man**	E1 5c
6	**The Exorcist**	E4 5c
7	**Glenwillie Grooves Direct**	MVS 4b
8	**Glenwillie Grooves**	HS 4b
9	**Harry's Arete**	E1 5b
10	**Harry's Groove**	HS 4b
11	**Smiling Faces**	VS 4b
12	**The Thirty-Nine Steps**	VD

RK

10
9
8
7
6
9
10
7
5
6
7
8
9
4
10
Sandy Bay

Glenwillie Grooves HS (page 447) Catherine Kenyon — RON KENYON

Central Buttress

This is the complex buttress nearest the riverside path. Bounded on the left by Hetherington's Bay - a popular bouldering area. On the right is a very open and interesting face with remarkable rock architecture, a fine towering arête on the right and a gigantic block overhang to the left. An open book corner marks the line of the superb *Flasherman*.

Descent: A narrow path along the top of the buttress (slippery when wet!) can be followed leftwards then down a steep grassy slope to meet the main approach path above the steps. Alternatively the narrow path right leads to a steep earthy gully, right of Domed Slab area.

13	**Flasherman**	VS 4b
14	**Flasherman Direct**	HVS 5a
15	**Erection**	E1 5a
16	**Viennese Oyster**	E3 5c

13 Flasherman 26m VS 4b ★★★
A classic! One of the best sandstone climbs anywhere! Low technicality, but a runout crux ensures an adventurous experience.
A Yarrow, S Wilson - May 1973

14 Flasherman Direct 25m HVS 5a ★
From the top of the corner instead of moving right, climb the steep continuation corner to gain a ledge; continue up and rightwards to finish.
P Whillance - Mar 1975

15 Erection 26m E1 5a ★★★
Little protection high up enhances the experience. Boulder the wall and move around the distinctive overhang to a stunning direct finish.
J Lamb, A Liddell - Jan 1974

16 Viennese Oyster 27m E3 5c ★
An daunting line; varied climbing in superb positions. Climb the steep wall and slab to below the lower block overhangs. Traverse right to an obvious jug on the bulge. Pull over then step left and move over a small, triangular roof (peg). Either span high and right for good holds then traverse steeply right round the arête to the top, or climb directly up the wall above.
G Brown, H Loughran - Sep 1987

Final Sector

A long section commences with the steep wall of *Free 'N' Easy*; further right, a large boulder abutting against the face forms a low tunnel. The deep corner on the right of this is *Barnacle Bill*. Attractive slabs steepen into pocketed walls containing *Pickpocket*.

Descent: Either end.

17 Free'N' Easy 12m E5 6a ★★★
An outstanding, absorbing and serious climb requiring technical competence and a cool approach. Reach good holds in the first break. A hard pull on the next break leads to a rest. Move slightly right onto the sloping holds in the break (wires) and ease up leftwards to use the best of a cluster of pockets to get established on sloping footholds below the top crack. Climb the crack with rising hopes that are soon shattered as the top is approached.
P Whillance, A Greig - May 1974

18 The Crescent 13m E3 5b ★★
The curving shelf forms the basis of this climb with its intimidating and unprotected crux; much easier for the tall. Start just left of the tunnel.
J Lamb, M Hetherington - Feb 1974

19 Jelly Terror 9m E1 5b ★★
A strenuous but protectable crack climb
J Lamb, M Hetherington - Feb 1974

20 Y-Front 11m E2 5b ★
A bold climb on generally positive holds.
P Botterill, M Hetherington - Mar 1974

21 Barnacle Bill 13m E1 5b ★★
A superb classic corner with a delicate and fairly bold crux.
R Kenyon, S Wilson - Summer 1973; FFA J Lamb -1974

22 Codpiece Left-Hand 12m E1 5b ★★
The more attractive finish to *Codpiece*. Climb the crack and gain the ramp, by a difficult step up, and follow this to easier climbing leftwards to the top.
A Yarrow, S Wilson - Summer 1973

23 Codpiece 12m E2 5c ★★
This offers poor jams, finger-locks and layaways. Direct, without resorting to the ramp, is **6a**.
A Yarrow, S Wilson, R May - Summer 1973; FFA J Lamb -1974

24 Pickpocket 10m E3 5c ★★
When clean this is a very fine climb of sustained difficulty and interest. Climb *Codpiece* to a line of foot pockets leading right; a difficult hand change and a long reach gain better holds in more pockets and a hand-ledge in a horizontal slot. Pull onto the wall above and climb this via a prominent protuberance.
P Whillance - Sep 1974

CHAPEL HEAD SCAR

OS Grid Ref: SD 443 862
Altitude: 70m

The crag is often in good condition, although some areas suffer from seepage after prolonged rain. It gets the sun in the afternoon and evening. Midges can occasionally be troublesome but of more concern are ticks; the whole area is infested. More likely to be found on your dog, humans will do just as nicely!

Access: Consult the BMC RAD. The site is an important site for rare plants, a National Nature Reserve within an SSSI and the Morecambe Bay SAC. The site is recognised as a climbing venue of national importance and climbers enjoy an excellent relationship with the National Park Rangers. This could easily be ruined by any selfish disregard of the agreed restrictions. Certain reasonable rules apply to climbing at the crag:

- No climbing left of Central Gully Wall.
- Use only marked paths.
- No gardening on or above the crag.
- Trees must not be damaged.
- Use lower-off points - Do not top-out from any route.
- Do not leave any litter whatsoever - finger tape, banana skins, orange peel, chalk wrappers, etc.
- Go before you go.

Approach: M6 - J36 - A590 Witherslack. Through the village follow the road for about 5km to the entrance to Witherslack Hall School; parking area on the right, P SD 43701 85948. The crag will be seen above the woods across the fields. Through a gate the path crosses the field to a second gate into the woods. Follow the track up and right for 200m, take the path on the left, cross a scree slope and up a short steep section to arrive at the crag between Moonchild Buttress and the Interstellar Area. See map page 444.

Tufa King Hard F6c (page 465) Michael kenyon — Ron Kenyon

Great Gully Wall

Routes start at the furthest left end of the accessible part of the crag. Right of the horribly vegetated Central Gully is Central Gully Wall with a number of enjoyable easier short routes.

1. **Cool Your Jets Mum** 7a
2. **Le Flange en Decomposition** 6b+
3. **Gully Wall** 6b
4. **Johnny No Mates** 6c
5. **Gully Wall Direct** 6c+
6. **Winter Pincher** 6b+
7. **Oddbods** 6b
8. **Strongbow** 6b
9. **Comedy Show** 6b

10
11
12
13
14
15
16
17
25m
AP

Interstellar Area

Steep climbing on solid clean rock with some of the best routes on the crag, lies immediately left of the point where the path arrives at the crag.

⑩ Jelly Head 7a ★

⑪ Interstellar Overdrive 6c ★★★
A great route, one of the best lower end sports routes on the crag.

⑫ Sun God 6a+ ★★
A good warm up, following the flake past the yew and up the bulging wall above.

⑬ Cement Head 7a+ ★★
Although this is only really half a route (the top half!), it does climb over superb rock. The start up the unbolted groove requires a couple of wires or climb *Interstellar Overdrive*.

Combat Plumber 7a ★
A worthwhile combination that allows easier access to the top of *War of the Worlds/Phantom Zone*. Good entertainment value. From the ledge below the Interstellar tree, step out right as for Cement Head but keep going until beneath the upper groove of *Phantom Zone*. Climb the thin wall to the overlap then step right to climb the groove above.

⑭ Zantom Phone 7c+ ★★

⑮ Phantom Zone 7b+ ★★★
Brilliant! Consider linking this with *Cement Head* for a tremendous outing.

⑯ Stan Pulsar 7b ★
A good route; Make the rock-over move to reach the tufa sidepull on *Phantom Zone* then swing steeply right.

⑰ Surfing with the Alien 8a ★
Even more steep and fingery than its neighbours!

18
19
20
21
22
23
24
25/35m
AP

Moonchild Buttress

The soaring buttress right of where the path arrives offers some of the longest routes at Chapel Head Scar.

18 Bleep and Booster 6c ★★

19 Moonchild 24m E4 5c ★★
A significant route in the early development of the crag which takes the obvious striking deep groove. The protection is good – where you can get it!

20 War of the Worlds 37m 6c+ ★★
Tie a knot in the end of the rope! A long route that winds its way up and left across the buttress, taking in a lot of excellent climbing along the way. Climb *Moonchild* into the groove and swing left into *Bleep and Booster*, keep traversing left to the groove of *Stan Pulsar*. Go up this to the resting place on the left. When you are ready, step down then head up and left above *Phantom Zone*, then up to the right-hand end of the roof, just left of the widest groove (*Phantom Zone*). Pull right into the groove and follow it to the belay up on the left.

21 62 West Wallaby Street 7a+ ★
The residents of this famous address would probably find some ingenious way of getting to the top – you will probably need to rely on power and technique!

22 War Hero F7a ★★
A great route. Starts up the wall behind the tree.

23 Tricky Prick Ears F7b ★★★
A tremendous route with a lot of climbing. Start a couple of metres up the slope from the tree at a shallow blank groove. Climb this to reach the obvious flake. Make a difficult move (crux) out left and up to easier ground. Move up and right, over the next bulge, to reach a resting position on the left. Move up and right across the steep white wall to reach the hanging groove. Make hard moves to enter and then follow this groove to the top. Awesome!

24 Maboulisme Merveilleux F7c+ ★★
A short spectacular route up incredibly steep rock way out there above Great Gully. It can be slow to dry but once it is dry there are no excuses left; you just have to do it. Start at a ledge with a bolt belay some way up the gully.

25 The Route of
26 Eraser Head
27 Cyborg
28 Mid-Air Collisi
29 The Borg
30 Omega Factor
31 Half-Life
32 Up Town
33 Witherslack A
25
26
27
28
29
30
25/30m
AP

F7a+
F7b+
(E2 5c) F6b+
F7b
F7a+
F6c
F6b+
F6c
F6c
31
32
33
25m
Langdale
Scafell
Gable
Buttermere
Borrowdale
Eastern
EV

Route of All Evil Wall

A solid wall of rock with an amazing headwall.

25 The Route of All Evil F7a+ ★★
A great route meandering up this excellent wall.

26 Eraser Head F7b+ ★★★
A more direct route up the wall, which includes the original direct finish to *The Route of All Evil*.

27 Cyborg 21m (E2 5c) F6b+ ★
Can be done on bolts alone, but very sporting!

28 Mid-Air Collision F7b ★★★
A companion route to *Eraser Head*, taking a parallel line to the right. Many variations are possible, using sections of the above routes e.g. some say follow *Mid-Air Collision* to *The Route of All Evil* traverse then head left to finish as for *Eraser Head*.

29 The Borg F7a+ ★★
Start up *Omega Factor*, climbing the crux moves of this before traversing left to the groove of *The Route of All Evil*. Follow this to the break then head right to climb the arête right of *Mid-Air Collision*.

30 Omega Factor F6c ★
A good steep direct start to *Cyborg*. Start below a white groove with an open niche containing a holly tree. Climb up into the niche then move steeply up and left to reach a good flake. Climb back right and up to join *Cyborg* (where the bolts run out!) continue to its ledge and lower-off.

Great Buttress

At first vertical, then becoming steeper as it continues rightwards, eventually becoming quite undercut. The rock on the main part of the buttress is fantastic with tufa pillars to help in places.

The next routes all share a common start, up the right-facing corner/flake directly below the large yew tree growing 5m up the crag. The tree prevents a good view of the wall above, and the climbs are better than might be expected.

31 Half-Life F6b+ ★

32 Up Town F6c ★★
An even better companion to *Half-Life* with possibly the best small tufa formation on the crag. Climb the corner and tree, then go up the wall to the horizontal break but move right and up, heading for the fabulous stalactite-like tufa (or start up *Witherslack Alice* to this point). Go up the tufa and the groove above until a very delicate puzzling move gains a standing position below the steeper upper bulge (*Half-Life* comes in from the left). Move up and right into another groove.

33 Witherslack Alice F6c
Takes a line starting right of the *Up Town* tree.

34 Shades of Mediocrity F7a ★
Stand on the tufa, move left at a small overlap then drift back right over some excellent rock.

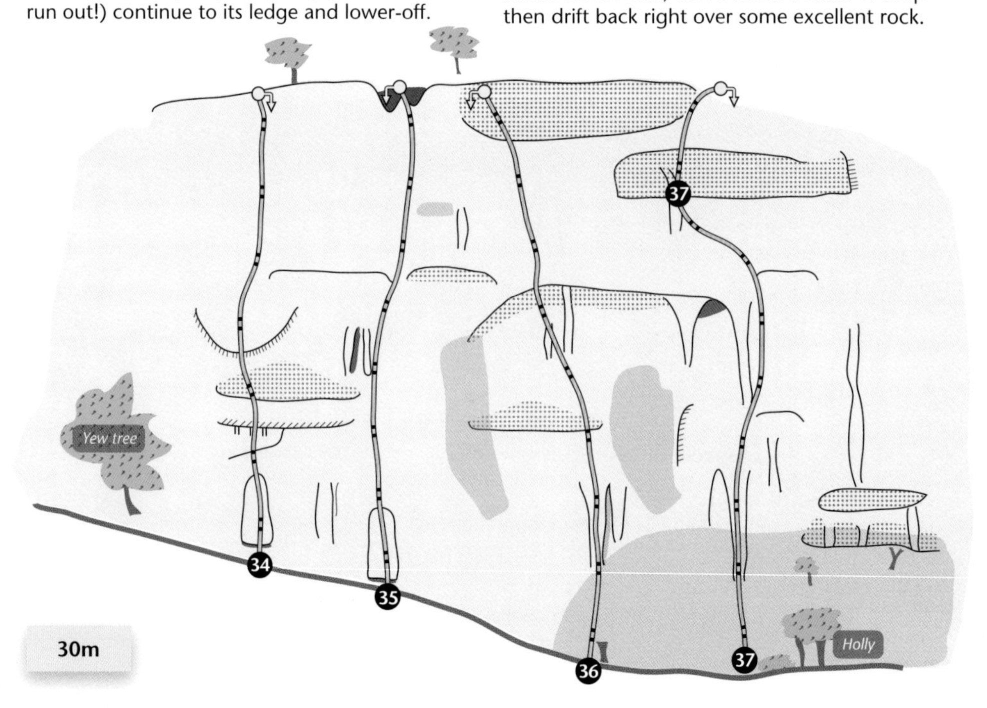

35 Gilbert Cardigan F7a+ ★
Take a more direct line from right of the right-hand stump.

36 Guloot Kalagna F7c ★
Hard and fingery climbing.

37 Electric Warrior Agent Provocateur 33m F7c ★★★
Big moves; fat tufas. The bulge has a very painful small hold.

38 Calling Mr Hall F8a ★★

39 Wargames F7b ★★★
Probably the best route on the crag. Steep to start but on good holds then more delicate in the upper half. Great value - sometimes wet but don't let that put you off. Fantastic!

40 More Games F7b+ ★

41 Stretchy Perineum F7b+ ★★
An excellent direct start to *Perverse Pépère*. Start at the large tufa stump "stuck" onto the wall.

42 Perverted Start F7b+ ★
A slightly harder right-hand variation to *Stretchy Perineum*. Finish up *Perverse Pépère* or, if you are feeling stronger, *Song For Europe*!

Remember the tree? In the middle of Great Buttress a tall dismal-looking ash tree grew from the base of the crag supported by a length of rope. It should have been treated with the respect and care that we give to gnarly oldtimers that have given such good service. Sadly, now gone, remember the Android Tree.

43 For When The Tree Goes F7b+ ★

44 Perverse Pépère F7b+ ★★
Excellent.

45 Song for Europe F7b+ ★★★
A magnificent way out of the the large scoop.

46 La Mangoustine Scatouflange F7b+ ★★★
A great route with a few hard finger-searing moves.

47 Super DuPont F7b+ ★★★

48 Super Duper DuPont F7c ★★★

49 Prime Evil F7c+ ★★★
Amazing climbing up a steep wall made entirely of Rice Krispies – beware of finger tendons going "Snap, Crackle and Pop!"

50 Unrighteous Doctors F7c+ ★★★
A fantastic route that provides a counter-diagonal to *Super Duper DuPont*.

51 Doctor Evil F8a ★★★
The hardest part of *Unrighteous Doctors* followed by the hardest part of *Prime Evil* was always going to be a hard sustained route.

52 Tufa King Hard F6c ★★
Not that hard!

53 Driller Killer F7a+ ★

54 Videodrome F7b+ ★
A harder variation finish to *Driller Killer*.

55 Warm Push 6b+

56 Reefer Madness 6c+

57 Doctor's Dilemma 6c+

38 Calling Mr Hall F8a
39 Wargames F7b
40 More Games F7b+
41 Stretchy Perineum F7b+
42 Perverted Start F7b+
43 For When The Tree Goes F7b+
44 Perverse Pépère F7b+
38
39
44
41
42
38
39
40
41
42
25/30m
AP

Langdale
Dow
Gable
Buttermere
Borrowdale
Eastern
EV

52 Tufa King Hard F6c
53 Driller Killer F7a+
54 Videodrome F7b+
55 Warm Push 6b+
56 Reefer Madness 6c+
57 Doctor's Dilemma 6c+
53
52
55
53
56
57
30m
NW

Cover Climbs

1.	**Flat Crags, Flat Iron Wall** (page 97)	E1
2.	**Dow Crag, The Balrog** (page 121)	E2
3.	**Esk Buttress, The Central Pillar** (page 164)	E2
4.	**Scafell Crag, Central Buttress - The Great Flake** (page 194)	E3
5.	**Napes Needle, The Wasdale Roof** (page 246)	E3
6.	**Grey Crag, Oxford and Cambridge Direct** (page 321)	S
7.	**Shepherd's Crag, The Bludgeon** (page 354)	E1
8.	**Dove Crag, Up Hellya** (FRCC Eastern Crags)	E8
9.	**Chapel Head Scar, Up Town** (page 464)	F6c

Cracked It

1.	**Gimmer Crag, The Crack** (page 88)	VS
2.	**Dow Crag, Hopkinson's Crack** (page 132)	HS
3.	**Esk Buttress, Black Sunday** (page 161)	HVS
4.	**Scafell East Buttress, Leverage** (page 207)	E1
5.	**The Napes, The Vikings** (page 240)	E3
6.	**High Crag, Samson** (page 310)	HVS
7.	**Eagle Crag, Post Mortem** (page 375)	E3
8.	**Castle Rock of Triermain, May Cay Cracks** (page 412)	HVS
9.	**Armathwaite, Codpiece** (page 453)	E2

Mega Classics

1.	**Bowfell, Bowfell Buttress** (page 102)	HS
2.	**Dow Crag, Eliminate 'A'** (page 123)	VS
3.	**Esk Buttress, Bridge's Route** (page 164)	HS
4.	**Scafell Crag, Moss Gill Grooves** (page 194)	MVS
5.	**Gable Crag, Engineer's Slabs** (page 250)	VS
6.	**Eagle Crag, Eagle Front** (page 317)	VS
7.	**Black Crag, Troutdale Pinnacle** (page 364)	S
8.	**Raven Crag Thirlmere, Communist Convert** (page 419)	VS
9.	**Armathwaite, Flasherman** (page 452)	VS

Obviously there are endless possibilities for linking routes to create memorable mountain experiences in the Lake District. However, the following examples may provide ideas for your own adventures or simply the basis for a grand day out in the fells!

Pavey Ark Integrales	page 56
The Picco-Harrison Integrale	page 56
Gimmer Integrales	page 84
Eskdale Enchainments	page 148
Fun Link-up Cragging	page 156
PSST! WANNA CLIMB?	page 170
Peascod's Ladies' Day Out	page 296
Grey Crag Link-ups	page 318
Ray McHaffie's Borrowdale Enchainement	page 366

The Lord of the Rings 342m E2 5c
Possibly one of the greatest expeditions in the Lakes: sumptuously long and arduous, offering some of the best pitches and situations on Scafell's East Buttress. Great care should be taken to protect the second on pitches 2, 3, 6 and 7. Pitches 2, 9 and 12 are probably the most taxing. Eight hours is the standard time taken on this route. Start in the square-cut corner with a crack at the back.
1 30m 5a Climb the groove for 12m then traverse right across sloping ledges to a pull up a wall onto a stance. (*Trinity*).
2 24m 5c Climb the corner behind, move right round the nose to a small spike which often sports a decaying runner. (Back-rope for second.) Climb downwards and rightwards to a ledge on the arête with high nut belays.
3 15m 5b Move right into the corner and traverse right to join p2 of *Hell's Groove*. Climb this pitch to the stance.
4 24m 5b Move right and climb down a groove until moves to the right lead to Morning Wall. Descend the easy gangway to the base of a large flake and climb the left side of this to its top. Make a thin move right along the narrow ledge and pull up to a stance on *Phoenix*.
5 15m 5b Follow *Phoenix* to a belay on the arête.
6 18m 5a Descend the wall for 8m and step right into *Ichabod*. Climb up this to protect the second and traverse right across the easy slab to belay on the shelf of *The Yellow Slab*.
7 30m 5b Climb straight down the easy slab to a recess. Descend the bottomless groove on the right of this for 2m to a tiny ledge. Move right around the arête to join *The Yellow Slab* at the foot of the crack. Move right and descend the rest of *The Yellow Slab* to a belay on *Great Eastern Route.*
8 24m 4c Follow the horizontal ledge line across the steep wall on the right until *The Centaur* is reached; follow this to its stance.
9 30m 5b Move right and climb the corner above (*The Centaur*) to pull onto a ledge above. Move right and pull onto a higher slab (peg). Continue traversing right into a white shallow chimney and climb this to a large ledge system.
10 27m 4b Follow a line of ledges round the corner to the large block in the middle of The White Slab. Descend to the foot of the slab.
11 21m 4c Move round the rib on the right, move down and step to the right. Climb up a little and descend rightwards to the arête. Step round this to the stance.
12 16m 5b Climb the crack above and step right into a corner. Climb to a good hold and traverse right to the arete which is followed to a ledge.
13 27m 5a Descend the slab, move below the overlap and traverse right into a groove. Move right round the rib and descend to below an overhang. Move right again, step down and join *Mickledore Grooves* at its stance.
14 42m 4c *Mickledore Grooves* provides a fitting finish.
J Adams, C Read - Jun 1969

Symbols

A

B

C

D

E

Kirk Fell and Pillar — Jon Allison

MOBILE GUIDEBOOK APP

The **Wired Guides** electronic guidebook application is available today.

Back in 1909, with Lliwedd, the Climbers' Club published the world's first "pocket size" climbing guidebook. Now the Club is perhaps helping to usher in a new era in guidebook publication. Imagine, with your support, in the very close future you could be carrying every route description you'll ever need on one small device in your shirt pocket!

All paid-for guidebook packages are associated with your ID so if you upgrade or loose your device all packages may be freely restored to your new device. Packages may also be selectively removed, and restored, to your device to save storage space as required.

Details of packages of guidebook information available are shown here:
www.climbers-club.co.uk/shop/mobile-guidebook-app/

If you are worried about taking your expensive smartphone onto the crags, perhaps consider picking up a secondhand device like a basic iPod Touch for a few quid.

iOS

The App is available on all Apple iOS devices (iPhone, iPod Touch, iPad and iPad Mini). Although please note that the App is designed for the smaller iPhone and iPod Touch devices as these are more likely to be taken to the crag.

itunes.apple.com/gb/app/guidebooks/id645218402?mt=8&uo=4

You can access the Guidebook Store directly on your device. There's is no need to ever use iTunes. Look for the Store icon on the home screen. Or, you may download using iTunes on your PC or Mac and synchronise to your iOS device in the normal way if you prefer.

Android

We will be launching on Android devices in the not too distant future. Stay tuned...